Essentials of
WIAT®-III and KTEA-II Assessment

Essentials of Psychological Assessment Series
Series Editors, Alan S. Kaufman and Nadeen L. Kaufman

Essentials of 16 PF® Assessment
by Heather E.-P. Cattell and James M. Schuerger
Essentials of Assessment Report Writing
by Elizabeth O. Lichtenberger, Nancy Mather, Nadeen L. Kaufman, and Alan S. Kaufman
Essentials of Assessment with Brief Intelligence Tests
by Susan R. Homack and Cecil R. Reynolds
Essentials of Bayley Scales of Infant Development–II Assessment
by Maureen M. Black and Kathleen Matula
Essentials of Behavioral Assessment
by Michael C. Ramsay, Cecil R. Reynolds, and R. W. Kamphaus
Essentials of Career Interest Assessment
by Jeffrey P. Prince and Lisa J. Heiser
Essentials of CAS Assessment
by Jack A. Naglieri
Essentials of Cognitive Assessment with KAIT and Other Kaufman Measures
by Elizabeth O. Lichtenberger, Debra Broadbooks, and Alan S. Kaufman
Essentials of Conners Behavior Assessments™
by Elizabeth P. Sparrow
Essentials of Creativity Assessment
by James C. Kaufman, Jonathan A. Plucker, and John Baer
Essentials of Cross-Battery Assessment, Second Edition
by Dawn P. Flanagan, Samuel O. Ortiz, and Vincent C. Alfonso
Essentials of DAS-II® Assessment
by Ron Dumont, John O. Willis, and Colin D. Elliot
Essentials of Evidence-Based Academic Interventions
by Barbara J. Wendling and Nancy Mather
Essentials of Forensic Psychological Assessment, Second Edition
by Marc J. Ackerman
Essentials of Individual Achievement Assessment
by Douglas K. Smith
Essentials of KABC-II Assessment
by Alan S. Kaufman, Elizabeth O. Lichtenberger, Elaine Fletcher-Janzen, and Nadeen L. Kaufman
Essentials of Millon™ Inventories Assessment, Third Edition
by Stephen Strack
Essentials of MMPI-A™ Assessment
by Robert P. Archer and Radhika Krishnamurthy
Essentials of MMPI-2 ™ Assessment
by David S. Nichols
Essentials of Myers-Briggs Type Indicator® Assessment, Second Edition
by Naomi Quenk

Essentials of NEPSY®-II Assessment
by Sally L. Kemp and Marit Korkman
Essentials of Neuropsychological Assessment, Second Edition
by Nancy Hebben and William Milberg
Essentials of Nonverbal Assessment
by Steve McCallum, Bruce Bracken, and John Wasserman
Essentials of PAI ® Assessment
by Leslie C. Morey
Essentials of Processing Assessment
by Milton J. Dehn
Essentials of Response to Intervention
by Amanda M. VanDerHeyden and Matthew K. Burns
Essentials of Rorschach ® Assessment
by Tara Rose, Nancy Kaser-Boyd, and Michael P. Maloney
Essentials of School Neuropsychological Assessment
by Daniel C. Miller
Essentials of Stanford-Binet Intelligence Scales (SB5) Assessment
by Gale H. Roid and R. Andrew Barram
Essentials of TAT and Other Storytelling Assessments, Second Edition
by Hedwig Teglasi
Essentials of Temperament Assessment
by Diana Joyce
Essentials of WAIS ®-IV Assessment
by Elizabeth O. Lichtenberger and Alan S. Kaufman
Essentials of WIAT ®-III and KTEA-II Assessment
by Elizabeth O. Lichtenberger and Kristina C. Breaux
Essentials of WISC-III ® and WPPSI-R ® Assessment
by Alan S. Kaufman and Elizabeth O. Lichtenberger
Essentials of WISC ®-IV Assessment, Second Edition
by Dawn P. Flanagan and Alan S. Kaufman
Essentials of WJ III™ Cognitive Abilities Assessment
by Fredrick A. Schrank, Dawn P. Flanagan, Richard W. Woodcock, and Jennifer T. Mascolo
Essentials of WJ III™ Tests of Achievement Assessment
by Nancy Mather, Barbara J. Wendling, and Richard W. Woodcock
Essentials of WMS®-III Assessment
by Elizabeth O. Lichtenberger, Alan S. Kaufman, and Zona C. Lai
Essentials of WNV ™ Assessment
by Kimberly A. Brunnert, Jack A. Naglieri, and Steven T. Hardy-Braz
Essentials of WPPSI ™-III Assessment
by Elizabeth O. Lichtenberger and Alan S. Kaufman
Essentials of WRAML2 and TOMAL-2 Assessment
by Wayne Adams and Cecil R. Reynolds

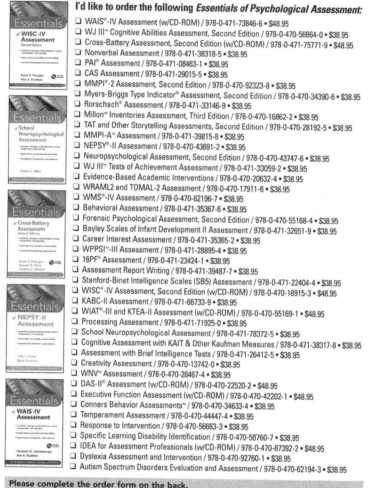

Essentials
of Psychological Assessment Series

ORDER FORM

Please send this order form with your payment (credit card or check) to:
John Wiley & Sons, Attn: J. Knott, 111 River Street, Hoboken, NJ 07030-5774

QUANTITY	TITLE	ISBN	PRICE
_____	_____	_____	_____
_____	_____	_____	_____
_____	_____	_____	_____
_____	_____	_____	_____
_____	_____	_____	_____

Shipping Charges:	Surface	2-Day	1-Day
First item	$5.00	$10.50	$17.50
Each additional item	$3.00	$3.00	$4.00

For orders greater than 15 items,
please contact Customer Care at 1-877-762-2974.

ORDER AMOUNT _____
SHIPPING CHARGES _____
SALES TAX _____
TOTAL ENCLOSED _____

NAME_____

AFFILIATION_____

ADDRESS_____

CITY/STATE/ZIP _____

TELEPHONE _____

EMAIL_____

❏ Please add me to your e-mailing list

PAYMENT METHOD:

❏ Check/Money Order   ❏ Visa   ❏ Mastercard   ❏ AmEx

Card Number _____ Exp. Date _____

Cardholder Name *(Please print)* _____

Signature _____

Make checks payable to **John Wiley & Sons.** *Credit card orders invalid if not signed.*
All orders subject to credit approval. • Prices subject to change.

To order by phone, call toll free 1-877-762-2974
To order online: www.wiley.com/essentials

Essentials

of WIAT®-III and KTEA-II

Assessment

Elizabeth O. Lichtenberger
Kristina C. Breaux

John Wiley & Sons, Inc.

Copyright © 2010 by John Wiley & Sons, Inc. All rights reserved.

Published by John Wiley & Sons, Inc., Hoboken, New Jersey.
Published simultaneously in Canada.

For general information on our other products and services please contact our Customer Care Department within the U.S. at (800) 762-2974, outside the United States at (317) 572-3993 or fax (317) 572-4002.

Wiley also publishes its books in a variety of electronic formats. Some content that appears in print may not be available in electronic books. For more information about Wiley products, visit our website at www.wiley.com.

Library of Congress Cataloging-in-Publication Data:

Lichtenberger, Elizabeth O.
  Essentials of WIAT-III and KTEA-II assessment/Elizabeth O. Lichtenberger, Kristina C. Breaux.
    p. cm. – (Essentials of psychological assessment series)
  Rev. ed. of: Essentials of WIAT-II and KTEA-II assessment/Elizabeth O. Lichtenberger, Donna R. Smith.
  Includes bibliographical references and index.
    ISBN 978-0-470-55169-1 (paper/cd-romess)
  1. Wechsler Individual Achievement Test. 2. Kaufman Test of Educational Achievement. 3. Ability–Testing. I. Breaux, Kristina C. II. Lichtenberger, Elizabeth O. Essentials of WIAT-II and KTEA-II assessment. III. Title. IV. Title: WIAT-III and KTEA-II assessment.
  LB3060.33.W47L53 2010
  153.9′4–dc22

                                                                                    2009038785

To Alan and Nadeen—
Your wisdom has taught me,
Your guidance has shaped me,
Your sincere kindness has astounded me, and
Your friendship has meant the world to me.
Thank you for all that you have given me.
Liz

To Gary,
With love and gratitude for your unfailing support
of all my projects and undertakings.
Kristina

CONTENTS

SERIES PREFACE

In the *Essentials of Psychological Assessment* series, we have attempted to provide the reader with books that will deliver key practical information in the most efficient and accessible style. The series features instruments in a variety of domains, such as cognition, personality, education, and neuropsychology. For the experienced clinician, books in the series will offer a concise yet thorough way to master utilization of the continuously evolving supply of new and revised instruments, as well as a convenient method for keeping up to date on the tried-and-true measures. The novice will find here a prioritized assembly of all the information and techniques that must be at one's fingertips to begin the complicated process of individual psychological diagnosis.

Wherever feasible, visual shortcuts to highlight key points are utilized alongside systematic, step-by-step guidelines. Chapters are focused and succinct. Topics are targeted for an easy understanding of the essentials of administration, scoring, interpretation, and clinical application. Theory and research are continually woven into the fabric of each book, but always to enhance clinical inference, never to sidetrack or overwhelm. We have long been advocates of "intelligent" testing—the notion that a profile of test scores is meaningless unless it is brought to life by the clinical observations and astute detective work of knowledgeable examiners. Test profiles must be used to make a difference in the child's or adult's life, or why bother to test? We want this series to help our readers become the best intelligent testers they can be.

In *Essentials of WIAT®-III and KTEA-II Assessment*, the authors have attempted to provide readers with succinct, straightforward, theory-based methods for competent clinical interpretation and application of the most recent editions of two widely used tests of individual achievement. Both the WIAT®-III and KTEA-II are normed for children, adolescents, and adults from Pre-Kindergarten through college. This book helps ease the transition of examiners who have been longtime users of the earlier editions of these tests, and provides a solid foundation for new examiners who are first discovering the abundance of information that can be gathered from these two individual assessment instruments. These tests of achievement both tap the important domains of academic ability required for assessment of learning disabilities. This book thoroughly integrates theory, research, clinical history, and clinical inference with sets of guidelines that enable the examiner to give, and then systematically interpret and apply, the 2004 KTEA-II and the brand-new 2009 WIAT®-III. This new edition, fully equipped with a CD-ROM to automate Lichtenberger and Breaux's thorough interpretive methods and to present a variety of additional interpretive aids, offers clinicians who routinely evaluate academic ability a cutting-edge resource that will optimize accurate assessment results and interpretation.

Alan S. Kaufman, PhD, and Nadeen L. Kaufman, EdD, Series Editors
Yale University School of Medicine

ACKNOWLEDGMENTS

We would like to acknowledge several people for their special and extraordinary contributions. We wish to express our deepest appreciation to Donna Smith, whose work on the first edition of this book helped develop an excellent foundation on which we were able to build this book. We are particularly grateful to Ron Dumont and John Willis, whose expert opinions and eagle eyes helped evaluate both the WIAT®-III and KTEA-II to create an unbiased chapter on the strengths and weaknesses of these instruments. We also appreciate the assistance that Mark Daniel and Haijiang Kuang of Pearson provided in creating the program for analyzing the GSV scores for inclusion in our CD-ROM. We are grateful for the input of Dawn Flanagan, Sam Ortiz, and Vinny Alfonso, who provided their expert advice on the sections of our book that integrated and described Cross-Battery Assessment (XBA). We are especially thankful to that XBA team of professionals for allowing us to adapt the CHC computer program for use in this book's CD-ROM.

Finally, the contributions of Isabel Pratt and the rest of the staff at Wiley are gratefully acknowledged. Their expertise and pleasant and cooperative working style made this book an enjoyable and productive endeavor.

One

OVERVIEW

O ver the past few years, there have been many changes affecting those who administer standardized achievement tests. New individually administered tests of achievement have been developed, and older instruments have been revised or renormed. The academic assessment of individuals from preschool to post-high school has increased over the past years due to requirements set forth by states for determining eligibility for services for learning disabilities. Individual achievement tests were once primarily norm-based comparisons with peers but now serve the purpose of analyzing academic strengths and weaknesses via comparisons with conormed (or linked) individual tests of ability. In addition, the focus of academic assessment has been broadened to include not only reading decoding, spelling, and arithmetic but also reading comprehension, arithmetic reasoning, arithmetic computation, listening comprehension, oral expression, and written expression (Smith, 2001).

These changes in the field of individual academic assessment have led professionals to search for resources that would help them remain current on the most recent instruments. Resources covering topics such as how to administer, score, and interpret frequently used tests of achievement and on how to apply these tests' data in clinical situations need to be frequently updated. Thus, in 2001, Douglas K. Smith published a book in the *Essentials* series titled *Essentials of Individual Achievement Assessment,* which devoted chapters to four widely used individually administered tests of achievement.[1] Smith's book was the inspiration for writing this book, which focuses on the recent second editions of two of the instruments written about in *Essentials of Individual Achievement Assessment:* the Wechsler Individual Achievement Test (WIAT) and the Kaufman Test of Educational Achievement

---

1. Another widely used achievement test, the Woodcock Johnson, Third Edition (WJ III) is the topic of its own book in the *Essentials* series entitled *Essentials of WJ III Tests of Achievement Assessment* (Mather, Wendling, & Woodcock, 2001).

(KTEA). Because both of these instruments are widely used achievement tests in school psychology and related fields, the third edition of the WIAT and the second edition of the KTEA are deserving of a complete up-to-date book devoted to their administration, scoring, interpretation, and clinical applications. *Essentials of WIAT-III and KTEA-II Assessment* provides that up-to-date information and includes rich information beyond what is available in the tests' manuals. An entire chapter is devoted to illustrative case reports to exemplify how the results of the WIAT-III and KTEA-II can be integrated with an entire battery of tests to yield a thorough understanding of a student's academic functioning. In a chapter devoted to clinical applications of the tests, the following topics are discussed: the integration of the KTEA-II and WIAT-III with their respective conormed tests of cognitive ability, focusing on the conceptual and theoretical links between tests, and the assessment of special populations, including specific learning disabilities and attention-deficit/hyperactivity disorder.

PURPOSES AND USES OF ACHIEVEMENT TESTS

The WIAT-III and KTEA-II are used for many reasons including diagnosing achievement, identifying processes, analyzing errors, planning programs, measuring academic progress, evaluating interventions or programs, making placement decisions, and conducting research. Some pertinent applications of these tests are described next.

Diagnosing Achievement

The WIAT-III and KTEA-II provide an analysis of a student's academic strengths and weaknesses in reading, mathematics, written expression, and oral language. In addition, these tests allow for the investigation of related factors that may affect reading achievement, such as Phonological Awareness and Naming Facility (RAN) on the KTEA-II and Early Reading Skills, Oral Word Fluency, Expressive Vocabulary, Receptive Vocabulary, and Oral Discourse Comprehension on the WIAT-III.

Identifying Processes

Pairwise comparisons of subtests on both the WIAT-III and KTEA-II allow examiners to better understand how students take in information (Reading Comprehension versus Listening Comprehension) and express their ideas (Written Expression versus Oral Expression).

Analyzing Errors

The KTEA-II provides a detailed quantitative summary of the types or patterns of errors a student makes on subtests in each of the achievement domains (Reading, Math, Written Language, and Oral Langauge), as well as for Phonological Awareness and Nonsense Word Decoding. Tracking error patterns can help examiners plan appropriate remedial instruction specifically targeting the difficulties a student displays, and the KTEA-II ASSIST software offers instructional strategies to help examiners design appropriate interventions based on a student's error pattern.

The WIAT-III provides skills analysis capabilities that also yield a detailed quantitative summary of the types of errors a student makes. This information helps examiners evaluate a student's error patterns and skill strengths and weaknesses. Each subtest includes sets of items that measure a specific skill or set of skills. The information yielded from analyzing the student's errors through the skills analysis can then be used in the design of an instructional plan or specific intervention for a student.

Planning Programs

The norm-referenced scores, along with the error analysis information, indicate a student's approximate instructional level. These results can help facilitate decisions regarding appropriate educational placement as well as appropriate accommodations or curricular adjustments. The information can also assist in the development of an individualized education program (IEP) based on a student's needs. For young adults, the results can help inform decisions regarding appropriate vocational training or general equivalency diploma (GED) preparation.

Measuring Academic Progress

The two parallel forms of the KTEA-II allow an examiner to measure a student's academic progress while ensuring that changes in performance are not due to the student's familiarity with the battery content. Academic progress can also be measured on the WIAT-III with a retest, taking into consideration any potential practice effect.

Evaluating Interventions or Programs

The WIAT-III and KTEA-II can provide information about the effectiveness of specific academic interventions or programs. For example, one or more of the composite scores could demonstrate the effectiveness of a new reading program within a classroom or examine the relative performance levels between classrooms using different math programs.

Making Placement Decisions

The WIAT-III and KTEA-II can provide normative data to aid in placement decisions regarding new student admissions or transfers from other educational settings.

Conducting Research

The WIAT-III and the KTEA-II Comprehensive Form are reliable, valid measures of academic achievement that are suitable for use in many research designs. Indeed, a brief search of the literature via the PsycINFO database yielded hundreds of articles that utilized the WIAT and the KTEA. The two parallel forms of the KTEA-II make it an ideal instrument for longitudinal studies or research on intervention effectiveness using pre- and post-test designs.

The KTEA-II Brief Form is also a reliable, valid measure of academic achievement that is ideal for research designs that call for a screening measure of achievement. The brevity of the KTEA-II Brief Form makes it useful in estimating the educational achievement of large numbers of prisoners, patients in a hospital, military recruits, applicants to industry training programs, or juvenile delinquents awaiting court hearings, where administering long tests may be impractical.

Screening

The KTEA-II Brief Form is intended for screening examinees on their global skills in mathematics, reading, and written language. The results of the screening may be used to determine the need for follow-up testing.

SELECTING AN ACHIEVEMENT TEST

Selecting the appropriate achievement test to use in a specific situation depends on a number of factors.[2] The test should be reliable, valid, and used only for the purposes for which it was developed. The *Code of Fair Testing Practices in Education*

---

2. Portions of this section were adapted from Chapter 1 of *Essentials of Individual Achievement Assessment* (Smith, 2001).

(Joint Committee on Testing Practices, 2004) outlines the responsibilities of both test developers and test users. Key components of the Code are outlined in Rapid Reference 1.1.

≡ *Rapid Reference 1.1*

Excerpts from the *Code of Fair Testing Practices in Education*

A. Selecting Appropriate Tests

Test users should select tests that meet the intended purpose and that are appropriate for the intended test takers.

1. Define the purpose for testing, the content and skills to be tested, and the intended test takers. Select and use the most appropriate test based on a thorough review of available information.
2. Review and select tests based on the appropriateness of test content, skills tested, and content coverage for the intended purpose of testing.
3. Review materials provided by test developers and select tests for which clear, accurate, and complete information is provided.
4. Select tests through a process that includes persons with appropriate knowledge, skills, and training.
5. Evaluate evidence of the technical quality of the test provided by the test developer and any independent reviewers.
6. Evaluate representative samples of test questions or practice tests, directions, answer sheets, manuals, and score reports before selecting a test.
7. Evaluate procedures and materials used by test developers, as well as the resulting test, to ensure that potentially offensive content or language is avoided.
8. Select tests with appropriately modified forms or administration procedures for test takers with disabilities who need special accommodations.
9. Evaluate the available evidence on the performance of test takers of diverse subgroups. Determine to the extent feasible which performance differences may have been caused by factors unrelated to the skills being assessed.

B. Administering and Scoring Tests

Test users should administer and score tests correctly and fairly.

1. Follow established procedures for administering tests in a standardized manner.
2. Provide and document appropriate procedures for test takers with disabilities who need special accommodations or those with diverse linguistic backgrounds. Some accommodations may be required by law or regulation.

(continued)

3. Provide test takers with an opportunity to become familiar with test question formats and any materials or equipment that may be used during testing.

4. Protect the security of test materials, including respecting copyrights and eliminating opportunities for test takers to obtain scores by fraudulent means.

5. If test scoring is the responsibility of the test user, provide adequate training to scorers and ensure and monitor the accuracy of the scoring process.

6. Correct errors that affect the interpretation of the scores and communicate the corrected results promptly.

7. Develop and implement procedures for ensuring the confidentiality of scores.

C. Reporting and Interpreting Test Results

Test users should report and interpret test results accurately and clearly.

1. Interpret the meaning of the test results, taking into account the nature of the content, norms or comparison groups, other technical evidence, and benefits and limitations of test results.

2. Interpret test results from modified test or test administration procedures in view of the impact those modifications may have had on test results.

3. Avoid using tests for purposes other than those recommended by the test developer unless there is evidence to support the intended use or interpretation.

4. Review the procedures for setting performance standards or passing scores. Avoid using stigmatizing labels.

5. Avoid using a single test score as the sole determinant of decisions about test takers. Interpret test scores in conjunction with other information about individuals.

6. State the intended interpretation and use of test results for groups of test takers. Avoid grouping test results for purposes not specifically recommended by the test developer unless evidence is obtained to support the intended use. Report procedures that were followed in determining who were and who were not included in the groups being compared and describe factors that might influence the interpretation of results.

7. Communicate test results in a timely fashion and in a manner that is understood by the test taker.

8. Develop and implement procedures for monitoring test use, including consistency with the intended purposes of the test.

D. Informing Test Takers

Test users should inform test takers about the nature of the test, test taker rights and responsibilities, the appropriate use of scores, and procedures for resolving challenges to scores.

1. Inform test takers in advance of the test administration about the coverage of the test, the types of question formats, the directions, and appropriate test-taking strategies. Make such information available to all test takers.

2. When a test is optional, provide test takers or their parents/guardians with information to help them judge whether a test should be taken—including indications of any consequences that may result from not taking the test (e.g., not being eligible to compete for a particular scholarship)—and whether there is an available alternative to the test.

3. Provide test takers or their parents/guardians with information about rights test takers may have to obtain copies of tests and completed answer sheets, to retake tests, to have tests rescored, or to have scores declared invalid.

4. Provide test takers or their parents/guardians with information about responsibilities test takers have, such as being aware of the intended purpose and uses of the test, performing at capacity, following directions, and not disclosing test items or interfering with other test takers.

5. Inform test takers or their parents/guardians how long scores will be kept on file and indicate to whom, under what circumstances, and in what manner test scores and related information will or will not be released. Protect test scores from unauthorized release and access.

6. Describe procedures for investigating and resolving circumstances that might result in canceling or withholding scores, such as failure to adhere to specified testing procedures.

7. Describe procedures that test takers, parents/guardians, and other interested parties may use to obtain more information about the test, register complaints, and have problems resolved.

Note: The Code was developed in 1988 and was revised in 2004 by the Joint Committee of Testing Practices, a cooperative effort of several professional organizations that has as its aim the advancement, in the public interest, of the quality of testing practices. The Joint Committee was initiated by the American Educational Research Association (AERA), the American Psychological Association (APA), and the National Council on Measurement in Education (NCME). In addition to these three groups, the American Association for Counseling and Development/Association for Measurement and Evaluation in Counseling and Development and the American Speech-Language-Hearing Association also now sponsor the Joint Committee.

The first factor to consider in selecting an achievement test is the purpose of the testing. Discern whether a comprehensive measure (covering the areas of achievement specified in the Individuals with Disabilities Improvement Act of 2004 [Public Law (PL) 108–446]) is needed or whether a less specific screening measure is appropriate. Another issue is whether an analysis for the identification of a specific learning disability (e.g., ability-achievement discrepancy) will need to be examined. Although PL 108–446 recently removed the requirement of demonstrating an achievement-ability discrepancy from determining eligibility for learning disabilities services, states still have the option to include this discrepancy if they choose. For this purpose, using achievement tests with conormed or linked ability tests is best. To gather diagnostic information and information about the level of skill development, you should use a test with skills analysis procedures.

The second factor to consider in selecting an achievement test is whether a particular test can answer the specific questions asked in the referral concerns. The specificity of the referral questions will help guide the test selection. For example, if the referral concern is about a child's reading fluency, the test you select should have a subtest or subtests that directly assess that domain.

The third factor to consider in selecting an achievement test is how familiar an examiner is with a certain test. Familiarity with a test and experience with scoring and interpreting it is necessary to ethically utilize it in an assessment. If you plan to use a new test in an assessment, you should ensure that you have enough time to get proper training and experience with the instrument before using it.

The fourth factor to consider in selecting an achievement test is whether the test's standardization is appropriate. Consider how recent the test's norms are. Most recent major tests of academic achievement are well standardized, but you should still review the manual to evaluate the normative group. See if students with disabilities were included in the standardization sample (which is important when assessing a student suspected of having a learning disability). Also see if appropriate stratification variables were used in the standardization sample.

The fifth factor to consider in selecting an achievement test is the strength of its psychometric properties. Consider whether the test's data have adequately demonstrated its reliability and validity. A test's internal consistency, test-retest reliability, and correlations with other achievement tests and tests of cognitive ability should all be examined. Additionally, consider the floor and ceiling of a test across age levels. Some tests have poor floors at the youngest age levels for the children with the lowest skills, and other tests have poor ceilings at the oldest age levels for the children with the highest skill levels. You can judge the adequacy of the floors and ceilings by examining the standard score range of the subtests and composites for the age range of the student you are assessing.

In Chapter 4 of this book, Ron Dumont and John Willis review what they feel are the strengths and weaknesses of the WIAT-III and KTEA-II, respectively. We encourage examiners to carefully review the test they select to administer, whether it is the WIAT-III, KTEA-II, or another achievement test, to ensure that it can adequately assess the unique concerns of the student for whom the evaluation is being conducted. Rapid Reference 1.2 summarizes the key points to consider in test selection.

≡ Rapid Reference 1.2

....

Key Points to Consider in Test Selection

Consider the Purpose of the Assessment and What Type of Test(s) It Demands

- Comprehensive assessment
- Screening assessment
- Ability-achievement discrepancy analysis
- Skills analysis

Consider Your Experience with the Assessment Instrument You Are Planning to Administer

- Administration (extensive, some, or no experience?)
- Scoring (extensive, some, or no experience?)
- Interpretation (extensive, some, or no experience?)

Consider the Adequacy of the Test's Standardization

- Are norms recent?
- Was the standardization sample appropriate?
- Were students with learning disabilities included?
- Was the norm sample appropriately stratified according to age, gender, geographic region, ethnicity, and socioeconomic status?

Consider the Psychometric Qualities of the Test

- Is the test's reliability adequate (internal consistency and test-retest reliability)?
- Is the test's validity adequate (correlations with other achievement tests, correlations with ability tests)?
- Does the test have an adequate floor for the age of the student you are assessing?
- Does the test have an adequate ceiling for the age of the student you are assessing?

ADMINISTERING STANDARDIZED ACHIEVEMENT TESTS

The WIAT-III and KTEA-II are standardized tests, meaning that they measure a student's performance on tasks that are administered and scored under known conditions that remain constant from time to time and person to person. Standardized testing allows examiners to directly compare the performance of one student to the performance of many other students of the same age who were tested in the same way. Strict adherence to the rules allows examiners to know that the scores obtained from the child they tested are comparable to those obtained from the normative group. Violating the rules of standardized administration renders norms of limited value. Being completely familiar with the test, its materials, and the administration procedures allows examiners to conduct a valid assessment in a manner that feels natural, comfortable, and personal—not mechanical. The specific administration procedures for the WIAT-III are discussed in Chapter 2, and those for the KTEA-II are discussed in Chapter 3.

Testing Environment

Achievement testing, like most standardized testing, should take place in a quiet room that is free of distractions. The table and chairs that are used during the assessment should be of appropriate size for the student being assessed. That is, if you are assessing a preschooler, then the table and chairs used should ideally be similar to those that you would find in a preschool classroom. However, if you are assessing an adolescent, adult-size table and chairs are appropriate. For the WIAT-III, the seating arrangement should allow both the examiner and the student to view the front side of the easel. For the KTEA-II, the seating arrangement should allow the examiner to see both sides of the easel. The examiner must also be able to write responses and scores discretely on the record form (out of plain view of the examinee). Many examiners find the best seating arrangement is to be at a right angle from the examinee, but others prefer to sit directly across from the examinee. The test's stimulus easel can be used to shield the record form from the student's view, but if you prefer, you may also use a clipboard to keep the record form out of view. Most importantly, you should sit wherever is most comfortable for you and allows you easy access to all of the components of the assessment instrument.

Establishing Rapport

In order to ensure that the most valid results are yielded from a testing, you need to create the best possible environment for the examinee. Perhaps more important than the previously discussed physical aspects of the testing environment is the relationship between the examiner and the student. In many cases, the examiner will be a virtual stranger to the student being assessed. Thus, the process of establishing rapport is a key component in setting the stage for an optimal assessment.

Rapport can be defined as a relationship of mutual trust or emotional affinity. Such a relationship typically takes time to develop. To foster the development of positive rapport, you need to plan on a few minutes of relaxed time with the student before diving into the assessment procedures. Some individuals are slow to warm up to new acquaintances, whereas others are friendly and comfortable with new people from the get-go. Assume that most students you meet will need time before being able to comfortably relate to you.

You can help a student feel more comfortable through your style of speech and your topics of conversation. Adapt your language (vocabulary and style) to the student's age and ability level (i.e., don't talk to a 4-year-old like you would a teenager, and vice versa). Use a friendly tone of voice, and show genuine personal interest and responsiveness. For shy children, rather than opening up immediately with conversation, try an ice-breaking activity such as drawing a picture or playing with an age-appropriate toy. This quiet interaction with concrete materials may provide an opening to elicit conversation about them.

In most instances, it is best not to have a parent, teacher, or other person present during the assessment, as it can affect the test results in unknown ways. However, when a child is having extreme difficulty separating, it can be useful to permit another adult's presence in the initial rapport-building phase of the assessment to help the child ease into the testing situation. Once the child's anxiety has decreased or once the child has become interested in playing or drawing with you, encourage the student to begin the assessment without the adult present.

Maintaining rapport requires diligent effort throughout an assessment. Watch students for signs of fatigue, disinterest, and frustration. These signs are clues that you need to increase your feedback, give a break, or suggest a reward for completing tasks. Using good eye contact will help you show interest and enthusiasm for the student's efforts. Use your clinical judgment about how much praise a child needs for their efforts. Some children will need more pats on the back than others. Always praise students for their efforts, not the correctness of their responses.

SUMMARY INFORMATION ABOUT THE TESTS AND THEIR PUBLISHERS

The WIAT-III is published by Pearson under the brand PsychCorp. The KTEA-II Comprehensive Form and KTEA-II Brief Form are published by Pearson Assessments. In Rapid References 1.3 and 1.4, we provide a summary of important

≡ Rapid Reference 1.3

Basic Information about the Wechsler Individual Achievement Test, Third Edition

Author	WIAT-III: Pearson
Publication Date	2009
What the Test Measures	WIAT-III measures the following achievement domains: Basic Reading, Reading Comprehension, Reading Fluency, Mathematics Calculation, Mathematics Problem Solving, Written Expression, Listening Comprehension, and Oral Expression.
Age Range	4–50 years (Adult norms for ages 20–50 available in 2010.)
Administration Time	Estimates based upon the time it took for 50 percent of the standardization sample to administer all grade-appropriate subtests. Pre-K–Kindergarten: 35–45 minutes Grades 1–3: 80–94 minutes Grades 4–12+: 104 minutes
Qualification of Examiners	Certification by or full active membership in a professional organization that requires training and experience in a relevant area of assessment. *or* A master's degree in psychology, education, occupational therapy, speech-language pathology, social work, or a field closely related to the intended use of the assessment and formal training in the ethical administration, scoring, and interpretation of clinical assessments.
Publisher	Pearson P.O. Box 599700 San Antonio, TX 78259 800.211.8378 http://www.PsychCorp.com
Price	**WIAT-III Kit: $625** Includes scoring assistant, audio CD, stimulus book, record form (package of 25), response booklet (package of 25), oral reading fluency booklet, word card, pseudoword card, scoring workbook, examiner's manual, and technical manual CD.

≡ Rapid Reference 1.4

Basic Information about the Kaufman Test of Educational Achievement, Second Edition

Author	Alan S. Kaufman and Nadeen L. Kaufman
Publication Date	KTEA-II Comprehensive Form: 2004 KTEA-II Brief Form: 2005
What the Test Measures	The following achievement domains are measured in both the Comprehensive and Brief Forms: Reading, Mathematics, and Written Language. The Comprehensive Form measures an additional fourth domain: Oral Language.
Age Range	4 ½ –25 years (Comprehensive Form) 4 ½ –90+ years (Brief Form)
Administration Time	Comprehensive Form: Pre-K–Kindergarten: 25 minutes Grades 1–2: 50 minutes Grades 3+: 70 minutes Brief Form: 4 ½ –90+ years: 20–30 minutes
Qualification of Examiners	User must have completed graduate training in measurement, guidance, individual psychological assessment, or special appraisal methods appropriate for an individual achievement test.
Publisher	Pearson Attn: Ordering Department P.O. Box 1416 Minneapolis, MN 55440 800.627.7271 http://www.pearsonassessments.com
Price *(retrieved from web site in July 2009)*	**KTEA-II Comprehensive Form** **A or B Kit: $351.50** Includes two easels, manual, norms book, Form A record forms (25), Form A student response booklets (25), Form A error analysis booklets (25), two each of three Form A WE booklets, all necessary stimulus materials, Form A administration CD, puppet, and tote bag. **KTEA-II Comprehensive Computer ASSIST: $267** Macintosh and Windows CD-ROM. **KTEA-II Brief Form Kit: $180** Includes one easel, one manual, 25 record forms, and 25 response booklets.

information about the WIAT-III, KTEA-II Comprehensive Form, and KTEA-II Brief Form. These Rapid References provide information on the following topics: test author, publisher, publication date, what the test measures, age range covered by the test, administration time, qualification of examiners, and test price.

Two

WIAT-III

The Wechsler Individual Achievement Test, Third Edition (WIAT-III; Pearson, 2009a) is a comprehensive, individually administered achievement test. It is designed for children and adolescents who are in Pre-Kindergarten (Pre-K) through grade 12 or aged 4:0 through 19:11 years. Adult norms for ages 20 through 50 years will be available as an automatic update to the Scoring Assistant software in 2010. This test can be administered by special educators, school psychologists, educational diagnosticians, speech-language pathologists, and similar professionals who have formal training and experience in the administration and interpretation of individually administered, norm-referenced tests. The WIAT-III provides information that enables educational and assessment professionals to meet the requirements of state regulations and the Individuals with Disabilities Education Improvement Act of 2004 (IDEA 2004; PL 108–446) when evaluating students for the following purposes:

To identify, classify, or qualify
- Identifying students at risk for academic failure or learning problems
- Diagnosing a learning disability
- Determining educational placement decisions or eligibility for special education services
- Reevaluating a student's achievement performance to revisit diagnostic and/ or eligibility decisions

To understand
- Evaluating profiles of skill strengths and weaknesses within and across achievement areas
- Analyzing patterns of errors to infer processing strengths and weaknesses, what the student knows and needs to be taught, and which strategies the student employs

- Comparing achievement strengths and weaknesses with cognitive strengths and weaknesses (when used in combination with an ability test)

To intervene
- Planning intervention and writing instructional goals
- Making curricular adjustments and providing accommodations
- Evaluating programs or interventions

HISTORY AND DEVELOPMENT

The first edition of the WIAT (The Psychological Corporation, 1992) was designed as a measure of academic achievement for students in kindergarten (K) through high school, aged 5:0 to 19:11, and contained eight subtests: Basic Reading, Mathematics Reasoning, Spelling, Reading Comprehension, Numerical Operations, Listening Comprehension, Oral Expression, and Written Expression. These subtests formed five composites: Reading, Mathematics, Language, Writing, and Total. These subtests corresponded to each of the areas of learning disability specified in the Education for All Handicapped Children Act of 1975 (PL 94–142). The WIAT was the only test of its kind to be linked with the Wechsler ability scales to facilitate the analysis of ability-achievement discrepancies.

The WIAT-II (The Psychological Corporation, 2001) was originally published in 2001, with updated scoring and normative materials published in 2002 and 2005. The WIAT-II was designed for students in grades Pre-Kindergarten through 12, college students in 2-year and 4-year institutions, and adults, extending the age range to 4 through 85 years. The second edition included significant updates to the eight subtests from the WIAT, changed the name of the Basic Reading subtest to Word Reading, and added one new subtest, Pseudoword Decoding. These subtests formed five composite scores: Reading, Mathematics, Written Language, Oral Language, and Total.

CHANGES FROM THE WIAT-II TO WIAT-III

The WIAT-III retains several features from its predecessor. The new edition preserves and updates many of the same subtests included in the WIAT-II and maintains content coverage in the areas of listening, speaking, reading, writing, and mathematics. The WIAT-III provides linkage (correlation data) with the *Wechsler Preschool and Primary Scale of Intelligence,* Third Edition (WPPSI-III; *Wechsler,* 2002), the *Wechsler Intelligence Scale for Children,* Fourth Edition (WISC-IV; Wechsler, 2003), the *Wechsler Adult Intelligence Scale,* Fourth Edition (WAIS-IV;

Wechsler, 2008), the *Wechsler Nonverbal Scale of Ability* (WNV; Wechsler & Naglieri, 2006), and the *Differential Ability Scales,* Second Edition (DAS-II; Elliott, 2007).

Age Range

The WIAT-III age range, 4 years through 50 years (adult norms will be provided in 2010), is narrower than that of the WIAT-II. A more restricted age range allows the WIAT-III to focus on the assessment needs of the school-age, adolescent, and college populations.

Subtest Modifications

Several subtests were updated with standard revisions, such as added and modified items, art, and/or administration instructions, but retain the basic structure and administration format as in the WIAT-II. These subtests include Spelling, Numerical Operations, Math Problem Solving, Word Reading, and Pseudoword Decoding. The latter two subtests each include new supplemental scores; however, the basic administration of the subtests is highly similar to the previous edition.

The Reading Comprehension subtest has updated comprehension questions and scoring rules and one new passage. The subtest no longer includes the supplemental scores from the WIAT-II (target words, reading speed).

The Listening Comprehension subtest includes Receptive Vocabulary and Oral Discourse Comprehension. Receptive Vocabulary was modified to include updated art and a new ceiling item. Oral Discourse Comprehension was adapted from the Listening Comprehension subtest from the original WIAT and updated with new floor items and an audio CD administration of item stimuli to improve administration reliability. The Oral Discourse Comprehension component replaces Sentence Comprehension from the WIAT-II. The Expressive Vocabulary component was moved to the Oral Expression subtest.

The Oral Expression subtest includes Expressive Vocabulary, Oral Word Fluency, and Sentence Repetition. Expressive Vocabulary includes updated art, simplified item definitions, and new floor and ceiling items. Oral Word Fluency includes updated administration directions and scoring rules and one new item (naming colors). Sentence Repetition includes new items and updated administration directions and scoring rules. Sentence Repetition is now administered to all grade levels. Visual Passage Retell and Giving Directions from the WIAT-II subtest were dropped due to the time required to administer and score these components.

The Alphabet Writing Fluency, Sentence Composition, and Essay Composition subtests are each based upon components of the WIAT-II Written Expression subtest. These components were updated and expanded to form distinct subtests that yield separate scores, allowing for improved interpretation of performance strengths and weaknesses. New administration directions and scoring rules are provided for Alphabet Writing Fluency, Sentence Composition, and Essay Composition. Unlike the WIAT-II subtest, Essay Composition includes one essay prompt for students in grades 3 through 12, and the same scoring rules are used across grades.

New Subtests

Five subtests are new to the WIAT-III: Early Reading Skills, Oral Reading Fluency, Math Fluency–Addition, Math Fluency–Subtraction, and Math Fluency–Multiplication. The Early Reading Skills subtest items are adapted from the early items from the WIAT-II Word Reading and Reading Comprehension subtests. In addition, the components that comprised the former Written Expression subtest now form distinct subtests: Alphabet Writing Fluency, Sentence Composition, and Essay Composition.

Composites

The WIAT-II included five composites: Total, Oral Language, Written Language, Mathematics, and Reading. The WIAT-III includes eight composites. Total Achievement, Oral Language, Written Expression, and Mathematics are similar to their WIAT-II counterparts, and Total Reading, Basic Reading, Reading Comprehension and Fluency, and Math Fluency are new composites.

Administration and Scoring Rules

The WIAT-III subtests with multiple start points include the same reverse rule as in the WIAT-II: If the first three items administered are scored 0 points, administer items in reverse order until three consecutive scores of 1 are obtained (or item 1 is reached). However, the discontinue rule has been shortened to four consecutive scores of 0. Unlike the WIAT-II, the discontinue rule is the same for all applicable subtests.

New scoring rules have been developed for all subjectively scored subtests (Reading Comprehension, Oral Expression, Alphabet Writing Fluency, Sentence Composition, Essay Composition). The new scoring rules are designed to be valid, reliable, clinically sensitive, and time efficient.

Skills Analysis

The WIAT-III provides item-level skills-analysis capabilities for four subtests—Reading Comprehension, Early Reading Skills, Numerical Operations, and Math Problem Solving—and within-item-level skills analysis for three subtests—Word Reading, Pseudoword Decoding, and Spelling. Item-level skills analysis provides the skill(s) measured by each item and requires the examiner to select those items that were answered incorrectly. Within-item-level skills analysis provides the skill(s) measured by each part within the item and requires the examiner to select the specific parts within each item that were answered incorrectly. Skills analysis may be completed by using the Scoring Assistant to produce an automated report or by manually using the worksheets provided in the manual.

Intervention Goal Statements

The WIAT-III Scoring Assistant includes a new functionality of providing intervention goal statements for 10 of the 16 subtests: Reading Comprehension, Early Reading Skills, Numerical Operations, Math Problem Solving, Word Reading, Pseudoword Decoding, Spelling, Oral Reading Fluency, Sentence Composition, and Essay Composition. The goal statements are provided for each subtest selected by the examiner.

Models for the Identification of Learning Disabilities

Federal regulations specify several criteria for determining the existence of a specific learning disability (SLD), including underachievement in one or more areas, failure to make sufficient progress in response to targeted intervention, and a pattern of strengths and weaknesses in performance, achievement, or both (34 CFR §300.309[a]). The IDEA 2004 introduces greater flexibility in the assessment process for identifying learning disabilities and/or determining eligibility for special services. Similar to the WIAT-II, the WIAT-III provides the capability of conducting an ability-achievement discrepancy analysis using either the simple difference or predicted achievement method. The WIAT-III also includes the capability of conducting a pattern of strengths and weaknesses discrepancy analysis, which most closely resembles the Concordance-Discordance Model of SLD identification presented by Hale and Fiorello (2004).

New Scores

Growth scale values (GSVs) are provided for tracking progress over time on each of the WIAT-III subtests. Growth score curves will also be provided as an enhancement to the Scoring Assistant in 2010 to assist examiners in plotting a student's growth trend relative to the average growth trend.

Supplemental standard scores are available for Word Reading, Pseudoword Decoding, Essay Composition, and Oral Reading Fluency. Word Reading and Pseudoword Decoding each provide an optional measure of reading speed. This score is calculated by recording the item number reached at 30 seconds and converting that item number to a standard score. Essay Composition yields a supplemental standard score for grammar and mechanics, which requires the calculation of correct minus incorrect word sequences (CIWS). Finally, Oral Reading Fluency yields two supplemental scores, Oral Reading Accuracy and Oral Reading Rate, that are most easily calculated using the Scoring Assistant.

Component Standard Scores

New to the WIAT-III are standard scores for components of subtests. This new feature provides greater interpretability of subtest performance. Four of the WIAT-III subtests are comprised of two or more components: (a) Listening Comprehension, (b) Oral Expression, (c) Sentence Composition, and (d) Essay Composition. For example, Listening Comprehension is comprised of two components: Receptive Vocabulary and Oral Discourse Comprehension. Evaluating standard scores for each component of the subtest allows the examiner to determine whether the student has a strength or weakness in listening comprehension at the level of vocabulary or discourse. Component standard scores do not typically have the same level of precision and reliability as subtest standard scores; for this reason, some of these scores may not be suitable for making educational placement decisions. (Refer to Table 2.3 later in this chapter for a comparison between the average subtest component reliabilities and the average subtest and composite reliabilities.)

Packaging

The packaging of components differs from the WIAT-II in several ways. First, the Scoring Assistant is included in the kit and does not need to be purchased separately. Second, only one stimulus book is required to administer the WIAT-III, and the stimulus book contains stimuli on both sides of the pages. As a result, both examiner and examinee view the same side of the stimulus book during administration. Third, all administration directions are included in the record form rather than the stimulus book. Finally, two new components are included: the Oral Reading Fluency booklet and the audio CD.

DESCRIPTION OF THE WIAT-III

As shown in Table 2.1, the 16 subtests included in the WIAT-III cover all eight areas of achievement specified by IDEA 2004.

As shown in Table 2.2, the WIAT-III subtests combine to form eight composites: Oral Language, Total Reading, Basic Reading, Reading Comprehension and Fluency, Written Expression, Mathematics, Math Fluency, and Total Achievement. As a broad measure of overall achievement, the Total Achievement composite is typically used as an indicator of a student's level of achievement in all

Table 2.1 IDEA 2004 and the WIAT-III

IDEA 2004 Areas of Achievement	WIAT-III Subtests	WIAT-III Subtest Administration Grade Levels
Oral Expression	Oral Expression	Pre-K–12
Listening Comprehension	Listening Comprehension	Pre-K–12
Written Expression	Alphabet Writing Fluency Sentence Composition Essay Composition Spelling	Pre-K–3 1–12 3–12 K–12
Basic Reading Skill	Early Reading Skills Word Reading Pseudoword Decoding	Pre-K–3 1–12 1–12
Reading Fluency Skills	Oral Reading Fluency	1–12
Reading Comprehension	Reading Comprehension	1–12
Mathematics Calculation	Numerical Operations	K–12
Mathematics Problem Solving	Math Problem Solving	Pre-K–12
	Math Fluency—Addition Math Fluency—Subtraction Math Fluency—Multiplication	1–12 1–12 3–12

Table 2.2 WIAT-III Subtests and Composites

Subtest (Administration Grade Levels)	Subtest Component	Composite (Grade Levels)	Total Achievement Composite (Grade Levels)
Listening Comprehension (Pre-K–12)	Receptive Vocabulary; Oral Discourse Comprehension	Oral Language (Pre-K–12)	Pre-K–12+
Oral Expression (Pre-K–12)	Expressive Vocabulary; Oral Word Fluency; Sentence Repetition	Oral Language (Pre-K–12)	Pre-K–12+
Early Reading Skills (Pre-K–3)	—	—	Pre-K–1
Word Reading (1–12+)	—	Total Reading (1–12+) Basic Reading (1–12+)	1–12+
Pseudoword Decoding (1–12+)	—	Total Reading (1–12+) Basic Reading (1–12+)	1–12+
Reading Comprehension (1–12+)	—	Total Reading (1–12+) Reading Comprehension and Fluency (2–12+)	1–12+
Oral Reading Fluency (1–12+)	—	Total Reading (2–12+) Reading Comprehension and Fluency (2–12+)	2–12+
Alphabet Writing Fluency (Pre-K–3)	—	Written Expression (K–2)	Pre-K–1
Spelling (K–12+)	—	Written Expression (K–12+)	K–2

Table 2.2 (Continued)

Subtest (Administration Grade Levels)	Subtest Component	Composite (Grade Levels)	Total Achievement Composite (Grade Levels)
Sentence Composition (1–12+)	Sentence Combining; Sentence Building	Written Expression (1–12+)	1–12+
Essay Composition (3–12+)	Theme Development and Text Organization; Word Count	Written Expression (3–12+)	3–12+
Math Problem Solving (Pre-K–12+)	—	Mathematics (K–12+)	Pre-K–12+
Numerical Operations (K–12+)	—	Mathematics (K–12+)	K–12+
Math Fluency—Addition (1–12+)	—	Math Fluency (1–12+)	—
Math Fluency—Subtraction (1–12+)	—	Math Fluency (1–12+)	—
Math Fluency—Multiplication (3–12+)	—	Math Fluency (3–12+)	—

academic areas relative to his or her age- or grade-mates. Each of the subtests, with the exception of the Math Fluency subtests, contributes to the Total Achievement composite for a particular grade range.

Note that the subtest administration grade levels do not always correspond to the composite grade levels. For example, Alphabet Writing Fluency is administered to grades pre-K through 3 but only contributes to the Written Expression composite for grades K through 2 and only contributes to the Total Achievement composite for grades Pre-K through 1.

STANDARDIZATION AND PSYCHOMETRIC PROPERTIES

The WIAT-III was standardized on a nationally stratified sample of 2,775 students in the grade-based sample (grades Pre-K–12) and 1,826 students in the age-based sample (ages 4:0–19:11). To establish a normative sample that is representative of the national school-age population, 4 percent of the normative sample consisted of students who met established criteria for a learning disorder in reading, writing, and/or mathematics; 1.9 percent of the sample consisted of students with expressive language disorder; and 1.8 percent of the sample included students with mild intellectual disability. A maximum of 1 percent of the sample at each grade level was permitted a diagnosis of attention-deficit/hyperactivity disorder (ADD/ADHD). In addition, 1.8 percent of the sample included students who qualified as academically gifted and talented.

Separate norms are provided for fall, winter, and spring for grades Pre-K through 12, enabling the examiner greater precision by measuring a student's performance against the normative sample at a specific semester of the school year.

Reliability

The internal-consistency reliability of the WIAT-III, using split-half reliability coefficients, is shown in Table 2.3 for subtests and composites. The average

Table 2.3 Average Grade-Based Reliability Coefficients of the WIAT–III Subtests and Composites

WIAT-III Subtests and Composites	Split-Half		Test-Retest (Corrected R^2)
	Fall	Spring	
Listening Comprehension	.84	.83	.75
Early Reading Skills	.90	.87	.82
Reading Comprehension	.88	.86	.90
Math Problem Solving	.92	.91	.85
Alphabet Writing Fluency			.69
Sentence Composition	.90	.87	.79
Word Reading	.97	.97	.94
Essay Composition	.87	.87	.84
Essay Composition: Grammar and Mechanics	.84	.84	.84
Pseudoword Decoding	.96	.96	.94
Numerical Operations	.93	.92	.89
Oral Expression	.87	.87	.89
Oral Reading Fluency			.94

Table 2.3 (Continued)

WIAT-III Subtests and Composites	Split-Half		Test-Retest (Corrected R²)
	Fall	Spring	
Oral Reading Accuracy			.83
Oral Reading Rate			.94
Spelling	.95	.95	.92
Math Fluency—Addition			.86
Math Fluency—Subtraction			.89
Math Fluency—Multiplication			.89
Subtest Components			
Receptive Vocabulary	.70	.69	.67
Oral Discourse Comprehension	.83	.82	.77
Sentence Building	.87	.82	.74
Sentence Combining	.81	.80	.76
Expressive Vocabulary	.71	.72	.82
Sentence Repetition	.85	.83	.83
Oral Word Fluency	.73	.73	.73
Theme Development and Text Organization	.79	.79	.79
Word Count	.80	.80	.80
Composites			
Oral Language	.91	.91	.87
Total Reading	.98	.97	.96
Basic Reading	.98	.98	.95
Reading Comprehension and Fluency	.93	.93	.94
Written Expression	.95	.94	.91
Mathematics	.96	.95	.93
Math Fluency	.95	.95	.93
Total Achievement	.98	.98	.96

internal-consistency reliability values for the WIAT-III composite scores and for Math Problem Solving, Word Reading, Pseudoword Decoding, Numerical Operations, Oral Reading Fluency, Oral Reading Rate, and Spelling are in the 0.90s. The average reliability coefficients for Listening Comprehension, Early Reading Skills, Reading Comprehension, Sentence Composition, Essay Composition, Essay Composition: Grammar and Mechanics, Oral Expression, and the Math Fluency subtests are predominantly in the 0.80s and 0.90s. Generally, reliabilities of 0.90 or higher support the use of a score for making educational decisions; however, scores with reliabilities between 0.80 and 0.90 may also be suitable for educational decision making.

The WIAT-III subtest reliabilities are comparable to the WIAT-II subtest reliabilities. For the subtests retained from the WIAT-II, the reliability coefficients in the WIAT-III are similar or improved, with the exception of Reading Comprehension, which has slightly lower reliability coefficients due to shortening the subtest to reduce administration time. The reliability coefficients for the new subtests—Early Reading Skills, Oral Reading Fluency, and the Math Fluency subtests—are generally comparable to the coefficients for the other reading and math subtests in the WIAT-II.

The split-half reliability method is not appropriate for measuring the reliability of subtests without item-level data (i.e., Essay Composition, Sentence Composition, Alphabet Writing Fluency, and Oral Reading Fluency) or subtests that are speeded (i.e., Alphabet Writing Fluency and Math Fluency subtests). Instead, test-retest stability coefficients were used as the reliability estimates for these subtests. The WIAT-III subtest and composite scores possess adequate stability across time for both grade bands. The average corrected stability coefficients are excellent (0.87–0.96) for the composite scores; excellent (0.90–0.94) for Reading Comprehension, Word Reading, Pseudoword Decoding, Oral Reading Fluency, Oral Reading Rate, and Spelling; good (0.82–0.89) for Early Reading Skills, Math Problem Solving, Essay Composition, Essay Composition: Grammar and Mechanics, Numerical Operations, Oral Expression, Oral Reading Accuracy, Math Fluency—Addition, Math Fluency—Subtraction, and Math Fluency—Multiplication; and adequate (0.75 and 0.79, respectively) for Listening Comprehension and Sentence Composition. A lower average stability coefficient (0.69) is expected for Alphabet Writing Fluency due to the speeded nature of this subtest and the restricted raw score range.

In general, average test-retest gains are more pronounced for the Oral Language subtests (4–7 points) and the Reading Comprehension subtests (4 points) and are less pronounced for the Written Expression subtests (3–7 points) than for the other subtests. For the Written Expression subtests, the diminished performance of the second testing may be explained by the relatively greater amount of time and/or effort involved in completing these subtests, which may lead to reduced motivation with subsequent testing sessions that follow closely in time.

Validity

The validity of the WIAT-III was demonstrated using multiple analyses. First, intercorrelations between the subtests and composites were calculated to test for expected relationships and discriminant evidence of validity. The subtests that comprise each composite are generally moderately correlated with one another. Correlations among the composites range from 0.45 to 0.93, with stronger correlations among the Reading composites and weaker correlations between the Math Fluency composite and other composites. The subtest intercorrelations confirm some expected relations between the subtests within composites. For example, relatively strong correlations are evident between Math Problem Solving and Numerical Operations and between Word Reading and Pseudoword Decoding. The intercorrelations also provide discriminant evidence of validity. For example, the Mathematics subtests correlate more highly with each other than with other subtests. Some examples of strong correlations across achievement domains are evident, such as the strong correlation between Word Reading and Spelling, which reflects the interrelatedness of some skills utilized across domains.

In addition, correlations with other instruments were conducted to evaluate construct validity. Correlations with the WIAT-II suggest that the two instruments are measuring similar constructs. The corrected correlations between the composite scores for the two instruments ranged from 0.76 (Oral Language) to 0.93 (Total Achievement), and correlations between the common subtests ranged from 0.62 (Oral Expression) to 0.86 (Spelling). Consistent with expectations, the corrected correlations were high for subtests that are highly similar in content and structure to the WIAT-II subtests—such as Word Reading (0.85), Pseudoword Decoding (0.84), Spelling (0.86), Math Problem Solving (Math Reasoning in the WIAT-II; 0.84), and Numerical Operations (0.81)—and were relatively low for subtests in which content and structure changed considerably—such as Reading Comprehension (0.69), Listening Comprehension (0.64), Oral Expression (0.62), and the Written Expression measures: Sentence Composition (0.56), Essay Composition (0.45), and Essay Composition: Grammar and Mechanics (0.59). Given that the WIAT-III is a revision of a previous edition and shows moderate to strong correlations in many achievement areas with the WIAT-II, most of the validity evidence reported in previous research related to the WIAT-II is still relevant and should be considered.

Correlations were also conducted between the WIAT-III and the Wechsler scales (WPPSI-III, WISC-IV, WAIS-IV, and WNV) and between the WIAT-III and the DAS-II. Consistent with expectations regarding typical correlations between ability and achievement measures, the correlations between the WIAT-III and the overall cognitive ability scores (full scale IQ [FSIQ] or general conceptual ability) range from 0.60 to 0.82. Such correlations also provide divergent evidence of validity, suggesting that different constructs are being measured by the WIAT-III than those measured by each cognitive ability test, and indicate varying degrees of overlap in the cognitive skills required.

> **DON'T FORGET**
> ....
> The WIAT-III shows moderate to strong correlations in many achievement areas with the WIAT-II. For this reason, most of the validity evidence reported in previous research related to the WIAT-II is still relevant and should be considered.

Finally, special population studies were conducted to examine the clinical utility of the WIAT-III. These studies included students identified as academically gifted and talented ($N = 91$), students with mild intellectual disability ($N = 70$), students with expressive language disorder ($N = 59$), and students with learning disabilities in the areas of Reading ($N = 108$), Written Expression ($N = 86$), and Mathematics ($N = 90$). The results of these studies, which are detailed in Chapter 5, show expected patterns of performance, providing evidence that the WIAT-III reliably differentiates between students in each of these special groups and their normally achieving peers.

HOW TO ADMINISTER THE WIAT-III

As with any standardized test, the WIAT-III should be administered according to the administration instructions explained in the examiner's manual and record form. The WIAT-III can be used to assess only in the area(s) of suspected disability or to comprehensively assess all areas of achievement when insufficient information is available regarding the student's achievement or when conducting an evaluation of a pattern of strengths and weaknesses in achievement. Examiners have the flexibility to select which subtests to administer and the order of administration; however, the preferred subtest order is the order of subtests in the record form because this order was used to standardize the test. Subtest selection is often determined by the referral question (or the hypothesis being tested), the educational data available, and local and state regulation requirements. For example, some school districts and educational agencies require the use of composite scores rather than subtest-level scores when making placement or eligibility decisions; for this reason, an examiner may select to administer the subtests that are necessary to yield a composite score in the area(s) of interest.

The essential materials required to administer the WIAT-III include the stimulus book, record form, response booklet, Oral Reading Fluency booklet, word card, pseudoword card, and audio CD. In addition, the examiner must supply an audio CD or MP3 player with speakers, an audio recorder (optional, to facilitate accurate recording of oral responses), a stopwatch that operates quietly, blank paper, and pencils without erasers.

DON'T FORGET
WIAT-III Administration Materials

1. Stimulus book
2. Record form
3. Response booklet
4. Oral Reading Fluency booklet
5. Word card
6. Pseudoword card
7. Audio CD
8. CD/media player with speakers
9. Audio recorder (recommended)
10. Stopwatch
11. Blank scratch paper
12. Pencils without erasers

Starting and Discontinuing Subtests

The WIAT-III provides four indicators that examiners must use in order to administer subtests correctly. These include start points, reverse rules, discontinue rules, and stop points.

Start Points
Start points are provided for every subtest on the WIAT-III. Some subtests have one start point for all grades (item 1), and other subtests have multiple start points,

depending upon the grade level of the student. A student who has completed a grade but not yet started the next grade should begin at the level of the completed grade. Generally, if the examiner is relatively certain that the grade-appropriate start point is much too easy or difficult for a particular student, then the student may begin a subtest at an earlier or later start point than the grade-appropriate start point; however, careful consideration must be given to the start points for the Reading Comprehension and Oral Reading Fluency subtests. Because these two subtests contain item sets, identifying the most appropriate item set for the student's skill level is very important for maximizing the utility of the scores. More information about identifying the most appropriate item set for these subtests is provided in the next section. Caution is also warranted when the examiner chooses to begin with item 1 rather than the grade-appropriate start point. An examiner may choose to begin with item 1 when testing a student who demonstrates significant limitations on grade-level material; however, if the student responds correctly to the grade-appropriate start point item and the next two items, the examiner must award full credit for items that precede the student's grade-appropriate start point (even if the student answered one or more items incorrectly). The student is awarded credit for these items because the student's performance indicated that he or she was able to answer items correctly at the grade-appropriate start point and did not need to begin at item 1; hence, the items are scored as if the student had begun at the grade-appropriate start point.

> ### DON'T FORGET
> ....
> If the student responds correctly to the grade-appropriate start point item and the next two items, award full credit for items that precede the grade-appropriate start point (even if the student answered one or more of these items incorrectly).

Reverse Rules

A reverse rule applies only when administration does not begin with item 1. The purpose of a reverse rule is to ensure that the easiest items administered to a student are not above that student's proficiency level. There are two types of reverse rules in the WIAT-III: (a) the standard reverse rule and (b) the item set reverse rule. The standard reverse rule specifies that if the student scores 0 points on any of the first three items given, the examiner administers earlier items in reverse order from the start point until three consecutive items are answered correctly (or until item 1 is administered). Alternatively, if the student receives credit for the first three items administered, the reverse rule is not applied, and the examiner awards credit for all preceding, unadministered items.

As shown in Rapid Reference 2.1, the item set reverse rule only applies to the two subtests containing item sets—Reading Comprehension and Oral Reading Fluency—and differs for each subtest. The purpose of an item set reverse rule is to better ensure that the student is administered the most appropriate item set for his or her ability level. Item set start points are determined by a student's grade of enrollment; however, the content within each item set may range from below grade level to slightly above grade level. For this reason, examiners are discouraged from beginning at an item set other than the student's grade-appropriate item set based upon the student's estimated grade of achievement. It is preferable to always begin at the grade-appropriate item set and follow the reverse rule to the most appropriate item set; however, if you believe that the student would perform poorly at the grade-appropriate item set and that beginning at that item set would discourage the student and/or damage rapport, it is permissible to begin one item set below the grade-appropriate item set.

An explanation of how to apply the reverse rules for the Reading Comprehension and Oral Reading Fluency subtests is provided in the section entitled "Subtest-by-Subtest Notes on Administration and Scoring."

≡ Rapid Reference 2.1

WIAT-III Reverse Rules by Subtest and (Subtest Component)

No Reverse Rule	Standard Reverse Rule	Item Set Reverse Rule
(Receptive Vocabulary)	(Oral Discourse Comprehension)	Reading Comprehension
Early Reading Skills	Math Problem Solving	Oral Reading Fluency
Alphabet Writing Fluency	Numerical Operations	
Sentence Composition	Spelling	
Word Reading		
Essay Composition		
Pseudoword Decoding		
Oral Expression		
Math Fluency		

Discontinue Rule

The discontinue rule is applied only to subtests with items of increasing difficulty. To minimize testing time and to help prevent the student from becoming frustrated or discouraged, the examiner stops administration of a subtest when the item difficulty exceeds the student's ability level. The WIAT-III uses the same discontinue rule across all applicable subtests: Discontinue administration of a subtest if the student receives 0 points on four consecutive items. If the student never receives 0 points on four consecutive items, continue administration until the last item of the subtest is administered.

Stop Points

A stop point indicates the completion of an item set; hence, the only subtests containing stop points are those with item sets (i.e., Reading Comprehension and Oral Reading Fluency). Stop points are labeled according to the grade level(s) associated with each item set. If the item set reverse rule is applied and the student is administered an item set other than his or her grade-appropriate item set, the examiner administers items up to the stop point for that particular item set—not the stop point for the student's grade level.

HOW TO SCORE THE WIAT-III

Generally, standard scores should be used when comparing performance on one WIAT-III subtest to another, one composite to another, and when comparing WIAT-III results to that of another test. The WIAT-III standard scores have a mean of 100 and a standard deviation (SD) of 15 points. The range of standard scores for the subtests and composites is 40 to 160. We assume that achievement is distributed on a normal curve with the majority of individuals scoring within +/−1 standard deviation of the mean. Thus, about two-thirds (68%) of examinees will score in the range of 85 to 115. Less than 3 percent of examinees score below 70 or above 130.

Obtaining Raw Scores

Items are objectively scored as correct (1 point) or incorrect (0 points) for a majority of the WIAT-III subtests: Listening Comprehension, Early Reading Skills, Math Problem Solving, Word Reading, Pseudoword Decoding, Numerical Operations, the Expressive Vocabulary component of Oral Expression, Spelling, and each of the Math Fluency subtests. A set of scoring rules, which employ subjective judgment, must be applied to score the remaining subtests.

Selection of Age-Based or Grade-Based Scores

Standard scores from the WIAT-III subtests are based upon norms that are either age based or grade based. The norms are reported within various age or grade bands. Ages or grades are grouped into larger bands for older students and adults for whom academic growth progresses at a slower rate. If grade-based scores are selected, the scores are based upon semester (fall, winter, or spring) norms for grades Pre-K through 12. If age-based scores are selected, the scores for ages 4 to 13 years are reported in 4-month intervals. The scores for ages 14 to 19 years are reported in 12-month (annual) intervals. The scores for high school students aged 17 to 19 years are based upon one 3-year age band norm.

Selecting age-based or grade-based scores determines the peer group with which the student's performance is compared, and the decision is influenced by a number of different factors, such as whether a particular skill develops according to age (i.e., developmental skills) or grade (i.e., curriculum-based skills), whether a student is outside of the typical age range for his or her grade level, and district/agency/state requirements. Some states currently require the use of age-based scores when evaluating for a specific learning disability because of the state's interpretation of the language of IDEA 2004 (34 CFR §300.309[a]): "The child does not achieve adequately for the child's age or to meet state-approved grade-level standards." Scores are often calculated and/or reported using both age-based and grade-based norms to allow for an evaluation of the difference between the two.

Derived Scores

Each of the subtest raw scores is converted to age-based or grade-based derived scores, including standard scores, percentile ranks, age or grade equivalents, normal curve equivalents, and stanines. Growth scale values are also yielded from the WIAT-III. The types of raw and derived scores yielded from the WIAT-III are summarized in Rapid Reference 2.2.

Derived scores from the WIAT-III can be obtained either with the Scoring Assistant software or by manually looking up scores in the published tables. Raw scores may be entered into the Scoring Assistant at the subtest level to yield the various derived scores (e.g., standard scores, percentiles) from the normative tables or at the item level to yield a more detailed error analysis. The Scoring Assistant also provides an evaluation report that summarizes the test results and can be exported to a word processor for expansion. Scores may be obtained manually by referring to the appropriate tables in the technical manual CD.

≡ *Rapid Reference 2.2*

Types of Scores Yielded from the WIAT-III

Type of Score	Use in WIAT-III
Raw Score	The raw score is the sum of points awarded for each subtest or subtest component. Raw scores should not be used to compare performance between tests or across subtests or composites.
Weighted Raw Score	A raw score on Reading Comprehension and Oral Reading Fluency is converted to a weighted raw score prior to conversion to a standard score or other derived score. Weighted raw scores are necessary because the total raw scores from different item sets are not directly comparable. When students of the same age or grade take different item sets, weighted scores are necessary in order to make the scores comparable. Weighted raw scores are not "weighted" in the traditional sense. No weights were applied; however, this term is used to differentiate these vertically scaled scores from traditional raw scores.
Standard Score	Standard scores are reported for both subtests and composites. The standard scores form a normal (bell curve) distribution, ranging from 40 to 160, with a mean of 100 and a standard deviation of 15. As an equal-interval measure, these standard scores can easily be compared with one another and with other standardized test scores. A standard score is a measure of performance but does not reflect growth over time.
Percentile Rank	Percentile ranks, ranging from <0.1 to 99.9, indicate the percentage of individuals of the same age or grade who scored at or below the performance of the examinee. Percentiles are not on an equal-interval scale, so they should not be averaged or used to demonstrate growth.
Age or Grade Equivalent	Age or grade equivalents indicate the age or grade level for which the examinee's score is typical (i.e., the median score of the age or grade group). Age equivalents are expressed in years and months; for example, an age equivalent of 10:3 refers to 10 years, 3 months. Grade equivalents are expressed in tenths of a grade; for example, a grade equivalent of 1.2 refers to the second month of first grade. Age and grade equivalents are based upon the median scores in the standardization reference group and do not reflect local curricula or classroom expectations. These scores are

	on a rank-order scale and do not increase at equal intervals. For these reasons, age/grade equivalents are not comparable across subtests or tests and are not suitable for making diagnostic, placement, or instructional decisions.
Normal Curve Equivalent	Normal curve equivalents (NCE), with a mean of 50 and a standard deviation of 21.06, range from <1 to >99 and reflect examinees' percentile rankings along a bell curve; however, unlike percentile ranks, NCE scores are on an equal-interval scale, allowing the scores to be averaged. These scores are typically used for evaluating and comparing the performance of groups of individuals.
Stanine	Stanines convert a raw score to a single-digit, normalized score between 1 and 9, with a mean of 5 and a standard deviation of 2. Stanines are not scaled at equal intervals. Due to the scale's limited range and unequal scaling, stanines are not sensitive to small differences in scores and are most useful for evaluating group performance. Stanines offer limited precision for describing the performance of an individual examinee or examinees with exceptionally high or low scores.
Growth Scale Value	Growth scale values (GSVs) are sample-independent scores on an equal-interval scale and are used to track achievement growth over time. In the WIAT-III, the average GSVs of third graders are anchored at 500 points.

Intervention Goal Statements

Intervention goal statements, written and reviewed by experts in the field of special education, are provided by the WIAT-III Scoring Assistant for those subtests selected by the examiner. Information about how to use the Scoring Assistant to obtain goal statements is provided in the next section.

The goal statements are displayed at the end of the clinician score report and include recommended intervention tasks and activities. The statements include multiple choice options and spaces to fill in the blank to assist examiners in writing goals that are specific, measurable, and customizable for a student's individualized education plan. A sample of a completed annual goal and short-term objective for the Word Reading subtest is shown in Figure 2.1. The ability to customize the goal statements allows the examiner to adjust the difficulty level of the goal based upon the needs of a particular student. In addition, it allows the

Word Reading

VCE Syllables

Items with Errors: 31

Annual Goal

Given a list of _30_ (circle/enter (one) two, three, ____) - syllable words containing one VCE syllable, the student will read the list aloud with no more than _3_ errors.

List examples: face, pace, lace; lake, bake, take; like, bike, hike; mine, wine, fine

Short-Term Objectives

Given a list of _20_ one-syllable word pairs, each pair including one VCE syllable word and the same word without the silent e, the student will pronounce the word pairs with no more than _4_ errors.

Word pair examples: win, wine; fin, fine; tap, tape; mop, mope; wip, wipe

Figure 2.1 Sample of WIAT-III Intervention Goal Statements.

examiner to formulate student goal statements that meet various school district or institutional standards and preferences. For example, some practitioners may generally prefer using goals that require a percent accuracy of at least 70 percent but may require a higher percent accuracy from a high-ability, low-achieving student who is likely to respond well to instruction.

If a subtest is selected that includes skills analysis, such as the Word Reading subtest, goal statements will be provided for each skill area in which the student made one or more errors. If a subtest is selected that does not include skills analysis, such as the Essay Composition subtest, the same goal statements will be provided, regardless of the student's performance on specific items or scoring criteria within that subtest. In either case, it is important that the examiner select those goal statements that are most relevant to the student's demonstrated strengths and weaknesses. For example, the examiner may determine that missing one item in a particular skill area is not sufficient to justify an annual goal statement and may decide to administer supplemental curriculum-based measures to test the hypothesis that instruction is needed in that skill area. Similarly, the examiner may decide not to use the Essay Composition intervention goal statement regarding essay planning because the student demonstrated above average planning skills by using a graphic organizer prior to writing the essay but may focus instead on the paragraph-writing goal statements.

Scoring Assistant

The Scoring Assistant is included as a standard component in every WIAT-III kit. Two score reports are available: (a) the clinician score report and (b) the parent report. A summary of the score report options for each report type is included in Rapid Reference 2.3. Only the clinician score report includes all of the reporting capabilities discussed in this section. The parent score report is a simplified report that provides subtest descriptions and summarizes subtest and composite performance. The parent report is intended to facilitate a discussion of assessment results between the examiner and parent(s)/caregiver(s).

The Scoring Assistant performs all of the basic scoring conversions and calculations and provides tables and graphs of the student's performance.

≡ Rapid Reference 2.3

WIAT-III Score Report Options and Report Types

Score Report Option or Feature	Description of Option or Feature	Report Type	
		Clinician Score Report	Parent Report
Tables and Graphs			
Subtest Score Summary	Optional table. Includes all subtests administered and the corresponding raw scores, standard scores, confidence intervals, percentile ranks, NCEs, stanines, age and grade equiv-alents, and, if selected, growth scores (GSVs).	X	
Subtest Standard Score Profile	Optional graph. Plots standard scores and confidence intervals for all subtests administered, organized by achievement area.	X	
Supplemental Subtest Score Summary	Optional table. Provides the same types of scores as the "Subtest Score Summary" for the supplemental scores: Oral Reading Accuracy and Oral Reading Rate.	X	

(continued)

Score Report Option or Feature	Description of Option or Feature	Report Type	
		Clinician Score Report	Parent Report
Cumulative Percentages	Optional table. Provides the cumulative percentages (base rates) and interpretive statements (statements that describe the student's performance) for the following scores: Word Reading Speed and Pseudoword Decoding Speed.	X	
Subtest Component Score Summary	Optional table. Provides raw scores, standard scores, percentile ranks, NCEs, stanines, and qualitative descriptions of performance for subtest components (e.g., Receptive Vocabulary and Oral Discourse Comprehension, which are components of the Listening Comprehension subtest).	X	
Composite Score Summary	Optional table. Provides sums of standard scores, confidence intervals, percentile ranks, NCEs, stanines, and qualitative descriptions for each of the composites.	X	
Composite Score Profile	Optional graph. Plots standard scores and confidence intervals for all available composites.	X	
Composite Standard Score Differences	Optional table. Lists all possible composite comparisons, standard score differences, critical values, whether the differences are significant (Y or N), and the base rates.	X	
Pattern of Strengths and Weaknesses Model	Optional table and graph. The table lists the two score comparisons, relative	X	

	strength standard scores, relative weakness standard scores, standard score differences, critical values, whether the differences are significant (Y or N), and whether the result supports the hypothesis of SLD (Y or N).The graph shows the comparisons between the processing strength and both the processing weakness and the achievement weakness, and indicates whether each comparison was discrepant (Y or N).		
Skills Analysis	Optional table. For each subtest, it lists the skills (and features, if applicable) measured, the total number of errors per skill, the maximum possible number of errors per skill, and the percent correct by skill (and feature, if applicable).	**X**	
Goal Statements	Optional table. For each subtest, it lists the skills measured, the items measuring each skill that included errors, the annual goals, and the short-term objectives.	**X**	
Subtest Descriptions	Standard table. Includes a brief description of each subtest administered that specifies what each subtest is designed to measure and what the student was asked to do.		**X**
Graph of Performance by Composite	Standard graph. Displays the student's performance on each composite (based upon standard scores that are not displayed) beneath a bell curve delineated by qualitative descriptions.		**X**

(*continued*)

Score Report Option or Feature	Description of Option or Feature	Report Type	
		Clinician Score Report	Parent Report
Graph of Performance by Subtest	Standard graph. Displays the student's performance on each subtest (based upon standard scores that are not displayed) beneath a bell curve delineated by qualitative descriptions.		X
Score Options			
Include Growth Scores	Indicates whether to include growth scores (GSVs) in the "Subtest Score Summary" and the "Supplemental Subtest Score Summary" tables.	X	
Age-Based or Grade-Based Norms	Indicates whether to report age-based or grade-based derived scores.	X	X
Significance Levels			
Confidence Intervals (95% or 90%)	Indicates whether to report 95 percent or 90 percent standard score confidence intervals in each applicable table in the report.	X	
Composite Level Differences (0.01 or 0.05)	Indicates whether to use critical values at the 0.01 or 0.05 significance level when comparing composite standard scores in the "Composite Standard Score Differences" table.	X	
Pattern of Strengths and Weaknesses Discrepancy (0.01 or 0.05)	Indicates whether to use critical values at the 0.01 or 0.05 significance level when comparing the processing strength with the processing weakness and the processing strength with the achievement weakness in the "Pattern of Strengths and Weaknesses Model" table and graph.	X	

Raw scores are converted into various derived scores (e.g., standard scores, percentiles) for subtest scores, supplemental subtest scores, and composite scores. If you use the Scoring Assistant, it is never necessary to look up weighted raw scores. Always enter raw scores rather than weighted raw scores for Reading Comprehension and Oral Reading Fluency, and the software will convert the raw scores into the necessary weighted raw scores before calculating the derived scores.

The WIAT-III Scoring Assistant can be used alone or in combination with other ability tests that use the same software platform, such as the DAS-II and WAIS-IV. Provision is made for comparing ability and achievement and conducting ability-achievement discrepancy (AAD) analyses so that results from both the WIAT-III and an ability test can be included in a single report.

Ability-Achievement Discrepancy and Pattern of Strengths and Weaknesses Analyses

To conduct an ability-achievement discrepancy analysis, you must have the Scoring Assistant installed for both the WIAT-III and a compatible ability test. However, you can conduct a pattern of strengths and weaknesses (PSW) discrepancy analysis with the WIAT-III Scoring Assistant alone or by creating a combination report with a compatible ability test.

Using the WIAT-III Scoring Assistant only, a PSW analysis can be calculated by manually entering scores from the WPPSI-III, WISC-IV, WAIS-IV, DAS-II, or KABC-II. Unlike the AAD analyses, the PSW analysis can only be calculated using the Scoring Assistant. To reduce the possibility of calculation errors and to ensure results that are accurate and time efficient, tables for manual calculation are not provided in the technical manual CD. For a more in-depth discussion of how to conduct a PSW analysis, refer to Chapter 5.

Scoring Guide

The Scoring Assistant includes an interactive scoring guide for scoring Essay Composition: Theme Development and Text Organization. It is highly recommended that examiners score the Essay Composition subtest using the Scoring Assistant scoring guide rather than using the printed version of the scoring guide included in the examiner's manual. The software version prevents scoring errors by helping the user to proceed from question to question correctly, skip questions as instructed, quit the scoring guide at the appropriate time, and calculate scores correctly. This version is also easier to use because each screen presents only the scoring criteria relevant to answering that particular question. This prevents the user from becoming overwhelmed by the amount of scoring information printed in the manual.

The scoring guide may be used to score every section of the Theme Development and Text Organization scoring rubric (i.e., Introduction, Conclusion, Paragraphs, Transitions, Reasons Why, and Elaborations) or just specific sections. After scoring many cases and attaining a high level of scoring proficiency, you may be able to score certain sections—such as Introduction, Conclusion, Paragraphs, and Transitions—quickly and easily without needing to use the scoring guide. If this is the case, you may enter the raw scores for these sections and only activate the scoring guide to score Reasons Why and Elaborations. Regardless of your level of scoring proficiency, use of the scoring guide is *always* recommended when scoring Reasons Why and Elaborations due to the number of scoring rules involved. You only need to click the icon beside either Reasons Why *or* Elaborations to score both sections, because Reasons Why and Elaborations are scored concurrently. When you complete the scoring guide for these sections, the raw scores for both Reasons Why and Elaborations will be entered automatically.

DON'T FORGET
....
Scoring Reasons Why and Elaborations

Using the Scoring Guide
1. Always use the scoring guide (in the Scoring Assistant or examiner's manual) to score Reasons Why and Elaborations rather than attempting to score from memory.
2. Reasons Why and Elaborations are both scored concurrently.
3. To score these sections, open the scoring guide by clicking the icon beside either one. When you complete the scoring guide, the raw scores for both sections will be entered automatically.

To activate the scoring guide for a particular section, from the "Raw Scores" tab, click on the icon next to the scoring section of interest, as shown in Figure 2.2. After a section has been scored using the scoring guide, you must close the scoring guide by clicking "Save and Close." To score another section of Theme Development and Text Organization, you must reopen the scoring guide by clicking the icon next to that section.

If you believe you have made a scoring error and would like to rescore a section, then you may reopen the scoring guide by clicking the icon next to the

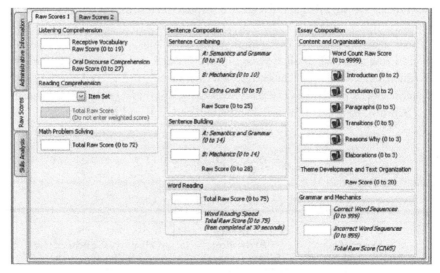

Figure 2.2 WIAT-III Scoring Assistant Raw Score Entry Screen 1.

Source: Wechsler Individual Achievement Test, Third Edition (WIAT-III). Copyright © 2009 NCS Pearson, Inc. Reproduced with permission. All rights reserved. "Wechsler Individual Achievement Test" and "WIAT" are trademarks, in the United States and/or other countries, of Pearson Education, Inc. or its affiliate(s).

section that was previously scored. A warning message will appear to verify that you want to override the previous score. Simply click "Yes," and the scoring guide will open. You can then change your previous responses and save the new score.

Similarly, if you want to review the information you have entered into the scoring guide for a particular section to double-score or verify a score, you may reopen the scoring guide by clicking the icon next to the section that was previously scored. A warning message will appear to verify that you want to override the previous score. Click "Yes," and the scoring guide will open. You can review your previous responses by clicking "Next" and proceeding from screen to screen. If all of your responses are correct, simply follow the instructions on the last screen to click "Save and Close."

Skills Analysis

To help practitioners evaluate a student's specific academic strengths and weaknesses and plan targeted interventions, the WIAT-III provides both item-level and within-item-level skills analysis capabilities. Rapid Reference 2.4 summarizes the two types of skills analysis by subtest. These capabilities are available with or without use of the Scoring Assistant. Skills analysis worksheets are provided in the technical manual CD and may be photocopied for repeated use; however, the Scoring Assistant offers the same capability in a format that is easier to use and that provides automatic error calculations. Conducting a skills analysis may be especially useful for evaluating the student's performance on subtests that are relevant to answering the referral question and/ or subtests that represent a normative weakness. To conduct a skills analysis using the Scoring Assistant, follow the steps outlined in Rapid Reference 2.5.

≡ *Rapid Reference 2.4*

WIAT-III Skills Analysis

Type of Skills Analysis	Subtests Providing Skills Analysis	How to Conduct the Skills Analysis
Item Level	Early Reading Skills Reading Comprehension Numerical Operations Math Problem Solving	Each item corresponds to a specific skill, and the examiner simply selects those items answered incorrectly.
Within-Item Level	Word Reading Pseudoword Decoding Spelling	The parts within a single item correspond to specific skills. This analysis requires the examiner to select which part(s) of an item was answered correctly. This information is recorded on the record form during administration, or, if the administration is audio recorded, shortly after administration is complete.

≡ *Rapid Reference 2.5*

Steps to Follow for Conducting Skills Analysis or Obtaining Intervention Goal Statements

1. Enter the subtest raw scores under the "Raw Scores" tab.
2. Click on the "Skills Analysis" tab.

3. On the summary page, select the subtests that you want to include for skills analysis and/or goal statements based upon the standard scores shown for each. Consider selecting subtests that are highlighted in yellow, which indicates below-average performance relative to the normative sample. This screen is shown in Figure 2.3.

Summary	Spelling		
Skills Analysis and Goal Statements			
Please select the subtest(s) for which skills analysis and/or intervention goal statements are desired.			
Subtest		Age-Based Standard Score	Grade-Based Standard Score
☐	Early Reading Skills	107	99
☐	Reading Comprehension	120	112
☐	Math Problem Solving	142	120
☐	Sentence Composition	86	77
☐	Word Reading	99	85
☐	Pseudoword Decoding	103	93
☐	Numerical Operations	130	112
☐	Oral Reading Fluency	103	89
☑	Spelling	77	69

Note: Subtests highlighted in yellow denote Skills Analysis and/or Goal Statements are recommended.

(Left sidebar tabs: Administrative Information, Raw Scores, Skills Analysis)

Figure 2.3 WIAT-III Scoring Assistant: Subtest Selection Screen for Skills Analysis and Goal Statements.

Source: Wechsler Individual Achievement Test, Third Edition (WIAT-III). Copyright © 2009 NCS Pearson, Inc. Reproduced with permission. All rights reserved. "Wechsler Individual Achievement Test" and "WIAT" are trademarks, in the United States and/or other countries, of Pearson Education, Inc. or its affiliate(s).

4. Click on each subtest tab that appears above the summary page.
5. For each subtest, either enter skills analysis information or select component areas for providing goal statements, as appropriate. A sample of this data-entry screen for the Spelling subtest is shown in Figure 2.4.
6. Click Save and Close.
7. Click Score and Report, and select WIAT-III from the drop-down menu.
8. Select a Clinician Report, select Skills Analysis and Goal Statements from the Tables and Graphs options, and create the score report.
9. After the score report is created, scroll to the end of the report to view the skills analysis summary table, as shown in Figure 2.5, and the goal statements table, as shown in Figure 2.1.

(continued)

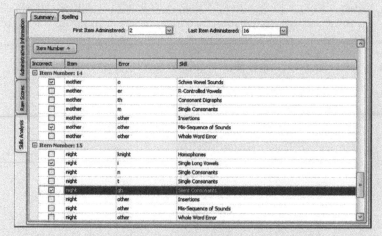

Figure 2.4 WIAT-III Scoring Assistant: Skills Analysis Entry Screen for Spelling Subtest.

Source: Wechsler Individual Achievement Test, Third Edition (WIAT-III). Copyright © 2009 NCS Pearson, Inc. Reproduced with permission. All rights reserved. "Wechsler Individual Achievement Test" and "WIAT" are trademarks, in the United States and/or other countries, of Pearson Education, Inc. or its affiliate(s).

Reading Comprehension
Grade 3 Item Set

Skill	Total Errors by Skill	Max. Errors by Skill	% Correct by Skill
Literal	4	12	67%
Inferential	6	9	33%

Word Reading

Feature	Skill	Total Errors by Skill	Max. Errors by Skill	% Correct By Skill	% Correct By Feature
Morphology Types	Common Prefixes/ Word Beginnings	0	5	100%	100%
	Common Suffixes/ Word Endings	0	10	100%	
Vowel Types	VCE Syllables	1	4	75%	93%
	Irregular Vowels	0	9	100%	
	Single Short Vowels	1	12	92%	
	Single Long Vowels	0	5	100%	
	Schwa Vowel Sounds	0	13	100%	
	Vowel Digraphs	0	8	100%	
	Diphthongs	0	2	100%	
	R-Controlled Vowels	0	3	100%	
	Silent Vowels	2	4	50%	

Figure 2.5 WIAT-III Scoring Assistant: Skills Analysis Score Report Sample.

Source: Wechsler Individual Achievement Test, Third Edition (WIAT-III). Copyright © 2009 NCS Pearson, Inc. Reproduced with permission. All rights reserved. "Wechsler Individual Achievement Test" and "WIAT" are trademarks, in the United States and/or other countries, of Pearson Education, Inc. or its affiliate(s).

The skills analysis report generated by the Scoring Assistant includes the specific skills that are measured by each subtest, the item number(s) that correspond to each skill, and, within each skill, the item numbers answered incorrectly and the percentage of items answered correctly. If the Scoring Assistant is not used, the skills analysis worksheets can be completed manually to provide this information.

Intervention Goal Statements

To obtain intervention goal statements using the Scoring Assistant, follow the steps outlined in Rapid Reference 2.5. The Scoring Assistant assists examiners in selecting subtests that are relative or normative weaknesses by displaying the standard scores of each subtest on the screen before the score report is generated. A sample of the goal statements generated by the score report is shown in Figure 2.1.

Subtest-by-Subtest Notes on Administration and Scoring

This section highlights pertinent information for administering and scoring each of the WIAT-III subtests and common errors to avoid. Subtests are listed in the order in which they appear in the WIAT-III record form.

Listening Comprehension

Administration of the Listening Comprehension subtest requires the administration of two components: Receptive Vocabulary and Oral Discourse Comprehension. It is preferable to administer the components in this order, because this is the order in which students in the standardization sample were administered the subtest.

Prior to administering Receptive Vocabulary, you should become familiar with how to pronounce each item correctly by listening to the audio CD (track 22) and referring to the pronunciation guide in the examiner's manual. Administration of Receptive Vocabulary requires use of the stimulus book. The subtest always begins with item 1 and continues until the student answers four consecutive items incorrectly.

Oral Discourse Comprehension is administered via the audio CD. The audio CD files can be played using a CD player, MP3 player, computer, or any other device that plays media files. Prior to administering Oral Discourse Comprehension, you should listen to the audio CD to adjust the volume of your media player and become familiar with when to push pause and how to change tracks in forward and reverse direction. Administration of Oral Discourse Comprehension requires use of the stimulus book. To improve the reliability of administration and maintain standard procedure, use of the audio CD is highly recommended; however, the subtest may be administered without use of the audio CD by reading the item passages from the record form. If the audio CD is not used, the item passages should be read aloud at a natural, conversational pace with a clear speaking voice.

Note that the reverse rule should not be applied too rigidly on Oral Discourse Comprehension. If the student has answered three consecutive items incorrectly and there is one additional item remaining that pertains to a given passage, do not reverse immediately to the preceding passage. Rather, administer the remaining question that pertains to the passage before reversing, and then reverse to the preceding passage, regardless of the student's performance on that item. This is important because passages cannot be repeated to administer items that were skipped.

Correct responses are provided in the record form. If the student paraphrases a correct response by conveying the same meaning using different words, score the response as correct.

DON'T FORGET

Oral Discourse Comprehension

Item passages may *not* be repeated, but questions may be repeated as needed.

Early Reading Skills

The Early Reading Skills subtest requires use of the stimulus book. Some items share a stimulus book page, so pay close attention to the record form and the item numbers printed on the stimulus book pages to ensure that you present the correct page for each item. All items must be administered; this subtest does not use a discontinue rule, because items are not ordered by difficulty. Rather, items are grouped by the type of skill being measured, and item difficulty varies within and across skills. Correct responses are included in the record form. Recording the student's verbatim response in the record form is recommended.

DON'T FORGET

Oral Discourse Comprehension

Administer all questions that pertain to a given passage before applying the reverse rule.

Reading Comprehension

The stimulus book contains the passages necessary to administer the Reading Comprehension subtest. Allow the student to review each passage while answering questions, and encourage the student to look back at the passage if he or she is hesitant to do so.

Applying the item set reverse rule correctly is necessary for properly administering the Reading Comprehension subtest. The item set reverse rule requires the student to reverse one start point if the sum of scores on all reversal items is 2, 1, or 0 points. It is recommended that you begin at the student's grade-appropriate start point whenever possible because it is important to find the most appropriate item set for the student. The most appropriate item set is the one closest to the grade-appropriate item set in which the student scores 3 or more points on the first passage. If you are certain that the student will not be able to read the passage and you believe that starting at the grade-appropriate start point would be detrimental to the student's subsequent motivation and performance, you may begin one start point below the grade-appropriate start point. If the student scores 2 or fewer points on the first passage of the item set, reverse one start point. You may reverse up to three item sets from the grade-appropriate item set if the student meets this criterion each time. After three reversals, you must administer the full item set.

Sample responses for 2-point and 1-point scores are included in the record form. Recording the student's verbatim response in the record form is recommended for later reference, particularly when the student's response is scored 1 point or 0 points.

Note that the answers that receive credit capture the correct responses given by a large sample of students from a national try-out study. It may be the case that alternative answers not listed may be considered acceptable or technically correct by some users; however, the answers listed only include high-quality responses that capture the most salient and pertinent features of the text. For example, item 76 of Reading Comprehension requires the student to identify the three consequences that would result if zoo prices are not raised. The answers that receive credit (i.e., zoo closes, animals sold off, children lose learning experiences, families lose entertainment) are the most salient consequences listed in the passage, because the passage clearly states that the zoo would close if zoo prices are not raised, and these are the consequences of the zoo closing. There are alternative responses that could be derived from the passage, such as the employees not receiving raises or the facilities not being kept up; however, these are not the most salient consequences because none of these would be relevant if the zoo were no longer open.

Understanding the design of this subtest and the purpose of the item set reverse rule is essential for correctly interpreting the subtest results when a student reverses to a preceding item set. Interpreting the results can be challenging when, for example, a student reverses to a preceding item set and receives a standard score in the average—or even above average—range. Initially, it may seem inaccurate that a student who was unsuccessful in completing his or her grade-appropriate item set could receive such a strong score; however, a prudent interpretation reveals this to be an accurate representation of some students' reading comprehension skills. Refer to Rapid Reference 2.6 for a summary of how to interpret performance on the Reading Comprehension subtest with students who do and do not reverse to a preceding item set.

When a student performs poorly on reading comprehension items with grade-level passages, it must be determined whether the student has a weakness in word identification skills, reading vocabulary, reading comprehension skills, or some combination of these. The first step is to allow the student to reverse to an item set with skill coverage that is comparable to the grade-appropriate item set but with passages at a lower readability level, placing fewer demands on word identification and vocabulary skills. If the student performs poorly on the preceding (lower) item set, then it is likely that the student has a weakness in the area of reading comprehension, and further assessment, error analysis, and intervention in this area should be pursued. On the other hand, if the student performs well on the preceding item set, the examiner may rule out reading comprehension as the area of weakness. It is important for the examiner to complete an error analysis to identify how word identification and vocabulary difficulties may have affected the student's ability to comprehend written material at the grade-appropriate start point. The examiner may want to examine the student's performance on reading text aloud and defining words. The student's performance on the Word Reading and the Listening Comprehension (Receptive Vocabulary) subtests should be evaluated in conjunction with the error analysis results to determine if intervention should include work in one or both of these areas.

When reporting results in which the student reversed to a preceding item set, you should communicate to parents, teachers, and other relevant school team members the ways in which the WIAT-III Reading Comprehension score differs

≡ Rapid Reference 2.6

Constructs Measured by the WIAT-III Reading Comprehension Subtest

For Readers Who Complete the Grade-Appropriate Item Set

For students who do not need to reverse to a preceding item set, this subtest measures reading comprehension of passages that are generally appropriate for the student's grade level. It is important to keep in mind that the passages within an item set generally cover a range of reading difficulty, from slightly below to slightly above grade level; as a result, it is inaccurate to assume, for example, that all passages in the first-grade item set are precisely at a first-grade reading level.

For Struggling Readers Who Reverse to a Preceding Item Set

The item set reverse rule allows you to measure reading comprehension of *below*-grade-level material relative to the performance of *same-age* or *same-grade* peers. Each passage (and item set) is composed of questions designed to measure a variety of comprehension skills. Each item set includes several types of factual and inferential questions, which simulate comprehension questions teachers ask students to demonstrate their understanding of reading materials. As a result, the types of questions included in each item set do not uniformly increase in difficulty, nor do comprehension questions measure increasingly complex skills from one item set to the next. A sampling of the same literal and inferential comprehension skills are distributed within and across item sets. This design, which differs in part from the designs of many other reading comprehension tests, enables a student to demonstrate reading comprehension skills on passages at a lower readability level and controls for potentially confounding weaknesses in word identification and vocabulary knowledge. Consequently, the Reading Comprehension subtest becomes a "purer" measure of reading comprehension for struggling readers.

from scores on many other reading achievement tests. You may wish to include this information in the description of the subtest in the report and in the presentation and discussion of the test results. Otherwise, persons reading the report are likely to assume that the score reflects reading comprehension skills with grade-level text rather than reading comprehension skills with texts at a lower reading level. Keep in mind that even if the student reverses to a preceding item set, the normative score is based upon a comparison with same-age or same-grade peers. As with any other assessment instrument, it is important for examiners to clearly explain and report the task demands and skills measured by this subtest to fully utilize its informative diagnostic characteristics and prevent readers from misinterpreting the test results.

Math Problem Solving

The Math Problem Solving subtest requires use of the stimulus book. Similar to the Early Reading Skills subtest, some items share a stimulus book page, so pay close attention to the record form and the item numbers printed on the stimulus book pages to ensure that you present the correct page for each item. If the student provides an answer that is equivalent to the correct answer listed in the record form, you should award credit for the response. If the student provides a response in a different response modality (i.e., oral or pointing) than the one listed beside the correct answer in the record form, you may query the student to tell you their answer or point to their answer as appropriate. The student is not permitted to use a calculator; however, for qualitative evaluation purposes, you may indicate those items for which the student used paper and pencil to solve the problem by circling "Y" (for "yes") under the "Paper and Pencil Used" column. This information may be used to assist in evaluating errors on individual items and for summing the percentage of items for which the student used paper and pencil. Correct answers are provided in the record form.

Note that some questions are structured to yield qualitative, behavioral observations as well as quantitative scores. For example, item 13 asks the student to count aloud and tell how many chips there are in total. They child may count the chips incorrectly but provide the correct total. The item should be scored correctly in this case, but the examiner should discuss this behavioral observation when reporting the results.

Alphabet Writing Fluency

The Alphabet Writing Fluency subtest has a 30-second time limit in which the student is asked to write as many letters of the alphabet as he or she can. This subtest requires the use of a stopwatch or clock with a second hand in order to discontinue after exactly 30 seconds; do not score responses written after this time limit. The student can write the letters in upper- or lowercase, in print or in cursive, and in any order. Each letter should be written only once. If the student begins writing the same letter in both upper- and lowercase or in both print and cursive, say, "Write each letter only once." If the student gives up before the time limit is reached, you may encourage him or her to keep trying. If the student asks for clarification of the directions or does not respond after you start timing, you may provide clarification by saying, "You can write the letters of the alphabet in order, starting with a-b-c, or you can write any letters you know, like the letters in your name." After you begin timing, do not stop timing to provide clarification. After administration is complete, refer to the scoring rules provided in the examiner's manual to score the student's response. Use the score box provided in the record form to record which letters received credit

> **DON'T FORGET**
> ....
> **Scoring Alphabet Writing Fluency**
>
> No credit is given for the letter "A," because it is provided as an example in the response booklet. (The maximum possible score is 25.)

(and whether the letters were upper- or lowercase) and the types of errors made. Examples of scored responses are included in the scoring workbook.

Sentence Composition

Administration of the Sentence Composition subtest requires the administration of two components: Sentence Combining and Sentence Building. It is preferable to administer the components in this order because this is the order in which students in the standardization sample were administered the subtest.

Administration of Sentence Combining always begins with item 1. If the student scores 0 points on the first two items, discontinue administration and proceed to Sentence Building. Otherwise, administer all items. If the student's response contains an abbreviation, texting language, or a symbol (e.g., "lol," "btw," "@," "&"), say, "Please write out the words instead of using symbols or abbreviations," and allow the student to correct his or her response. Do not provide any additional assistance. If he or she does not correct his or her response, proceed to the next item. This prompt may be administered once per item. Do not give this prompt if the student uses numerals in his or her response; use of numerals is not penalized.

> **DON'T FORGET**
> ....
> Before scoring Sentence Composition or Essay Composition, refer to the "Basic Rules of Written Grammar and Mechanics" in Appendix B of the examiner's manual for guidance in identifying grammar and mechanics errors.

> **DON'T FORGET**
> ....
> When scoring Sentence Combining and Sentence Building, errors that could be attributed to dialect or slang are penalized, except when oral language is being quoted or explicitly referenced.

Sentence Combining is scored after administration is complete. Scoring rules are provided in the examiner's manual for scoring three skill areas: (a) Syntax and Semantics, (b) Mechanics, and (c) Extra Credit. Use the score box provided in the record form to record errors and scores. Examples of scored responses are included in the scoring workbook.

DON'T FORGET
....
Sentence Combining Includes a Score for "Extra Credit"

This score awards 1 extra point for each item in which the student (a) combined the original sentences into one sentence that means the same thing, (b) did not use poor sentence structure, and (c) did not use the word "and" to join two independent clauses/sentences.

Meeting these criteria indicates a level of syntactic maturity and efficiency that was characteristic of high-achieving students in the standardization sample.

Item: Cats are pets. Dogs are pets.

Sample response that receives extra credit:

Cats and dogs are pets.

Sample responses that do not receive extra credit:

Cats are pets and dogs are pets.

Cats and birds are pets.

Administration of Sentence Building always begins with item 1 and follows the same discontinue rule: If the student scores 0 points on the first two items, discontinue administration. Otherwise, administer all items. If the student's response contains an abbreviation, texting language, or a symbol, administer the same prompt as described for Sentence Combining. If the student's response uses the target word within a title or as the subject or object of the sentence (e.g., for the target word "as": "*As* is a word"; "I just said *as*"; "As *the World Turns* is a show"), say, "Please write a new sentence that uses this word in a different way." Do not provide additional assistance. If he or she does not write a new sentence, proceed to the next item. The purpose of this prompt is to discourage students from writing sentences that fail to use the target word with meaningful context. Only use this prompt under the conditions specified, and do not give the prompt simply because the student used the target word incorrectly. Both prompts may be administered once per item.

Sentence Building is scored after administration is complete. Scoring rules are provided in the examiner's manual for scoring Mechanics, and Syntax and Semantics. Note that unlike Sentence Combining, Sentence Building does not include a score for extra credit. Use the score box provided in the record form to record errors and scores. Examples of scored responses are included in the scoring workbook.

Word Reading

Prior to administering the Word Reading subtest, you should become familiar with the acceptable pronunciation(s) of each item by listening to the audio CD (track 23) and referring to the pronunciation guide in the examiner's manual. This will prepare you to score the student's responses quickly and efficiently during administration. Recording responses accurately is essential, particularly if you plan to conduct a skills analysis for this subtest, and use of an audio recorder is highly recommended. Many students provide responses at a rapid pace, making it difficult to score and record errors accurately. If you use a recorder, you can play back the recording after administration is complete to score the responses in the record form and record errors for the skills analysis. Always begin administration with item 1 and continue administration until the discontinue rule is met.

To obtain a measure of the speed of word reading, you may choose to obtain a supplemental Word Reading Speed score by recording the item completed at 30 seconds. This score is provided as a cumulative percentage and is optional; recording this information is not required to obtain the Word Reading subtest standard score. To record the item completed at 30 seconds during administration, it is recommended that you simply mark the item reached at 30 seconds and then continue administration until the discontinue rule is reached. After administration is complete, you can record this item number completed at 30 seconds in the space provided in the record form. Alternatively, you may play back the audio recording of the administration to obtain this information. If the student skips a word or row, redirect the student immediately. If the student makes multiple attempts to read a word, score only the last attempt. If the student does not say a word clearly, circle or star the item, and after administration is complete, point to the row containing the item in question and say, "I did not hear you clearly. Please read these words again." Score only the item in question; do not rescore any other items in that row. Asking the student to repeat a row rather than a single item is done to avoid the implication that a particular word was read incorrectly and should be read differently the second time. If the student reads a word slowly or

≡ *Don't Forget*

Do not discontinue administration after the item completed at 30 seconds is recorded. Continue administration until the discontinue rule is met.

in parts, prompt the student once per item to "say it all together." Pronunciations that are not read fluently are scored 0 points. For qualitative evaluation purposes, you may record which items took the student longer than 3 seconds to complete and which items elicited a self-correction from the student by recording check marks in the columns provided in the record form.

Essay Composition

The Essay Composition subtest has a 10-minute time limit in which the student is asked to write an essay. This subtest requires the use of a stopwatch or clock with a second hand in order to discontinue after exactly 600 seconds; do not score any part of the response written after this time limit. Prompt the student as directed at 5 minutes and 1 minute before the time limit expires to help the student pace his or her work and avoid running out of time. If the student finishes early, you should stop timing and verify that the student has written at least 30 words; if not, prompt the student to "try to write a full page." If the student finishes early and has written more than 30 words, record the elapsed time and discontinue the subtest.

All scoring for this subtest occurs after administration is complete. Read through the student's essay before scoring to become familiar with its content and structure, and make a photocopy of the essay to write on for scoring purposes. To obtain the Essay Composition score, score Word Count (the number of words written) and Theme Development and Text Organization. Scoring Theme Development and Text Organization is easiest using the scoring guide included in the Scoring Assistant (see previous section on the Scoring Assistant for more information). If you are not using the Scoring Assistant, follow the scoring guide printed in the examiner's manual. In order to obtain the Grammar and Mechanics score, refer to the scoring rules in the examiner's manual to count the number of correct word sequences and incorrect word sequences.

Excellent interscorer reliabilities are reported in the WIAT-III technical manual for Essay Composition as a whole (0.92–0.99) and for Theme Development and Text Organization specifically (0.92). Practice using the scoring workbook and the scoring guide is recommended to acquire this level of proficiency.

Refer to the CD-ROM for a step-by-step demonstration of how to score a student's essay using the scoring guide feature of the Scoring Assistant.

Pseudoword Decoding

Prior to administering the Pseudoword Decoding subtest, you should become familiar with the acceptable pronunciation(s) of each item by listening to the audio CD (track 24) and referring to the pronunciation guide in the examiner's manual. This will prepare you to score the student's responses quickly and efficiently during administration. Recording responses accurately is essential, particularly if you plan to conduct a skills analysis for this subtest, and use of an audio recorder is highly recommended. Many students provide responses at a rapid pace, making it difficult to score and record errors accurately. If you use a recorder, you can play back the recording after administration is complete to score the responses in the record form and record errors for the skills analysis. Always begin administration with the sample items and continue administration until the discontinue rule is met.

> **DON'T FORGET**
>
> When scoring Theme Development and Text Organization, do not penalize for spelling, capitalization, and punctuation errors.
> When scoring Essay Composition: Grammar and Mechanics, errors that could be attributed to dialect or slang are penalized, except when oral language is being quoted or explicitly referenced.

To obtain a measure of the speed of decoding skill, you may choose to obtain a supplemental Pseudoword Decoding Speed score by recording the item completed at 30 seconds. This score is provided as a cumulative percentage and is optional; recording this information is not required to obtain the Pseudoword Decoding subtest standard score. To record the item completed at 30 seconds during administration, it is recommended that you simply mark the item reached at 30 seconds and then continue administration until the discontinue rule is reached. After administration is complete, you can record this item number completed at 30 seconds in the space provided in the record form. Alternatively, you may play back the audio recording of the administration to obtain this information. If the student skips a word or row, redirect the student immediately. If the student makes multiple attempts to read a word, score only the last attempt. If the student does not say a word clearly, circle or star the item, and after administration is complete, point to the row containing the item in question and say, "I did not hear you clearly. Please read these

> **DON'T FORGET**
>
> **Pseudoword Decoding**
>
> Do not discontinue administration after the item completed at 30 seconds is recorded. Continue administration until the discontinue rule is met.

words again." Score only the item in question; do not rescore any other items in that row. Asking the student to repeat a row rather than a single item is done to avoid the implication that a particular word was read incorrectly and should be read differently the second time. If the student reads a word slowly or in parts, prompt the student once per item to "say it all together." Pronunciations that are not read fluently are scored 0 points.

Numerical Operations

In order to apply the discontinue rule, you may choose to allow the student to complete as many problems as he or she can and then score the responses later, or you may score the student's responses during administration and discontinue the subtest after the student receives four consecutive scores of 0. If you allow the student to attempt all items, do not award credit for any items completed after the first four consecutive scores of 0. If you score during administration, it is important to avoid making a student feel uncomfortable or nervous by watching him or her work each problem. Instead, it may be helpful to allow the student to work on an item without feeling watched and then review the response after he or she is finished. However, if the child is comfortable, valuable behavioral observations may be obtained by observing the student at work. The student is not permitted to use a calculator.

> **DON'T FORGET**
> ....
> **Pseudoword Decoding**
>
> If the student skips a word or row, redirect the student immediately.
> If the student makes multiple attempts to read a word, score only the last attempt.

Note that item 2 requires the student to write the number of balls he or she counted in the preceding item. If the number of balls was miscounted, the student will not receive credit for either item. Item 1 is designed to measure counting skills, and item 2 is designed to measure both counting and numeral writing skills.

> **DON'T FORGET**
> ....
> **Expressive Vocabulary**
>
> Ambiguous but possibly correct responses, related synonyms, and slang terms should be queried by saying, "Tell me another word."

Oral Expression

Administration of the Oral Expression subtest requires the administration of three components: Expressive Vocabulary, Oral Word Fluency, and Sentence Repetition. It is preferable to administer the components in this order, because this is the order in which students in the standardization sample were administered the subtest.

The stimulus book is required to administer Expressive Vocabulary, and administration always begins with item 1. Item prompts may be repeated if the student requests a repetition or does not respond within a reasonable amount of time. The student must provide a one-word response. If more than one word is given, prompt the student by saying, "Tell me one word." If the student gives a slang term or closely related term (e.g., "cape" for "peninsula), say, "Tell me another word." However, do not prompt the student after an incorrect response.

Oral Word Fluency is a timed subtest that requires the use of a stopwatch or clock with a second hand. You must discontinue each item after exactly 60 seconds; do not record or score responses after this time limit. Both items must be administered in the order presented in the record form.

> # DON'T FORGET
> ···
> ## Oral Word Fluency
>
> Recording responses accurately is essential, and use of an audio recorder is highly recommended.

If a student gives up before the time limit is reached, you may encourage him or her to keep trying and repeat the item prompt as needed. Recording responses accurately is essential, and use of an audio recorder is highly recommended. Many students provide responses at a rapid pace, making it difficult to write all responses accurately. If you use a recorder, you can play back the recording after administration is complete to record the responses in the record form.

Administration of Sentence Repetition always begins with item 1. You may choose to administer all 15 items and apply the discontinue rule after administration and scoring are completed, or you may score responses during administration and discontinue administration after four consecutive scores of 0. Use of an audio recorder is recommended for recording responses accurately for Sentence Repetition. This subtest requires careful recording of three error types: Additions, Substitutions/Omissions, and Transpositions. Prior to administration, review the recording and scoring directions carefully. Recording errors incorrectly could result in an early discontinue; for this reason, it is a good idea to administer additional items past the discontinue rule if you are unsure about whether you have recorded or scored the responses correctly.

The most common scoring errors are illustrated in the following text and are organized by scoring rule:

1. Scoring rule: Forming or separating contractions are not scored as errors.

a. *Example:* Saying "you're" for "you are" is not an error. It is acceptable to either record "you're" in parentheses above the item, as in the following example, or to not record it at all.

(You're)
you are not

2. Scoring Rule: Changing verb form/tense is scored as one error.
   a. *Example:* Changing the verb "wanted" to "had hoped" is one error.

   (had hoped)
   man ~~wanted~~ to keep

3. Scoring Rule: Adding two or more words is scored as one error.
   a. *Example:* Adding the words "from the" is scored as one error.

   (from the)
   stop her ∧ crying

4. Scoring Rule: Each deleted/substituted word is scored as one error.
   a. *Example:* If the student says, "I don't remember the rest" or "something about a bus" or "they couldn't move" instead of "when the bus got stuck," simply count the number of words omitted/substituted from the item. In this case, "when the bus got stuck" is five words, so this would be scored as five errors.

   ~~When the bus got stuck~~

Oral Reading Fluency

The Oral Reading Fluency subtest is administered by item sets that use grade-based start and stop points. The student reads passages aloud from the Oral Reading Fluency booklet and is allowed to review each passage while answering the comprehension question. The comprehension questions are for qualitative evaluation purposes only and do not contribute to the subtest score; however, the comprehension questions are not optional and must be administered according to the directions in the record form. The purpose of the comprehension questions is to structure the subtest in a way that encourages the student to read for meaning. After all passages and

> **DON'T FORGET**
> ····································
> The comprehension questions are for qualitative evaluation purposes only and do not contribute to the subtest score. However, the comprehension questions are *not* optional and must be administered according to the directions in the record form.

comprehension questions have been administered for the student's item set, you may complete the Prosody Scale at the end of this subtest for qualitative evaluation purposes.

Prior to administration, review the recording and scoring directions carefully. This subtest requires careful recording of four error types: Supplied Words, Additions, Substitutions/

DON'T FORGET

If the student skips a line of text, redirect the student to the appropriate line, but do not stop timing, and do not score as an error.

If the student skips a word, do not redirect the student; rather, record the omitted word as an error.

Omissions, and Transpositions. Supplied Words are words that the examiner provides to the student after the student spends 5 seconds attempting to read a word. Record a "G" (for "given") above each word supplied to the student. Recording and scoring Additions, Substitutions/Omissions, and Transpositions follow similar rules as described for Sentence Repetition. You may choose to record errors as the student is reading, or you may create an audio recording of the subtest administration and review the recording after administration is complete to record reading errors. Use of an audio recorder is recommended to ensure accurate recording and scoring.

To avoid scoring errors, you may opt not to record deviations from print that are not scored as errors, such as repetitions of words, forming or separating correct contractions, and self-corrections. A stopwatch is recommended to time how long it takes the student to read each passage. Record the elapsed time in seconds.

Applying the item set reverse rule correctly is necessary for properly administering this subtest. This subtest includes an item set reverse rule that requires the student to reverse one start point if the reading time on the first passage of the item set exceeds the specified time limit. If so, you may choose to interrupt the student's reading to reverse to the preceding item set, or you may allow the student to finish reading the passage before reversing. Use your clinical judgment to determine the best way to maintain rapport, sustain the student's motivation, and avoid causing the student undue frustration. The reverse rule may be applied a maximum of two times from the grade-appropriate item set if the student meets the

DON'T FORGET

The item set reverse rule for Reading Comprehension allows you to reverse a maximum of three item sets.

The item set reverse rule for Oral Reading Fluency allows you to reverse a maximum of two item sets.

reverse rule criteria each time. After two reversals, the full item set must be administered.

It is recommended that you begin at the student's grade-appropriate start point whenever possible because it is important to find the most appropriate item set for the student. The most appropriate item set is the one closest to the grade-appropriate item set in which the student reads the passage within the given time limit. If you are certain that the student will not be able to read the passage and you believe that starting at the grade-appropriate start point would be detrimental to the student's subsequent motivation and performance, you may begin one start point below the grade-appropriate start point.

Scoring the Oral Reading Fluency subtest is greatly facilitated by using the Scoring Assistant. Using the Scoring Assistant requires that you enter the following information for each passage in the item set: elapsed time (in seconds), the number of Addition errors, and the number of other errors (which includes Supplied Words and Substitution/Omission and Transposition errors). If scoring by hand, you must incorporate the preceding information into the formulas provided in the record form in order to calculate the Fluency and Accuracy raw scores.

Spelling

Prior to administering the Spelling subtest, you should become familiar with how to pronounce each item correctly by listening to the audio CD (track 25) and referring to the pronunciation guide in the examiner's manual. Read each item prompt at a natural, conversational pace, and pronounce each spelling word according to the pronunciation guide. Do not pronounce the target word slowly or with unusual emphasis, because this may help or hinder the student's performance. Item prompts may be repeated if the student requests a repetition or has not responded in an appropriate time frame. Responses that contain letter reversals are scored 0 points unless the student is in kindergarten or first grade. If the student is in kindergarten or first grade, letter reversals are not penalized as long as the reversal does not form a different letter. In order to apply the discontinue rule, you must be able to score the student's responses during administration. However, it is important to avoid making a student feel uncomfortable or nervous by watching him or her spell each word. Instead, it may be helpful to allow the student to work on an item without feeling watched and then review the response after he or she is finished.

Math Fluency

The Math Fluency subtests may be administered individually or together. If all three Math Fluency subtests are administered, it is preferable to administer the subtests in the order presented in the record form because this is the order in which students in the standardization sample were administered the subtests. As specified in the record form, the full administration instructions must be read before administering Math Fluency— Addition and before each subsequent Math Fluency subtest if there is a delay

between subtest administrations. If more than one Math Fluency subtest is administered and there is no delay between subtest administrations, the brief (abbreviated) administration instructions may be read before administering each of the following: Math Fluency—Subtraction and/or Math Fluency—Multiplication. For all Math Fluency subtests, when administering the three Math Fluency subtests, make sure the student completes the problems from left to right, row by row, down the first page and then from left to right, row by row, down the second page. If the student does not complete the problems in the order specified, do not stop timing, but immediately redirect the student to the correct item order by pointing to the appropriate item and reminding the student to solve the problems in that order. If the student solves the problems in a different order than the instructions specify but does not complete all items in the subtest, the validity of the results may be compromised and should be interpreted with caution. Order of administration is important, because item difficulty varies within each subtest, so following a different order may result in exposure to a subset of items before the time limit is reached that differs in difficulty from the subset of items that would have been administered according to the standard order. If the student solves the problems in a different order than the instructions specify but completes all items in the subtest before the time limit, the validity of the results should not be affected.

HOW TO INTERPRET THE WIAT-III

Interpretation of the WIAT-III results should be purposeful by responding to the original referral question(s) and testing one or more hypotheses. The score comparisons and subsequent analyses should be evaluated according to these purposes.

Qualitative Data

Both quantitative and qualitative information should be considered when interpreting test results. Qualitative information can be obtained by recording general behavioral observations during testing and through the use of skills analysis (discussed in the preceding Scoring Assistant section). A qualitative analysis helps clarify why an individual might achieve a set of scores. Investigate whether test behaviors are typical of the individual's performance by talking with teachers, parents, or others who are familiar with the examinee. Determine if there are mitigating circumstances such as illness or anxiety that might have affected test performance. Note if test behaviors are consistent from one subtest to another. Pay close attention to comments that an examinee may make regarding his or her academic interests and strengths and weaknesses. Record the use of problem-solving strategies. For example, an examinee that uses subvocalization when writing a spelling word is probably using a different strategy than an examinee who writes a word with various spellings, commenting, "That doesn't look right." Qualitative observations are important, because they provide information that can serve as a cross-check on the validity of the examinee's scores (Glutting, Oakland, & Konold, 1994) and provide valuable information for linking assessment results to instructional planning.

When recording behavioral observations, pay close attention to the student's performance on each subtest. Observe how the student approaches a task and responds to perceived success or failure. Is an error the result of carelessness, inattentiveness, lack of self-monitoring, or lack of effort? Does the examinee use self-monitoring by checking his or her work, by rereading what has been written, or by rechecking a passage prior to answering a comprehension question? Does frustration set in once errors begin to occur? Does the examinee seek out your encouragement and approval?

Compare the student's performance across subtests, and observe how task demands affect performance. For example, observe how the examinee decodes unfamiliar words when reading from a list on Word Reading and Pseudoword Decoding in comparison to reading unfamiliar words in context on Oral Reading Fluency.

Review the student's responses to determine where the problem-solving process may break down. Because examinees are required to write their responses with a pencil without an eraser, you can more easily identify how errors were made on written responses.

By understanding why an error occurs or under what conditions an individual achieves success, an individualized intervention plan can be developed. For example, knowing that a student's spelling problem is related to morphology (word form, such as root word, suffix, prefix) rather than phonology (sound-symbol relationship) can direct the teacher to provide explicit, systematic instruction in that area.

Age Norms versus Grade Norms

The norm-referenced scores obtained on the WIAT-III represent the individual's performance in comparison to others of the same age or in the same grade. When achievement is compared to ability, age-based norms are recommended to quantify student performance on the achievement measure. However, with the WIAT-III as well as other measures of academic achievement, there are times when age-based scores can be misleading. For example, when a student has been retained in a grade, comparing him or her to age-mates assumes that the equivalent instructional opportunity has been provided. In such a case, the individual might have lower scores because some skills have not been taught. For this reason, grade-based scores are typically preferred for students with a history of grade retention. When talking with teachers, it also makes more sense to discuss where a student performs in relation to others in the same grade.

If a student is considered very young or old for his or her grade level, age norms may not be available for all subtests or composites. For example, age norms are not available for a 7-year-old third grader who is administered the Essay Composition subtest (administered to grades 3–12), because this student's age is considered unusually young (out of level) for third grade. However, it is possible to yield age norms for this student for subtests such as Listening Comprehension and Oral Expression, because these subtests are administered at every age and grade. Grade norms must be used to obtain scores for certain subtests and composites when a student's age is out of level.

> # CAUTION
> ....
> ## Using Age Norms with Students Who Are Young or Old for Grade
>
> Out-of-level age norms are *not* provided. If a student is unusually young or old for their grade, age norms may not be available for all subtests or composites. Use of grade norms is necessary to yield some scores for these students.

Confidence Intervals

When interpreting and reporting standard scores for subtests and composites, it is recommended that you use the confidence interval information provided, which allows you to report scores within a range. For example, using the tables provided in the technical manual, if a 13-year-old student obtained a Word Reading age-based standard score of 100, the examiner can be 90 percent confident that the student's true score is in the range of 95 to 105 (100 ± 5) and 95 percent confident that the student's true score is in the range of 94 to 106 (100 ± 6).

Subtest and Composite Score Comparisons

One of the first steps in interpreting test results is to compare scores across subtests and composites. Specific learning disabilities are characterized by patterns of strengths and weaknesses, and score comparisons facilitate accurate diagnoses and effective intervention planning.

For example, students with certain types of reading disorders have trouble with both encoding (spelling) and decoding (Lyon, Shaywitz, & Shaywitz, 2003). Compare performance on the Word Reading and Pseudoword Decoding subtests to performance on the Spelling subtest. Determine if similar types of errors occur across these subtests. For example, does the individual show a pattern of errors with a particular letter-sound relationship? Are there similar morphological errors (e.g., omission of word suffixes)?

In the area of mathematics, comparing a student's performance on the Numerical Operations and the Math Problem Solving subtests helps identify whether difficulties in math are specific to calculation or to using math skills to solve real problems.

In the area of oral language, compare Listening Comprehension performance to Oral Expression performance. Evaluate whether weaknesses are specific to certain tasks (e.g., expressive vocabulary but not receptive vocabulary) and whether difficulties are demonstrated on receptive tasks, expressive tasks, or both. Next, compare performance in the area of oral language with performance in the area of written language (reading and writing subtests). For example, a student with weaknesses in Reading Comprehension and Listening Comprehension (Oral Discourse Comprehension) requires instruction in language comprehension. In contrast, a student who performs poorly on Reading Comprehension, Oral Reading Fluency, and Word Reading but demonstrates average performance on Listening Comprehension would likely benefit from instruction in word identification and reading fluency rather than language comprehension. To give another example, a student who performs poorly on the Word Reading subtest may have underlying oral language weaknesses in word retrieval (measured by Oral Word Fluency and Expressive Vocabulary) and vocabulary (measured by Receptive Vocabulary and Expressive Vocabulary) that contribute to a weakness in word identification, and intervention should be planned accordingly.

Subtest and composite score comparisons can be evaluated using the score reports generated by the Scoring Assistant or by completing the tables provided in the record form (pp. 1–3). Completing the following steps will help you properly interpret the composite scores and the score comparisons:

1. Evaluate whether the composite scores are consistent with the level of achievement across composite areas or if there is variation in performance across composite areas.
2. Evaluate the consistency or variability in subtest scores within achievement areas (and composites) and across achievement areas.
3. Determine whether each composite and subtest score is a normative strength (standard scores above 115) or a normative weakness (standard scores below 85).
4. Evaluate whether the differences between pairs of composite standard scores are statistically significant at the desired level of confidence.
5. For any statistically significant differences, determine if the differences are typical or rare by looking up the cumulative percentages of the standardization sample that obtained the same or similar composite score discrepancies.
6. Intersubtest scatter can be evaluated in the same way.

When comparing subtest scores, it is also important to consider whether there is restricted range with any of the subtests. The distributions of the following scores are slightly skewed in the lower ages and grades due to the natural floor that exists before skills are acquired: Early Reading Skills; Reading Comprehension; Alphabet Writing Fluency; Sentence Composition; Word Reading; Pseudoword Decoding; Numerical Operations; and Math Fluency–Addition, Subtraction, and Multiplication. For example, many students in first grade (age 6) are not yet able to write sentences; hence, 6-year-olds who earn a raw score of 0 on the Sentence Composition subtest earn a score that is less than 2 standard deviations below the mean because their performance is not far below average relative to their same-age peers. Rapid Reference 2.7 reports by age the lowest possible score for each subtest based on a raw score of 0.

The distributions of the following scores are slightly skewed in the upper ages and grades due to the natural ceiling that is reached as skills are acquired: Early Reading Skills; Alphabet Writing Fluency; Word Reading; and Math Fluency–Addition, Subtraction, and Multiplication. In other words, once a level of mastery is reached in

DON'T FORGET

Restricted Range of Subtest Standard Scores

Many subtests that show a restricted range have a natural floor or ceiling that is reasonable to expect, given the timing or trajectory of skill acquisition.

Rapid Reference 2.7

Minimum Subtest Scores by Age (Based on Raw Score of 0)

Age	LC	ER	RC	MP	AW	SC	WR	EC	PD	NO	OE	OR	SP	MA	MS	MM
4:0–4:3	67	72	—	65	80	—	—	—	—	—	58	—	—	—	—	—
4:4–4:7	66	67	—	59	77	—	—	—	—	—	56	—	—	—	—	—
4:8–4:11	64	63	—	56	73	—	—	—	—	—	54	—	—	—	—	—
5:0–5:3	60	54	—	51	70	—	—	—	—	71	52	—	70	—	—	—
5:4–5:7	58	42	—	45	66	—	—	—	—	68	49	—	66	—	—	—
5:8–5:11	54	40	—	43	62	—	—	—	—	63	47	—	64	—	—	—
6:0–6:3	52	40	86	40	60	88	84	—	84	59	45	55	60	75	88	—
6:4–6:7	52	40	79	40	58	82	78	—	76	57	43	51	58	65	83	—
6:8–6:11	49	40	69	40	55	77	70	—	73	52	42	48	54	63	78	—
7:0–7:3	46	40	63/65	40	52	72	63	—	71	48	40	42/66	50	59	73	—
7:4–7:7	45	40	56/58	40	49	69	59	—	69	44	40	40/61	48	57	67	—
7:8–7:11	43	40	50/52	40	46	66	57	—	66	40	40	40/54	44	55	63	—
8:0–8:3	41	40	49/55	40	43	63	55	58	64	40	40	51/57	42	53	59	87
8:4–8:7	40	40	46/52	40	42	60	53	55	63	40	40	49/55	40	49	58	79
8:8–8:11	40	40	44/50	40	41	59	52	54	61	40	40	47/53	40	49	56	73
9:0–9:3	40	40	48/51	40	40	57	51	50	60	40	40	51	40	48	56	68
9:4–9:7	40	40	47/50	40	40	56	51	48	59	40	40	49	40	47	55	63

Age																	
9:8–9:11	40	40	45/48	40	40	55	50	46	59	40	40	47	40	44	40	54	60
10:0–10:3	40	—	47/48	40	—	55	48	44	59	40	40	46/51	40	42	40	51	57
10:4–10:7	40	—	46/47	40	—	54	46	42	58	40	40	44/49	40	40	40	50	54
10:8–10:11	40	—	45/46	40	—	53	45	40	56	40	40	43/47	40	40	40	50	52
11:0–11:3	40	—	45/46	40	—	52	43	40	54	40	40	46/49	40	40	40	49	52
11:4–11:7	40	—	44/45	40	—	51	41	40	53	40	40	45/48	40	40	40	48	51
11:8–11:11	40	—	44/45	40	—	50	40	40	53	40	40	44/47	40	40	40	46	50
12:0–12:3	40	—	44/46	40	—	50	40	40	51	40	40	46/47	40	40	40	45	49
12:4–12:7	40	—	43/45	40	—	48	40	40	51	40	40	45/46	40	40	40	44	48
12:8–12:11	40	—	42/44	40	—	47	40	40	50	40	40	44/45	40	40	40	43	47
13:0–13:3	40	—	44/42	40	—	45	40	40	49	40	40	44	40	40	40	41	46
13:4–13:7	40	—	44/42	40	—	43	40	40	49	40	40	43	40	40	40	40	45
13:8–13:11	40	—	43/41	40	—	43	40	40	48	40	40	42	40	40	40	40	43
14:0–14:11	40	—	40	40	—	42	40	40	47	40	40	41/49	40	40	40	40	41
15:0–15:11	40	—	40	40	—	41	40	40	46	40	40	48	40	40	40	40	41
16:0–16:11	40	—	40	40	—	41	40	40	44	40	40	46	40	40	40	40	41
17:0–19:11	40	—	40	40	—	40	40	40	42	40	40	44	40	40	40	40	41

Note: LC = Listening Comprehension; ER = Early Reading Skills; RC = Reading Comprehension; MP = Math Problem Solving; AW = Alphabet Writing Fluency; SC = Sentence Composition; WR = Word Reading; EC = Essay Composition; PD = Pseudoword Decoding; NO = Numerical Operations; OE = Oral Expression; OR = Oral Reading Fluency; SP = Spelling; MA = Math Fluency—Addition; MS = Math Fluency—Subtraction; MM = Math Fluency—Multiplication. Data are from Appendix C of the *WIAT-III Technical Manual* (Pearson, 2009b). Shaded cells indicate standard scores that are less than 2 standard deviations below the mean. Cells with two standard scores (e.g., 43/41) include scores for both possible grade-level item sets within an age band for subtests with weighted raw scores.

≡ Rapid Reference 2.8

Maximum Subtest Scores by Age

Age	LC	ER	RC	MP	AW	SC	WR	EC	PD	NO	OE	OR	SP	MA	MS	MM
4:0–4:3	160	152	—	160	160	—	—	—	—	—	160	—	—	—	—	—
4:4–4:7	160	148	—	160	160	—	—	—	—	—	160	—	—	—	—	—
4:8–4:11	160	145	—	160	160	—	—	—	—	—	160	—	—	—	—	—
5:0–5:3	160	141	—	160	159	—	—	—	—	160	160	—	160	—	—	—
5:4–5:7	160	135	—	160	156	—	—	—	—	160	160	—	160	—	—	—
5:8–5:11	160	130	—	160	153	—	—	—	—	160	160	—	160	—	160	—
6:0–6:3	160	127	155	160	151	160	160	—	160	160	160	160	160	160	160	—
6:4–6:7	160	123	151	160	148	160	160	—	160	160	160	160	160	160	160	—
6:8–6:11	160	121	146	160	145	160	160	—	160	160	160	160	160	160	160	—
7:0–7:3	160	118	141/149	160	142	160	160	—	160	160	160	157/154	160	160	160	—
7:4–7:7	160	118	135/143	160	139	160	160	—	160	160	160	153/150	160	160	160	—
7:8–7:11	160	118	130/138	160	136	160	160	—	159	160	160	150/147	160	158	160	—
8:0–8:3	160	116	136/145	160	134	160	159	160	155	160	160	145/158	160	155	160	160
8:4–8:7	160	115	134/143	160	132	157	158	160	152	160	160	143/157	160	152	160	160
8:8–8:11	160	114	133/141	160	130	153	155	160	150	160	160	141/155	160	152	159	160
9:0–9:3	160	114	141/154	160	128	151	153	160	149	160	160	153/157	160	149	156	160
9:4–9:7	160	114	141/154	160	127	149	151	160	148	160	160	152/156	160	145	152	160
9:8–9:11	160	114	141/154	160	126	148	149	160	148	160	160	150/154	160	143	149	156
10:0–10:3	160	—	153/160	160	—	148	147	160	148	160	160	153/160	160	141	149	151

Age																
10:4–10:7	160	—	152/160	160	—	147	145	160	146	160	160	152/160	160	139	147	148
10:8–10:11	159	—	150/160	160	—	145	144	160	144	160	160	150/160	160	138	145	145
11:0–11:3	158	—	160	160	—	145	142	160	143	160	160	160	158	135	142	141
11:4–11:7	156	—	157/160	160	—	143	140	160	142	160	160	160	155	132	139	137
11:8–11:11	155	—	155/160	160	—	143	138	160	141	160	160	160	153	131	136	135
12:0–12:3	151	—	160	160	—	143	137	160	140	160	160	160	152	130	134	133
12:4–12:7	153	—	160	160	—	141	136	160	140	160	160	160	150	127	133	132
12:8–12:11	152	—	158/160	160	—	140	135	160	139	160	160	160	149	127	132	131
13:0–13:3	151	—	160	157	—	138	134	160	138	160	160	160	147	126	132	130
13:4–13:7	150	—	160/158	154	—	136	132	160	137	160	160	160	145	126	130	128
13:8–13:11	149	—	160/156	149	—	135	130	160	137	160	160	159	143	125	129	126
14:0–14:11	148	—	153/160	146	—	134	129	160	136	160	159	158/140	141	123	127	126
15:0–15:11	147	—	160	145	—	134	127	160	135	160	157	137	141	120	125	125
16:0–16:11	145	—	160	143	—	133	125	159	133	153	155	134	138	118	123	123
17:0–19:11	144	—	160	138	—	133	123	159	132	142	153	132	136	117	122	123

Note: LC = Listening Comprehension; ER = Early Reading Skills; RC = Reading Comprehension; MP = Math Problem Solving; AW = Alphabet Writing Fluency; SC = Sentence Composition; WR = Word Reading; EC = Essay Composition; PD = Pseudoword Decoding; NO = Numerical Operations; OE = Oral Expression; OR = Oral Reading Fluency; SP = Spelling; MA = Math Fluency—Addition; MS = Math Fluency—Subtraction; MM = Math Fluency—Multiplication. Data are from Appendix C of the *WIAT-III Technical Manual* (Pearson, 2009b). Shaded cells indicate standard scores that are less than 2 standard deviations above the mean. Cells with two standard scores (e.g., 43/41) include scores for both possible grade-level item sets within an age band for subtests with weighted raw scores.

each of these areas, there is little room for differentiation between students who are proficient and students who are excellent. Hence, it is reasonable to expect that the highest standard scores obtainable on these subtests are often less than 160 in the upper ages and grades. Rapid Reference 2.8 reports by age the highest possible score based on the maximum raw score for each subtest.

Growth Scale Values

When considered in conjunction, growth scale values and standard scores (or percentile ranks) can provide a meaningful sense of a student's progress. Rapid Reference 2.9 presents three possible combinations of changes in GSVs and standard scores and how to interpret each combination. Comparing standard scores (and percentile ranks) across time indicates whether the student has improved faster, slower, or at the same rate as his or her peers in the normative sample. In contrast, comparing GSVs over time indicates whether the student's performance, or skill level, has changed relative to his or her own previous performance. In addition, multiple GSVs can be used to plot a growth curve, which can be compared to the average growth curve of the student's peers. GSVs can be subtracted or averaged, and are well suited for progress monitoring; however, do not average or compare GSVs across different subtests because the range of GSVs varies from subtest to subtest, depending on the nature of each subtest's raw score distribution.

When using GSVs for progress monitoring, use caution when interpreting scores if fewer than 3 months have passed between testing sessions because growth rates may be inflated due to practice effects. In addition, use caution when interpreting only two GSVs; three or more GSVs are typically needed to form a reliable growth trend.

CAUTION

Using Growth Scale Values

- Comparing, subtracting, and averaging GSVs from the same subtest is encouraged—but *not* across different subtests.
- Three or more months between testing sessions is recommended to avoid practice effects.
- Three or more GSV scores are recommended to form a reliable growth trend.

≡ *Rapid Reference 2.9*

Interpreting GSVs and Standard Scores

GSV Change	Standard Score Change	Interpretation
Increase	Increase	The increase in the GSVs suggests that the student's achievement skills have improved. The increase in standard scores across testing sessions suggests that the student's achievement skills improved *at a faster rate* than his or her peers'.
Increase	No Change	The increase in the GSVs suggests that the student's achievement skills have improved. The consistency of standard scores across testing sessions suggests that the student's achievement skills improved *at the same rate* relative to his or her peers'.
Increase	Decrease	The increase in the GSVs suggests that the student's achievement skills have improved. The decrease in standard scores indicates that the student's peers improved even more during the same time period. In other words, the student improved but at a slower rate than his or her peers.
No Change	Decrease	The consistency of GSVs across testing sessions indicates that the student has not shown growth or decline in the achievement area. The decrease in standard scores suggests that during the same time period, his or her peers' skills improved.

Note: This table includes the most likely combination patterns of change for GSVs and standard scores. Less likely combinations (e.g., GSV scores decrease, standard scores increase) are intentionally omitted.

🐟 TEST YOURSELF 🐟

1. The WIAT-III normative sample includes representative proportions of students with clinical diagnoses and a representative proportion of students identified as academically gifted.

True or False?

(continued)

2. **Average test-retest gains are *least* pronounced for subtests in which of the following achievement areas?**

   (a) Oral Language

   (b) Basic Reading

   (c) Reading Comprehension

   (d) Reading Fluency

   (e) Written Expression

   (f) Mathematics

3. **Average test-retest gains are *most* pronounced for subtests in which of the following *two* achievement areas?**

   (a) Oral Language

   (b) Basic Reading

   (c) Reading Comprehension

   (d) Reading Fluency

   (e) Written Expression

   (f) Mathematics

4. **Goal statements are only provided for subtests with skills analysis data.**
   True or False?

5. **After selecting the item set administered, what type of score should be entered into the Scoring Assistant for Reading Comprehension and Oral Reading Fluency?**

   (a) Raw score

   (b) Weighted raw score

6. **The pattern of strengths and weaknesses (PSW) analysis may be calculated using WIAT-III scores and scores from which of the following ability tests?**

   (a) WPPSI-III

   (b) WISC-IV

   (c) WAIS-IV

   (d) DAS-II

   (e) KABC-II

   (f) All of the above

   (g) A through D only

7. **Which of the following subtests does not have a discontinue rule and must be administered in its entirety?**

   (a) Word Reading

   (b) Reading Comprehension

   (c) Early Reading Skills

   (d) Numerical Operations

8. **Which of the following should be followed in order to determine the correct start point for Reading Comprehension?**

   (a) The examiner can select the appropriate start point based upon the student's performance on the Word Reading subtest.

   (b) The examiner can select the appropriate start point based upon the student's current reading level in the classroom.

   (c) Students who score 2 or fewer points on the reversal items at their grade-appropriate start point should reverse two start points.

   (d) Students who score 2 or fewer points on the reversal items at their grade-appropriate start point should reverse one start point.

9. **If an examiner obtains a grade-based standard score for a ninth-grade student who reversed to the eighth-grade item set on the Reading Comprehension or Oral Reading Fluency subtest, which comparison group is used to derive that standard score?**

   (a) Ninth-grade peers who took the eighth-grade item set

   (b) Ninth-grade peers who took the ninth-grade item set

   (c) Eighth-grade students who took the eighth-grade item set

   (d) Eighth-grade students who took the ninth-grade item set

10. **Which type of norms is generally preferred when interpreting assessment results from a student who is unusually young or old for his or her grade?**

    (a) Age-based norms

    (b) Grade-based norms

11. **Use of an audio recorder to record student responses is highly recommended when administering which of the following subtests?**

    (a) Oral Expression

    (b) Word Reading

    (c) Pseudoword Decoding

    (d) Oral Reading Fluency

    (e) All of the above

12. **The audio CD is used to administer the items for which of the following subtest components?**

    (a) Oral Discourse Comprehension

    (b) Receptive Vocabulary

    (c) Sentence Repetition

    (d) Oral Word Fluency

(*continued*)

13. **How many growth scale value (GSV) scores are recommended to form a reliable growth trend?**

(a) At least 1

(b) At least 2

(c) At least 3

14. **Which of the following describes interscorer reliabilities for the Essay Composition subtest?**

(a) Excellent (0.90s)

(b) Good (0.80s)

(c) Acceptable (0.70s)

Answers: 1. True; 2. e; 3. a, c; 4. False; 5. a; 6. f; 7. c; 8. d; 9. a; 10. b; 11. e; 12. a; 13. c; 14. a

Three

KTEA-II

DESCRIPTION OF THE KTEA-II

The Kaufman Test of Educational Achievement–Second Edition (KTEA-II; Kaufman & Kaufman, 2004) was developed to assess the academic achievement of children and adolescents ages 4½ through 25. The KTEA-II has two versions: the Brief Form and the Comprehensive Form (the Comprehensive Form is comprised of two independent parallel forms, A and B). The Brief Form assesses three academic domains (reading, math, and written expression), and the Comprehensive form assesses an additional fourth domain (oral language). Although the Brief and Comprehensive forms tap three of the same academic domains, there is no overlap in items between the two forms of the test. This chapter reviews the content of the KTEA-II Comprehensive and Brief forms.

History and Development

Over a 4-year period beginning in 1981, Drs. Alan and Nadeen Kaufman developed the first edition of the Kaufman Test of Educational Achievement (K-TEA). During those years, items were developed and tried out in 1981, 1982, and 1983. The K-TEA was standardized in both the spring and fall of 1983. The normative groups comprised of 1,409 students in the spring and 1,067 in the fall. Upon completion of the standardization, the K-TEA was published in 1985. Then, in the mid-1990s, American Guidance Service, publisher of the K-TEA, restandardized the original K-TEA to match the 1994 U.S. Bureau of the Census estimates of the population. No changes were made to the items and scales of the K-TEA during the restandardization, but the norms were thoroughly updated. The renorming project involved four achievement batteries: the K-TEA, the Peabody Individual Achievement Test–Revised (PIAT-R), KeyMath–Revised

(KeyMath-R), and the Woodcock Reading Mastery Tests–Revised (WRMT-R). The instruments all measured one or more domains of academic achievement. During the renorming, each student was administered one of the primary batteries along with subtests from the other instruments. Thus, each of the primary batteries was administered to approximately one-fifth of the standardization sample (with 3,429 total participants in the Age-Norm sample and 3,184 total participants in the Grade-Norm sample). The renorming of the K-TEA was finalized with the publication of the K-TEA/Normative Update (K-TEA/NU) by Nadeen and Alan Kaufman in 1997.

Because professionals in school psychology and related fields used the K-TEA and K-TEA/NU so frequently, the test authors decided to revise the test beginning in 1995. Indeed, studies of test usage have shown that both the K-TEA and the K-TEA/NU are used frequently in educational and clinical settings (Archer et al., 1991; Hammill et al., 1992; Hutton et al., 1992; Laurent & Swerdlik, 1992; Stinnett et al., 1994; Wilson & Reschley, 1996). To ensure that the KTEA-II provided the most useful and practical information to clinicians, the Kaufmans developed their plan for the second edition based on current research and clinical practice. Four main goals were identified for the revision of the K-TEA, which are outlined in Rapid Reference 3.1.

Chapter 5 of the *KTEA-II Comprehensive Form Manual* (Kaufman & Kaufman, 2004a) discusses the content development for each subtest in depth. Generally, the first step in the development of each subtest was to define at a conceptual level which skills should be measured for a particular academic domain. Both literature reviews and expert opinion were used to determine what should be measured within each academic domain. The original K-TEA items were reviewed to determine which item formats should be retained and which should be modified. Since four new achievement areas were added in the KTEA-II,

---

≡ *Rapid Reference 3.1*

Goals of KTEA-II Revision

Improve the measurement of the achievement domains measured by the original K-TEA.	Add content that is appropriate for preschool and college-age students.
Add subtests to assess written and oral expression, listening comprehension, and reading-related skills.	Make error analysis more informative through the systematic representation of skills, and, on some subtests, a more fine-grained approach to classifying errors.

expert advisors contributed suggestions for content and item formats for written expression, oral expression, listening comprehension, and reading-related skills. Part of the content development of the subtests involved making sure that certain skills were systematically represented. Developing subtests in this manner helped to make error analysis more informative and also allowed a more fine-grained approach to classifying errors on some subtests.

Changes from K-TEA to KTEA-II

The Comprehensive form of the K-TEA was modified in a number of ways to create the KTEA-II: The age range assessed was increased from 6:0 to 18:11 on the K-TEA to 4:6 to 25:11 on the KTEA-II, the number of academic domains assessed increased from two on the K-TEA to eight on the KTEA-II, and several new subtests were added to assess abilities related to learning disabilities (five K-TEA subtests were retained and modified and nine new subtests were added to the KTEA-II Comprehensive Form). The Don't Forget box reminds readers of these changes from the K-TEA to the KTEA-II and

DON'T FORGET

Changes from the K-TEA to the KTEA-II

Increased Age Range	
KTEA Age Range: 6:0 to 18:11	**KTEA-II Age Range:** 4:6 to 25:11
Increased Number of Academic Domains Measured	
K-TEA Composites: Reading Mathematics	**KTEA-II Composites:** *Domain Composites* Reading Mathematics Written Language Oral Language *Reading-Related Composites* Sound-Symbol Decoding Oral Fluency Reading Fluency
Modified Existing Subtests and Added New Subtests	
Number of K-TEA Subtests: 5	**Number of KTEA-II Subtests:** 14

Note: Subtests of the K-TEA and KTEA-II are listed in Rapid Reference 3.2.

Rapid Reference 3.2 describes the KTEA-II subtests that were retained from the K-TEA, as well as those that are new to the KTEA-II.

≡ Rapid Reference 3.2

Brief Description of KTEA-II Comprehensive Form Subtests

Reading Subtest	Range	Description
Letter & Word Recognition	Ages 4:6–25:11	The student identifies letters and pronounces words of gradually increasing difficulty. Most words are irregular to ensure that the subtest measures word recognition (reading vocabulary) rather than decoding ability.
Reading Comprehension	Grade 1–Age 25:11	For the easiest items, the student reads a word and points to its corresponding picture. In following items, the student reads a simple instruction and responds by performing the action. In later items, the student reads passages of increasing difficulty and answers literal or inferential questions about them. Finally, the student rearranges five sentences into a coherent paragraph and then answers questions about the paragraph.
Phonological Awareness	Grades 1–6	The student responds orally to items that require manipulation of sounds. Tasks include rhyming, matching sounds, blending sounds, segmenting sounds, and deleting sounds.
Nonsense Word Decoding	Grade 1–Age 25:11	The student applies phonics and structural analysis skills to decode invented words of increasing difficulty.
Word Reading Fluency	Grade 3–Age 25:11	The student reads isolated words as quickly as possible for 1 minute.
Decoding Fluency	Grade 3–Age 25:11	The student applies decoding skills to pronounce as many nonsense words as possible in 1 minute.
Associational Fluency	Ages 4:6–25:11	The student says as many words as possible in 30 seconds that belong to a semantic category or have a specified beginning sound.
Naming Facility (RAN)	Ages 4:6–25:11	The student names objects, colors, and letters as quickly as possible.
Math Subtest	**Range**	**Description**
Math Concepts & Applications	Ages 4:6–25:11	The student responds orally to test items that focus on the application of mathematical principles to real-life situations. Skill categories include number

		concepts, operation concepts, rational numbers, measurement, shape and space, data investigations, and higher math concepts.
Math Computation	Grade K– Age 25:11	The student computes solutions to math problems printed in a student response booklet. Skills assessed include addition, subtraction, multiplication, and division operations; fractions and decimals; square roots, exponents, signed numbers, and algebra.

Written Language Subtest	**Range**	**Description**
Written Expression	Ages 4:6– 25:11	Kindergarten and Pre-Kindergarten children trace and copy letters and write letters from dictation. At grade 1 and higher, the student completes writing tasks in the context of an age-appropriate storybook format. Tasks at those levels include writing sentences from dictation, adding punctuation and capitalization, filling in missing words, completing sentences, combining sentences, writing compound and complex sentences, and, starting at spring of grade 1, writing an essay based on the story the student helped complete.
Spelling	Grade 1– Age 25:11	The student writes words dictated by the examiner from a steeply graded word list. Words were selected to match acquired spelling skills at each grade level and for their potential for error analysis. Early items require students to write single letters that represent sounds. The remaining items require students to spell orthographically regular and irregular words of increasing complexity.

Oral Language Subtest	**Range**	**Description**
Listening Comprehension	Ages 4:6– 25:11	The student listens to passages played on a CD and then responds orally to questions asked by the examiner. Questions measure literal and inferential comprehension.
Oral Expression	Ages 4:6– 25:11	The student performs specific speaking tasks in the context of a real-life scenario. Tasks assess pragmatics, syntax, semantics, and grammar.

Note: Five of the 14 KTEA-II Comprehensive Form subtests were retained and expanded from the K-TEA, including: Math Concepts & Applications (originally called Mathematics Applications), Letter & Word Recognition (originally called Reading Decoding), Spelling, Reading Comprehension, and Math Computation (originally called Mathematics Computation). Subtest descriptions are from Table 2004a of the *KTEA-II Comprehensive Form Manual* (Kaufman & Kaufman, 2004a, p. 4).

Like the Comprehensive Form, the KTEA-II Brief Form has also been modified from its original form. The changes mainly involved modifying subtests to integrate several types of items to provide more thorough skill coverage. The *KTEA-II Brief Form Manual* (Kaufman & Kaufman, 2005a) lists the following as the key changes in the subtests:

- The **Writing** subtest replaces the Spelling subtest, providing a much broader measure of the examinee's skill in written expression (including spelling, sentence structure, grammar, capitalization, and punctuation). The K-TEA/ NU Spelling subtest and KTEA-II Writing subtest correlate .68, reflecting the moderate differences in what these subtests measure.
- The **Reading** subtest has been expanded into two distinct parts: Recognition and Comprehension. The Recognition part retains letter and word recognition that were part of the original KTEA Brief, but the Comprehension part presents passage comprehension items along with the "following directions" item type. The K-TEA/NU and KTEA-II Reading subtests correlate .81, which demonstrates the similarities between the original and revised versions of this subtest.
- The **Math** subtest includes the same types of items as the original version, but computation and application items are interspersed throughout the subtest, and new colored illustrations replaced the original ones. The K-TEA/NU and KTEA-II Math subtests correlate .88, which demonstrates the strong similarities between the original and revised versions of this subtest.

Despite the many changes in the revision of the K-TEA Comprehensive Form, the original version correlates very highly with the KTEA-II Comprehensive Form. For example, in a sample of 68 children in grades 2 through 6, the K-TEA Battery Composite and the KTEA-II Comprehensive Achievement Composite correlated .94, and the correlation between these two composites for 62 seventh through eleventh grade children was .88. These correlations are quite strong despite the fact that the KTEA-II Comprehensive Achievement Composite contains subtests that were not part of the K-TEA Battery Composite (i.e., Written Expression and Listening Comprehension).

The two K-TEA composites also correlated very highly with their like-named composites on the KTEA-II Comprehensive. For example, the correlations between the K-TEA and KTEA-II Reading Composites were .88 and .86 for grades 2 through 6 and grades 7 through 11, respectively. The correlations between the K-TEA and KTEA-II Mathematics Composites were .85 and .93 for grades 2 through 6 and grades 7 through 11, respectively. Similar to the relationships found among the composites, the five K-TEA subtests correlated

≡ Rapid Reference 3.3

Correlations between K-TEA and KTEA-II Comprehensive Form Subtests of the Same Name and Composites of the Same Name

Subtest or Composite	Adjusted r	
	Grades 2–6 (N = 68)	Grades 7–11 (N = 62)
Letter & Word Recognition	.84	.87
Reading Comprehension	.77	.68
Math Concepts and Applications	.83	.82
Math Computation	.77	.91
Spelling	.85	.86
Reading Composite	.88	.86
Mathematics Composite	.85	.93
Comprehensive Achievement Composite	.94	.88

Note: All values are corrected for the variability of the norm group, based on the standard deviation obtained on the KTEA-II, using the variability correction of Cohen et al. (2003, p. 58). Coefficients are from Tables 7.15 and 7.16 of the *KTEA-II Comprehensive Form Manual* (Kaufman & Kaufman, 2004a, p. 103).

strongly with their KTEA-II counterparts. For grades 2 through 6 the correlations between K-TEA and KTEA-II Comprehensive Form subtests ranged from .77 for Reading Comprehension and Math Computations to .85 for Spelling. For grades 7 through 11, correlations between K-TEA and KTEA-II subtests ranged from .68 for Reading Comprehension to .91 for Math Computation. Rapid Reference 3.3 provides the correlations between K-TEA and KTEA-II subtests of the same name.

Scales and Composites of the KTEA-II

The KTEA-II Comprehensive Form has 14 subtests that are grouped into four domain composites and four Reading-Related composites. The four KTEA-II Comprehensive domain composites are Reading, Mathematics, Written

Language, and Oral Language, and the four Reading-Related composites are Sound-Symbol, Decoding, Oral Fluency, and Reading Fluency. The composition of the KTEA-II Comprehensive varies slightly according to grade level (or age). For example, for grade 1 through age 25, six of the eight subtests contribute to the Comprehensive Achievement Composite, but for ages 4½ through kindergarten, four of the eight subtests come together to yield the Comprehensive Achievement Composite (Figure 3.1 details which subtests contribute the Comprehensive Achievement Composite and the domain composites).

For children in Pre-Kindergarten (Pre-K is defined as children who have not yet begun kindergarten), the KTEA-II Comprehensive yields two domain composites: Written Language and Oral Language. Although no math domain composite is calculated at the Pre-K level, Math Concepts and Applications (a math subtest) is administered to these children. In addition, three reading-related subtests are administered to Pre-K children: Letter and Word Recognition, Associational Fluency, and Naming Facility. One Reading-Related Composite may be calculated for Pre-K children: Oral Fluency. Seven total subtests can be administered to children at the Pre-K level.

For kindergarteners, the KTEA-II Comprehensive yields three domain composites: Math, Written Language, and Oral Language. No Reading domain composite is obtained for kindergarteners, but three reading-related subtests are administered: Letter and Word Recognition, Associational Fluency, and Naming Facility. Similar to Pre-K children, one Reading-Related Composite may be calculated for kindergarteners: Oral Fluency. At the kindergarten level, eight subtests can be administered in total.

For children and adolescents in grades 1 through 12 and above, the four aforementioned domain composites are calculated based upon scores yielded from eight KTEA-II Comprehensive subtests. From grade 1 to 12+, two of the reading-related composites are calculated for the entire age range: Decoding and Oral Fluency. However, Sound-Symbol is calculated only from grades 1 through 6, and Reading Fluency is calculated only from grades 3 through 12 and above. Rapid Reference 3.4 lists which of the reading-related subtests contribute to the four reading-related composites.

The KTEA-II Brief Form offers three subtests for children, adolescents, and adults spanning the age range from 4½ to 90. Although these subtests are parallel to those in the Comprehensive Form, the Brief Form contains a completely different set of items than the Comprehensive Form. One global score is yielded from the Brief Form subtests: The Brief Achievement Composite. For Pre-K children that composite is comprised of only the Reading and Math subtests, but for children in kindergarten through those in grade 12 and above the Brief

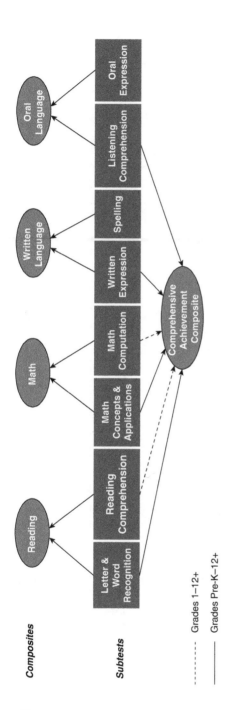

Figure 3.1 Structure of the KTEA-II Comprehensive Form.

Note: The ages at which subtests may first be administered vary from Pre-K to grade 1. Five subtests are administered beginning at the Pre-K level: Letter and Word Recognition, Math Concepts and Applications, Written Expression, Listening Comprehension, and Oral Expression. One subtest is first administered at the kindergarten level: Math Computation; two subtests are first administered at the grade 1 level: Reading Comprehension and Spelling. At the Pre-K level, two domain composites can be obtained: Written Language and Oral Language. At the kindergarten level, three domain composites can be obtained: Math, Written Language, and Oral Language. From grade 1 on, all four domain composites can be obtained.

≡ Rapid Reference 3.4

Composites Formed by the KTEA-II Comprehensive Form Reading-Related Subtests

Subtests	KTEA-II Reading-Related Composites			
	Sound Symbol (Grades 1–6)	Decoding (Grades 1–12+)	Oral Fluency (Pre-K–Grade 12+)	Reading Fluency (Grades 3–12+)
Phonological Awareness (Grades 1–6)	X			
Nonsense Word Decoding (Grades 1–12+)	X	X		
Letter and Word Recognition (Pre-K–Grade 12+)		X		
Associational Fluency (Pre-K–Grade 12+)			X	
Naming Facility (RAN) (Pre-K–Grade 12+)			X	
Word Recognition Fluency (Grades 3–12+)				X
Decoding Fluency (Grades 3–12+)				X

Achievement Composite is derived from all three subtests. The Brief Form subtests are described in the section on subtests that follows.

Subtests

The KTEA-II Comprehensive and Brief Forms provide much flexibility for examiners. If only one particular domain of academic functioning is of concern, examiners may choose to administer a single subtest or any combination of subtests in that domain in order to assess a student's academic achievement. If multiple domains need to be measured, then all of the age-appropriate subtests can be administered to obtain the desired composite score(s). Brief descriptions of each of the KTEA-II Comprehensive Form subtests are given in Rapid Reference 3.2, which is organized by content area. The age range for each subtest varies, so the table indicates the age and grade range at which each subtest may be administered. Regardless of whether grade or age norms are being used, examiners should use student's grade level to guide selection of subtests.

The subtests of the KTEA-II Brief Form cover content that is similar to that of the Comprehensive Form, but the item sets are different. Descriptions of each of the three Brief Form subtests follow:

1. **Reading.** Part 1 contains 27 recognition items. In these items the examinee identifies letters and pronounces words of gradually increasing difficulty. Most words are irregular to ensure that the subtest measures word recognition reading vocabulary more than decoding ability. Part 2 contains 46 comprehension items. Some of these items require an examinee to read a simple instruction and then do what the instruction says. Other items require examinees to read passages of increasing difficulty and answer a literal or inferential question about them.
2. **Math.** In the 67 Math items, examinees respond orally to items that focus on the application of mathematical principles to real-life situations. The examinee is also required to work on computation items by writing solutions to math problems printed in the Response Booklet. A variety of mathematical skills are assessed from addition and subtraction to higher level skills such as square roots, exponents, and algebra.
3. **Writing.** The 46 writing items vary according to age. Children who are kindergarten and younger are required to copy letters and write letters from dictation. Students or adults from grade 1 on complete writing tasks in the context of an age-appropriate newsletter format. Tasks at those levels involve adding punctuation and capitalization, filling in

missing words, completing sentences, combining sentences, and writing complex sentences. The examinees also spell regular and irregular words dictated by the examiner.

STANDARDIZATION AND PSYCHOMETRIC PROPERTIES OF THE KTEA-II

This section of the chapter describes the standardization samples of the KTEA-II Comprehensive and Brief Forms and reliability and validity information about the tests.

Standardization

The KTEA-II Comprehensive Form was standardized with an age-norm sample of 3,000 examinees ages 4.5 through 25, and a grade-norm sample of 2,400 students in kindergarten through grade 12. For each grade level, the sample size ranged from 140 to 220 students (with more examinees contributing to the earlier grades). For each age level, the sample sizes ranged from 100 to 220 students (with the exception of age 19 that had a sample of only 80 examinees). The KTEA-II Comprehensive Form contains two parallel forms, so approximately half of the norm sample was administered Form A and the other half was administered Form B. The standardization sample was chosen to closely match the U.S. population. Thus, on the variables of gender, ethnicity, parental education, geographic region, and special education or gifted placement the standardization sample closely corresponded to data from the 2001 Current Population Survey of the Bureau of the Census.

Similar to the Comprehensive Form, the KTEA-II Brief Form was standardized on a large representative sample that closely corresponded to the 2001 Current Population Survey of the Bureau of the Census. The Brief Form normative sample matched the U.S. population on the variables of gender, education level of examinee or parent, race/ethnicity, and geographic region. The grade-norm sample consisted of 1,645 students from kindergarten through grade 12. The number of students sampled from each grade ranged from 75 to 90 for grades 9 through 12 to 110 to 125 for grades 3 through 8, and 210 students were sampled for grades 1 and 2. The size of the Brief Form total age sample (N = 2,495) was larger than that of the grade sample. At each age, for children under age 15, the samples included 100 to 210 children. For ages 15 through 25, the samples included 75 to 150 children, and the adult samples over age 25 (to age 90) included 50 to 60 individuals for each age group.

Reliability

The internal-consistency reliability of the KTEA-II Comprehensive is strong for both Forms A and B. The average internal-consistency reliability value across grades and forms for the Comprehensive Achievement Composite was .97. The averages for the Reading, Math, and Decoding Composites were .96, .96, and .97, respectively. The average reliability values for the Written Language Composite and Sound-Symbol Composite were .93. For Oral Language and Oral Fluency composites, the average reliabilities were .87 and .85, respectively. Reliability values based on age groups were very similar to what was reported for the reliability values found with the grade-level samples. Table 3.1 presents the internal consistency reliability values of the KTEA-II Comprehensive Form subtests and composites averaged across forms.

Table 3.1 Average Split-Half Reliability Coefficients for Subtests and Composites

KTEA-II Subtest or Composite	Mean Grade-Level Reliability	Mean Age-Level Reliability
Letter & Word Recognition	.96	.97
Reading Comprehension	.93	.93
Reading Composite	**.96**	**.97**
Math Concepts & Applications	.92	.93
Math Computation	.93	.94
Mathematics Composite	**.96**	**.96**
Written Expression	.85	.87
Spelling	.93	.94
Written Language Composite	**.93**	**.94**
Listening Comprehension	.85	.85
Oral Expression	.78	.79
Oral Language Composite	**.87**	**.87**
Phonological Awareness	.86	.88
Nonsense Word Decoding	.94	.94
Sound-Symbol Composite	**.93**	**.93**

(Continued)

Table 3.1 (Continued)

KTEA-II Subtest or Composite	Mean Grade-Level Reliability	Mean Age-Level Reliability
Decoding Composite	**.97**	**.97**
Associational Fluency	.73	.72
Naming Facility (RAN)	.89	.89
Oral Fluency Composite	**.85**	**.87**
Comprehensive Achievement	**.97**	**.97**
Reading (Brief Form)	.94	.95
Math (Brief Form)	.90	.91
Writing (Brief Form)	.86	.90
Brief Achievement Composite	**.96**	**.96**

Note: From Tables 7.1 and 7.2 of the *KTEA-II Comprehensive Form Manual* (Kaufman & Kaufman, 2004a) and Tables 6.1 and 6.2 of the *KTEA-II Brief Form Manual* (Kaufman & Kaufman, 2005). All reliabilities are based on the standard deviation of scores for both forms combined. Reliabilities of composites were computed using the formula provided by Nunnally (1978, p. 248). Mean grade-level values and mean age-level values were calculated using Fisher's z transformation.

The KTEA-II Brief Form also had strong average internal-reliability values. For the individual subtests scored via grade norms (grades K through 12) the average reliability values were .94, .90, and .86 for the Reading, Math, and Writing subtests, respectively. For the individual subtests scored via age norms (ages 4:6 through 90) the values were .95, .91, and .90 for the Reading, Math, and Writing subtests, respectively. The split-half reliability values for the Brief Achievement Composite were .96 for both the grade and age norms.

Alternate-form reliability values were calculated by administering the two forms of the KTEA-II Comprehensive to a sample of 221 children. The forms were administered approximately $3\frac{1}{2}$ to 4 weeks apart, on average. Similar to the internal-consistency reliability values, the values for the alternate-form reliability were also high. The Comprehensive Achievement Composites showed very high consistency across time and forms (low to mid .90s). The Reading, Math, Written Language, Decoding, and Reading Fluency Composites have alternate-form reliabilities in the high .80s to mid .90s. These strong values indicate that the alternate forms of the KTEA-II will be useful for reducing practice effects when the test is administered more than once. Table 3.2 shows the alternate form reliability values.

Table 3.2 Alternate Form Reliability Coefficients for Subtests and Composites

KTEA-II Subtest or Composite	Pre-Kindergarten to Grade 1		Grade 2 to Grade 6		Grade 7 to Grade 12	
	N	r^a	N	r^a	N	r^a
Letter & Word Recognition	62	.97	83	.85	79	.89
Reading Comprehension	27	.88	83	.76	79	.80
Reading Composite	27	.94	83	.87	79	.89
Math Concepts & Applications	62	.84	80	.84	79	.89
Math Computation	45	.86	80	.87	79	.90
Mathematics Composite	45	.87	80	.90	79	.94
Written Expression	62	.79	83	.82	79	.79
Spelling	27	.87	80	.91	79	.88
Written Language Composite	27	.85	80	.90	79	.90
Listening Comprehension	62	.50	80	.56	79	.73
Oral Expression	62	.62	80	.54	79	.58
Oral Language Composite	62	.64	80	.68	79	.81
Phonological Awareness	60	.77	83	.58	—	—
Nonsense Word Decoding	27	.74	83	.90	79	.89
Sound-Symbol Composite	27	.84	83	.80	—	—
Word Recognition Fluency	—	—	61	.89	79	.87
Decoding Fluency	—	—	63	.92	78	.88
Reading Fluency	—	—	61	.95	78	.91

(Continued)

Table 3.2 (Continued)

KTEA-II Subtest or Composite	Pre-Kindergarten to Grade 1		Grade 2 to Grade 6		Grade 7 to Grade 12	
	N	r^a	N	r^a	N	r^a
Decoding Composite	27	.90	83	.92	79	.93
Associational Fluency	61	.47	80	.55	73	.64
Naming Facility (RAN)	54	.65	75	.76	71	.76
Oral Fluency Composite	54	.59	75	.67	70	.78
Comprehensive Achievement	62	.92	80	.94	79	.95

Note: From Table 7.5 of the *KTEA-II Comprehensive Form Manual* (Kaufman & Kaufman, 2004a). The KTEA-II scores are based on age norms.

[a] All reliability coefficients were corrected for the variability of the norm group, based on the standard deviation obtained on the first testing, using the variability correction of Cohen et al. (2003, p. 58).

For the KTEA-II Brief Form, test-retest reliability was examined by administering the test twice within a 2 to 8 week period (mean interval 3.7 weeks) to 327 students. Across the grade-norm and age-norm samples, the average adjusted test-retest reliabilities were as follows: Reading = .93, Math = .90, Writing = .81, and Brief Achievement Composite = .94.

Validity

The validity of the KTEA-II was demonstrated via multiple methods. Intercorrelations between the subtests and composites were calculated to show the relationships between the academic domains. Factor analyses were conducted to show that the structure of the test was empirically grounded. Correlations with other instruments were also conducted to evaluate the construct validity of the test. Finally, special population studies were conducted to show the efficacy of applying the KTEA-II to the assessment of children with learning disabilities, Mental Retardation, Attention-Deficit/Hyperactivity Disorder, and of children with other special qualities such as deafness or giftedness. The results of these special studies are detailed in the chapter in this book on Clinical Applications.

Confirmatory factor analysis was conducted to investigate the relationships between the KTEA-II Comprehensive form subtests and composites in a systematic manner. The factor analysis proceeded in a stepwise fashion with the eight primary subtests yielding a final model comprised of four factors. The final model had good fit statistics and all subtests had high loadings on their factors. The results of the factor analysis are shown in Figure 3.2.

The KTEA-II Comprehensive and Brief Forms were administered along with other tests of achievement and cognitive ability during standardization. In addition to the results of the correlational data already reported with the original K-TEA (see Rapid Reference 3.4), correlations were calculated between the KTEA-II Comprehensive and Brief Forms. In a sample of 1,318 students administered both the Comprehensive and Brief Forms, the correlations were .85, .86, .78, and .89 for Reading, Math, Writing, and Achievement Composite, respectively. Further correlations were calculated between the KTEA-II Comprehensive Form and the following achievement

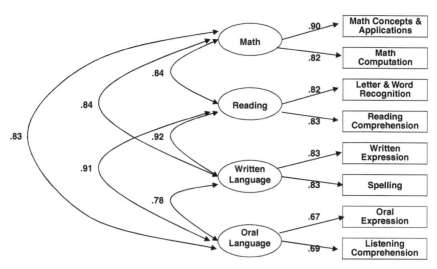

Figure 3.2 Results of Confirmatory Factor Analysis of Eight KTEA-II Comprehensive Form Subtests.

Note: Figure is adapted from Figure 7.1 of the KTEA-II Comprehensive Form Manual (Kaufman & Kaufman, 2004a, p. 101). Results are based on the complete norm sample (age norms) at grade 1 and above (N = 2,560). Factors are shown in the ovals on the left, and subtests are in rectangles on the right. The numbers represent factor intercorrelations or factor loadings.

tests: WIAT-II, *Woodcock-Johnson Tests of Achievement*, Third Edition (WJ III AcH; Woodcock, McGrew, & Maher, 2001), the *Peabody Individual Achievement Test–Revised, Normative Update* (PIAT-R/NU; Markwardt, 1998), and the *Oral and Written Language Scales* (OWLS; Carrow-Woolfolk, 1996). A summary of the KTEA-II Comprehensive Form correlational studies with the WIAT-II[1] and WJ III are provided in Table 3.3 (for grades 1 through 5 and grades 6 through 11). The results of the studies with the WIAT-II and WJ III are very similar to those found with the original K-TEA. That is, most correlations between like-named composites were in the mid- to high-.80s, and correlations between most of the total achievement scores hovered around .90. The correlations with the PIAT-R/NU overall composite score were .86 for both grades K through 5 and grades 6 through 9. For domain composites, the PIAT-R/NU's highest correlations were for reading, ranging from .89 to .78, and lower correlations were found for mathematics and spelling (ranging from .67 to .70). The OWLS has three subtests, and the highest correlation with the KTEA-II was between the tests of Written Expression (.75); the instruments' measures of Oral Expression and Listening Comprehension correlated only at a modest level (in the .40s).

Table 3.3 Correlations of KTEA-II Comprehensive Composites with Other Achievement Test Composites

KTEA-II Composite	WIAT-II [a]		WJ III	
	Grades 1–5	Grades 6–11	Grades 1–5	Grades 6–10
Reading Composite	.85	.85	.82	.76
Mathematics Composite	.82	.87	.87	.87
Written Language Composite	.87	.87	.92	.84
Oral Language Composite	.52	.70	.71	.74
Comprehensive Achievement Composite	.89	.90	.84	.89

Note: Data are from Tables 7.17, 7.18, 7.19, and 7.20 of the *KTEA-II Comprehensive Form Manual* (Kaufman & Kaufman, 2004a). All correlations were corrected for the variability of the norm group, based on the standard deviation obtained on the KTEA-II, using the variability correction of Cohen et al. (2003, p. 58). Sample sizes for grades 1–5 were N = 82 for the WIAT-II study and N = 33 for the WJ III study. Sample sizes for grades 6–11 were N = 89 for the WIAT-II study and N = 47 for the WJ III study.
[a] Correlational data with the WIAT-III were not available at the time of publication.

---

1. Correlations were not available with the WIAT-III.

The correlations between the KTEA-II Brief Form and other achievement tests were also examined (Kaufman & Kaufman, 2005). Specifically, the *Woodcock Johnson–Third Edition Tests of Achievement* (WJ III Ach; Mather & Woodcock, 2001) and the *Wide Range Achievement Test–Third Edition* (WRAT3; Wilkinson, 1993) were administered together with the KTEA-II Brief Form to samples of 25 and 80 students, respectively. (Table 3.4 details these correlations.) Correlations between the WJ III Ach and KTEA-II Brief Form subtests ranged from .74 to .79, with the correlation between the Brief Achievement Composite and WJ III Academic Skills composite being slightly higher (.89). When comparing the WRAT3 to the KTEA-II Brief, the strongest correlation was between Reading subtests of the two measures (.84) and the weakest was between the Writing subtest of the KTEA-II Brief and the Spelling subtest of the WRAT3 (.64). As the KTEA-II Brief Writing subtest measures more than simply spelling ability, the lower correlation is not surprising.

In addition to the correlational data showing the relationships between the KTEA-II and other tests of academic achievement, the *KTEA-II Comprehensive Form Manual* provides data showing the correlations between the KTEA-II and three tests of cognitive ability: the KABC-II, the *Wechsler Intelligence Scale for Children–Third Edition* (WISC-III; Wechsler, 1991), and the *Woodcock-Johnson Tests of Cognitive Abilities, Third Edition* (WJ III CoG; Woodcock, McGrew, & Mather, 2001). A very large sample ($N = 2,520$) was used in the study with the KABC-II, as this test was conormed with the KTEA-II. Sample sizes were 97 and 51 for the studies with the WISC-III and WJ III COG, respectively.

Table 3.4 Correlations of KTEA-II Brief Composites with Other Achievement Test Composites

KTEA-II Brief Subtests/Composite	WRAT3	WJ III Ach
Reading	.84	.78
Mathematics	.75	.74
Writing	.64[a]	.79
Brief Achievement Composite	—	.89

Note: Data are from Tables 6.19 and 6.15 of the *KTEA-II Brief Form Manual* (2005). All correlations were corrected for the variability of the norm group, based on the standard deviation obtained on the KTEA-II, using the variability correction of Cohen et al. (2003), p. 58). Sample sizes were $N = 80$ for the WRAT3 study and $N = 25$ for the WJ III Ach study. Data on the WRAT3 are for ages 7–19, and data for the WJ III Ach are for ages 7–16. The WJ III correlations are based on the following: Broad Reading, Broad Math, Broad Written Language, and Academic Skills.

[a]This is the correlation between WRAT3 Spelling and KTEA-II Brief Writing.

The KTEA-II Comprehensive Achievement Composite correlates .79 with the KABC-II Fluid Crystallized Index (FCI), .74 with the KABC-II Mental Processing Index (MPI), and .69 with the KABC-II Nonverbal Index (NVI) for the total sample. Very similar correlations were found between the Comprehensive Achievement Composite and global cognitive scores on the WISC-III and WJ III COG. The Comprehensive Achievement Composite correlated .79 with the WISC-III Full Scale IQ (FSIQ) and .82 with the WJ III COG General Intellectual Ability (GIA). For all three tests of cognitive ability, the KTEA-II's Reading Composite and Mathematics Composites had the strongest relationship to overall cognitive ability. Correlations with the Reading Composite were .74, .69, and .72 for the KABC-II FCI, WISC-III FSIQ, and WJ III GIA, respectively. Correlations with the Mathematics Composite were .71, .65, and .76 for the KABC-II FCI, WISC-III FS-IQ, and WJ III GIA, respectively. The other academic domains measured by the KTEA-II did not correlate as strongly with overall cognitive ability. For example, Written Language and Oral Language correlated .66 and .67, respectively, with the KABC-II FCI. A summary of KTEA-II and KABC-II correlations is provided in Table 3.5.

Correlational data were also analyzed for KTEA-II Brief Form and three measures of cognitive ability: the KABC-II, the *Kaufman Brief Intelligence Test–Second Edition* (KBIT-2; Kaufman & Kaufman, 2004c), and the *Wechsler Abbreviated Scale of Intelligence* (WASI; The Psychological Corporation, 1999). Patterns of correlation between the KTEA-II Brief Form and the measures of cognitive ability were similar to what was found on the Comprehensive Form. That is, the KTEA-II Brief Form Reading and Math subtests correlated more

Table 3.5 KTEA-II Composites correlations with KABC-II Global Scales

KTEA-II Composite	KABC-II Global Scale		
	FCI	MPI	NVI
Reading			
Ages 4 ½–6	.67	.68	.57
Ages 7–18	.74	.68	.61
Total Sample	.74	.69	.61
Math			
Ages 4 ½–6	.70	.71	.65
Ages 7–18	.71	.68	.67
Total Sample	.71	.68	.67
Written Language			
Ages 4 ½–6	.67	.70	.56

	KABC-II Global Scale		
KTEA-II Composite	FCI	MPI	NVI
Ages 7–18	.66	.62	.56
Total Sample	.66	.63	.56
Oral Language			
Ages 4 ½–6	.62	.57	.52
Ages 7–18	.67	.61	.56
Total Sample	.67	.60	.55
Comprehensive Achievement			
Ages 4 ½–6	.75	.73	.65
Ages 7–18	.80	.74	.70
Total Sample	.79	.74	.69

Note: FCI = Fluid Crystallized Index; MPI = Mental Processing Index; NVI = Nonverbal Index. All correlations were corrected for the variability of the norm group, based on the standard deviation obtained on the KTEA-II, using the variability correction of Cohen et al. (2003, p. 58). Data are adapted from Table 7.25 and Appendix J of the *KTEA-II Comprehensive Form Manual* (Kaufman & Kaufman, 2004a).

strongly with global cognitive ability than did the Writing subtest (see Table 3.6). The Brief Achievement Composite correlated most strongly with the KBIT-2 IQ Composite ($r = .78$) and correlated about equally with the WASI FSIQ (.71) and the KABC-II FCI (.70).

HOW TO ADMINISTER THE KTEA-II

As with any standardized test, when administering the KTEA-II you should follow closely the test administration instructions contained in the test manual and easels. Chapter 2 of both the *KTEA-II Comprehensive Form Manual* (Kaufman & Kaufman, 2004a) and the *KTEA-II Brief Form Manual* (Kaufman & Kaufman, 2005) reviews the general administration procedures and the test easels list specific administration directions.

The KTEA-II Comprehensive Form offers much flexibility to examiners in terms of the subtests that can be administered and the order in which those subtests are administered. The entire battery may be administered or you may choose to administer only select composites or subtests. Once you have decided whether the KTEA-II Brief Form battery or a complete or partial KTEA-II Comprehensive Form battery will be administered, then you need to determine the sequence of the subtests. The easels and record form provide the suggested

Table 3.6 KTEA-II Brief Form Correlations with Measures of Global Cognitive Ability

| Measure of Global Cognitive Ability | N | KTEA-II Brief Form | | | |
		Reading	Math	Writing	Brief Achievement Composite
KABC-II FCI	1,266	.65	.63	.60	**.70**
KABC-II MPI	1,266	.61	.63	.60	**.70**
KBIT-2 IQ Composite	747	.74	.71	.54	**.78**
WASI Full Scale IQ-4 (FSIQ)	142	.73	.65	.48	**.71**

Note: FCI = Fluid Crystallized Index; MPI = Mental Processing Index. Data are from Tables 6.20–6.31 of the *KTEA-II Brief Form Manual* (Kaufman & Kaufman, 2005). All correlations were corrected for the variability of the norm group, based on the standard deviation obtained on the KTEA-II using the variability correction of Cohen et al. (2003, p. 58). The WASI FSIQ is based on four subtests: Vocabulary, Block Design, Similarities, and Matrix Reasoning.

CAUTION

Remember that the last subtests listed in the Record Form, Associational Fluency and Naming Facility (RAN), must be administered intermittently throughout the battery. Thus, do not wait until the end of the battery to administer them (see Rapid Reference 3.5 for a suggested administration order).

administration order, but you may select a different administration order if you prefer (see Caution). For the KTEA-II Comprehensive, if you choose to follow the sequence of subtests presented in the record form and easels, you must plan to administer two subtests out of easel order: Associational Fluency (13th subtest) and Naming Facility (14th subtest). These two subtests are administered together in four separate "task pairs," which include one Fluency task and one Naming Facility task together as a pair. You should administer each pair intermittently among the other subtests. A suggested order for interspersing these task pairs with the other subtests is presented in Rapid Reference 3.5. The Caution box reminds you not to wait until the end of the battery to administer the Associational Fluency and Naming Facility tasks.

CAUTION

If you depart from the suggested subtest administration sequence, you must always:
1. Administer Letter & Word Recognition before Reading Comprehension.
2. Administer Word Recognition Fluency and Nonsense Word Decoding before Decoding Fluency.

≡ Rapid Reference 3.5

....

Suggested Subtest Administration Order when Administering Associational Fluency and Naming Facility

Subtest Number	Subtest	Grade Range for Administration
1	Phonological Awareness	K–6
2	Letter & Word Recognition	Pre-K–12+
13 & 14	Associational Fluency and Naming Facility (RAN): Task Pair 1	Pre-K–12+
3	Math Concepts and Applications	Pre-K–12+
13 & 14	Associational Fluency and Naming Facility (RAN): Task Pair 2	Pre-K–12+
4	Nonsense Word Decoding	1–12+
5	Math Computation	K–12+
13 & 14	Associational Fluency and Naming Facility (RAN): Task Pair 3	1–12+
6	Reading Comprehension	1–12+
7	Written Expression	Pre-K–12+
14	Associational Fluency: Task 4	1–12+
8	Spelling	1–12+
9	Listening Comprehension	Pre-K–12+
10	Oral Expression	Pre-K–12+
11	Word Recognition Fluency	3–12+
12	Decoding Fluency	3–12+

Note: Associational Fluency and Naming Facility (RAN) Task Pairs must be given out of easel order and should be administered intermittently among other subtests. Subtests may be administered in alternative orders as well. "Pre-K" refers to children aged 4:6 or older who have not yet entered kindergarten. "Grade 12+" indicates that the subtests can be administered up to the top of the age range (age 25:11).

Starting and Discontinuing Subtests

Like most standardized tests of individual achievement, the KTEA-II items are ordered by difficulty with the easiest items first. Grade-based starting points are listed in the record form and on the first page of a subtest's directions in the easel. If you have knowledge or suspicion based on clinical judgment that the child you are testing will benefit from an earlier or later start point, you may select a different start point.

If you have started administering a subtest from a starting point other than item 1, you must make sure that the examinee is able to achieve a basal. That is, the examinee must demonstrate proficiency on the task by getting the first few items correct in order to achieve the basal. If the examinee does not meet the basal criterion, then you must drop back to the preceding start point. The basal rules are listed in the record form as well as on the first page of the directions for a subtest in the easel. Some subtests on the KTEA-II do not have traditional basal rules because the items are grouped into item sets. These Comprehensive form subtests with item sets include Reading Comprehension, Listening Comprehension, and Oral Expression. The Writing subtest on the KTEA-II Brief Form also is administered with item sets. The Don't Forget box describes the administration procedures for these subtests that do not have traditional basal rules.

Sample and Teaching Items

Unlike many cognitive tests, such as the KABC-II, very few KTEA-II subtests include sample or teaching items. These items are intended to communicate the nature of the task by allowing the examiner to give feedback and explain the task further in order to teach the task. Three KTEA-II Comprehensive Form subtests include either sample or teaching items: Phonological Awareness, Nonsense Word Decoding, and Oral Expression. Sample items or teaching items are indicated on the record form by an apple icon. Each of the five sections of Phonological Awareness has one or two sets of sample items. The first two scored items on Nonsense Word Decoding are teaching items and the third and sixth items on Oral Expression are teaching items.

Recording Responses

Accurately recording responses during administration of KTEA-II subtests is very important—especially if you intend to conduct error analysis after scoring

DON'T FORGET

....

Starting Points, Basal Rules, and Discontinue Rules for Reading Comprehension, Listening Comprehension, and Oral Expression

Subtest	Start Point	Basal	Discontinue
Reading Comprehension	Determined by raw score on Letter & Word Recognition (see Start Point Table on record form or easel)	If start point is Set B, examinee must pass first three items. If start point is Set C or above, examinee must pass two items in the first passage administered.	Discontinue at a stop point for a set *if* there are at least four failures and four passes in a set or pair of sets *or* if there are five consecutive failures.
Listening Comprehension	Determined by grade (see Start Point Table on record form or easel)	Must pass at least 2 items in the first passage administered	
Oral Expression	Determined by grade (see Start Point Table on record form or easel)	At least four preliminary scores of 1 in the first set	

the subtests is complete. On 3 of the 14 Comprehensive Form subtests, the examinees write their responses themselves (i.e., Written Expression, Spelling, and Math Computation), requiring no recording on the examiner's part until scoring is conducted. Phonological Awareness and Math Concepts and Applications require simple recording of either a zero for incorrect or a one for correct, or recording a one-word response. Reading Comprehension and Listening Comprehension require that the gist of the examinee's responses are recorded with as much detail as possible, but Oral Expression and Associational Fluency require that an examinee's responses are recorded verbatim (and may be recorded via a tape recorder). Letter and Word Recognition and Nonsense Word Decoding require careful listening in order to correctly record the child's responses. Mispronunciations on these two subtests should be recorded using the phoneme key provided on the record form or by writing the student's response phonetically. Recording responses either by the phonetic key or by phonetically spelling the child's response takes some practice. Chapter 4 of the *KTEA-II Comprehensive Form Manual* (Kaufman & Kaufman, 2004a) describes in more detail how to record responses for use with the error analysis system.

Timing

Most subtests on the KTEA-II are not timed. However, four of the Reading-Related subtests do require timing. Specifically, for Word Recognition Fluency, Decoding Fluency, and Associational Fluency, the student's performance within the specified time is the basis of the score. For Naming Facility (RAN), the time taken by the student to complete each trial is converted to a point score.

Querying

Occasionally, examinees' responses may be missing an essential detail or qualifier to be 100 percent correct. These instances will most commonly occur during Reading Comprehension and Listening Comprehension and will require you to query the examinee to clarify his or her response. Specific queries are listed right in the easel, and, when querying is done, a notation should be made on the record form (e.g., "Q"). Occasionally, students give multiple responses and it is unclear which response is the final answer. In such instances you should ask the examinee which is the intended response.

Subtest-by-Subtest Notes on Administration

This section highlights pertinent information for administering each of the KTEA-II subtests and points out common errors in administration. Subtests are listed in the order in which they appear in the KTEA-II Comprehensive Form easels. Because administrative procedures for the Brief Form are very similar to those of the Comprehensive Form, we review notes on administration of the Brief Form subtests under the sections on the related Comprehensive Form subtests to reduce redundancy. The Don't Forget box reminds you where to look for administrative information on the Brief Form subtests.

DON'T FORGET

··

Where to Look for Administrative Information on Brief Form Subtests

Brief Form Subtest	Look under the Following Subsection in "Subtest-by-Subtest Notes on Administration"
Reading (Part 1)	Letter & Word Recognition
Reading (Part 2)	Reading Comprehension
Math (Concepts & Applications Items)	Math Concepts & Applications
Math (Computation Items)	Math Computation
Writing	Written Expression

Note: Although the KTEA-II Brief and Comprehensive Forms are similar in general content and administrative procedures, they do not have overlapping items.

Phonological Awareness

Phonological Awareness has five sections: (a) Rhyming; (b) Sound Matching; (c) Blending; (d) Segmenting; and (e) Deleting Sounds. All five sections are administered to children in kindergarten, but only Sections 1, 4, and 5 are administered to children in first through sixth grades. Beginning in Section 3, this subtest requires use of Pepper, the dog puppet, as well as the KTEA-II Easel 1 for administration. The CD that accompanies this subtest is very useful for ensuring that you understand how to properly administer Section 3 (Blending) and Section 5 (Deleting Sounds). Most children find Pepper the puppet quite engaging, but some are distracted and seem to more easily go off task when it is their turn to make Pepper talk. With such children, remind them to stay on task, but suggest that they can have a few minutes to "play with Pepper" after the task is over (a nice built-in reward of the task). Occasionally, children may struggle with trying to make Pepper's mouth move. Encourage these children to focus on segmenting the word properly and worry less about getting Pepper to move his mouth.

Since this task is purely auditory (except for Section 2 that has pictorial stimuli, too), ensure that the child is paying attention prior to beginning an item. If necessary, during the task you may repeat an item.

Letter and Word Recognition

The key to properly administering Letter and Word Recognition from the Comprehensive Form and Reading Part 1 from the Brief Form is having knowledge of the proper pronunciation of all the stimuli words. If you are unsure of how a word should be pronounced, you will undoubtedly struggle with whether an examinee correctly pronounced it and will therefore not know whether or not to continue. This problem is less of an issue when testing younger children, but when assessing older children and adolescents, they may be administered the highest levels of words, which are quite challenging. Thus, before administering the subtest, listen to the CD provided with the test kit to hear the correct pronunciations of the most difficult words.

Most of the stimuli words are presented six to a page, and examinees should be allowed to attempt to pronounce all words on a page, even if they have met the discontinue rule before reaching the sixth word on a page. Such administration methods will continue to foster good rapport. Sometimes children will pronounce words in disconnected pieces, but to receive credit, a child must pronounce words as a connected, relatively smooth whole. Thus, they should be instructed to "Say it all together" if they pronounce a word in disconnected pieces and then stop.

Math Concepts and Applications

On the Comprehensive Form, an entire subtest is devoted to assessing mathematical concepts and applications, and, on the Brief Form, items measuring math concepts and applications are interspersed among computation items in a single subtest. Regardless of whether you are administering the Comprehensive or Brief Form, you will find that some children require more concrete ways to process the problems in Math Concepts and Applications, and such children will more often count with their fingers or use the pictures to aid them in coming up with a response. Fingers are an acceptable tool for problem solving during math computation and application items, but calculators are not. On the Brief Form, paper and pencil are allowed for all Math subtest items. However, prior to item 34 on the Comprehensive Form subtest, children are not allowed to use paper and pencil, but beginning with item 34 children should be offered paper and pencil should they wish to use them. In the latter half of the subtest there are several word problems; although the word problems are printed on the easel for the examinee to see, you should read each of these problems aloud to the examinee.

Nonsense Word Decoding

Similar to Letter and Word Recognition, the key to properly administering Nonsense Word Decoding is having knowledge of the proper pronunciation of all the stimuli words. Thus, it is crucial to listen to the CD provided with the test kit that demonstrates how the words should be pronounced. Most of the stimuli words are presented six on an easel page. To maintain rapport and minimize frustration for children, it is best to administer an entire easel page (all six words) even if a child has discontinued before reading the sixth word. However, only the words read before the discontinue rule was met should be counted toward the final raw score. As the nonsense words become more challenging for children, some children will get stuck on a particular word with which they are struggling. In such cases, you should encourage children to try the next one so that the test continues without multiple lengthy delays.

Nonsense Word Decoding is one of the few KTEA-II subtests that allows teaching of the task. On items 1 and 2, you are to tell the student the correct answer if they respond incorrectly (you are reminded that they are teaching items with the apple icons on the record form). Before you administer this subtest, it is advisable to practice how to record children's responses (whether you choose to do so using the phonemic key on the record form or another method). At times children will rapidly read the words, requiring you to increase your pace for recording their responses. In addition to recording the responses to specific items, you may record what the student's general approach to pronouncing the nonsense words was by marking one of three boxes at the bottom of the record form (letter-by-letter, chunking, or whole word). However, if a child doesn't use the same general approach to most of the items, checking these "Response Style" boxes will not be that useful.

Math Computation

The Student Response Booklet and a pencil with an eraser are needed to administer the Math Computation subtest on the Comprehensive Form and the computation items of the Brief Form's Math subtest. The Student Response Booklet should be folded so that the examinee can only see the page that they are currently working on. Some children will impulsively turn the page to see what comes next, but encourage such children not to worry about the next problems and rather just focus on finishing the page in front of them. Children may work out problems by counting on their fingers or by writing notes on the paper, but they may not use calculators. If necessary, remind children that it is okay to erase. Children with disabilities that cause difficulty with writing should be allowed to respond orally.

It is important to closely observe children as they solve the problems. Some children will fill the entire square with scratch notes, and it may be unclear which number is their final response. If you are uncertain about which number the child intended as their final answer, ask the child to circle his or her final response before the next item has been started. As you are observing the child work out the problems make notes about repeated erasures, verbal mediation of the problems, or other notable behaviors.

Reading Comprehension

To determine the starting point on the Comprehensive Form's Reading Comprehension subtest, you must first administer Letter and Word Recognition and then enter the child's raw score on that subtest into the "Start Point Table" on page 12 of the KTEA-II record form or on the first page of the Reading Comprehension subtest in the easel. Items 1 through 5 require that examinees point to a picture of a word that they read and items 6 through 12 require the examinee to read a command and do what it says (e.g., "Stand up"). On items 6 through 12, some examinees may require you to encourage them to pretend or make believe in response to the command that they read (the first six items of Reading Part 2 of the Brief Form are also "command" items). Items 13 through 87 of Reading Comprehension and items 7 through 25 of the Brief Form's Reading Part 2 subtest require the examinee to read a paragraph and answer questions about what they read. Examinees may read the paragraphs and questions silently or aloud, but they are not penalized if they make mistakes while they read aloud. However, such mistakes while reading aloud are noteworthy, especially if they are made frequently. In the remaining few items of Reading Comprehension on the Comprehensive Form, examinees must read a series of sentences and decide the correct order of the sentences (items 88 and 90). Examinees are allowed to use paper and pencil to organize the sentence numbers for these two items if they wish. While reading the paragraphs or questions, examinees sometimes ask for clarification of a term or help to read a particular word. In such cases, you should not give them help, but rather encourage them to just try their best.

Some of the passage questions are multiple choice and require only recording a letter response (e.g., a, b, c, d). However, other questions are open-ended and in such cases the examinee's responses should be recorded verbatim. Generally, querying is not necessary for most responses, but if the examinee provides multiple responses and you are unsure which is their intended final response, then ask for clarification.

Written Expression

Although there are many similarities in the skills tapped in the Comprehensive Form's Written Expression subtest and the Brief Form's Writing subtest, there are some important differences in administration, so we discuss each subtest in turn in this section. For the Comprehensive Form, examinees' responses to items on the Written Expression subtest are recorded in the appropriate Written Expression Booklet (grades 1 through 12) or in the Student Response Booklet (Pre-K and kindergarten). The first easel page of Written Expression lists which of the booklets examinees should use, based upon their grade level (the Caution box reminds examiners of an important point for administering to students in grade 1). The booklets, *Pam and Don's Adventure, The Little Duck's Friend, Kyra's Dragon, The Amazing Scrapbook, A Day on the Set,* and *The News at Six,* each tell a story with the goal of engaging the student in the writing tasks. Thus, when presenting the subtest, the examiner's directions written in the easel emphasize the fact that the booklets are stories. Before administering any level of Written Expression, you should familiarize yourself with the response booklet so that you know where to point to the words as you read them and so that you know where the student should write his or her response to each item (indicated by numbers printed in small boxes). The last item for each of the stories requires the examinee to write a summary of the story (items 30, 49, and 60). For each of these items the examinees are given 5 to 10 minutes to write their summary; thus, you will need a watch or clock to time these final items.

In Written Expression on the Comprehensive Form, you are allowed to repeat story segments or item instructions if it is necessary. As noted in the Don't Forget, you may also tell a student how to spell a word, if they ask (spelling is not scored in this subtest). However, you should not spontaneously correct a child's spelling or offer similar assistance unless asked by the examinee.

To administer the Brief Form's Writing subtest, you need the Response Booklet, a pencil, and the KTEA-II Brief Easel. Students are administered an item set based on their grade. After a student has completed a set, if they have earned 4 or more scores of 0, then stop testing,

CAUTION

If administering Written Expression to children in the spring of grade 1, Booklet 2 must be tentatively scored at the midpoint (after item 23 in Form A and item 24 in Form B) in order to decide whether the student should continue to the end. If you are uncertain about whether the preliminary score is adequate to necessitate administration of the rest of Level 2, it is best to on the side of caution and continue with the test.

DON'T FORGET
....
Spelling in the Written Expression Subtest

Spelling is not scored in the Comprehensive Form's Written Expression subtest. Therefore, you are allowed to tell an examinee how to spell a word if he or she asks.

but if they have earned 3 or fewer scores of 0, then continue until the next stop point. In the Writing subtest, spelling items are interspersed among items that demand skills such as capitalization, punctuation, and word form. Because spelling is an important component of the Brief Form's Writing subtest, you may not help students spell words during the subtest (which is unlike the rules of administration for the Comprehensive Form's Written Expression subtest).

Spelling

Spelling is administered to children in first grade and beyond. Examinees write their responses in the Student Response Booklet using a pencil with an eraser (it is a good idea to have extras on hand in case of broken pencil points). The first four items require examinees to write a letter to complete a word, but the remaining items require the spelling of complete words. Watch the child on each item to make sure that they are writing their response on the correct line. You should ask the child to clarify what they wrote if their handwriting is unclear or if you suspect they have reversed a letter (e.g., writing *b* for *d* or *p* for *q*). Children will not be penalized for such reversals if they say the correct letter. Children are allowed to erase and correct a response if they want. If a child does not respond immediately after you have said a word or if the child asks you to repeat something, you may repeat the word or sentence.

If the child you are testing has a motor disability or an inability to write for another reason, then you may permit the child to respond orally. If a child responds orally, then write their response on the record form as they spell it. However, this alternative procedure for responding should only be used after every attempt is made to have the student give a written response.

Listening Comprehension

Listening Comprehension is administered via a CD player. In an emergency or if you experience technical problems with your CD player, you can read the subtest's passages aloud yourself, as they are written in the test easel. Similar to Reading Comprehension, Listening Comprehension items are grouped into item sets, and the child's grade level determines where to begin. Prior to beginning this subtest, you should check the volume on your CD player to ensure that the examinee will be able to hear adequately, and cue the CD to the proper track. Before playing each passage, be sure that the child is ready to listen because examinees are not allowed to hear the passage more than once. Immediately after the passage has been played, pause the CD player and ask the questions about the story. Although the passage itself may not be replayed, you may repeat a test question at the student's request. The Don't Forget box reminds you of important points about administering Listening Comprehension.

DON'T FORGET
··

Reminders for Administering Listening Comprehension

INTRODUCE THE TEST BEFORE BEGINNING THE FIRST PASSAGE.

Say, "You are going to hear a short story. Listen carefully, and then I will ask you some questions about the story. Ready? Listen."

READ THE RESPONSE CHOICES FOR MULTIPLE-CHOICE QUESTIONS TWICE.

When administering multiple-choice questions, say the letter as well as the text of each answer choice, and then pause slightly after each choice. After completing the list of choices, say the list a second time.

PROMPT EXAMINEES FOR A SECOND ANSWER ON QUESTIONS WITH TWO-PART ANSWERS.

If a question asks for a two-part answer and the students only gives one part, then say: "Yes, and what else?"

PLAY THE PASSAGE ONLY ONE TIME.

You may play the passage only once and may not answer any questions that the student asks about the story.

TEST QUESTIONS MAY BE REPEATED.

You may repeat a test question if a child asks for repetition or if you suspect that the student did not hear the question the first time.

Oral Expression

Oral Expression is administered in item sets and begins with the set determined by the child's grade (these starting points are listed in the easel). During administration, you may repeat an item if the child requests or if you believe that he or she did not hear it. Some items require examinees to start their response with a particular word. If a child does not start with the requested word, then you should give the child a second trial and give credit if they respond correctly upon the second administration of the item.

Word Recognition Fluency

Prior to administering Word Recognition Fluency make sure that you have the Word Recognition Fluency Card and a stopwatch in hand. Some of the words in this subtest are quite challenging, and it is recommended that you review the pronunciation of these words on the CD prior to administering the subtest. The starting point for Word Recognition Fluency is based on a child's performance on Letter and Word Recognition. Children who reached item 84 on Letter and Word Recognition start Word Recognition Fluency at item 31 and all other children begin Word Recognition Fluency at item 1.

Introduce the test with the verbiage printed in the easel (also on the record form). Once you say "Go," then begin timing. After 60 seconds, say, "Stop," and draw a line in the record form after the last word attempted. Some children may complete the task before 60 seconds have elapsed. For these children, record their completion time on the record form. During administration of this subtest, children may hesitate or get stuck on a word. When such a pause occurs, encourage the examinee to keep going and move onto the next word. As children read the words, record any words that they misread or skip by putting a slash through the appropriate word on the record form. However, do not penalize examinees for articulation errors or variations due to regional speech patterns.

Decoding Fluency

Administration of Decoding Fluency is very similar to administration of Word Recognition Fluency. For administration, you need the Decoding Fluency Card and a stopwatch or watch that shows seconds. Prior to administration, you should listen to the CD to hear examples of how to pronounce the nonsense words. To begin administration, you should introduce the subtest with the instructions printed in the manual and the record form. After you say, "Go," immediately begin timing the examinee, and, after 60 seconds, instruct the examinee to "Stop." Make a slash on the record form after the last word that the examinee read. If an examinee pauses or hesitates during the task, encourage them to keep going or move onto the next one. As the examinee is reading the words, make a slash through any of the words that are mispronounced or skipped. If a child completes the Decoding Fluency Card before 60 seconds have elapsed, then record the completion time in seconds.

Associational Fluency and Naming Facility

As mentioned earlier in this chapter, Associational Fluency and Naming Facility are administered together in task pairs (one Associational Fluency task with one Naming Facility task). Although these are the final tests listed in the easel and in the record form, they must be administered throughout the test battery and each of the four task pairs should be separated by other subtests. In Rapid Reference 3.5, we provide a suggested order for subtests administration order when these two tasks are included in the battery.

The specific directions to administer each of the task pairs are listed in the record form. Generally, on the Associational Fluency tasks (naming foods, naming objects, and two phonemic fluency tasks), you give the children 30 seconds to say as many of the words in a category that they can think of. If children stop or say that they cannot think of more, you should encourage them to try to say more if they have more time left. Children under grade 1 are administered only the first two Associational Fluency tasks: semantic fluency but not phonemic fluency. You should attempt to record the examinee's words verbatim, but sometimes a child responds so rapidly that such recording is difficult. In those instances, you should simply make a checkmark on a line of the record form to indicate that the child gave a correct response.

For the Naming Facility tasks, you first need to determine that the examinee knows the names of the objects, colors, and letters. If the examinee uses a different name for one of the objects, tell them the correct name to use. However, on the color and letter naming tasks, if the student does not name a color or letter correctly, then do not administer that task (see Caution). Students in Pre-K and kindergarten should only be administered the first two Naming Facility (RAN) tasks (not letter naming). As the examinee is responding, you should mark on the record form any stimulus that the examinee names incorrectly. When the child completes naming all of the stimuli on the card, you should record the child's completion time.

CAUTION

Prior to administering Naming Facility (RAN), check to make sure that the student knows the names of the objects, colors, and letters. You may tell them the correct name of an object if they use a different term. However, do not administer the task if the student does not correctly name a color or letter.

HOW TO SCORE THE KTEA-II

The KTEA-II yields several types of scores: raw scores, standard scores (subtests, domain composites, and Comprehensive Achievement Composite or Brief Achievement Composite), grade equivalents, age equivalents, and percentile ranks. Raw scores reflect the number for points earned by the student on each subtest. These scores, by themselves, are meaningless because they are not norm-based scores. When they are converted to standard scores, which are norm-based, they then allow the student's performance to be compared to that of others. The KTEA-II standard scores have a mean of 100 and a SD of 15. The range of standard scores for the subtests and composites is 40 to 160. We assume that achievement-test performance is distributed on a normal curve, with the majority of students scoring within +/– 1 SD of the mean. Thus, about two-thirds (68 percent) of students score in the range of 85 to 115. Less than 3 percent of students score above 130 or below 70.

Types of Scores

Each type of the KTEA-II's scores is described below.

Raw Scores

Subtest raw scores are calculated in a variety of ways. Five of the KTEA-II Comprehensive Form subtests' raw scores are calculated by subtracting the number of errors from the ceiling item (i.e., Letter and Word Recognition, Math Concepts and Applications, Math Computation, Nonsense Word Decoding, and Spelling). Phonological Awareness and Associational Fluency require examiners to sum the scores from various sections to determine the raw scores. Similarly, the raw scores for the Math and Reading subtests of the Brief Form are calculated by subtracting the total number of errors from the ceiling number. Some subtests require examiners to use a table to convert the total number of points in a section to the final raw score (i.e., Reading Comprehension, Written Expression, Listening Comprehension, Oral Expression, and the Writing subtest of the Brief Form). Three tasks that are timed (Word Recognition Fluency, Decoding Fluency, and Naming Facility) require examiners to use a chart to convert an examinee's completion time to a point value that is then part of the calculation of the raw score.

Standard Scores

To be meaningfully interpreted, the raw scores of the KTEA-II must be converted to standard scores. When converting from raw to standard scores, you must first decide whether to use age-based or grade-based norms. This decision depends on whether you want to compare the student's test performance with that of the same-age peers or same-grade peers. In most cases, the resulting standard scores will be similar. However, important differences can occur if the student has been retained or has received an accelerated grade placement, or if the student began school earlier or later in the year than is typical. In these cases, the age-based norms are probably more relevant. However, if you are planning on comparing performance on the KTEA-II with performance on an ability measure such as the KABC-II, always use age-based norms because they are the basis for the standard scores on ability measures. The Caution box provides further information about the differences between age-based and grade-based standard scores.

CAUTION

QUESTION:

I recently administered the KTEA-II to a child age 8:11 that just completed third grade. I looked up her standard scores according to age norms (as is typically my practice), but then, out of curiosity, I looked up her scores according to grade norms, too. The scores were quite different in some cases (e.g., both Reading Comprehension and Math Computation were 9 points lower when calculated according to the grade norms). Could you tell me why age and grade norms may yield different scores and give me your opinion about when each type of norm is most useful?

ANSWER:

The explanation of the difference is pretty simple. Assuming that children start kindergarten when they are 5 years old, then children start grade 3 when they are 8 years old. Therefore, virtually all children aged 8:11 are in grade 3. Children turn 8:11 at a steady rate throughout the grade 3 school year—some turn 8:11 in September, others in June. Therefore, about half of the students turn 8:11 in the fall, and about half in the spring. Thus, the norm sample for age 8:11 contains students from the beginning through the end of grade 3. That sample performs lower, as a group, than the norm sample for the spring of grade 3.

   Thus, for a student who turns 8:11 in the spring, the age norms will give higher standard scores than the grade norms. The reverse is true for a student who turns 8:11 in the fall. (The direction of the difference by time of year can't be generalized: It depends on what the "month" of age is. For a student aged 8:3 in the fall, age-based scores are higher than grade-based scores, because some students who turn 8:3 in the fall are in grade 2.)

   In principle, there is no good, practical solution for taking curriculum exposure into account in age norms, and all of the achievement batteries have this problem.

The ideal might be to have age-by-grade norm tables (e.g., age 8:6 in the fall of grade 3, age 8:6 in the spring of grade 3, age 8:6 in the spring of grade 2), but that is too complex. Simply subdividing age norms into fall and spring, as we used to do, is flawed because at most "months" of age a student could be in either of two grades, which would be an even greater distortion for some students.

The bottom line is that the situation is complicated—the deeper you look into it, the messier it becomes. In these days when grade retention is rare, there might be a good argument to be made for using grade norms rather than age norms for clinical evaluations. The concern used to be that grade norms would make a student who had repeated a grade or two look "too good." These days, there would seem to be a better argument that age norms are problematic because they mix students with different amounts of curriculum exposure. However, examiners must follow requirements set forth by their state and school district based on IDEA Reauthorized, so for some that will mean using age norms for special-ed classification and for others that will require using grade norms. Examiners should just be aware that occasionally differences do occur between them.

Note: The "Answer" is based on a personal communication from Mark Daniel (7/13/2004), Executive Director of Assessment Development and Director of the KABC-II/KTEA-II Project at AGS.

When selecting grade norms to convert raw scores to standard scores, you must select from one of two sets: Fall (indicating that a child was assessed in August to January) or Spring (indicating that a child was assessed in February to July). The front of the record form has a box that you can check to indicate whether you have used the Fall or Spring grade norms or the age-norms. In addition to separating each of the grade-norms into Fall and Spring, the *KTEA-II Comprehensive Form Norms Book* also has two columns for each subtest (one for Form A and one for Form B). Carefully select the correct column and the correct page of the norms book when you are determining the standard scores. The Don't Forget box reminds examiners about which tables to use to find various standard scores.

Because scores have error associated with them, it is wise to report standard scores with a band of error or within a confidence interval. The KTEA-II allows you to choose from 85 percent, 90 percent, or 95 percent confidence levels (the record form directs you to circle which level of confidence you are reporting). Tables N.6 and N.7 in the *KTEA-II Comprehensive Form Norms Book* provide the bands of error for age-based standard scores and grade-based standard scores.

Grade and Age Equivalents

Grade and age equivalents may be found in tables N.9 and N.10, respectively, in the *KTEA-II Comprehensive Form Norms Book* (similar tables are also available in the *Brief Form Manual*). However, we recommend that they be reported with

DON'T FORGET
....

Where to Find Standard Scores

	Fall Grade Norms	Spring Grade Norms	Age-Based Norms
Subtest Standard Scores	Table N.1	Table N.2	Table N.4
Domain Composites	Table N.3		Table N.5
Comprehensive Achievement Composite	Table N.3		Table N.5

Note: Tables referenced here are from the *KTEA-II Comprehensive Form Norms Book*. Table N.1 is found on pages 2–53, Table N.2 is found on pages 54–105, Table N.3 is on pages 107–115, Table N.4 is on pages 116–283, and Table N.5 is on pages 284–299.

caution, as they are frequently misunderstood. They are not precise like standard scores or percentile ranks and often suggest large differences in performance, when the differences are insignificant. For example, a raw score of 71 on Reading Comprehension yields an age equivalent of 14-years, 8-months, and earning just two more points for a raw score of 73 corresponds to an age equivalent of 16-years, 6 months. On the same subtest, an examinee age 15:5 would earn an age-based standard score of 99 (for a raw score of 71) and an age-based standard score of 101 (for a raw score of 73). Thus, this 2-point standard score difference appears much smaller than the nearly 2-year difference in age-equivalents, when comparing scores based on the same raw scores.

Percentile Ranks

Percentile ranks are an excellent metric to communicate results to parents, teachers, and other non-psychologists. They are often readily understood and interpreted. Regardless of whether age-based standard scores or grade-based standard scores are used, the percentile rank has the same meaning: It is the percentage of individuals that the student outperformed at his or her age (age norms) or grade level (grade norms). For example, a 12-year-old who scored at the 75th percentile on Nonsense Word Decoding performed better than 75 percent of 12-year-olds on that subtest. A first grader who scored at the 5th percentile on Phonological Awareness scored better than only 5 percent of first graders. Each standard score can be converted to a percentile rank by using Table N.8 of the *KTEA-II Comprehensive Form Norms Book* or Table C.9 in the *KTEA-II Brief Form Manual*.

CAUTION

....

Percentile Ranks Are Not Percent Correct

Clearly communicate to parents that a percentile rank is the percent of children that an examinee scored better than. A percentile rank is not the percentage of items answered correctly.

Descriptive Categories

Rapid Reference 3.6 presents the descriptive categories that the test authors selected for KTEA-II subtests and composites. These verbal descriptions correspond to commonly used standard score ranges. The categories shown in this table are intended to reflect in words the approximate distance of each range of scores from the group mean—a verbal translation of the normal curve. This system differs from the system used for the original KTEA-II and from many other classification systems, such as Wechsler's (2002, 2003).

The KTEA-II system depends on the standard deviation of 15 to define its categories, with the Average range of 85 to 115 corresponding to ±1 SD from the mean (100 ± 15), Below Average defined as 1 to 2 SDs below the mean (70 to 84), and so forth. You should use these categories to describe standard scores on the global scales and scale indexes. This system avoids the narrow 10-point categories (e.g., 70 to 79, 110 to 119) that appear frequently in other systems (including the one used previously for the original K-TEA). One problem with 10-point categories is that, when confidence intervals are used to provide a reasonable band of error, it is common for the confidence interval to span three different categories. That broad span of ability levels can be confusing, for example, when explaining a child's test performance to a parent.

It is inappropriate to overwhelm readers of a case report by providing descriptive categories for each standard score. These labels serve best when they either summarize an individual's performance on all scales via a composite score or highlight significant discrepancies among the scales. Generally, the use of descriptive labels with subtests should be reserved for standard scores that are significantly above or below the child's own mean values or for standard scores that are high or low relative to other children of the same age.

Growth Scale Values

The KTEA-II's Growth Scale Values (GSV) are based on Item Response Theory (IRT) ability scale. The GSVs are designed for measuring change. These scores specifically reflect absolute performance like a raw score, and therefore do not provide relative standing (i.e., normative data). One of the advantages of this metric is that it allows direct comparison of GSV scores obtained on the alternate forms of a subtest. The KTEA-II provides the GSV for each raw score value on each subtest by form (see Table I.13 in Appendix I of the KTEA-II Manual). Professionals can use the GSV scores to track academic progress over time. Conceptually, GSV scores are much like "inches" are an equal-interval scale of length, but the GSV scale is an equal-interval scale of academic ability. Thus, GSV scores can be used as a "yardstick" by which academic progress can be measured throughout the school years. The GSV metric can also be used to compare a student's academic ability to a reference group of all the students in a particular grade. Because standard scores take into account "normal" growth, over time, the standard score will be the same if the child is growing at a "typical" rate. However, GSV scores will reflect even small amounts of academic improvement over time (see the Don't Forget box on this page).

DON'T FORGET

GSV scores will reflect even small amounts of academic improvement over time. However, if a child's ability is growing at a "typical" rate, the standard score will appear relatively unchanged over time.

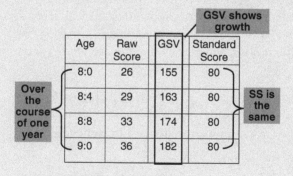

	Age	Raw Score	GSV	Standard Score	
Over the course of one year	8:0	26	155	80	
	8:4	29	163	80	SS is the same
	8:8	33	174	80	
	9:0	36	182	80	

GSV shows growth

Subtest-by-Subtest Scoring Keys

Most of the items on the KTEA-II have a simple dichotomous scoring system, requiring examiners to circle either a 1 (for correct) or a 0 (for incorrect) on the record form. However, there are differences in how raw scores are

≡ Rapid Reference 3.6

Descriptive Category System

Range of Standard Scores	Name of Category	SDs from Mean
131–160	Upper Extreme	+2 to +4
116–130	Above Average	+1 to +2
85–115	Average Range	−1 to +1
70–84	Below Average	−1 to −2
40–69	Lower Extreme	−2 to −4

calculated across the subtests. Regardless of how the raw score is calculated, you need to score the items (at least in a preliminary fashion) as you are testing. This score-as-you-go procedure is necessary so that you know when to discontinue a subtest or when you need to drop back to an earlier start point. We recommend that you double-check the accuracy of each item's score when you are completely done with the test administration, prior to calculating the raw score. The Caution box lists some common errors in scoring. Scoring keys for each of the Comprehensive Form subtests are listed in the following pages and scoring keys for the Brief Form subtests are listed in the Don't Forget box.

CAUTION

Common Errors in Scoring

- calculating the raw score incorrectly
- transferring the raw score to the front page of the record form incorrectly
- adding the subtest standard scores incorrectly when calculating the sum for the composite scores
- using the wrong tables for standard score conversions.
- misreading the norms tables (e.g., using the wrong line or wrong column)
- subtraction errors in comparing composites and subtest scores
- errors in conducting the error analysis (e.g., totaling the error columns incorrectly)

DON'T FORGET

....

Scoring Keys for the Brief Form Subtests

Brief Form Subtest	Scoring Keys
Reading Part 1	• Each correctly pronounced word is awarded 1 point. • To be correct, the word must be said as a connected, relatively smooth whole, with accent properly placed. • Multiple pronunciations are not penalized, as long as the final pronunciation is correct. • Be aware that some words have multiple correct pronunciations. • Although there is no error analysis in the Brief Form, examiners should still carefully record incorrect responses as part of their qualitative observations.
Reading Part 2	• Each correct response is awarded 1 point. • Parts of some responses may be optional and not required to earn credit (e.g., responses shown in parentheses in the manual). • Refer to the complete scoring rules on the easel when scoring. • Mispronunciations due to regional speech patterns are not penalized. • Total Reading score is based on the sum of correct scores for Parts 1 and 2 for children in grades 1–12 but only includes Part 1 for children under first grade.
Math	• Each correct response is awarded 1 point. • Credit can be given even if a response is not reduced to the lowest terms. • Units of measurement are not required to credit a correct response. • Total score is based on the total number of correct items. (Any nonadministered items before the basal are also given credit.)

(Continued)

Brief Form Subtest	Scoring Keys
Writing	• Items are scored 1 point for each scoring criteria correctly met (i.e., some items have more than one scoring criteria, such as "correctly spelled" and "no punctuation errors"). • Specific scoring criteria are listed on the easel and in the record form. • Calculate the raw score by totaling the number of points earned in the item set and using the table on page 8 of the record form to convert that point total to the raw score.

Phonological Awareness

Children should not be penalized for articulation errors or for variations in speech due to regional speech patterns. In Sample A and items 1 through 4, children's responses should be scored as correct if they rhyme with the stimulus word, even if they are nonsense words (e.g., if a child says "*jook* rhymes with *book*"). The Phonological Awareness total raw score is the sum of scores from sections one through six for kindergartners but is the sum of only sections 1, 4, and 5 for children in first grade and above. However, the Long form can be administered and scored for students in first grade and above if deemed clinically necessary.

Letter and Word Recognition

Similar to proper administration of this subtest, the key to properly scoring Letter and Word Recognition is having knowledge of the proper pronunciation of all the stimulus words. You need to be proficient in how to record a response phonetically (either with the phonetic key or sound-by-sound). A bright child or adolescent may rapidly read the six words listed on a stimulus page, and if you struggle with how to record what they say, you will undoubtedly run into trouble with scoring.

Note that some words have multiple correct pronunciations (e.g., items 72, 74, 85, 88, and 95), and the various pronunciations are listed on both the record form and the easel. Sometimes examinees will sound out a word two or three times (perhaps incorrectly) before they read it smoothly as their final response. Give credit to children for their final response if it is correctly pronounced in a relatively smooth manner with the accent properly placed. However, if a child's regional speech pattern leads to a different pronunciation, give credit for an item if it is the region's common pronunciation. For example, reading "car" with a

Bostonian accent of "caw." To calculate the raw score, subtract the number of errors (0 scores) from the ceiling item. An error analysis may be conducted after the test is administered.

Math Concepts and Applications

Some Math Concepts and Applications items have multiple questions, and, to give credit, examinees must answer all parts of the question correctly (e.g., items 27 and 28). Some items have multiple ways that the child can correctly respond (e.g., $\frac{3}{5}$ or 60 percent or 0.6). Note that the record form only lists one of the correct ways, but the manual lists all the possible correct ways of responding. Some items are problems requiring calculations with units of measure (e.g., inches, feet, pounds). In most instances children are not required to include the unit of measurement in their response. For such items, the fact that the unit of measurement is optional is indicated on the record form by being printed in parentheses. To calculate the raw score, subtract the number of errors (0 scores) from the ceiling item. An error analysis may be conducted after the test is administered.

Nonsense Word Decoding

Scoring for this subtest is very similar to that of Letter and Word Recognition. Correct recording of the examinee's responses is crucial if you intend to complete detailed error analysis. Each item is scored 1 point for a correct response and 0 points for an incorrect response. Six of the 50 items have more than one correct pronunciation, and all of these correct pronunciations are listed on both the record form and in the easel. Children should not be penalized for misplacing the accent of a word or if they have articulation errors. Correct responses are those in which the child pronounces the word in a connected, relatively smooth whole (even if they must make several attempts before being able to finally pronounce the word in that manner). To calculate the raw score, subtract the number of errors (0 scores) from the ceiling item. An error analysis may be conducted after the test is administered.

Math Computation

Binary scoring is used for Math Computation, with 1 point given for correct responses and 0 points for incorrect responses. You should score examinees' responses as they finish each problem so that you know when to discontinue the subtest. As mentioned in the section of this text on administration, it is important to watch examinees as they write their responses to ensure that you know which number is their final response and also to ensure that you can read their handwriting.

When handwriting is unclear, you should ask examinees what their final written response is. Some items allow different versions of a number as a correct response. For example, a response reduced to the lowest terms is correct (e.g., $1\frac{1}{2}$), but also an equivalent improper fraction is correct (e.g., $\frac{3}{2}$), or an equivalent decimal (e.g., 1.5). Acceptable versions of a response are printed in the record form. To calculate the raw score, subtract the number of errors (0 scores) from the ceiling item. An error analysis may be conducted after the test is administered.

Reading Comprehension

Reading Comprehension is one of the few KTEA-II subtests that requires a bit of judgment in scoring. The first 12 items requiring a pointing response and following a specific command are easy to score as correct or not correct. Of the remaining items, 22 are multiple-choice questions, which are also straightforward to score. The passage items that have open-ended questions generally are not difficult to score, as the easel has examples of correct and incorrect answers, and the general criteria that is necessary for an item to be scored correct. In most cases, the reasons behind the decisions regarding correct and incorrect responses are implicitly clear. However, for nine Reading Comprehension items, additional information is provided in Appendix C of the *KTEA-II Comprehensive Form Manual* regarding the explanation for scoring decisions. Additional examples of correct and incorrect responses are also provided in Appendix C of the *KTEA-II Comprehensive Form Manual* for these nine items.

To calculate the total raw score for Reading Comprehension, you first compute the number of points obtained on the set (or last pair of adjacent sets) that the examinee took. Then you must use the conversion table on pages 12 and 13 of the record form to convert this point total to the raw score.

Written Expression

Thorough scoring must be completed after the test is administered. Detailed item-by-item Written Expression scoring instructions are provided in Appendix E of the *KTEA-II Comprehensive Form Manual* (pages 159 to 222). The one exception to scoring at the end of the test is for first-grade students in the spring: For these children, Level 2 must be preliminarily scored after item 23 to determine whether the rest of Level 2 should be administered. Each item of this subtest has one or more scoring categories that is scored 1 or 0. The most common categories include task, sentence structure, capitalization, punctuation, grammar, and other mechanical errors. In addition to the specific error categories, you should familiarize yourself with the general scoring guidelines for Written Expression (see the Don't Forget box for a review of these).

DON'T FORGET
··
General Scoring Guidelines for Written Expression

ERROR CATEGORIES ARE INDEPENDENT.

Score each error category independently of the others. Try not to let poor performance in one category influence the scores for other categories in that item.

STRUCTURE AND GRAMMAR ERRORS SHOULD BE OBVIOUS.

Score 0 for sentence structure and word form (grammar) only if the error is obvious and would stand out in semi-formal writing such as a class paper.

USE JUDGMENT TO CHOOSE BEST-FITTING CATEGORY.

Sometimes a response is clearly erroneous, but it is not immediately evident which category should be scored 0. In those instances, choose the category that in your judgment best fits the error. The overall subtest score will not be affected.

MOST OFTEN, IGNORE EXTRA WRITING.

If the task criterion specifies a limited product (e.g., one word or one sentence) and the student produces a response, part of which satisfied this criterion, ignore any additional material the student has written when scoring the task criterion. However, if the task criterion is open-ended (e.g., "one or more sentences"), score according to the entire response. For the sentence structure criterion, scoring usually is based on the student's entire response, except when the scoring rule for an item specifies otherwise.

GIVE NO CREDIT FOR INCOMPREHENSIBLE RESPONSES OR NO RESPONSE.

If a student doesn't respond to an item, or if the response is incomprehensible (the meaning cannot be understood), score 0 on all categories for that item.

GIVE NO CREDIT FOR TASK CRITERION AND SENTENCE STRUCTURE FOR MISPLACED SENTENCE PARTS.

On later items, misplacement of a part of the sentence can cause failure on both the task criterion (because the sentence does not make sense or says something false) and the sentence structure criterion (because of the misplacement). In such cases, score 0 for both criteria.

IF A WORD IS RECOGNIZABLE IT IS PHONETICALLY READABLE.

"Phonetically readable," a term used in Level 2 and 3 scoring, is not a technical term; it means that the word is recognizable.

TRY NOT TO PENALIZE FOR POOR HANDWRITING OR POOR SPELLING.

If a response is difficult to read due to poor spelling or poor handwriting, score as much of it as possible.

Note: From Appendix E of *KTEA-II Comprehensive Form Manual* (Kaufman & Kaufman, 2004a, p. 162).

Once you have scored each of the categories 1 or 0, then you must sum the total number of points obtained within the item set administered. This total number of points is then converted to a raw score using a conversion table. The table that converts the total points earned at a particular level of the Written Expression subtest to the raw score is provided on pages 223 and 224 of the *KTEA-II Comprehensive Form Manual.* Some children will end up taking more than two sets of items; in such cases, use the last two sets administered for scoring purposes. An error analysis may be conducted after the test is administered.

Spelling

Scoring for spelling is straightforward: Score 1 for correctly spelled words and 0 for misspelled words. Poorly formed letters, capitalization, and mixing printing with handwriting are not penalized. They key to scoring Spelling is making sure that you know what the child intended to write during administration. Thus, as mentioned in the administration section, you must carefully watch children write their responses and ask children to name any letters that are unclear or ambiguous. To calculate the raw score, subtract the number of errors (0 scores) from the ceiling item. An error analysis may be conducted after the test is administered.

Listening Comprehension

The record form lists correct responses (that is, the most common correct responses). However, other correct responses are listed in the easel. For some items, specific criteria that a response must satisfy in order to be scored correct are listed (along with examples). Some responses have optional portions, which are shown in parentheses in the easel. When scoring, you should not penalize students for immature speech or articulation errors.

The total number of points for Listening Comprehension is based on the scores from administration of a complete item set or a pair of adjacent tests. You should base the final score on the last two item sets administered. Once you have calculated the total points, then use the conversion table on pages 20 and 21 of the record form to convert the point total to the raw score.

Oral Expression

Similar to Written Expression, the *KTEA-II Comprehensive Form Manual* provides detailed, item-by-item scoring instructions, which should be applied after the subtest is administered. However, you must give a preliminary score while the subtest is being administered to determine if the basal or discontinue rules have been met (preliminary scores are listed on the left side of the record form just beside the item number). When you are unsure whether a preliminary item score should be 0 or 1, you should err on the side of caution and give the child credit. This procedure is less likely to lead you to prematurely discontinue the subtest.

The item-by-item scoring categories listed in Appendix F of the manual (pp. 225 to 257) are four-fold: task (pragmatics), sentence structure (syntax), word meaning (semantics), and word form (grammar). These categories are explained in depth and exemplified in the manual. General scoring guidelines are also provided and summarized in the Don't Forget box. Once scoring is complete, total the points in the item set (or last pair of adjacent item sets) taken by the examinee. Then use the conversion table on pages 258 and 259 of the *KTEA-II Comprehensive Form Manual* to determine the raw score based upon the total points in the set.

DON'T FORGET
....
General Scoring Guidelines for Oral Expression

ERROR CATEGORIES ARE INDEPENDENT.

Score each error category independently of the others. Try not to let poor performance in one category influence the scores for other categories in that item.

BASE SCORING ON COMMONLY HEARD SPEECH.

Score 0 for sentence structure, word meaning, and word form (grammar) only if the error is obvious and would stand out in semi-formal speech such as speaking to the class.

USE JUDGMENT TO CHOOSE BEST-FITTING CATEGORY.

Sometimes a response is clearly erroneous, but it is not immediately evident which category should be scored 0. In those instances, choose the category that in your judgment best fits the error. The overall subtest score will not be affected.

GIVE NO CREDIT FOR INCOMPREHENSIBLE RESPONSES OR NO RESPONSE.

If a student doesn't respond to an item, or if the response is incomprehensible (the meaning cannot be understood), score 0 on all categories for that item.

DO NOT PENALIZE FALSE STARTS, SELF-CORRECTIONS, OR INTERJECTIONS.

For example, give credit if a child says: "Before she went home—I want to go home—she went to the grocery store with her mom."

MOST OFTEN, IGNORE EXTRANEOUS WORDS OR SENTENCES.

If the student says something that is not related to the task, but the child gives a correct response, ignore anything else he or she says.

(Continued)

GIVE NO CREDIT FOR TASK CRITERION AND SENTENCE STRUCTURE FOR MISPLACED SENTENCE PARTS.

On later items, misplacement of a part of the sentence can cause failure on both the task criterion (because the sentence does not make sense or says something false) and the sentence structure criterion (because of the misplacement). In such cases, score 0 for both criteria.

DO NOT PENALIZE FOR ARTICULATION ERRORS.

Note: From Appendix F of *KTEA-II Comprehensive Form Manual* (Kaufman & Kaufman, 2004a, p. 225).

Word Recognition Fluency

Scoring for this subtest involves calculating the number of correct items read within the time limit. The scores are calculated in a slightly different manner for children who start with item 31, in contrast to those who start with item 1 (see the Don't Forget box). Children who reach the end of the card in less than a minute and have a total raw score of 83 or greater will have extra points added to their total raw score at the end.

DON'T FORGET

How to Calculate Word Recognition Fluency's Raw Score

If examinee started at item 1	If examinee started at item 31, but did not reach the end of the card in less than 60 seconds	If examinee started at item 31, reached the end of the card in less than 60 seconds, and has a total raw score of 83 or
1. Subtract the number of errors (and skips) from the number of the last item reached to calculate the raw score.	1. Subtract the number of errors (or skips) from the last item number reached. 2. Subtract 6 from the result.	1. Subtract the number of errors (or skips) from the last item number reached. 2. Subtract 6 from the result. 3. Use the Completion Time Table in the record form to determine how many extra points to add to the raw score.

Decoding Fluency

The total raw score for Decoding Fluency is calculated by subtracting the number of errors (which includes the number of words skipped) from the number of the last item reached. However, if an examinee finishes reading all of the words in less than 60 seconds and has a total raw score of 45 or greater, you add extra points to his or her score. The number of extra points to add is determined by referring to the Completion Time chart in the record form, which states how many extra points are awarded for various completion times. There are a maximum of 13 possible extra points for the fastest responses.

Associational Fluency

Scoring for the four associational fluency tasks (foods, noisy, /d/, /t/, or animals, toys, /k/, /m/) is based on the number of different responses spoken by the examinee in 30 seconds that meet the task demand. Appendix G of the *KTEA-II Comprehensive Form Manual* (pp. 261 to 263) lists the specific requirements for each of the Associational Fluency tasks. For all tasks, credit is not given for made-up words or words that were given as examples. Although words that are repetitions are not credited, you may give a child credit if he or she uses a homophone (words that sound the same but have different meanings—e.g., too, two, to; seem, seam). Total raw scores for children in Pre-K and kindergarten are based only on the sum of the two semantic fluency tasks, but the total raw scores for children in first grade and above are based on the sum of the two semantic fluency tasks plus the two phonemic fluency tasks.

Naming Facility

The raw score for each of the three Naming Facility tasks is based on the examinee's completion time as well as the number of errors that they make. If an examinee makes more than three errors on a task, then you should not score that task. If a child makes two or fewer errors, then you should convert the examinee's completion time to a point score using the table on the record form. The total raw score for Naming Facility for children in Pre-K and kindergarten is based only on the first two Naming Facility tasks, and the total raw score for children in grades one and above is based on the sum of all three Naming Facility tasks.

Computer Scoring Procedures

The KTEA-II ASSIST™ computer scoring program offers an alternative to hand scoring the test. Raw scores can quickly be converted to derived scores with the KTEA-II ASSIST™. The software contains both Macintosh and Windows programs on one CD-ROM. The printout from the KTEA-II ASSIST™ includes a summary of student performance by composite or subtest, comparisons of skill areas or subtests for easy interpretation of results, achievement/ability comparisons, and error analysis for all standard subtests. It also offers additional information, including: best practices instructional suggestions for designing IEP goals that match students' score information with remediation strategies and lists of math problems or reading or spelling words similar to those that were difficult for the student. The KTEA-II ASSIST^{TM} works on the same platform as the KABC-II ASSIST^{TM}, so examinee information (e.g., name, date of birth, dates of testing) will be saved and can transfer from one program to the next.

HOW TO INTERPRET THE KTEA-II

Once you have completed administration and scoring, then you may begin a systematic method of interpreting the scores yielded from the KTEA-II. Because the KTEA-II Comprehensive Form yields so much information—14 possible subtest scores, 4 domain composites, 4 Reading-Related composites, and a Comprehensive Achievement Composite—examiners need to methodically employ an efficient process of interpretation to glean the most from the data. In this section of the book, we provide readers with such a systematic method.

Introduction to Interpretation

A child's or adolescent's reason for referral typically dictates the battery of tests administered during an assessment. In the case of the KTEA-II, either the full battery may be administered or a partial battery may be administered to answer a question about a particular area of academic functioning. We present an approach to interpreting the comprehensive battery of the KTEA-II and an alternative approach if only part of the KTEA-II Comprehensive Form is administered. The interpretive approaches advocated in this book begin at the global level by looking at the Comprehensive Achievement Composite (CAC) and domain composites then move to subtests and finally to specific patterns of errors. One goal of KTEA-II interpretation is to identify and promote understanding of the student's strong and weak areas of academic functioning, from both *normative* (age-based or grade-based) and *ipsative* (person-based) perspectives. Similar to interpretive approaches presented for various cognitive instruments such as the KABC-II (Kaufman, Lichtenberger, Fletcher-Janzen, & Kaufman, 2005) and the WISC-IV (Flanagan & Kaufman, 2004), we support the notion of backing interpretive hypotheses with multiple pieces of supportive data. Such supportive data may be in the form of multiple test scores, behavioral observations, teacher reports, school records, or parent reports. In other words, test scores are not interpreted in isolation.

Interpretation of the complete KTEA-II Comprehensive Form involves five steps:

1. Interpret the Comprehensive Achievement Composite.
2. Interpret domain composites and subtest scores.
3. Identify domain composite strengths and weaknesses.
4. Identify subtest strengths and weaknesses.
5. Determine the significance and unusualness of planned comparisons.

When you administer only portions of the KTEA-II Comprehensive Form, you may conduct an abbreviated interpretation, as the CAC and some domain composites will not be available for the interpretive analyses. In the abbreviated interpretation of a partial battery you will conduct only two of the steps listed earlier:

2. Interpret domain composites and subtest scores.
5. Determine the significance and unusualness of planned comparisons.

Interpretation of the KTEA-II Brief Form is analogous to what we describe for interpreting a partial KTEA-II Comprehensive Form battery. The KTEA-II Brief Form was designed to be a screening instrument that can determine when further, more comprehensive assessment is necessary; therefore, the level of interpretation is not as in-depth as it is with the Comprehensive Form (e.g., no error analysis is available on the KTEA-II Brief Form). There are two steps to interpreting the Brief Form: (a) Interpret the Brief Achievement Composite, and (b) compare subtest standard scores. Readers are directed to Step 1 on the following page for interpreting the Achievement Composite for both the Brief and the Comprehensive Forms. For information on how to conduct a comparison of subtest scores in the Brief Form, readers are directed to Step 5 on page 135.

The data and calculations needed to conduct each of the interpretive steps outlined in this chapter are recorded on the KTEA-II record form. For the Comprehensive Form, the data for Steps 1 and 2 are recorded on pages 1 and 3 of the record form. The data for Steps 3 and 4 are recorded on page 3 of the record form, and the data for Step 5 are recorded on the back page of the record form. All data for the Brief Form are recorded on the front cover of the record form.

After the interpretation of either the complete or the partial KTEA-II Comprehensive Form battery, examiners may wish to obtain more detailed information by analyzing an examinee's errors. The final section on interpretation details a process of error analysis for each KTEA-II subtest.

Step 1. Interpret the Comprehensive Achievement Composite (CAC)

The CAC is comprised of four subtests for preschoolers and kindergarteners and six subtests for students in grades 1 and above. The CAC subtests for these two groups are shown earlier in this chapter in Figure 3.1. If a partial KTEA-II battery is administered, and all four or six of the subtests that comprise the CAC are not obtained, then the CAC cannot be calculated, and this interpretive step can be skipped. The function of the CAC and the Brief Achievement Composite (BAC) on the Brief Form is to provide a global overview of a student's academic achievement across four domains: reading, math, written language, and oral language. The CAC standard score is also used in later interpretive steps as it represents a student's "average" academic ability or the "midpoint" of all their academic skills. Thus, in the later interpretive steps, the CAC is the basis of comparison for determining the student's relatively strong and weak areas of achievement.

When interpreting the CAC or BAC in written reports, you should report the CAC or BAC standard score, the confidence interval, percentile rank, and descriptive category. If the BAC's or CAC's confidence interval spans more than one descriptive category, we suggest reporting the descriptive category as a range (e.g., if the confidence interval is 111 to 119, then write in the report: "Eliza's CAC was in the Average to Above Average range of academic functioning").

In addition to reporting the CAC standard score, confidence interval, percentile rank, and descriptive category, you should report whether the CAC is a Normative Strength or Normative Weakness. A Normative Strength (NStr) is defined as a standard score that is greater than 115 and a Normative Weakness (NWk) is defined as a standard score that is lower than 85. Thus, Normative Strengths and Weaknesses are those scores that fall outside of the Average range of academic functioning. Page 3 of the KTEA-II Comprehensive Record Form has a place to record whether the CAC is a Normative Strength or Normative Weakness by circling the appropriate abbreviation (see Figure 3.3).

Some children's CAC (or BAC) standard scores are comprised of scores that vary widely across the four academic domains. In such cases, the CAC should be interpreted with an appropriate explanation. For example:

Tomás earned Reading Comprehension and Letter Word Recognition standard scores of 74 and 75, respectively, but he also earned much higher Math Computation and Math Concepts and Applications standard scores of 124 and 125, respectively. His CAC standard score was 100, which represents the midpoint of very diverse abilities. Because of the variability in the scores that comprise Tomás' CAC scores, a more meaningful understanding of his diverse academic abilities can be

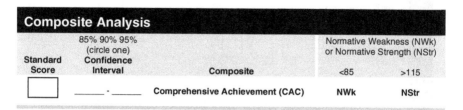

Figure 3.3 Analysis of Comprehensive Achievement Composite.

Note: Excerpt from page 3 of the *KTEA-II Comprehensive Form* record form that can be used to record data for interpretive Step 1.

obtained by examining his performance on the separate academic domain composites.

Thus, the examiner's written report will communicate that, although Tomás earned a CAC in the Average range, his academic skills are highly variable, ranging from Below Average to Above Average. The report will then go on to focus on those separate academic domains, as the Average CAC does not provide as much useful and meaningful information as his scores on the separate academic domains.

Step 2. Interpret the Domain Composite Scores and Subtest Scores

In the second interpretive step, a procedure similar to that of Step 1 is followed for interpreting the domain composite scores and the subtest scores. Step 2 is conducted whether a complete or partial KTEA-II battery was administered. For whichever subtests were administered, report the standard score, the confidence interval, and the percentile rank. We do not recommend reporting the descriptive categories for each of the subtests, as that amount of information (scores plus descriptive categories) is a bit overwhelming and unnecessary. However, we do recommend reporting the descriptive categories for the four domain composites and four Reading-Related composites, in addition to the standard scores, the confidence intervals, and the percentile ranks.

The final part of Step 2 for each composite and subtest is to determine whether each is a Normative Strength or a Normative Weakness. Like interpretation of the CAC, you can circle NWk (scores < 85) and NStr (scores > 115) on page 3 of the record form to indicate the Normative Weaknesses and Strengths (see Figure 3.4).

Composite Analysis

Standard Score	Confidence Interval 85% 90% 95% (circle one)	Composite	Normative Weakness (NWk) or Normative Strength (NStr)		Personal Weakness (PWk) or Personal Strength (PStr)		
			<85	>115	Diff. from CAC	Sig. ($p < 0.05$)	Infrequent (<10%)
☐	_ – _	Comprehensive Achievement (CAC)	NWk	NStr			☐
☐	_ – _	Reading	NWk	NStr	⎯⎯	PWk PStr	☐
☐	_ – _	Math	NWk	NStr	⎯⎯	PWk PStr	☐
☐	_ – _	Written Language	NWk	NStr	⎯⎯	PWk PStr	☐
☐	_ – _	Oral Language	NWk	NStr	⎯⎯	PWk PStr	☐
☐	_ – _	Sound Symbol	NWk	NStr	⎯⎯	PWk PStr	☐
☐	_ – _	Decoding	NWk	NStr	⎯⎯	PWk PStr	☐
☐	_ – _	Reading Fluency	NWk	NStr	⎯⎯	PWk PStr	☐
☐	_ – _	Oral Fluency	NWk	NStr	⎯⎯	PWk PStr	☐

Figure 3.4 Analysis of Domain Composites.

Note: Excerpt from page 3 of the *KTEA-II Comprehensive Form* record form that can be used to record data for interpretive Steps 3 and 4.

Step 3. Identify Domain Composite Strengths and Weaknesses

In Steps 1 and 2 you compare the examinee's abilities to that of the normative group (i.e., determining Normative Strengths and Weaknesses), but in Step 3 you compare the examinee's abilities to his or her own average level of academic performance (i.e., determining Personal Strengths and Weaknesses). The CAC standard score is used as the value that represents a student's "average level of performance," which is compared to the student's performance on the separate domain composites (Rapid Reference 3.7 gives the rationale for using the CAC to represent the student's "average" level of performance). Thus, for each of the four domain composites (Reading, Math, Written Language, and Oral Language) and the four Reading-Related composites (Sound Symbol, Oral Fluency, Decoding, and Reading Fluency), subtract the domain composite standard score from the CAC standard score. Then record this difference on page 3 of the record form in the column labeled "Diff. from CAC." A student's domain composite that is significantly higher than the CAC is labeled a Personal Strength (PStr) and a domain composite that is significantly lower than the CAC is labeled a Personal Weakness (PWk). Tables in the *KTEA-II Comprehensive Form Manual* provide the specific difference values necessary to be considered significant at the .05 level (refer to the "Significance" column of Table I.1 for grade norms or Table I.3 for age norms). If the difference between the CAC and a domain composite is equal to or greater than the value indicated in the table then

≡ *Rapid Reference 3.7*

Rationale for Using CAC as Student's Average Level of Performance

Interpretive Steps 3 and 4 suggest using the CAC as the midpoint or average level of student's academic performance when conducting comparisons with specific academic skill areas. This procedure is slightly different than that suggested in the previous version of the K-TEA, which compared subtest scores to the mean score on all subtests. By using the CAC rather than the mean of the subtests administered, examiners are not burdened with having to calculate the mean composite or mean subtest scores. The CAC includes one or two subtests from each of the academic domains, and it serves as an appropriate reference point for evaluating a broad range of individual composites and subtests.

Note: This explanation is adapted from pages 30 and 31 of the *KTEA-II Comprehensive Form Manual* (Kaufman & Kaufman, 2004a). Further detail regarding the technical procedures used in the interpretive procedures can also be found on pages 30 and 31 of the Manual.

that composite is deemed significantly different. A significant difference in which the domain composite is greater that the CAC is a Personal Strength and a significant difference in which the domain composite is less than the CAC is a Personal Weakness.

After determining which composites are Personal Strengths and Personal Weaknesses, you must determine how usual the difference is in the norm sample. If the value of the difference is unusually large (occurring in fewer than 10 percent of the norm sample cases), then you should check the box in the column labeled "Infrequent" on page 3 of the record form. To determine whether a discrepancy is unusually large, refer to the "Frequency" column of Table I.1 or Table I.3 of the *KTEA-II Comprehensive Form Manual.*

Personal Strengths or Weaknesses that are also "Infrequent" and a Normative Strength or Weakness are especially noteworthy and demand special attention when translating scores to diagnostic and educational considerations. Personal Strengths and Weaknesses by definition are scores that are significantly different than a student's CAC—that is, the differences are very unlikely to have occurred by chance. Some significant differences may be quite common in the population. Thus, these significant differences, in and of themselves, may not be of particular clinical interest. However, if a difference is so large that it rarely occurs in the population (i.e., it is "Infrequent"), then it is usually worth investigating further.

Step 4. Identify Subtest Strengths and Weaknesses

Step 4 is similar to Step 3 in that you are comparing a student's performance to their own average level of performance. However, Step 3 determined Personal Strengths and Weaknesses for domain composites and Step 4 determines them for subtest scores. To identify subtest strengths and weaknesses, follow the same procedure outlined in Step 3: Subtract each subtest standard score from the CAC standard score. Record the absolute difference between the scores on page 3 of the record form in the appropriate blank under "Diff. from CAC." Then refer to Table I.2 (grade norms) or I.4 (age norms) in Appendix I of the *KTEA-II Comprehensive Form Manual* to determine whether each difference is statistically significant at the .05 level. If a difference is large enough to be considered significant and the subtest score is higher than the CAC score, then that subtest is a Personal Strength (circle PStr on the record form). If a difference is large enough to be considered significant and the subtest score is lower than the CAC score, then that subtest is a Personal Weakness (circle PWk on the record form).

If a difference is statistically significant (deeming a subtest a Personal Strength or Personal Weakness), then determine how unusual it is in the norm sample. Refer to the columns labeled "Frequency" in Table I.2 (grade norms) or Table I.4 (age norms) in Appendix I of the *KTEA-II Comprehensive Form Manual*. If the value of the difference occurs in fewer than 10 percent of the norm sample cases, put a checkmark on page 3 of the record form in the "Infrequent" column. The subtests that are both a Personal Strength or Weakness and labeled "Infrequent" are worthy of further investigation, as they may provide useful diagnostic information or information related to educational considerations.

Step 5. Determine the Significance and Unusualness of Planned Comparisons

Step 5 is useful for evaluating hypotheses about specific strong and weak areas of achievement or for evaluating a comparison between particular academic or reading-related skills. At times, specific planned comparisons of composites or subtests may provide useful information for diagnosis or instructional planning.

On the Comprehensive form, there are numerous planned comparisons that can be made depending on the examiner's needs. However, the test authors recommend routinely making at least two comparisons in the Comprehensive Form: (a) Oral Expression subtest with Written Expression subtest, and (b) Reading Comprehension subtest with Listening Comprehension subtest. The

DON'T FORGET

What can be learned from the Expression and Comprehension Comparisons?

Oral Expression vs. Written Expression	Reading Comprehension vs. Listening Comprehension
These two expression subtests both require students to use expressive language in realistic situations. Both subtests are scored along similar dimensions: task (pragmatics), sentence structure (syntax), and word form (grammar). Thus, the comparison between these tasks may point to a particular difficulty in either written or spoken expression.	These two comprehension tasks both assess the literal and inferential comprehension of connected text (particularly the passage-reading tasks of Reading Comprehension and Listening Comprehension). Thus, the comparison between these subtests may help identify a problem specific to reading (that is distinct from a more general language problem).

Don't Forget box reminds readers what can be learned from these expression and comprehension comparisons.

On the KTEA-II Brief Form, there are three subtest comparisons to make: (a) Reading versus Math, (b) Reading versus Writing, and (c) Math versus Writing. These three comparisons should be routinely made to discover if there are any relative academic strengths or weaknesses.

The methods for evaluating planned comparisons between composites or subtests is very similar to those employed in Steps 3 and 4. Once you have determined which comparisons you would like to make, follow the substeps of Step 5 outlined in Rapid Reference 3.8. You will calculate the difference between the scores, and then determine the significance and frequency of that difference. The back page of the KTEA-II Comprehensive record form and the front page of the KTEA-II Brief Form have places to record the data for these planned comparisons.

≡ *Rapid Reference 3.8*

....

Substeps of Interpretive Step 5

A. Record the standard scores for the two composites or subtests of each comparison in the appropriate boxes of the back page of the KTEA-II Comprehensive record form or the front page of the KTEA-II Brief record form.

B. Record the absolute value of the difference between them in the space between the boxes.

C. Determine whether the difference is statistically significant by referring to the appropriate table (I.5 through I.8 in Appendix I of the *KTEA-II Comprehensive Form Manual* or Tables C.14 and C.15 of the *KTEA-II Brief Form Manual*). Find the column for the smallest significance level in which the observed difference computed in Step B above is equal to or greater than the value in the table, and circle the appropriate number (.05 or .01) on the record form. Then draw a circle around the name of the composite or subtest having the higher score.

D. If the difference is statistically significant, refer again to the appropriate table in the manual (Table I.5, I.6, I.7, or I.8 in Appendix I of the *KTEA-II Comprehensive Form Manual* or Tables C.16 and C.17 of the *KTEA-II Brief Form Manual*) to see whether the difference is also unusually large, meaning that it occurred infrequently in the norm sample. Find the column for the smallest percentage frequency in which the observed difference (computed in Step B) is equal to or grater than the value in the table, and circle the appropriate number (15%, 10%, or 5%) on the record form.

Clinical Analysis of Errors

The KTEA-II authors believe that understanding test performance by studying the student's incorrect responses is a profitable method of helping a student's progress, and that efforts to objectify and substantiate the value of various error analysis methods should be intensified (Kaufman & Kaufman, 2004a). Many good teachers intuitively apply error analysis skills in their everyday teaching. In today's schools, however, where psychologists, educational diagnosticians, special educators, and classroom teachers exchange information about students, a more formal systematic approach to error analysis, using a common language, is necessary for effective communication of information about students' academic functioning and teachers' instructional strategies (Kaufman & Kaufman, 2004).

During development of the original K-TEA Comprehensive Form and its revision, the KTEA-II, the authors were aided by curriculum experts in reading, mathematics, spelling, writing, and oral language in defining the specific skills making up each subtest and examining the types of errors students are likely to make on subtest items. Based on the recommendations of these experts, a review of the literature on instructional theory and practice, discussions with many practicing school psychologists and educational diagnosticians, and the actual errors made by students participating in the standardization programs, the KTEA-II error analysis method was developed (Kaufman & Kaufman, 2004a). It is built on the method used with the original K-TEA, but for some subtests it has been enhanced to provide a greater amount of detail. This procedure uses information documented on the record form during KTEA-II administration to identify specific areas in which the student demonstrates strong, weak, or average skill development as defined by the performance of the standardization sample.

The error analysis procedures provide examiners with more specific information about a student's performance than can be obtained from composite or subtest standard scores or comparisons. Some uses for the error analysis data are described by Kaufman and Kaufman (2004a) as:

- obtaining a more precise level of diagnostic information than subtest standard scores
- determining the concentration of skill problems
- determining the location of weak skills on a skill continuum
- gauging the severity of skill deficiencies
- identifying common sources of difficulty underlying several skill areas
- integrating results from multiple subtests to help substantiate hypotheses about the sources of skill difficulties
- error analyses are a valuable part of the interpretive process

Thus, the *KTEA-II Comprehensive Form* offers detailed information beyond the examinee's subtest and composite scores that can provide important and specific information that becomes a basis for intervention. The details about a child's skills come from a system for analyzing specific errors made on 10 of the KTEA-II's 14 subtests. The system of error analysis determines both strong and weak skill areas across global skills (such as reading and math) and more specific skills (such as Math Computation and Math Concepts and Applications).

The *KTEA-II Comprehensive Form* error analysis uses norm-referenced methodology to determine a child's relative mastery of specific skills that can then lead to effective remediation of skill deficiencies. Each student's performance on certain skills is labeled: "strong," "average," or "weak," compared to other students in the same grade level. The Don't Forget box explains how each of these levels of skill status are defined and what the implications are for each.

DON'T FORGET

Skill Status Defined According to Number of Errors

Skill Status Category	Definition	Implications for Obtaining Each Level of Skill Status
Strong	Average number of errors made by the top 25 percent of the national grade-level reference group.	A student's skill acquisition is considerably above that of typical students at that grade level. These areas require less instructional attention and may be used to teach to the student's strengths.
Average	Average number of errors made by the middle 50 percent of the national grade-level reference group (i.e., those between the 25th and 75th percentiles).	The student has demonstrated acquisition of that skill to a degree typical for pupils at that grade level. These areas require less instructional attention and may be used to teach to the student's strengths.
Weak	Average number of errors made by the bottom 25 percent of the national grade-level reference group.	The student has a possible deficiency in that skill area, and further diagnostic evaluation is warranted. Appropriate remediation strategies may be needed to help the student with the deficiency.

There are two basic types of error classification methods: item-level error classification and within-item classification. In the item-level error classification, each item is classified according to the process, concept, or skill that it assesses. If an item is incorrect, the error type is automatically assigned. For example, each of the Reading Comprehension and Listening Comprehension items are classified as either literal or inferential. Thus, if a student's response to Reading Comprehension item 13 is incorrect, it is automatically classified as a "literal error," where as an incorrect response to item 15 is automatically counted as an "inferential" error. Other item-level classifications are conducted on Written Expression items (items are classified in the following categories: task, structure, word form, capitalization, and punctuation). Oral Expression items are classified along similar categories: task, sentence structure, word meaning, and word form. In contrast to item-level classification's automatic error assignment, within-item classification requires judgment on the part of the examiner to determine the error type. That is, the specific details of the student's response will lead examiners to select which of many types of errors that the examinee made. For example, on Letter and Word Decoding, examiners must examine the incorrect pronunciation of a word to determine if an error was made in categories such as: short vowel, long vowel, silent letter, prefix, suffix, and more. Multiple error categories may be marked in the within-item classification. The Don't Forget lists the types of error analysis that are used for the KTEA-II subtests.

DON'T FORGET
....

Types of Error Analysis Methods for KTEA-II Subtests

Subtests Using Item-Level Error Classification	Subtests Using Within-Item[a] Error Classification
Reading Comprehension Listening Comprehension Written Expression Oral Expression Phonological Awareness Math Concepts and Applications Math Computation	Math Computation Letter & Word Recognition Nonsense Word Decoding Spelling

Note: Subtests with errors categorized according to item-level error classifications are automatically assigned an error category when an item is incorrect. Subtests with errors categorized according to within-item error classification are assigned an error category or categories according to the examiner's qualitative analysis of the student's incorrect response.

[a] Because within-item error analysis has a large number of error categories, the grids for classifying and counting errors on these four subtests are too large to be included in the record form. Thus, a separate error analysis booklet contains the worksheets for tabulation errors on these subtests.

General Procedures for Using the Error Analysis System

The error analysis system differs according to whether the subtest is being analyzed by item-level classification or by within-item classification. However, there are some general procedures that should be followed in any of the error analysis methods. Rapid Reference 3.9 lists the general procedures for conducting error analysis. The Caution box reminds examiners about when the appropriate time is to conduct the error analysis. In the next several

---

≡ *Rapid Reference 3.9*

General Procedures for Using the Error Analysis System

1. After test administration, place one or more check marks in the appropriate error category column for each item answered incorrectly.

   a. For **item-level error analysis**, make a mark in every column with an open (unshaded) box if an item was incorrectly answered.

   b. For **within-level error analysis**, make a mark in the open (unshaded) boxes in columns that apply to the student's incorrect responses.

2. After error categories have been checked for all failed items, sum the number of checks in each column and record the total number for each category.

3. Transfer the error totals for the 10 subtests to pages 28 and 29 of the *KTEA-II Comprehensive Record Form* under the column labeled "Student's # of Errors."

4. Refer to the error analysis norm tables in Appendix K of the *KTEA-II Comprehensive Form Manual* and record the following on the record form:

   a. The number of items that the examinee attempted. Calculate this number by counting the number of white boxes in the column between item 1 and the discontinue point, even if the examinee was not administered all of the earliest items.

   b. The "Average Number of Errors" for each error category made by students in the norm sample, who are in the same grade and who attempted the same items.[a]

   c. If the examinee made more than the "Average Number of Errors" then mark that error category as a weakness (circle *W*) on the record form.

   d. If the examinee made fewer than the "Average Number of Errors" then mark that error category as a strength (circle *S*) on the record form.

   e. If the number of errors made by the examinee was equal to or within the range of the "Average Number of Errors" then mark that error category as average (circle *A*) on the record form.

Note: The four subtests analyzed by within-level error categorizations are Letter & Word Recognition, Nonsense Word Decoding, Math Computation, and Spelling.

[a]In the norms tables, the "average" is defined as the number of errors made by the middle 50 percent of students.

Rapid References (3.10 through 3.15), specific information about the conducting error analysis for each of the subtests is outlined. These Rapid References are grouped according to subtests with similar error analysis procedures.

Error Analysis in Reading Comprehension and Listening Comprehension
Reading comprehension can be defined as the process of deriving meaning from text by reflecting on what is read. On the KTEA-II, items from reading comprehension and listening comprehension are divided into literal and inferential comprehension. Literal comprehension requires recognizing or recalling ideas, information, or events that are explicitly stated in an oral or written text. In contrast, inferential comprehension requires the generation of new ideas from those stated in the text. Students derive inferences from relating different concepts presented in the text or combining information with previously acquired knowledge. Sometimes inferences require students to evaluate the writer's or speaker's viewpoint. Literal questions do not require the student to go beyond the viewpoints of the writer or speaker and are usually

≡ *Rapid Reference 3.10*

Using the Error Analysis System for Reading Comprehension and Listening Comprehension

	Reading Comprehension	Listening Comprehension
Where Error Analysis Is Recorded	Record form on pp. 12–13 and summarized on p. 28	Record form on pp. 20–21 and summarized on p. 28
Types of Errors Recorded	Either literal or inferential	
Items for Which Errors Are Recorded	Error analysis is based on the set, or pair of adjacent sets, used for scoring the case.	

paraphrased portions of the text. The questions asked on the KTEA-II Reading Comprehension subtest (except for the simple "command" items) and the Listening Comprehension subtest either demand literal comprehension or inferential comprehension, and errors on the items are categorized accordingly.

Error Analysis in Written Expression and Oral Expression

Students are required to communicate their ideas in words for KTEA-II's both Written Expression and Oral Expression. The skills needed to communicate orally are similar to those needed to communicate in written form. However, oral communication is typically more spontaneous and natural and writing is more deliberate and structured. Difficulty in both oral and written communication can be caused by a variety of errors, which the error analysis procedures attempt to quantify.

To quantify students' communication ability, the error analysis examines several aspects of communication:

≡ Rapid Reference 3.11

Using the Error Analysis System for Written Expression and Oral Expression

	Written Expression	Oral Expression
Where Error Analysis Is Recorded	Record form on pp. 14–18 and summarized on p. 29	Record form on pp. 22–25 and summarized on p. 29
Types of Errors Recorded	Task Structure Word Form Capitalization (written only) Punctuation (written only) Word Meaning (oral only)	
Items for Which Errors Are Recorded	Error analysis is based on a level (or booklet) administered.	Error analysis is based on the set, or pair of adjacent sets, used for scoring the case.

- how well the writing or speech adheres to the task demands to communicate in a comprehensible and functional manner (pragmatics)
- how well-constructed the student's sentences are (syntax)
- appropriateness of the word forms (grammar)
- correct use of words (semantics)
- mechanics (capitalization and punctuation for written expression)

When contrasting the errors made in Written Expression with those from Oral Expression, examiners can differentiate language structure problems from writing problems. Some children have deficits in their basic knowledge of language (which will likely be evident in errors on both tests), but some children with intact oral language skills may have strong language structure, yet have deficits in their written expression.

Errors Analysis in Phonological Awareness

The particular aspects of sound awareness and manipulation that a student has and has not mastered will be evident in the errors that are made on the Phonological Awareness subtest. The development of skills tapped in this subtest—rhyming, sound matching, blending, segmenting, and deleting sounds—are important precursors to reading. Teachers can use information about deficits in certain areas of phonological awareness when trying to teach early reading skills.

Phonological awareness involves skills that allow students to manipulate phonemes heard in spoken language. Children with poor phonological awareness

≡ Rapid Reference 3.12

Using the Error Analysis System for Phonological Awareness

	Phonological Awareness
Where Error Analysis Is Recorded	Record form on p. 5 and summarized on p. 29
Types of Errors Recorded	Rhyming, sound matching, blending, segmenting, and deleting sounds
Items for Which Errors Are Recorded	Error analysis is based on the set, or pair of adjacent sets, used for scoring the case.

may be unable to identify sounds in words, manipulate sounds in words, perceive a word as a sequence of sounds, or isolate beginning, medial, or final sounds. These subskills are assessed by the error analysis, which is divided into either three or five skills, depending on the child's grade. Error analysis of the kindergarten form of Phonological Awareness (the long form) contains five task categories: rhyming, sound matching, blending, segmenting, and deleting sounds. For grades 1 through 6, errors are analyzed for a short form containing rhyming, segmenting, and deleting sounds.

Error Analysis in Math Concepts and Applications

This subtest contains two related sets of abilities: concepts and applications. Concepts are the basic ideas and relationships on which the system of mathematics are built. Acquisition of math concepts is hierarchical, which requires students to master basic concepts before more advanced concepts can be learned. Applications involve using these concepts and skills to solve actual and hypothetical problems (e.g., reading graphs, balancing a checkbook). If a child has not yet mastered a certain concept or skill, he or she will not be able to apply that concept to solve an actual or hypothetical problem.

≡ Rapid Reference 3.13

Using the Error Analysis System for Math Concepts and Applications

	Math Concepts and Applications
Where Error Analysis Is Recorded	Record form on pp. 8–9 and summarized on p. 29
Types of Errors Recorded	Number concepts, addition, subtraction, multiplication, division, tables and graphs, time and money, geometry, measurement, fractions, decimals and percents, data investigation, advanced operations, multistep problems, word problems
Items for Which Errors Are Recorded	Error analysis is based on all administered items until the ceiling is reached.

Each Math Concepts and Applications item is associated with one primary skill. Thus, if a child responds incorrectly to an item, then in the error analysis that item is marked as an error in 1 of 15 categories. However, the final skill category (Word Problems) will be marked as an additional error along with one other error category. That is, on the six items that are word problems, children who respond incorrectly will have an error in "Word Problems" as well as one of the other 14 skill categories (such as addition, multiplication, division, etc.).

Error Analysis in Math Computation

The error analysis system for Math Computation gives information about nine skill areas (such as addition, multiplication, fractions) and about 10 specific processes (such as regrouping, converting to common denominators, or placing decimal points) in which the student has made errors. Useful information is gleaned from understanding students' skill deficits, but even more instructionally relevant information may be revealed from the process errors that students make. Understanding the reason that a child missed an item (e.g., because they added when they should have subtracted, because they made an error when regrouping) can help determine how and where to provide additional remedial instruction for a child.

≡ Rapid Reference 3.14

Using the Error Analysis System for Math Computation

	Math Computation
Where Error Analysis Is Recorded	Error analysis booklet on pp. 6–7 and summarized in record form on p. 29
Types of Errors Recorded	*Item-level errors*: addition, subtraction, multiplication, division, fraction, decimal, exponent or root, algebra *Within-item errors*: wrong operation, factor computation, regrouping addition, regrouping subtraction, subtract smaller from larger, add or subtract numerator and denominator, equivalent fraction/common denominator, multiply/divide fraction, mixed number, incorrect sign
Items for Which Errors Are Recorded	Error analysis is based on all administered items until the ceiling is reached.

DON'T FORGET
....

Dividing Words into Parts Based on Orthographically Predictable Patterns for Error Analysis

Number of Syllables	How Words Are Divided	Example
One-Syllable Words	Divided into vowel and consonant parts.	*what* is divided into: *wh* (consonant digraph) *a* (short vowel) *t* (single consonant)
Multisyllabic Words	Divided into words with roots and affixes, with the affixes as whole words and the roots further divided into vowel and consonant parts.	*roasted* is divided into: *r* (single consonant) *oa* (vowel team) *st* (medial/final consonant blend) *ed* (suffixes and inflections)

The first two error categories of the specific processes (listed under Within-Item Errors) are *Wrong Operation and Fact* or *Computation Error*. These two error categories can be applied to all items. However, if an error is better described by another type of error category, then the *Wrong Operation* category should not be marked. For example, if the child solves a problem involving division by a fraction by dividing the numerators and denominators instead of inverting and multiplying, then you should make the *Multiply/Divide Fraction* category instead of the *Wrong Operation* category. Pages 44 and 45 of the *KTEA-II Comprehensive Form Manual* define and give examples of the within-item errors.

Error Analysis in Letter and Word Recognition, Nonsense Word Decoding, and Spelling

The decoding of words requires that students connect speech sounds to letter patterns. Three subtests tap this skill in slightly different ways. Nonsense Word Decoding assesses a student's ability to apply decoding and structural analysis skills to typically occurring letter patterns. Spelling requires students to relate speech sounds that they hear to letter patterns that they write. Letter and Word Recognition taps a student's ability to read words with unpredictable letter patterns.

The error analysis system for Letter and Word Recognition, Nonsense Word Decoding, and Spelling is made up of "categories corresponding to letters and

≡ Rapid Reference 3.15

Using the Error Analysis System for Letter and Word Recognition, Nonsense Word Decoding, and Spelling

	Letter & Word Recognition	Nonsense Word Decoding	Spelling
Where Error Analysis Is Recorded	Error analysis booklet on pp. 2–3 and summarized in record form on p. 28	Error analysis booklet on pp. 4–5 and summarized in record form on p. 28	Error analysis booklet on p. 8 and summarized in record form on p. 28
Types of Errors Recorded[a]	Single/double consonant; initial blend; consonant blend; medial/final blend; consonant digraph; wrong vowel; short vowel; long vowel; vowel team/diphthong; r-controlled vowel; silent letter; prefix/word beginning; suffix/inflection/hard or soft C, G, S; unpredictable pattern; initial/final sound; insertion/omission; nonphonetic; misordered sounds		
Items for Which Errors Are Recorded	Error analysis is based on all administered items until the ceiling is reached.		

[a]Errors for these subtests are defined and exemplified on page 48 of the *KTEA-II Comprehensive Form Manual*. From "Kaufman Test of Educational Achievement Comprehensive Form Manual (2nd ed.)," by A. S. Kaufman and N. L. Kaufman, (2004), Circle Pines, MN: AGS. Some error categories are not scored for each of these subtests. Specifically, nonphonetic errors are only scored for the Spelling subtest, and errors due to an unpredictable pattern are scored for Letter & Word Recognition and Spelling only. Errors due to a wrong vowel and initial or final sounds are only scored in Letter & Word Recognition and Nonsense Word Decoding.

letter combinations that have a predictable relationship to their sound. Errors involving unpredictable letter-sound relationships are qualitatively different from the other error categories, because by definition those errors are not generalizable to other words" (Kaufman & Kaufman, 2004, p. 46). A separate error category is provided for words with unpredictable patterns, which gives a cleaner indication of the student's problem areas in the decoding or spelling of predictable patterns.

The error analysis system is set up in such a way that words are divided into parts based on orthographically predictable patterns. The Don't Forget box

CAUTION

....

Differences between Skill Categories for Letter & Word Recognition, Nonsense Word Decoding, and Spelling

- All three subtests include a category for *Consonant Blends*, but in Nonsense Word Decoding and Spelling this category is divided into *Initial and Medial/ Final* consonant blends because these subtests include a large number of instances of each subtype.

- Because the pseudowords in Nonsense Word Decoding were created to be decodable based on predictable patterns, error analysis for this subtest does not include the *Unpredictable Pattern* category.

- Spelling error analysis does not contain the *Wrong Vowel* category. Writing a wrong vowel is categorized as a short or a long vowel error.

- All three subtests include *Prefixes and Word Beginnings* and *Suffixes and Inflections* categories. They are merged into one category in Nonsense Word Decoding because that subtest has few prefixes.

- In Spelling, if a student inserts a grapheme (smaller than a syllable) that is not in the sound of the word, count this is a *silent letter* error.

Note: This information is adapted from the *KTEA-II Comprehensive Form Manual* (Kaufman & Kaufman, 2004a, p. 47).

explains how words are divided within this system. Other error categories include those such as: incorrect initial or final sound or letter, wrong vowel, omitted or incorrectly inserted syllables, or, in Spelling, a non-phonetic misspelling. In the *KTEA-II Comprehensive Form Manual*, definitions and examples of the error categories for these three subtests are outlined in Table 4.2 (Kaufman & Kaufman, 2004a, p. 48). Although the categories are very similar for Letter and Word Recognition, Nonsense Word Decoding, and Spelling, some differences do exist, which are articulated in the Caution box.

The last category in Letter and Word Recognition, Nonsense Word Decoding, and Spelling is *Whole Word Error*. Generally, if an examinee's response is significantly different from the stimulus word, then it is usually better to mark the item as a *Whole Word Error* rather than trying to identify numerous specific errors. There are several times when it is best to mark a student's response in the *Whole Word Error* category (Kaufman & Kaufman, 2004a, p. 50):

1. If the response contains more than four incorrect parts, don't try to identify them, but write UN (unclassifiable) in the *Whole Word Error* box.

2. If the response is a different word or a read word that approximates the stimulus word or nonsense word, use the word-parts error analysis grid for those errors that can be easily identified, and write *WS* (word substitution) in the *Whole Word Error* box. If the response contains more than four identifiable errors, follow guideline 1 above.

3. In Letter and Word Recognition, if the mispronunciation contains a misplaced accent, write MPA (misplaced accent) in the *Whole Word Error* box.

4. If the student doesn't know or doesn't respond, write *NR* (no response) in the *Whole Word Error* box. If a student stops before finishing a set of items on the easel page, fill in the remaining items for that set with *NR*.

As we stressed in the administration and scoring sections, recording a student's exact responses is crucial for these subtests. In addition to being familiar with how to record students' responses phonetically, you should be familiar with the error categories before testing, as this will aid you during the error analysis.

USING THE KTEA-II COMPREHENSIVE FORM WITH THE KABC-II

Earlier in this chapter we described the relationship between the KTEA-II Comprehensive Form and the KABC-II that was revealed by the psychometric data. These data (see Table 3.5 in the section on validity) showed moderate relationships between the two measures (KTEA-II CAC correlations of .74 to .80 with the KABC-II's global scores—the FCI and MPI), which are indicative of the concurrent validity of the tests. In practical terms, these data mean that you can interpret the two test batteries together and be confident that they relate to each other very well. In addition to examining correlational data, another quantitative method of understanding the relationship between the KABC-II and the KTEA-II can be gained by examining significant differences between standard scores on both batteries. One of the benefits of conorming an achievement battery with a measure of cognitive abilities is that it provides a basis for more accurate comparisons between achievement and ability.

In the past, many states and school districts required that a discrepancy between achievement and ability be documented in order to qualify for the diagnosis of a specific learning disability under the Education for All Handicapped Children Act of 1975 (Public Law 94–142) and the Individuals with Disabilities Education Act (IDEA) Amendments of 1997. However, changes in how learning disabilities are identified occurred on December 3, 2004, when President Bush signed into law new IDEA reforms under the Individuals with Disabilities Education Improvement Act (making it officially known as Public Law No. 108–446). The signing marked the end of a 3-year IDEA reauthorization process and represented the first update to the nation's special education law in 7 years. The ramifications for PL 108–446 on learning disability identification, including the elimination of the IQ–achievement discrepancy requirement, are discussed in the Clinical Applications chapter of this book. Although the new law does not require the IQ–achievement discrepancy, it does not prohibit its use as a mechanism to identify children for services. States, in collaboration with local education agencies, will determine the criteria for determining a specific learning disability. Bearing these changes in mind, in the following section, we present the procedures for determining whether significant discrepancies exist between global cognitive ability and achievement for examiners who desire to use them.[2] In the Clinical Applications chapter of this book, we present alternative ways to examine the KTEA-II together with the KABC-II and other tests.

Calculating Significant Differences between KTEA-II and KABC-II Scores

The two primary methods of comparing ability with achievement are the simple-difference method and the regression (or predicted-score) method. In the former, a standard score from an ability test is compared with achievement standard scores, and the differences may be evaluated for statistical significance or unusualness. In the regression method, the correlation in the population between the ability and achievement scores is used to calculate the expected (average) achievement standard score for students having a given ability score, and the individual student's actual achievement score is compared with this predicted value (Rapid Reference 3.16 outlines the steps for using the regression method). Both the simple-difference method and the regression method require that the achievement test be scored using age

---

2. Typically achievement–ability discrepancy analyses are not conducted when administering a screening measure like the KTEA-II Brief Form. Such analyses are more appropriate when conducting a comprehensive assessment with the KTEA-II Comprehensive Form. However, examiners may administer a brief test of cognitive ability along with the KTEA-II, such as the conormed *Kaufman Brief Intelligence Test–Second Edition* (KBIT2; Kaufman & Kaufman, 2004c) in order to have an understanding of a person's general level of cognitive functioning.

norms because ability tests typically do not provide grade norms. Interpretive tables for both methods are provided in the *KTEA-II Comprehensive Form Manual* (Appendix I, Kaufman & Kaufman, 2004a), although we prefer the regression approach to the simple-difference method because it has a stronger psychometric rationale.

≣ *Rapid Reference 3.16*

Steps for Using the Regression Model in Ability-Achievement Discrepancy Analysis

1. Record the student's KABC-II standard score (either FCI, MPI, or NVI) and the KTEA-II standard score in the designated boxes on the back page of the KTEA-II Comprehensive record form.

2. Refer to Table I.9 in Appendix I of the *KTEA-II Comprehensive Form Manual* to find the correlation between the KABC-II ability scale and the achievement composite or subtest.

3. Using that correlation value, refer to Table I.10 in Appendix I of the *KTEA-II Comprehensive Form Manual* to obtain the predicted achievement score corresponding to the ability standard score, and write the predicted achievement score in the designated box on the KTEA-II Comprehensive record form.

4. If the actual achievement score is lower than the predicted score, compute the difference between the predicted and actual achievement scores, and write it on the designated line of the KTEA-II Comprehensive record form.

5. Refer to Table I.11 Appendix I of the *KTEA-II Comprehensive Form Manual* to find the values of the difference required for statistical significance. Find the column for the smallest significance level in which the observed difference (computed in Step 4 above) is equal to or greater than the values in the table, and circle the appropriate number (.05 or .01) on the KTEA-II Comprehensive record form.

6. If the difference between the predicted and actual achievement scores is statistically significant, refer again to Table I.11 to determine whether the difference is unusual. Find the column for the smallest percentage frequency in which the observed difference (computed in Step 4 above) is equal to or greater than the value in the table, and circle the appropriate number (10 percent, 5 percent, 2 percent, or 1 percent) on the record form. The frequencies in Table I.11 are one-tailed, meaning that they represent the percentage of the population having an actual achievement score that is lower than the predicted achievement score by the specified amount or more.

Note: Steps are adapted from p. 32 of the *KTEA-II Comprehensive Form Manual* (Kaufman & Kaufman, 2004a)

TEST YOURSELF

1. **In addition to Reading, Mathematics, Written Language, and Oral Language composite standard scores, the KTEA-II offers four Reading-Related composites.**
   True or False?

2. **Which two domain composites does the KTEA-II yield for children who have not yet begun kindergarten?**
   (a) Reading and Mathematics
   (b) Mathematics and Written Language
   (c) Oral Language and Reading
   (d) Written Language and Oral Language

3. **Knowledge of proper pronunciation of all the stimuli words is key to administering which KTEA-II subtests?**

4. **Students are not penalized for misspelled words on the Written Expression subtest.**
   True or False?

5. **All KTEA-II subtests offer an error analysis.**
   True or False?

6. **What value is used to represent a student's overall "average level of performance" on the KTEA-II during the interpretive process?**
   (a) the mean of all domain composites
   (b) the Comprehensive Achievement Composite (CAC)
   (c) the mean of only Reading and Math Composites
   (d) the mean of Reading, Math, and Writing Composites

7. **The suggested KTEA-II interpretive steps base academic strengths on normative comparisons as well as ipsative (person-based) comparisons.**
   True or False?

8. **Of the two primary methods of comparing ability with achievement, the simple-difference method and the regression method, which has a stronger psychometric rationale (and is therefore the preferred approach)?**
   (a) Regression method
   (b) Simple-difference method

9. **Pairs of KTEA-II Comprehensive subtests (i.e., Reading Comprehension and Listening Comprehension, and Written Expression and Oral Expression) were developed specifically to have similar formats to enable useful comparisons that can help the examiner distinguish specific problems in reading or writing from more general language problems.**
   True or False?

10. Which one of the four academic domains measured in the KTEA-II Comprehensive Form is *not* measured by the KTEA-II Brief Form?

(a) Reading

(b) Mathematics

(c) Written Language

(d) Oral Language

Answers: 1. True; 2. b; 3. Letter & Word Recognition, Nonsense Word Decoding, Word Recognition Fluency, and Decoding Fluency; 4. True; 5. False; 6. b; 7. True; 8. a; 9. True; 10. d

Four

CLINICAL APPLICATIONS

I n this chapter we focus on some key clinical applications of the WIAT-III and KTEA-II. In the first half of this chapter, we discuss topics related to utilizing the relationship between measures of achievement and intelligence. The WIAT-III and KTEA-II were designed to work in tandem with specific cognitive instruments to identify skill deficits as well as potential process deficits; for this reason, the WIAT-III and KTEA-II included linking and conorming studies, respectively, with tests of cognitive ability. When the KTEA-II is used together with the KABC-II or the WIAT-III is used together with other cognitive ability instruments (e.g., WISC-IV, DAS-II) and specialized instruments such as the Process Assessment of the Learner–Second Edition (Berninger, 2007) examiners can develop a more comprehensive understanding of the reasons for under-achievement. (At the same time, WIAT-III and KTEA-II are widely used in the assessment of children for placement in accelerated or gifted programs, and use of these instruments with individuals with varying levels of achievement is discussed later in this chapter.)

The linking of these achievement measures with other assessment measures provides for efficient collection of in-depth data that can help the examiner to test hypotheses, to formulate a diagnosis, to make decisions related to eligibility, but most importantly, to bridge the gap between assessment and intervention. Although an ability-achievement discrepancy is no longer required to identify learning disabilities, understanding the consistencies and inconsistencies between cognitive abilities and academic achievement serves an important role in under-standing all of the issues that place a student at risk for academic failure. Here we provide information on the conceptual and theoretical relationships between achievement and ability as measured by the WIAT-III and WISC-IV, and the KTEA-II and KABC-II.

In the second half of this chapter, we review some of the data on the clinical application of the WIAT-III and KTEA-II in special populations, including reading, math, and writing disabilities, as well as attention-deficit/hyperactivity disorder. Based on these special population studies, we attempt to draw inferences about the relationships between WIAT-III–WISC-IV and KTEA-II–KABC-II to provide useful information for clinicians who assess such children and strive to develop the best possible interventions for them. In addition, we describe how the results from either the WIAT-III and WISC-IV or the KTEA-II and KABC-II may be used within contemporary models for identifying specific learning disabilities.

WIAT-III AND THE WECHSLER INTELLIGENCE SCALES

David Wechsler based his original Wechsler-Bellevue on the premise that intelligence is a *global* entity because it characterizes the individual's behavior as a whole, and it is also *specific* because it is composed of elements or abilities that are distinct from each other. Wechsler developed subtests that highlighted the cognitive aspects of intelligence: verbal comprehension, abstract reasoning, perceptual organization, quantitative reasoning, memory, and processing speed, and all of these areas have been confirmed as important in more contemporary theories and measures of intelligence (Carroll, 1993, 1997; Horn, 1991). A significant change in the Wechsler Scales occurred with the publication of the WISC-IV in that instead of reporting scores within two domains, Verbal and Performance, emphasis was placed on the measure of more discrete domains of cognitive functioning (e.g., verbal comprehension, perceptual reasoning, processing speed, working memory), while continuing to provide a measure of global intelligence (FSIQ). The new four-factor structure of the cognitive measure is appropriate for several reasons. First of all, cognitive functions are interrelated, functionally and neurologically, making it difficult to measure a pure domain. Various aspects of cognition are required to perform the tasks used to measure a domain. For example, a measure of processing speed such as the WISC-IV's Coding subtest requires visual scanning and discrimination of the information, short-term memory, paired-associative learning, and a grapho-motor response. Second, including subtests that require the use of multiple cognitive abilities is ecologically valid in that cognitive tasks are rarely performed in isolation. As Wechsler (1975) observed:

> . . . the attributes and factors of intelligence, like the elementary particles in physics, have at once collective and individual properties, that is, they appear to behave differently when alone from what they do when operating in concert (p. 138).

The measurement of general intelligence (g) is supported by its strong ecological validity in predicting such things as academic achievement, job performance, and overall psychological well-being. Measures of more discrete domains do not show the same degree of predictive ability (Gottfredson, 1998). Measuring psychometrically pure factors of discrete domains may be useful to research, but it does not necessarily result in information that is useful for real-world application (Zachary, 1990). Because it is unreasonable to expect any single measure of intelligence to adequately test all domains of cognitive functioning in a meaningful and practical way (Carroll, 1997), Wechsler selected measures that sampled a wide variety of domains (e.g., verbal comprehension, perceptual organization, memory) that have since proven to be important aspects of cognitive functioning. He also acknowledged the possibility of obtaining invalid results when examiners or examinees become fatigued. As a result, he selected a sufficient number of subtests to provide clinically meaningful information about an individual's cognitive functioning in a reasonable time period. Wechsler believed that other related factors such as achievement, executive functioning, and motor skills that could impact performance on an intelligence test should be assessed by tests specifically designed to measure those abilities. Finally, Wechsler recognized that performance on measures of cognitive ability reflects only a portion of what comprises intelligence. He defined intelligence as the "capacity of the individual to act purposefully, to think rationally, and to deal effectively with his environment" (p. 3). He avoided defining intelligence in purely cognitive terms because he believed that these factors only comprised a portion of intelligence. He proposed that attributes such as planning and goal awareness, enthusiasm, field dependence and independence, impulsiveness, anxiety, and persistence, which are not directly tapped by standard measures of intelligence, influence a person's performance on these measures as well as his or her functioning in the real world (Wechsler, 1975). Assessing an individual's intelligence involves more than simply obtaining a score on an intelligence test. As Wechsler (1975) noted:

> What we measure with tests is not what tests measure—not information, not spatial perception, not reasoning ability. These are only a means to an end. What intelligence tests measure is something much more important; the capacity of the individual to understand the world about him and his resourcefulness to cope with its challenges. (p. 139)

The WIAT-III was designed to be used with the three age-specific Wechsler Scales and the *Wechsler Nonverbal Scale of Ability* (WNV) (Wechsler & Naglieri, 2006), in addition to the *Differential Ability Scales–Second Edition* (DAS–II) (Elliott, 2007), as the foundation of a psychoeducational assessment. Consequently, subsets of the

WIAT-III standardization sample were administered the appropriate cognitive measures according to age. The data related to the linking samples of the WIAT-III and the WPPSI-III, WISC-IV, WAIS-IV, WNV, and DAS-II published with the WIAT-III in 2009. As a result, WIAT-III can be used with any of the Wechsler Scales to identify ability-achievement discrepancies and to explore the relationship between higher-order cognitive ability domains and acquired achievement skills. Special attention will be placed on using WIAT-III with WISC-IV in this section as this is the predominant pairing of the tests for school-age children.

Description of the WISC-IV

Because WISC-IV and WIAT-III were designed to be used together, it is important to understand the structure of the WISC-IV and the WISC-IV Integrated (Wechsler, 2004), and to identify the cognitive abilities measured by each index. Correlational studies between the WISC-IV and the WIAT-III and the WISC-IV Integrated and the WIAT-II are discussed. Clinical studies, which are addressed later in this chapter, reveal unique patterns of performance between the WIAT-II and the WISC-IV and the WISC-IV Integrated.

Rapid Reference 4.1 presents the four-factor structure of the WISC-IV. The subtests were designed to measure a broad range of cognitive abilities. The new framework of the WISC-IV is based on theory and supported by clinical research

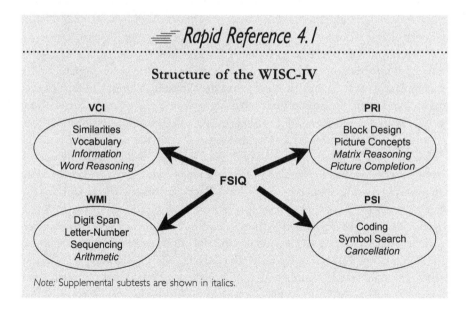

≡ Rapid Reference 4.1

Structure of the WISC-IV

VCI
Similarities
Vocabulary
Information
Word Reasoning

PRI
Block Design
Picture Concepts
Matrix Reasoning
Picture Completion

FSIQ

WMI
Digit Span
Letter-Number
Sequencing
Arithmetic

PSI
Coding
Symbol Search
Cancellation

Note: Supplemental subtests are shown in italics.

and factor-analytic results (see a discussion in Chapter 23 of the *WISC-IV Technical and Interpretive Manual*). The framework is similar to that of the WAIS-III, which was published in 1997. Subtests are either *core* (required for calculation of the index scores and FSIQ) or *supplemental* (intended to substitute for a core under certain conditions, or to extend the range of cognitive skills measured by the core), and an individual's performance can be evaluated using the index scores (Verbal Comprehension Index (VCI), Perceptual Reasoning Index (PRI), Working Memory Index (WMI), Processing Speed Index (PSI), the composite Full Scale IQ (FSIQ), and an alternate General Ability Score (GAI), which is a composite of VCI and PRI). Each subtest yields a scaled score ($M = 10$; $SD = 3$) and each index produces a derived standard score ($M = 100$; $SD = 15$). In addition to the WISC-IV subtest and composite scores, seven *process* scores (i.e., Block Design No Time Bonus, Digit Span Forward, Digit Span Backward, Longest Digit Span Forward, Longest Digit Span Backward, Cancellation Random, and Cancellation Structured) can be obtained for the purpose of providing more in-depth information about an examinee's performance.

The WISC-IV introduced new subtests to improve the measurement of fluid reasoning, working memory, and processing speed. The importance of fluid reasoning is emphasized in many theories of cognitive functioning (Carroll, 1997; Cattell, 1943, 1963; Cattell & Horn, 1978; Sternberg, 1995). Tasks that require *fluid reasoning* involve the process of "manipulating abstractions, rules, generalizations, and logical relationships" (Carroll, 1993, p. 583). The measurement of fluid reasoning is incorporated in the new subtests: Matrix Reasoning, Picture Concepts, and Word Reasoning. The first two appear on the PRI index, whereas the latter is a VCI supplemental subtest. *Working memory* is the ability to actively maintain information in conscious awareness, perform some operation or manipulation with it, and produce a result. Working memory is an essential component of fluid reasoning and other higher-order cognitive processes and is closely related to achievement (Fry & Hale, 1996; Perlow, Jattuso, & Moore, 1997; Swanson, 1996). Working memory is assessed with the new Letter-Number Sequencing subtest and by the reworking of the former Arithmetic subtest to increase working memory demands. Because research indicates greater demands on working memory occur for Digit Span Backward than Digit Span Forward, separate process scores were developed for this subtest. Speed of processing is dynamically related to mental capacity (Kail & Salthouse, 1994), reading performance (Berninger, 2001), reasoning, and the efficient use of working memory for higher-order fluid reasoning tasks (Fry & Hale, 1996). Processing speed is also sensitive to such neurological conditions as epilepsy, ADHD, and traumatic brain injury (Donders, 1997). In children, more rapid processing of information may reduce demands on working memory and facilitate reasoning. The new Cancellation subtest was developed for the WISC-IV as a supplemental measure of processing speed. By comparing performance on Cancellation when stimulus materials are structured (CAS) as opposed to when they are random (CAR), additional information related to visual selective attention, visual neglect, response inhibition, and motor perseveration is acquired.

Description of the WISC-IV Integrated

Rapid Reference 4.2 shows the structure of the WISC-IV Integrated (2004), which adds 16 process subtests to the WISC-IV battery. Seven of the process subtests are *adaptations* of the core and supplemental subtests of the WISC-IV (i.e., Similarities Multiple Choice, Vocabulary Multiple Choice, Picture Vocabulary Multiple Choice, Comprehension Multiple Choice, Information Multiple Choice, Arithmetic Process Approach and Written Arithmetic). These subtests contain the same item content as their corresponding core or supplemental subtests, but they contain modifications to the mode of presentation or response format. Six of the process subtests are *variations* of the core and supplemental subtests (i.e., Block Design Multiple Choice, Block Design Process Approach, Visual Digit Span, Spatial Span, Letter Span, and Letter-Number Sequencing Process Approach). The variations include new item content and modifications to the mode of presentation or response format. Three process subtests are designed to expand the scope of construct coverage (e.g., Elithorn Mazes) or to provide information that can be used to better understand a child's performance on other subtests (e.g., Coding Recall and Coding Copy). The process subtests provide additional measures of cognitive abilities and may be used to test specific hypotheses regarding underlying cognitive processes and test-taking behaviors that contribute to performance on the core and supplemental subtests. On occasion, a process subtest may not measure the same construct as the core and supplemental subtest within a cognitive domain. For example, if a child performs poorly on Coding B (a measure of processing speed), the examiner may elect to administer Coding Recall (a measure of incidental learning) to see if the child remembers the pairings of numbers and symbols on Coding B. Although it is not a measure of processing speed, Coding Recall is included in the Processing Speed domain because it provides additional information about the cognitive processes contributing to performance on Coding B.

One of the primary benefits of adding select subtests from the WISC-IV Integrated to a pscyhoeducational battery that includes the WIAT-III is to delve more deeply into the role played by executive functions, working memory, and

≡ Rapid Reference 4.2

....

Structure of the WISC-IV Integrated

Verbal Domain

Core Subtests
—Block Design
—Picture Concepts
—Matrix Reasoning

Supplemental Subtests
—Picture Completion

Process Subtests
—Block Design Multiple Choice
—Block Design Process Approach
—Elithorn Mazes

Perceptual Domain

Core Subtests
—Similarities
—Vocabulary
—Comprehension

Supplemental Subtests
—Information
—Word Reasoning

Process Subtests
—Similarities Multiple Choice
—Vocabulary Multiple Choice
—Picture Vocabulary Multiple Choice
—Comprehension Multiple Choice
—Information Multiple Choice

Working Memory Domain

Core Subtests
—Digit Span
—Letter-Number Sequencing

Supplemental Subtests
—Arithmetic

Process Subtests
—Visual Digit Span
—Spatial Span
—Letter Span
—Letter-Number Sequencing Process Approach
—Arithmetic Process Approach
—Written Arithmetic

Processing Speed Domain

Core Subtests
—Coding
—Symbol Search

Supplemental Subtests
—Cancellation

Process Subtests
—Coding Recall
—Coding Copy

processing speed in learning. For example, empirical data gathered from clinical populations suggest that working memory may be affected differentially by neurodevelopmental problems or brain injury. Studies have identified distinct neuroanatomical locations for verbal, visuospatial, and executive working memory functions (Gathercole et al., 2004). The WISC-IV Integrated measures both the auditory-verbal (e.g., Digit-Span and Letter-Number Sequencing Process Approach) and the visuospatial (i.e., Visual Digit Span and Spatial Span) components. Further, several of the subtests (e.g., Block Design and Block Design No Time Bonus, Arithmetic and Arithmetic With Time Bonus) provide scaled scores that are derived from total raw scores with and without time-bonus points. This type of information is especially helpful when making recommendations for instruction and accommodations in the classroom.

INTEGRATING THE WIAT-III AND WISC-IV— QUANTITATIVE ANALYSES

When comparing ability, as measured by the WISC-IV, to achievement measured by WIAT-III, FSIQ or GAI and individual achievement subtest standard scores or composites are typically used. With some achievement tests it is necessary to use the composite scores to identify ability-achievement discrepancies because of the lower reliability scores on the individual achievement subtests. This is not the case with the WIAT-III because nearly all average subtest reliabilities across the fall, spring, and age samples range from good (.83–.89) to excellent (.90–.97). Reliabilities of .90 or higher provide strong support for the use of a subtest score for making educational decisions. Subtest scores with reliabilities between .80 and .90 are also suitable for making educational decisions in most settings. In fact, there are times when a discrepancy among subtests contributing to a composite exists, and individual subtest scores should be used because the composite score could mask important weaknesses and be misleading.

Coefficients of correlation between WIAT-III scores and WISC-IV scores demonstrate the strong relationship between the Wechsler tests of cognitive ability and achievement. The WISC-IV and the WIAT-III were administered to 117 children aged 6–16 years with a testing interval between 1 and 53 days. The correlations between the two tests are highest at the composite level ranging from .32 (for PRI and Math Fluency) to .82 (for FSIQ and Total Achievement). The VCI was moderately to highly correlated with all of the WIAT-III composites (range of .48 for Written Expression and Mathematics to .70 for Oral Language) except the Math Fluency composite (.28), with a .66 correlation between VCI and Total Achievement. The low to moderate correlations between PRI and the WIAT-III composites range from a low of .32 with Math Fluency to a high of .58 with Oral Language, with a .57 correlation between PRI and Total Achievement. At the subtest level, the strongest relationships are found between WISC-IV FSIQ and the Oral Expression (.74) and Early Reading Skills (.71) subtests, and between the WISC-IV VCI and the Oral Expression subtest (.72). See Table J.1 in the *WIAT-III Technical Manual* (Wechsler et al., 2009) for the complete correlation data.

Conceptually and psychometrically, the WISC-IV and WISC-IV Integrated paired with the WIAT-III have enhanced clinical utility especially in the assessment of children with various types of learning disabilities, children with ADHD, children with language disorders, children with open or closed head injury, children with Autistic Disorder, and children with Asperger's Disorder. Later in this chapter, information related to some of these clinical groups will be presented.

WIAT-III AND PROCESS ASSESSMENT OF THE LEARNER–SECOND EDITION (PAL-II)

The Process Assessment of the Learner - Second Edition: Diagnostic Assessment for Reading and Writing (PAL-II RW) may be used as a companion to the WIAT-III and provides in-depth assessment of the processing skills that are necessary for the development of the academic skills measured by the WIAT-III reading and writing subtests. The PAL-II RW is a norm-referenced tool, designed for assessing the development of reading and writing processes in children in kindergarten through grade 6. One of its primary functions is to be used for diagnosing the *nature* of reading- or writing-related processing problems in students who have exhibited a discrepancy between ability and achievement or have other indicators of a possible learning disability. Preliminary research has also indicated that the PAL-II RW process measures can be used to identify processing problems in older students with average or better intelligence who are functioning at developmental levels below grade placement. The PAL-II RW does not target all reading- or writing-related processes; rather, it provides measures of many of the processes that have been shown to be the best predictors of reading and writing achievement. A description of the PAL-II RW subtests is found in Rapid Reference 4.3. Rapid Reference 4.4 presents a model of how the PAL-II RW subtests can be used to better understand performance on the WIAT-III subtests by focusing on the processing skills required to perform the reading or writing tasks. The PAL-II RW may be used as a follow-up assessment when deficits in reading and/or writing are identified using the WIAT-III. The purpose of the follow-up testing is to identify those processing weaknesses that require remediation as part of an intervention plan. Once a process weakness is identified, the PAL-II RW provides targeted research-based interventions.

Additional testing using the PAL-II RW is not warranted for every examinee; however, for those students referred for possible reading and/or writing

≡ Rapid Reference 4.3

Description of PAL-II RW Subtests

Subtest	Description	Measures
Alphabet-Writing	The child is asked to write the lowercase letters of the alphabet in order, quickly and accurately.	Measures the child's automaticity in writing (including the ability to retrieve from long-term memory).
Copy Task A	The child is asked to copy a sentence quickly and accurately that contains all of the letters of the alphabet.	Measures the child's handwriting and ability to copy accurately without memory requirements.
Copy Task B	The child is asked to copy a paragraph quickly and accurately.	Measures the child's handwriting and ability to copy longer text accurately without memory requirements.
Receptive Coding	The child is asked to compare whole words, single letters, and letter groups to the target words presented visually in the stimulus booklet.	Measures the child's ability to quickly code written words into short-term memory and then to segment each word into units of different size.
Expressive Coding	The child is presented with the word in the stimulus booklet and then asked to write the whole word or targeting single letter or letter group from the word by memory.	Measures the child's ability to quickly code whole written words into short-term memory and then to reproduce the words or parts of words in writing.
Rhyming	The child is asked to listen to three words and to select the word that does not rhyme with the other two. Then, the child is asked to generate a list of words that rhyme with a spoken target word.	Measures phonological awareness (the child's ability to discriminate between words that have the same ending sounds and to generate real words that have the same ending sounds).

(continued)

Subtest	Description	Measures
Syllables	The child is asked to repeat a polysyllabic word presented by the examiner and then to say the syllable(s) remaining when a targeted syllable is omitted.	Measures the child's ability to segment spoken words into syllables.
Phonemes	The child is asked to repeat a monosyllabic or polysyllabic word presented by the examiner to provide the phonemes remaining when a targeted phoneme is omitted.	Measures the child's ability to segment spoken words into phonemes.
Rimes	The child is asked to say the portions of a monosyllabic or polysyllabic word remaining when the targeted rime is omitted.	Measures the child's understanding of rimes. A rime is the portion of the syllable that is left when the initial phoneme or phonemes of the syllable are omitted.
Are They Related?	For each item, the child decides whether a word is derived and related in meaning to another given word.	Measure's the child's ability to understand morphemes.
Does It Fit?	The child selects the pseudoword with the suffix that makes sense in a given sentence.	Measure's the child's ability to understand morphemes and syntax.
Sentence Structure	For each item, the child chooses the one sentence out of three that makes sense.	Measure's the child's ability to understand morphemes and syntax.
Pseudoword Decoding[a]	The child is asked to read aloud from a list of printed nonsense words. The pseudowords are designed to mimic the phonological structure of words in the English language.	Measures the child's ability to apply phonological decoding skills.
Find the True Fixes	The child is asked to identify words in which a prefix or suffix is being used as a morpheme.	Measures the child's ability to differentiate spelling patterns that are and are not morphemes.

Morphological Decoding Fluency	The child is asked to read base words with different suffixes under timed conditions.	Measures the child's ability to fluently read words that vary by morphological ending.
Word Choice	The child is presented with a response booklet and asked to circle from a choice of three the word that is spelled correctly.	Measures the child's ability to identify the correct spelling of a word presented with two misspelled distractors that have the same or nearly the same pronunciation as the correctly spelled word.
Sentence Sense	Each item requires the child to identify the meaningful (correct) sentence from among three very similar sentences, which contain only real words and which differ by only one word. Each of the two distractor sentences has one erroneous word (e.g., homonym) that does not make sense in the sentence context.	Measures the child's ability to coordinate word-recognition and sentence-comprehension processes when reading for meaning under timed conditions.
Compositional Fluency	The child writes about two given topics, each for 5 minutes.	Measures narrative compositional fluency.
Expository Note Taking and Report Writing	The child reads source materials, takes notes on the materials, and then writes a report using his or her notes.	Measures the integration of reading and writing skills.
Letters	The child listens to a letter spoken aloud and then provides the letter that comes one, two, or three letters before or after that letter.	Measures the ability to store and manipulate letters in working memory.
Words	The child spells words backward and identifies letters in various positions within words.	Measures the ability to store and manipulate words in working memory.

(continued)

Subtest	Description	Measures
Sentences: Listening	The child listens to a series of sentences, answers questions about them, and then repeats them back.	Measures the ability to manipulate sentences in working memory.
Sentences: Writing	The child listens to sentences read aloud and then writes sentences that come before, between, and/or after them.	Measures the ability to store sentences in working memory and to plan and write new sentences.
RAN	The child is asked to name aloud familiar letters, letter groups, or words quickly and accurately.	Measures automaticity of naming letters, letter groups, or highly frequent words that cannot be completely decoded on the basis of the alphabet principle.
RAS	The child is asked to alternately name aloud familiar words and double-digit numbers quickly and accurately.	Measures the executive functions required to coordinate cross-category naming processes.
Oral Motor Planning	The child repeats different syllables and then the same syllable.	Compares planning and execution times for repeating alternating sounds and the same sounds.
Finger Sense	Four tasks are included to elicit repetition, succession, localization, recognition, and finger-tip writing for both hands.	Measures the child's finger function related to written output.

[a]Pseudoword Decoding is a different subtest from the one included in the WIAT-III.

Rapid Reference 4.4

PAL-II RW Subtests for Measuring Processes Underlying WIAT-III Subtest Skills

Component Reading or Writing Skill (WIAT-III Subtest)	Process	PAL-II Subtest(s)
Decoding Accuracy (Pseudoword Decoding)	1. Orthographic coding in short-term memory 2. Phonological awareness at the syllable level 3. Phonological awareness at the phoneme level 4. Orthographic loop of working memory	1. Receptive Coding 2. Syllables 3. Phonemes 4. Expressive Coding
Decoding Speed (Pseudoword Decoding Speed)	1. Orthographic coding in short-term memory 2. Phonological awareness at the syllable level 3. Phonological awareness at the phoneme level 4. Rapid Automatic Naming (RAN)/phonological loop of working memory 5. Orthographic loop of working memory	1. Receptive Coding 2. Syllables 3. Phonemes 4. RAN Letters and Letter Groups 5. Expressive Coding
Word Recognition Accuracy (Word Reading)	1. Orthographic coding in short-term memory 2. Phonological awareness at the syllable level 3. Phonological awareness at the phoneme level 4. Recognizing morphemes 5. Recognizing the grammatical role of suffixes 6. Orthographic loop of working memory	1. Receptive Coding 2. Syllables 3. Phonemes 4. Are They Related? 5. Does It Fit? 6. Expressive Coding

(continued)

Component Reading or Writing Skill (WIAT-III Subtest)	Process	PAL-II Subtest(s)
Word Recognition Speed (Word Reading Speed)	1. Orthographic coding in short-term memory 2. Phonological awareness at the syllable level 3. Phonological awareness at the phoneme level 4. Long-term memory of written spelling of words 5. Recognizing morphemes 6. Recognizing the grammatical role of suffixes 7. Rapid Automatic Naming (RAN)/ phonological loop of working memory 8. Orthographic loop of working memory	1. Receptive Coding 2. Syllables 3. Phonemes 4. Word Choice 5. Are They Related? 6. Does It Fit? 7. RAN Letter Groups and Words 8. Expressive Coding
Oral Reading Fluency (Oral Reading Fluency, Oral Reading Accuracy, Oral Reading Rate)	1. Orthographic coding in short-term memory 2. Phonological awareness 3. Long-term memory of written spelling of words 4. Recognizing morphemes 5. Recognizing the grammatical role of suffixes 6. Rapid Automatic Naming (RAN) 7. Orthographic loop of working memory 8. Constructing sentence syntax 9. Accessing letter forms from long-term memory 10. Holding and processing words in working memory 11. Holding and processing sentences in working memory 12. Speed of integrating word decoding and syntax comprehension at the sentence level	1. Receptive Coding 2. Syllables 3. Phonemes 4. Word Choice 5. Are They Related? 6. Does It Fit? 7. RAN Letter Groups and Words 8. Expressive Coding 9. Sentence Structure 10. RAS Words and Double Digits 11. Letters 12. Words 13. Sentence Sense
Reading Comprehension (Reading Comprehension)	1. Orthographic coding in short-term memory 2. Phonological awareness at the phoneme level	1. Receptive Coding 2. Phonemes 3. Word Choice 4. Are They Related?

	3. Long-term memory of written spelling of words 4. Recognizing morphemes 5. Recognizing the grammatical role of suffixes 6. Constructing sentence syntax 7. Rapid Automatic Naming (RAN)/switching attention or mental set 8. Accessing letter forms from long-term memory 9. Holding and processing words in working memory 10. Holding and processing sentences in working memory 11. Speed of integrating word decoding and syntax comprehension at the sentence level	5. Does It Fit? 6. Sentence Structure 7. RAS Words and Double Digits 8. Letters 9. Words 10. Sentence: Listening (grades 4–6) 11. Sentence Sense
Handwriting/Letter Formation (Alphabet Writing Fluency)	1. Orthographic coding in short-term memory 2. Execution of finger movements 3. Planning, execution, and sequencing of finger movements	1. Receptive Coding 2. Finger Sense: Finger Repetition 3. Finger Sense: Finger Succession
Spelling (Spelling, Sentence Composition, Essay Composition)	1. Orthographic coding in short-term memory 2. Phonological awareness at the syllable level 3. Phonological awareness at the phoneme level 4. Accessing letter forms from long-term memory 5. Holding and processing words in working memory 6. Long-term memory of written spelling of words 7. Orthographic loop of working memory	1. Receptive Coding 2. Syllables 3. Phonemes 4. Letters 5. Words 6. Word Choice 7. Expressive Coding 8. Rimes 9. Are They Related? 10. Does It Fit?

(continued)

Component Reading or Writing Skill (WIAT-III Subtest)	Process	PAL-II Subtest(s)
	8. Phonological awareness of rimes 9. Recognizing morphemes 10. Recognizing the grammatical role of suffixes	
Written Composition Quality (Sentence Composition, Essay Composition)	1. Handwriting automaticity 2. Execution of finger movements 3. Planning, execution, and sequencing of finger movements 4. Accessing letter forms from long-term memory 5. Holding and processing words in working memory 6. Orthographic loop of working memory 7. Holding and processing sentences in working memory 8. Recognizing morphemes 9. Recognizing the grammatical role of suffixes 10. Constructing sentence syntax	1. Alphabet Writing (especially automaticity score) 2. Finger Sense: Finger Repetition 3. Finger Sense: Finger Succession 4. Letters 5. Words 6. Expressive Coding 7. Sentence: Writing 8. Are They Related? 9. Does It Fit? 10. Sentence Structure

Source: Adapted from Tables 4.1–4.7 of the PAL-II Administration and Scoring Manual for Reading and Writing (The Psychological Corporation, 2007).

disabilities, the use of the PAL-II RW with the WIAT-III can provide both diagnostic data and instructional clues for improving learning outcomes.

KTEA-II AND THE KAUFMAN ASSESSMENT BATTERY FOR CHILDREN, SECOND EDITION

The KTEA-II and the KABC-II are designed to fit hand-in-glove.[1] The advantages of conorming the two batteries are numerous: the theoretical basis for the ability test and the achievement tests are similar and cohesive; administration and interpretive systems are similar in design; more accurate comparisons can be made between achievement and ability; each test can enhance the diagnostic "reach" of the other; and the combination of tests conveniently provides a cohesive and large portion of a comprehensive assessment.

This section introduces the reader to the design and make-up of the KABC-II and the Cattell-Horn-Carroll (CHC) broad and narrow abilities that both the KTEA-II and KABC-II were designed to assess. Different aspects of the integration of the KTEA-II and the KABC-II are explored by examining theoretical, quantitative, clinical, qualitative, and procedural points of view. It should be noted that the formal integration of the KTEA-II and the KABC-II is in its infancy because the batteries have just been published. There are limits to the amount of prepublication research that can be performed. We look forward to the future field research that will explore and define the boundaries of KTEA-II/KABC-II integration.

Description of the KABC-II

The KABC-II is a measure of the processing and cognitive abilities of children and adolescents between the ages of 3 years 0 months and 18 years 11 months. The KABC-II is founded in two theoretical models: Luria's (1966, 1970, 1973) neuropsychological model, featuring three Blocks, and the Cattell-Horn-Carroll (CHC) approach to categorizing specific cognitive abilities (Carroll, 1997, Flanagan, McGrew, & Ortiz, 2000). The KABC-II yields a separate global score for each of these two theoretical models: the global score measuring general mental processing ability from the Luria perspective is the Mental Processing Index (MPI), and global score measuring general cognitive ability from the

---

1. The section titled "KTEA-II and the Kaufman Assessment Battery for Children, Second Edition" is adapted with permission from Chapter 6 of *Essentials of KABC-II Assessment* (Kaufman, Lichtenberger, Fletcher-Janzen, & Kaufman, 2005).

Cattell-Horn-Carroll perspective is the Fluid-Crystallized Index (FCI). The key difference between these two global scores is that the MPI (Luria's theory) *excludes* measures of acquired knowledge, whereas the FCI (CHC theory) *includes* measures of acquired knowledge. Only one of these two global scores is computed for any examinee. Prior to testing a client, examiners choose the interpretive system (i.e., Luria or CHC) that best fits with both their personal orientation and the reason for referral.

In addition to the MPI and FCI, the KABC-II offers from one to five scales depending on the age level of the child and the interpretive approach that the clinician chooses to take. At age 3, there is only one scale, a global measure of ability, composed of either five subtests (Mental Processing Index [MPI]) or seven subtests (Fluid-Crystallized Index [FCI]). For ages 4–6, subtests are organized into either three scales (Luria model) or four scales (CHC model): Sequential/*Gsm*, Simultaneous/*Gv*, and Learning/*Glr* are in both models, and Verbal/*Gc* is only in the CHC model. For ages 7–18, four scales (Luria) or five scales (CHC) are available, with the Planning/*Gf* scale joining the aforementioned KABC-II scales. The KABC-II scales for each age level are shown in Rapid Reference 4.5.

From the Luria perspective, the KABC-II scales correspond to learning ability, sequential processing, simultaneous processing, and planning ability. From the vantage point of the CHC model, as applied to the KABC-II, the scales measure the following Broad Abilities: Short-term memory, visualization, long-term memory, fluid reasoning, and crystallized ability (Rapid Reference 4.6 describes

≡ *Rapid Reference 4.5*

KABC-II Scales at Each Age Level

Age 3	Ages 4–6	Ages 7–18
MPI, FCI, or NVI	MPI, FCI, or NVI	MPI, FCI, or NVI
(no additional scales are obtained at age 3)	Learning/*Glr*	Learning/*Glr*
	Sequential/*Gsm*	Sequential/*Gsm*
	Simultaneous/*Gv*	Simultaneous/*Gv*
	Knowledge/*Gc*	Planning/*Gf*
		Knowledge/*Gc*

Note: The MPI from the Luria system *excludes* Knowledge/*Gc* subtests (age 3) and scale (ages 4–18). The FCI of the CHC system *includes* the Knowledge/*Gc* subtests (age 3) and scale (ages 4–18).

≡ *Rapid Reference 4.6*

Definitions of Luria and CHC Terms

Luria Term	CHC Term
Learning Ability	Long-Term Storage & Retrieval *(Glr)*
Reflects an integration of the processes associated with all three Blocks, placing a premium on the attention-concentration processes that are in the domain of Block 1, but also requiring Block 2 coding processes and Block 3 strategy generation to learn and retain the new information with efficiency. Sequential and simultaneous processing are associated primarily with Luria's Block 2 and pertain to either a step-by-step (sequential) or holistic (simultaneous) processing of information.	Storing and efficiently retrieving newly learned or previously learned information
Sequential Processing	Short-Term Memory *(Gsm)*
Measures the kind of coding function that Luria labeled "successive" and involves arranging input in sequential or serial order to solve a problem, where each idea is linearly and temporally related to the preceding one.	Taking in and holding information and then using it within a few seconds
Simultaneous Processing	Visual Processing *(Gv)*
Measures the second type, or simultaneous, coding function associated with Block 2. For its tasks, the input has to be integrated and synthesized simultaneously (holistically), usually spatially, to produce the appropriate solution. As mentioned earlier, the KABC-II measure of simultaneous processing deliberately blends Luria's Block 2 and Block 3 to enhance the complexity of the simultaneous syntheses that are required.	Perceiving, storing, manipulating, and thinking with visual patterns
Planning Ability	Fluid Reasoning *(Gf)*
Measures the high-level, decision-making, executive processes associated with Block 3. However, as Reitan (1988) states, "Block 3 is involved in no sensory, motor, perceptual, or speech functions and is devoted exclusively to analysis, planning, and organization of programs for behavior" (p. 335). Because any cognitive task involves perception of sensory input and	Solving novel problems by using reasoning abilities such as induction and deduction

(continued)

Luria Term	CHC Term
either a motor or verbal response, the KABC-II measure of planning ability necessarily requires functions associated with the other two Blocks as well.	
(Crystallized ability does not have an analogous ability that is included in the Luria model.)	Crystallized Ability (*Gc*)
	Demonstrating the breadth and depth of knowledge acquired from one's culture

Note: The names of the KABC-II scales were chosen to reflect both their Luria and CHC underpinnings. Verbal/*Gc* is included in the CHC system for the computation of the FCI, but it is *excluded* from the Luria system for the computation of the Mental Processing Index (MPI). The Planning/*Gf* scale is for ages 7–18 only. All other scales are for ages 4–18. Only the MPI and FCI are offered for three-year-olds.

how the scales are conceptualized by each theoretical perspective). The names of the KABC-II scales reflect both the Luria process it is believed to measure and its CHC Broad Ability, as indicated in Rapid Reference 4.6: Learning/*Glr*, Sequential/*Gsm*, Simultaneous/*Gv*, and Planning/*Gf*. However, the Verbal/*Gc* scale that measures crystallized ability reflects only CHC theory, as it is specifically excluded from the Luria system.

In addition to the MPI and FCI, and the five scales, the KABC-II has a Nonverbal Scale, composed of subtests that may be administered in pantomime and responded to motorically. The Nonverbal Scale permits valid assessment of children who are hearing impaired, have limited English proficiency, have moderate to severe speech or language impairments, and other disabilities that make the Core battery unsuitable. This special scale comprises a mixture of Core and supplementary subtests for all age groups. The interested reader can find more information about this scale in *Essentials of KABC-II Assessment* (Kaufman, Lichtenberger, Fletcher-Janzen, & Kaufman, 2005).

The KABC-II includes 18 subtests (described in Rapid Reference 4.7), which comprise a Core battery and an Expanded battery. The Expanded battery offers supplementary subtests to increase the breadth of the constructs that are measured by the Core battery, to follow up hypotheses, and to provide a comparison of the child's initial learning and delayed recall of new learning. The scale structure for each age group varies slightly, and is described in detail in the *KABC-II Manual* (Kaufman & Kaufman, 2004b).

≡ *Rapid Reference 4.7*

....

Description of KABC-II Subtests

Sequential/*Gsm* Subtests	*Description*
Word Order	The child touches a series of silhouettes of common objects in the same order as the examiner said the names of the objects; more difficult items include an interference task (color naming) between the stimulus and response.
Number Recall	The child repeats a series of numbers in the same sequence as the examiner said them, with series ranging in length from two to nine numbers; the numbers are single digits, except that 10 is used instead of 7 to ensure that all numbers are one syllable.
Hand Movements	The child copies the examiner's precise sequence of taps on the table with the fist, palm, or side of the hand.
Simultaneous/*Gv* Subtests	
Rover	The child moves a toy dog to a bone on a checkerboard-like grid that contains obstacles (rocks and weeds) and tries to find the "quickest" path—the one that takes the fewest moves.
Triangles	For most items, the child assembles several identical rubber triangles (blue on one side, yellow on the other) to match a picture of an abstract design; for easier items, the child assembles a different set of colorful rubber shapes to match a model constructed by the examiner.
Conceptual Thinking	The child views a set of four or five pictures and identifies the one picture that does not belong with the others; some items present meaningful stimuli, and others use abstract stimuli.
Face Recognition	The child attends closely to photographs of one or two faces that are exposed briefly and then selects the correct face or faces, shown in a different pose, from a group photograph.
Gestalt Closure	The child mentally "fills in the gaps" in a partially completed "inkblot" drawing and names (or describes) the object or action depicted in the drawing.

(continued)

Simultaneous/Gv Subtests	
Block Counting	The child counts the exact number of blocks in various pictures of stacks of blocks; the stacks are configured such that one or more blocks is hidden or partially hidden from view.
Planning/Gf Subtests	
Pattern Reasoning[a]	The child is shown a series of stimuli that form a logical, linear pattern, but one stimulus is missing; the child completes the pattern by selecting the correct stimulus from an array of four to six options at the bottom of the page. (Most stimuli are abstract, geometric shapes, but some easy items use meaningful.)
Story Completion[a]	The child is shown a row of pictures that tell a story, but some of the pictures are missing. The child is given a set of pictures, selects only the ones that are needed to complete the story, and places the missing pictures in their correct locations
Learning/Glr Subtests	
Atlantis	The examiner teaches the child the nonsense names for fanciful pictures of fish, plants, and shells; the child demonstrates learning by pointing to each picture (out of an array of pictures) when it is named.
Atlantis—Delayed	The child demonstrates delayed recall of paired associations learned about 15–25 minutes earlier during Atlantis by pointing to the picture of the fish, plant, or shell that is named by the examiner.
Rebus Learning	The examiner teaches the child the word or concept associated with each particular rebus (drawing) and the child then "reads" aloud phrases and sentences composed of these rebuses.
Rebus Learning—Delayed	The child demonstrates delayed recall of paired associations learned about 15–25 minutes earlier during Rebus Learning by "reading" phrases and sentences composed of those same rebuses.
Knowledge/Gc Subtests	
Riddles	The examiner provides several characteristics of a concrete or abstract verbal concept and the child has to point to it (early items) or name it (later items).

Expressive Vocabulary	The child provides the name of a pictured object.
Verbal Knowledge	The child selects from an array of six pictures the one that corresponds to a vocabulary word or answers a general information question.

[a] At ages 5–6, Pattern Reasoning and Story Completion are categorized as Simultaneous/*Gv* subtests.
Note: Descriptions are adapted from the *KABC-II Technical Manual* (Kaufman & Kaufman, 2004).

Integrating the KTEA-II and KABC-II—Quantitative Analyses

Coefficients of correlation between KTEA-II global scores and scores on cognitive tests were presented and discussed in the validity section of Chapter 3 in this book. Overall, the KABC-II FCI and MPI correlated substantially (mean $r = .74–.79$) with the KTEA-II CAC. The KTEA-II Comprehensive Form Reading and Math Composites also strongly correlated with the KABC-II FCI and MPI (ranging from .68–.74). KTEA-II Written Language and Oral Language had slightly lower correlations with the KABC-II (e.g., ranging from .60–.67).

To further examine the cognitive-achievement relationships we can study how each KABC-II Scale Index correlates with major KTEA-II Composites. Rapid References 4.8 and 4.9 show these correlations and asterisks are used to indicate

≡ *Rapid Reference 4.8*

KABC-II Scale Index Correlations with KTEA-II Composites (Ages 7–18 Years)

KABC-II Scale	KTEA-II Composite				
	Total	Reading	Math	Written Language	Oral Language
Learning/*Glr*	.58	.55	.49	.53*	.48
Sequential/*Gsm*	.50	.48	.44	.44	.44
Simultaneous/*Gv*	.54	.47	.53	.40	.43
Planning/*Gf*	.63*	.56*	.59*	.51	.51*
Knowledge/*Gc*	.75**	.71**	.62**	.59**	.68**

** *Highest* correlate of each KTEA-II Achievement Composite.
* *Second-highest* correlate of each KTEA-II Achievement Composite.

Note: Total = Comprehensive Achievement Composite; $N = 2,025$. All correlations were corrected for the variability of the norm group, based on the standard deviation obtained on the KTEA-II, using the variability correction of Cohen et al. (2003, p. 58). Data are adapted from Kaufman and Kaufman (2004b).

≡ *Rapid Reference 4.9*

....

KABC-II Scale Index Correlations with KTEA-II Composites (Ages 4½–6 Years)

KABC-II Scale	KTEA-II Composite				
	Total	Reading	Math	Written Language	Oral Language
Learning/*Glr*	.54	.58**	.52	.62**	.42
Sequential/*Gsm*	.59	.57*	.57*	.58	.49
Simultaneous/*Gv*	.65**	.57*	.65**	.59*	.50*
Knowledge/*Gc*	.60*	.49	.49	.47	.62**

** *Highest* correlate of each KTEA-II Achievement Composite.
* *Second-highest* correlate of each KTEA-II Achievement Composite.

Note: Total = Comprehensive Achievement Composite; N = 491 for Total and Oral Language;
N = 301 for Math; N = 122–124 for Written Language. All correlations were corrected for the variability of the norm group, based on the standard deviation obtained on the KTEA-II, using the variability correction of Cohen et al. (2003, p. 58). Data are adapted from Kaufman and Kaufman (2004b).

the KABC-II Index that correlates highest (**) and second highest (*) with each KTEA-II composite.

For the older children, ages 7–18 years, the Knowledge/*Gc* scale was the strongest correlate of all areas of achievement (Rapid Reference 4.9). For this age group, the Knowledge/*Gc* Index correlated .75 with KTEA-II Comprehensive Achievement, about .70 with Reading and Oral Language, and about .60 with Math and Written Language. The second-best correlate for ages 7–18 was typically Planning/*Gf* (*r*'s of .51–.63), although Learning/*Glr* was the second-best correlate of Written Language (.53). The poorest relationships with all areas of academic achievement for ages 7–18 tended to be analogs of the original KABC-II processing scales—Sequential/*Gsm* and Simultaneous/*Gv* (*r*'s of .40-.54).

Given that the KABC-II's Knowledge/*Gc* Index is designed to measure the depth and breadth of knowledge acquired from one's culture (including schooling), the strong relationship between it and all areas of achievement for school-age children and adolescents was not surprising. The good correlations with achievement for the new KABC-II scales—Planning/*Gf* and Learning/*Glr*—attest to the importance in the classroom of the ability to solve problems and learn new material during a clinical evaluation of general cognitive ability.

Intriguingly, the patterns of relationship between ability and achievement observed for school-age children and adolescents differed quite a bit from the patterns seen at ages 4½–6 years (Rapid Reference 4.9), when academic abilities are first emerging. Despite its obvious link to vocabulary and acquisition of facts, the Knowledge/*Gc* Index was *not* the highest correlate of achievement for young children. That distinction went to the Simultaneous/*Gv* Index ($r = .65$ with KTEA-II Comprehensive Achievement) with Knowledge/*Gc* (.60) and Sequential/*Gsm* (.59) in a virtual deadlock for second best. So contrary to ages 7–18, the KABC-II Sequential/*Gsm* and Simultaneous/*Gv* Indexes were among the best correlates of achievement for ages 4½ to 6 years. In addition, rather than the Knowledge/*Gc* scale emerging as the automatic best predictor of each area of achievement, the highest correlates for young children varied by area. Simultaneous/*Gv* was the highest correlate of Math (.65), Learning/*Glr* was best for Written Language (.62), and Knowledge/*Gc* was best for Oral Language (.62). Three of the four Indexes (all *except* Knowledge/*Gc*) were about equal as predictors of Reading (.57-58).

Thus, for ages 7–18, mental processes such as reasoning and planning were important for academic achievement, but not as important as a child's previously acquired knowledge. For ages 4½–6, the roles were reversed. During the stage when school skills are emerging, the amount of knowledge a child has already acquired is secondary to the cognitive processes that are needed to learn to read, write, compute, and speak. Indeed, the one aspect of achievement for which Knowledge/*Gc* was easily the best predictor was Oral Language—undoubtedly relating to the fact that both subtests for this age group (Riddles and Expressive Vocabulary) emphasize children's oral language skills.

The increase in the Knowledge/*Gc* scale's importance from ages 4½–6 to 7–18 probably reflects the increased experience with language and academic information as age increases. Also, the strong correlations at ages 4½–6 between Simultaneous/*Gv* and achievement most likely relates to the fact that this scale measures *both* Visual Processing (*Gv*) and Fluid Reasoning (*Gf*) for young children, because a separate Planning/*Gf* scale does not emerge until age 7.

Further examination of Rapid References 4.8 and 4.9 indicates that coefficients between KABC-II Scale Indexes and the five major KTEA-II composites ranged from .40 to .75 with median values of .53 (ages 7–18) and .57 (4½–6). Most values (about 70 percent) were in the .50 to .75 range indicating an acceptable level of relationship between the individual scales of the KABC-II major KTEA-II Composites. If the majority of values were below this moderate range then there would be a concern that there would not be a reasonable level of association between the two tests. On the other hand, individual scales indicating much higher levels would raise the issue of redundancy and the possibility that the tests measure the same constructs. Even the highest correlation of .75 between Knowledge/Gc and total KTEA-II achievement for ages 7–18 denotes an overlap of 56 percent, indicating that each test has its own uniqueness. Therefore, the fact that the majority of coefficients fall in this moderate to strong area indicates an acceptable level of relationship between the two tests.

The KABC-II scales that correlate most highly with the Comprehensive Achievement scale of the KTEA-II differ, again, by age level. The Knowledge scale, as expected, has the highest correlation coefficients with the Comprehensive Achievement scale across all age levels except ages 4:6 and grade 1. The latter groups have highest coefficients on the Simultaneous and Sequential scales, respectively, rather than the Knowledge scale. This is another way of reflecting the make-up of the FCI, MCI, and Comprehensive Achievement relationship. The increase in Knowledge scale importance probably reflects the increased experience with language and academic information as age increases.

USING A CHC FRAMEWORK TO INTEGRATE WIAT-III WITH WISC-IV AND KTEA-II WITH KABC-II

The integration of both the WIAT-III with the WISC-IV and the KTEA-II with the KABC-II allows examiners to sample the spectrum of Broad and Narrow Abilities defined by the Cattell-Horn-Carroll (CHC) model. The CHC model includes 10 Broad Abilities and about 70 Narrow Abilities (Flanagan & Ortiz, 2001; Flanagan, Ortiz, & Alfonso, 2007). Both the WISC-IV and the KABC-II address five or six of the CHC broad abilities: Short-Term Memory (Gsm), Visual Processing (Gv), Fluid Reasoning (Gf), Crystallized Ability (Gc), and Long-Term Storage and Retrieval (Glr) (Flanagan & Kaufman, 2009; Kaufman et al., 2005).[2] Processing Speed (Gs) is also measured by the WISC-IV. The WIAT-III and the KTEA-II Comprehensive Form measure three additional broad abilities: Auditory Processing (Ga), Reading and Writing (Grw), and Quantitative Knowledge/ Gq ability. These achievement tests also measure Glr Narrow Abilities that increase the breadth of the Glr Narrow Abilities measured by the WISC-IV and KABC-II when the achievement batteries are administered together with their corresponding test of intelligence. The WISC-IV and KABC-II also provide measures of Gq Narrow Abilities. WISC-IV Arithmetic taps Mathematics Achievement. The KABC-II also indirectly measures one of the Gq Narrow

---

2. Flanagan and Kaufman (2009) report that some experts include Glr as a broad ability that the WISC-IV measures, whereas other experts do not.

Abilities (i.e., Mathematics Achievement, by virtue of the fact that Rover and Block Counting each require the child to count).

The WISC-IV Processing Speed subtests, Symbol Search, Coding, and Cancellation, and the WIAT-III Math Fluency subtests provide measures of Processing Speed (*Gs*); however, neither *Gs* nor Decision Speed/Reaction Time (*Gt*) are measured by either the KABC-II or the KTEA-II. These two Broad Abilities were purposefully excluded from the Kaufman test batteries because these abilities are only concerned with speed, not quality, of processing; they lack the requisite complexity for inclusion; and they are weak measures of *g* in Carroll's (1993) factor-analytic survey (Kaufman & Kaufman, 2004b). *Gt* is not measured by any major test battery.

Of the 70 or so Narrow Abilities hypothesized, and often documented empirically, by Carroll (1993), the WISC-IV and WIAT-III measure 28 unique Narrow Abilities (40 percent of all Narrow Abilities) and the KABC-II and KTEA-II measure 33 unique Narrow Abilities (roughly 47 percent of all Narrow Abilities).

Figure 4.1 displays the alignment of Narrow Abilities measured by the KABC-II and KTEA-II, grouped by the pertinent Broad Ability. Alone, the KTEA-II measures 19 Narrow Abilities and six Broad Abilities. For the KABC-II, the 14 Narrow Abilities are measured, including two or more associated with each of five Broad Abilities.

Figure 4.2 displays the alignment of Narrow Abilities measured by the WISC-IV and WIAT-III, grouped by the pertinent Broad Ability. Alone, the WIAT-III measures 19 Narrow Abilities and eight Broad Abilities. The WISC-IV measures 14 Narrow Abilities and six Broad Abilities.

Rapid References 4.10 through 4.17 provide specific information regarding the precise WISC-IV, WIAT-III, KABC-II, and KTEA-II subtests that are believed to measure specific Narrow Abilities. The Rapid References are organized by Broad Ability (e.g., Rapid Reference 4.10 covers the subtests that measure *Glr* Narrow Abilities, Rapid Reference 4.11 is confined to *Gsm* Narrow Abilities, and so forth). The Broad Abilities of *Glr, Gsm, Gv, Gf,* and *Gc* were defined earlier in Rapid Reference 4.7. The Broad Ability of *Gs* plus remaining three Broad Abilities, which are measured only by the WIAT-III and KTEA-II, are defined as follows (Flanagan, McGrew, & Ortiz, 2000):

- **Processing Speed (*Gs*):** This is the ability to fluently and automatically perform cognitive tasks, especially when under pressure to maintain focused attention and concentration. *Attentive speediness* encapsulates the essence of *Gs*, which is measured typically by fixed-interval, timed tasks that require little in the way of complex thinking or mental processing.

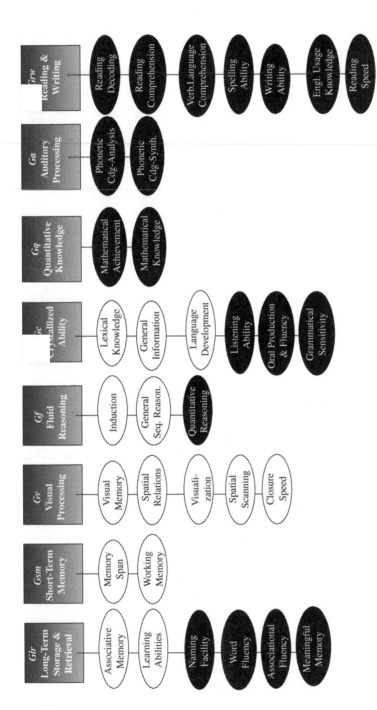

Figure 4.1 CHC Broad and Narrow Abilities Measured by the KABC-II and the KTEA-II.

Note: The CHC Broad Abilities are shown in gray squares. The CHC Narrow Abilities that are measured by only KABC-II subtests are represented by white ovals; Narrow Abilities that are measured only by KTEA-II subtests are represented by black ovals. Two KABC-II subtests also measure math achievement but are primarily measures of other Narrow Abilities.

Source: Kaufman, Lichtenberger, Flectcher-Janzen, and Kaufman (2005).

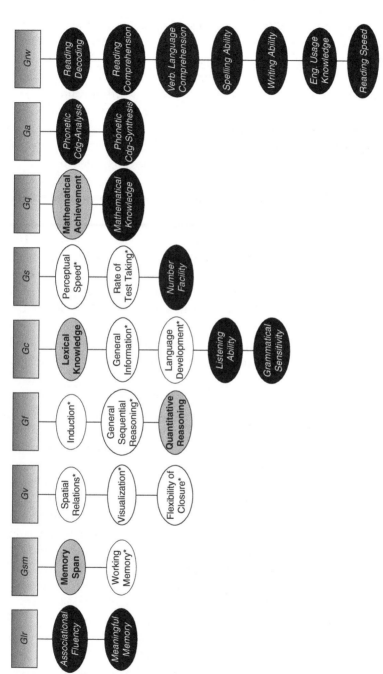

Figure 4.2 CHC Broad and Narrow Abilities Measured by the WISC-IV and the WIAT-III.

Note: The CHC Broad Abilities are shown in gray squares. The CHC Narrow Abilities that are measured by both the WISC-IV and the WIAT-III are represented by gray ovals; Narrow Abilities that are measured only by WISC-IV subtests are represented by white ovals; Narrow Abilities that are measured only by WIAT-III subtests are represented by black ovals.

- **Quantitative Knowledge (*Gq*):** The *Gq* store of acquired knowledge represents the ability to use quantitative information and manipulate numeric symbols.
- **Auditory Processing (*Ga*):** Auditory processing is the ability to perceive, analyze, and synthesize patterns among auditory stimuli, and discriminate subtle nuances in patterns of a sound and speech when presented under distorted conditions. *Ga* subsumes most of those abilities referred to as phonological awareness/processing.
- **Reading/Writing Ability (*Grw*):** The *Grw* ability is an acquired store of knowledge that includes basic reading and writing skills required for the comprehension of written language and the expression of thought via writing. It includes both basic (e.g., reading decoding, spelling) and complex abilities (e.g., reading comprehension and the ability to write a story).

One of the most important expectations that you may have about using CHC theory for interpretation of the WISC-IV with the WIAT-III and the KABC-II together with the KTEA-II is that there is a cohesive theoretical umbrella over the pairs of tests. When using a CHC framework, the explanation for what is cognitive processing and what is achievement on the WISC-IV, WIAT-III, KABC-II, and KTEA-II is theoretically based and evidence-based, and the results of combining the test batteries will give the examiner a comprehensive and fruitful examination of the child's cognitive abilities and how they translate into academic skills.

That is not to say that the achievement and cognitive batteries do not overlap in Broad or Narrow Abilities. As is evident from Figures 4.1 and 4.2 and Rapid References 4.10–4.17, there is some overlap. However, there is minimal redundancy overall. For example, both the KABC-II and KTEA-II measure *Glr* and *Gc* Narrow Abilities, but each measures a separate set. When they do measure the same Narrow Ability, they do it in quite different ways: Mathematical Achievement is a minor aspect of two KABC-II subtests, but this *Gq* ability is the major thrust of Mathematics Computation; in contrast, the *Gf* Narrow Ability of Induction is a key component of the KABC-II Planning/*Gf* subtests. Similarly, the WISC-IV and WIAT-III both provide measures of *Gsm*, *Gf*, *Gc*, *Gs*, and *Gq*, but each measures unique Narrow Abilities with minimal overlap. The WISC-IV and WIAT-III overlap in the measurement of four Narrow Abilities (i.e., Memory Span, Quantitative Reasoning, Lexical Knowledge, and Mathematical Achievement); however, each measures these Narrow Abilities very differently. For example, WISC-IV Arithmetic and WIAT-III Math Problem Solving both measure Mathematical Achievement. However, Math Problem Solving was designed primarily as a measure of Mathematical Achievement, whereas

Quantitative Reasoning (*Gf*) is the primary Narrow Ability measured by Arithmetic and Mathematical Achievement is a secondary aspect.

Flanagan and colleagues (Flanagan & Ortiz, 2001; Flanagan, Ortiz, & Alfonso, 2007) suggest that you need at least two different primary Narrow Ability measures to adequately measure a Broad Ability from a cross-battery perspective. Examiners who integrate the WISC-IV with the WIAT-III or the KABC-II with the KTEA-II should easily be able to achieve adequate measurement of eight Broad Abilities: *Glr*, *Gsm*, *Gv*, *Gf*, *Gc*, *Gs* (WISC-IV and WIAT-III only), *Gq*, and *Grw*. However, assessment of *Ga* (Phonetic Coding) depends on a single KTEA-II subtest (Phonological Awareness) that is only normed from age 4 ½ to grade 6 or a single WIAT-III subtest (Early Reading Skills) that is normed for grades Pre-K–3(ages 4–9).

Of course, no one battery can cover the CHC model in its entirety, but the WISC-IV with the WIAT-III and the KABC-II with the KTEA-II—like the WJ III Cognitive and Achievement Batteries—provide a substantially positive start for the clinician to examine a child's performance from a CHC perspective. To supplement the WISC-IV, WIAT-III, KABC-II, and KTEA-II via Cross Battery Assessment, using CHC theory as a foundation, consult publications by Flanagan and her colleagues (Flanagan & Kaufman, 2004; Flanagan, McGrew, & Ortiz, 2000; Flanagan & Ortiz, 2001; Flanagan, Ortiz, & Alfonso, 2007; Flanagan, Ortiz, Alfonso, & Mascolo, 2002; McGrew & Flanagan, 1998). These works provide an in-depth study of CHC theory and the Cross Battery Assessment approach, which is valuable for linking the Wechsler and Kaufman batteries with each other and with other instruments.

Long-Term Storage and Retrieval (*Glr*)

Long-term storage and retrieval requires the child to engage in activities that measure the efficiency of how well information is stored and retrieved. Examiners can obtain a rich measurement of *Glr* by administering a variety of WIAT-III, KTEA-II, and KABC-II subtests. The WIAT-III subtests that measure *Glr* include the Oral Discourse Comprehension component of the Listening Comprehension subtest and the Oral Word Fluency component of the Oral Expression subtest. The WISC-IV subtests do not measure *Glr* Narrow Abilities. The KTEA-II subtests that measure *Glr* include Listening Comprehension, Associational Fluency, and Naming Facility/RAN. The KABC-II Core Battery measures a single *Glr* Narrow Ability (Associative Memory); an additional Narrow Ability is assessed when examiners administer the supplementary Delayed Recall scale (Atlantis Delayed and Rebus Delayed each measure *both* Associative Memory and Learning Abilities).

The WIAT-III Oral Discourse Comprehension component of the Listening Comprehension subtest requires the student to listen and encode oral passages of increasing length and then answer open-ended comprehension questions about each one. Similarly, KTEA-II Listening Comprehension demands that the child listens and encodes a story and then manipulates the information to answer questions about the story. Although, "long-term storage and retrieval" implies that there is a long time between encoding and retrieval, this is not necessarily the case because the information has to be retrieved by association for whatever time interval has lapsed. The CHC model calls the Narrow Ability measured by the WIAT-III and KTEA-II Listening Comprehension subtests "Meaningful Memory."

The WIAT-III Oral Word Fluency component of the Oral Expression subtest measures Associational Fluency by requiring the student to name as many items within a given category (i.e., animals, colors) as he or she can within 60 seconds. This component yields a separate standard score to allow examiners to interpret performance on this component apart from performance on the other components of the Oral Expression subtest.

The KTEA-II Naming Facility/RAN subtest was given its label based both on the CHC Narrow Ability that it measures (Naming Facility) and on the popular neuropsychological subtest that inspired it (Rapid Automatized Naming, or RAN). The KTEA-II Associational Fluency subtest is also named after a CHC Narrow Ability, but, in actuality, this subtest measures two different Narrow Abilities. The category items (e. g., name as many kinds of toys as you can) measure Associational Fluency, whereas the items that focus on naming as many words as possible that start with a specific sound (such as/k/) measure Word Fluency. For purposes of reliability, these two Narrow Abilities are subsumed by a single standard score. Inferences about the separate Narrow Abilities are only possible if the child performs at notably different levels on the two kinds of items (e.g., a child who can reel off a string of words that begin with particular sounds, but is stymied and hesitant when retrieving categorical words). See Rapid Reference 4.10 for an outline of the Long-Term Storage and Retrieval (*Glr*) Narrow Abilities.

Short-Term Memory (*Gsm*)

Short-term memory is required by the WIAT-III Sentence Repetition component of the Oral Expression subtest. This subtest is primarily designed to measure oral syntactic knowledge using a task that is constrained by auditory short-term memory. The student is required to listen to sentences of increasing length and syntactic complexity, and then repeat each sentence verbatim.

≡ *Rapid Reference 4.10*

CHC Analysis: Long-Term Storage & Retrieval (*Glr*) Narrow CHC Abilities Measured by WIAT-III Subtests and KTEA-II and KABC-II Subtests (WISC-IV Subtests Do Not Measure Any *Glr* Narrow Abilities)

Glr Narrow Ability

Associative Memory
   KABC-II Atlantis
   KABC-II Rebus
   KABC-II Atlantis Delayed
   KABC-II Rebus Delayed

Learning Abilities
   KABC-II Atlantis Delayed
   KABC-II Rebus Delayed

Naming Facility
   KTEA-II Naming Facility/RAN

Associational Fluency
   KTEA-II Associational Fluency (category items; e.g., foods, animals)
   WIAT-III Oral Expression (Oral Word Fluency component)

Word Fluency
   KTEA-II Associational Fluency (category items; e.g., words that start with the /d/ sound)

Meaningful Memory
   KTEA-II Listening Comprehension
   WIAT-III Listening Comprehension (Oral Discourse Comprehension component)

The WISC-IV Digit Span and Letter-Number Sequencing subtests measure two *Gsm* Narrow Abilities. Digit Span provides a measure of Memory Span (auditory short-term memory) by requiring the child to repeat numbers in the same order as presented aloud by the examiner (Digit Span Forward). This subtest also measures (auditory) Working Memory with a different task that requires the child to repeat numbers in the reverse order of that presented aloud by the examiner (Digit Span Backward). Letter-Number Sequencing provides an additional measure of (auditory) Working Memory with a task that requires the child to listen to a sequence of numbers and letters and then recall the numbers in ascending order and the letters in alphabetical order.

The primary subtest that measures auditory short-term memory on the KABC-II is Number Recall. The CHC model mostly mentions auditory short-term memory tests for *Gsm*, but visual and haptic activities such as Hand Movements also measure *Gsm*. The three subtests together measure different modalities of short-term memory and also how short-term memory can evolve into working memory.

All three KABC-II *Gsm* subtests (Number Recall, Word Order, and Hand Movements) measure Memory Span. In addition, Word Order has a color interference task that definitely requires the Narrow Ability of Working Memory. Consequently, for young children (ages 3 to 5 or 6), who are not likely to reach the color interference items in Word Order, the KABC-II measures only a single CHC Narrow Ability—Memory Span. However, for children 6–7 years or older, the KABC-II measures both Memory Span and Working Memory. See Rapid Reference 4.11 for an outline of the Short-Term Memory (*Gsm*) Narrow Abilities.

Visual Processing (Gv)

The WISC-IV measures three *Gv* Narrow Abilities with Block Design (Spatial Relations and Visualization) and Picture Completion (Flexibility of Closure). The

---

≡ Rapid Reference 4.11

CHC Analysis: Short-Term Memory (*Gsm*) Narrow CHC Abilities Measured by WIAT-III, WISC-IV, and KABC-II (KTEA-II Subtests Do Not Measure Any *Gsm* Narrow Abilities)

Gsm Narrow Ability

Memory Span
  WIAT-III Oral Expression (Sentence Repetition component)
  WISC-IV Digit Span
  KABC-II Word Order (without color interference)
  KABC-II Number Recall
  KABC-II Hand Movements

Working Memory
  WISC-IV Digit Span
  WISC-IV Letter-Number Sequencing
  KABC-II Word Order (with color interference)

Note: Success on WIAT-III Early Reading Skills and the Oral Discourse Comprehension component of Listening Comprehension and KTEA-II Phonological Awareness and Listening Comprehension is also dependent, to some extent, on *Gsm*.

KABC-II provides measurement of five *Gv* Narrow Abilities, although examiners need to administer supplementary subtests such as Gestalt Closure (Closure Speed) and Hand Movements (Visual Memory) to measure all five. See Rapid Reference 4.12 for an outline of the Visual Processing (*Gv*) narrow abilities.

Fluid Reasoning (*Gf*)

Fluid reasoning is measured by the WISC-IV Matrix Reasoning, Picture Concepts and Arithmetic subtests. Matrix Reasoning and Picture Concepts both measure Induction, but Matrix Reasoning also measures General Sequential Reasoning

---

≡ *Rapid Reference 4.12*

....

CHC Analysis: Visual Processing (*Gv*) Narrow CHC Abilities Measured by WISC-IV and KABC-II (WIAT-III and KTEA-II Subtests Do Not Measure Any *Gv* Narrow Abilities)

Gv Narrow Ability

Visual Memory
  KABC-II Face Recognition
  KABC-II Hand Movements

Spatial Relations
  WISC-IV Block Design
  KABC-II Triangles

Visualization
  WISC-IV Block Design
  KABC-II Triangles
  KABC-II Conceptual Thinking
  KABC-II Block Counting
  KABC-II Pattern Reasoning
  KABC-II Story Completion

Spatial Scanning
  KABC-II Rover

Closure Speed
  KABC-II Gestalt Closure

Flexibility of Closure
  WISC-IV Picture Completion

Note: Success on WIAT- III Numerical Operations and KTEA-II Written Expression is also dependent, to some extent, on Visual Processing.

(deduction). Arithmetic primarily measures the Narrow Ability of Quantitative Reasoning.

Fluid reasoning is specifically measured by the subtests that constitute the KABC-II Planning/*Gf* scale (Pattern Reasoning, Story Completion), and also by subtests on the Simultaneous/*Gv* scale (Rover, Conceptual Thinking) and the Knowledge/*Gc* scale (Riddles). On the Planning/*Gf* scale, Pattern Reasoning primarily measures the Narrow Ability of Induction whereas Story Completion measures *both* Induction (figuring out what the story is about) and General Sequential Reasoning or deduction (selecting and sequencing the correct pictures).

KTEA-II Mathematics Concepts and Applications and WIAT-III Math Problem Solving are primarily *Gq* tasks, but each also requires considerable *Gf* for success, specifically the Narrow Ability Quantitative Reasoning. See Rapid Reference 4.13 for an outline of the Fluid Reasoning (*Gf*) Narrow Abilities.

≡ *Rapid Reference 4.13*

CHC Analysis: Fluid Reasoning (*Gf*) Narrow CHC Abilities Measured by KTEA-II and KABC-II Subtests

Gf Narrow Ability

Induction
  WISC-IV Matrix Reasoning
  WISC-IV Picture Concepts
  KABC-II Conceptual Thinking
  KABC-II Pattern Reasoning
  KABC-II Story Completion

General Sequential Reasoning
  WISC-IV Matrix Reasoning
  KABC-II Story Completion
  KABC-II Rover
  KABC-II Riddles

Quantitative Reasoning
  WISC-IV Arithmetic
  WIAT-III Math Problem Solving
  KTEA-II Mathematics Concepts & Applications

Note: Success on WIAT-III Listening Comprehension (Oral Discourse Comprehension component), Reading Comprehension, and Essay Composition; KABC-II Rebus; and four KTEA-II subtests (Reading Comprehension, Listening Comprehension, Oral Expression, and Written Expression) is also dependent, to some extent, on Fluid Reasoning.

Crystallized Ability (Gc)

The WISC-IV measures three *Gc* Narrow Abilities: (a) Lexical Knowledge, measured by the Vocabulary, Word Reasoning, and Similarities subtests; (b) General Information, measured by the Information and Comprehension subtests; and (c) Language Development, measured by the Comprehension and Similarities subtests. The Narrow Ability of Lexical Knowledge is measured by all three KABC-II Knowledge/*Gc* subtests, with Riddles (Language Development) and Verbal Knowledge (General Information) each measuring an additional *Gc* Narrow Ability as well.

When the WISC-IV and WIAT-III are administered together, five *Gc* Narrow Abilities are measured. Similarly, when the KABC-II and KTEA-II are administered together, the measurement of *Gc* Narrow Abilities expands to six. Hence, administering these tests together provides greater breadth of coverage of this Broad Ability. See Rapid Reference 4.14 for an outline of Crystallized Ability (*Gc*) Narrow Abilities.

Processing Speed (Gs)

Gs measures the ability to fluently and automatically perform relatively simple cognitive tasks under timed conditions (Flanagan, McGrew, & Ortiz, 2000). The WISC-IV measures two *Gs* Narrow Abilities: Perceptual Speed and Rate of Test Taking. Perceptual Speed is the ability to rapidly search, identify, and compare visual information. This Narrow Ability is measured by the WISC-IV Symbol Search subtest and a supplemental subtest, Cancellation. Rate of Test Taking, the ability to perform tests quickly and accurately, is also measured by WISC-IV Cancellation and Symbol Search subtests in addition to the Coding subtest.

The WIAT-III measures an additional *Gs* Narrow Ability, Number Facility, with three Math Fluency subtests: Math Fluency—Addition, Math Fluency—Subtraction, and Math Fluency—Multiplication. See Rapid Reference 4.15 for an outline of Processing Speed (*Gs*) Narrow Abilities.

Quantitative Knowledge (Gq)

Gq measures the individual's store of accumulated mathematical knowledge (Flanagan & Ortiz, 2001). It is different from the *Gf* Narrow Ability of Quantitative Reasoning because *Gq* is more about what the child knows than how the child reasons with quantitative information. WIAT-III Math Problem Solving and KTEA-II Math Concepts and Applications each measure Quantitative Reasoning to some extent but primarily measure *Gq*. WIAT-III Numerical Operations and KTEA-II Mathematics Computation also provide measures of *Gq*. Both WIAT-III subtests

≡ *Rapid Reference 4.14*

CHC Analysis: Crystallized Ability (*Gc*) Narrow CHC Abilities Measured by KTEA-II and KABC-II Subtests

Gc Narrow Ability

Lexical Knowledge
  WISC-IV Vocabulary
  WISC-IV Word Reasoning
  WISC-IV Similarities
  WIAT-III Listening Comprehension (Receptive Vocabulary component)
  WIAT-III Oral Expression (Expressive Vocabulary component)
  KABC-II Riddles
  KABC-II Verbal Knowledge (items that measure vocabulary)
  KABC-II Expressive Vocabulary
General Information
  WISC-IV Information
  WISC-IV Comprehension
  KABC-II Verbal Knowledge (items that measure general information)
  KABC-II Story Completion
Language Development
  WISC-IV Comprehension
  WISC-IV Similarities
  KABC-II Riddles
Listening Ability
  WIAT-III Listening Comprehension (Oral Discourse Comprehension component)
  KTEA-II Listening Comprehension
Oral Production and Fluency
  KTEA-II Oral Expression
Grammatical Sensitivity
  KTEA-II Oral Expression
  KTEA-II Written Expression

Note: Success on KABC-II Rebus is also dependent, to some extent, on Grammatical Sensitivity.

that comprise the Mathematics composite and both KTEA-II subtests that make up the Math Composite measure the two *Gq* Narrow Abilities, providing thorough measurement of the *Gq* Broad Ability. See Rapid Reference 4.16 for an outline of Quantitative Knowledge (*Gq*) narrow abilities.

≡ *Rapid Reference 4.15*
....

CHC Analysis: Processing Speed (*Gs*) Narrow CHC Abilities Measured by WIAT-III and WISC-IV Subtests (KTEA-II and KABC-II Subtests Do Not Measure Any *Gs* Narrow Abilities)

Gs Narrow Ability

Perceptual Speed
  WISC-IV Symbol Search
  WISC-IV Cancellation
Rate of Test Taking
  WISC-IV Symbol Search
  WISC-IV Cancellation
  WISC-IV Coding
Number Facility
  WIAT-III Math Fluency—Addition
  WIAT-III Math Fluency—Subtraction
  WIAT-III Math Fluency—Multiplication

≡ *Rapid Reference 4.16*
....

CHC Analysis: Quantitative Knowledge (*Gq*) Narrow CHC Abilities Measured by WIAT-III, WISC-IV, KTEA-II, and KABC-II Subtests

Gq Narrow Ability

Mathematical Knowledge
  WIAT-III Math Problem Solving
  KTEA-II Mathematics Concepts & Applications
Mathematical Achievement
  WIAT-III Math Fluency—Addition
  WIAT-III Math Fluency—Subtraction
  WIAT-III Math Fluency—Multiplication
  WIAT-III Math Problem Solving
  WIAT-III Numerical Operations
  KTEA-II Mathematics Computation
  KABC-II Rover
  KABC-II Block Counting

Auditory Processing (Ga)

Ga "requires the perception, analysis, and synthesis of patterns among auditory stimuli as well as the discrimination of subtle differences in patterns of sound" (Flanagan & Ortiz, 2001, p. 18). Both the analytic and synthetic Narrow Abilities associated with the *Ga* Broad Ability are measured by WIAT-III Early Reading Skills and by KTEA-II Phonological Awareness.

The WIAT-III subtest is normed for young children (Pre-K to grade 3) and does not provide separate scores for performance on analytic and synthetic items; however, skills analysis capabilities allow the examiner to evaluate performance at the item level and compare performance on items measuring analytic and synthetic Phonetic Coding.

Similarly, the KTEA-II subtest is of appropriate difficulty primarily for young children (Pre-K to grade 2), and is only standardized through grade 6. It yields an overall score rather than separate scores for its two Narrow Abilities. Nonetheless, the KTEA-II Error Analysis procedure for Phonological Awareness permits examiners to determine whether the child performed at a "Strong," "Average," or "Weak" level on the separate sections of the subtest (Kaufman & Kaufman, 2004a). Hence, the error analysis allows examiners to compare the child's ability on the two *Ga* Narrow Abilities that it measures. See Rapid Reference 4.17 for an outline of Auditory Processing (*Ga*) Narrow Abilities.

≡ *Rapid Reference 4.17*

CHC Analysis: Auditory Processing (*Ga*) Narrow CHC Abilities Measured by WIAT-III and KTEA-II (WISC-IV and KABC-II Subtests Do Not Measure Any *Ga* Narrow Abilities)

Ga Narrow Ability

Phonetic Coding—Analysis
  WIAT-III Early Reading Skills
  KTEA-II Phonological Awareness (Section 1—Rhyming; Section 2—Sound Matching; Section 4—Segmenting; Section 5—Deleting Sounds)

Phonetic Coding—Synthesis
  WIAT-III Early Reading Skills
  KTEA-II Phonological Awareness (Section 3—Blending)

Note: Deficits in certain *Ga* Narrow Abilities like Speech Sound Discrimination (US) may impact performance negatively on such tests as WIAT-III Listening Comprehension; KABC-II Riddles, Word Order, and Number Recall; and KTEA-II Listening Comprehension.

Reading and Writing (*Grw*)

Grw is measured by achievement tests (Flanagan & Ortiz, 2001). The WIAT-III and KTEA-II provides thorough measurement of five key *Grw* Narrow Abilities: Reading Decoding, Reading Comprehension, Spelling Ability, Writing Ability, and Reading Speed. Each test also measures two additional *Gc* abilities to some extent—Verbal (Printed) Language Comprehension and English Usage Knowledge. Seven *Grw* Narrow Abilities are measured by eight WIAT-III subtests: Word Reading, Pseudoword Decoding, Reading Comprehension, Early Reading Skills, Spelling, Sentence Composition, Essay Composition, and Oral Reading Fluency. Several of the new subtests added to the KTEA-II Comprehensive Form (Nonsense Word Decoding, Written Expression, Word Recognition Fluency, and Decoding Fluency) greatly enriched the measurement of *Grw* Narrow Abilities relative to the original K-TEA. See Rapid Reference 4.18 for an outline of Reading and Writing (*Grw*) Narrow Abilities.

≡ Rapid Reference 4.18

CHC Analysis: Reading & Writing (*Grw*) Narrow CHC Abilities Measured by WIAT-III and KTEA-II (WISC-IV and KABC-II Subtests Do Not Measure Any *Grw* Narrow Abilities)

Grw Narrow Ability

Reading Decoding
    WIAT-III Word Reading
    WIAT-III Pseudoword Decoding
    KTEA-II Letter & Word Reading
    KTEA-II Nonsense Word Decoding

Reading Comprehension
    WIAT-III Reading Comprehension
    KTEA-II Reading Comprehension (paragraph items)

Verbal (Printed) Language Comprehension
    WIAT-III Early Reading Skills (items requiring matching words with pictures)
    KTEA-II Reading Comprehension (items requiring student to do what a sentence tells them to do)

Spelling Ability
    WIAT-III Spelling
    KTEA-II Spelling
    WIAT-III Alphabet Writing Fluency

(continued)

Writing Speed (fluency)
  WIAT-III Alphabet Writing Fluency
Writing Ability
  WIAT-III Sentence Composition
  WIAT-III Essay Composition
  KTEA-II Written Expression
English Usage Knowledge
  WIAT-III Sentence Composition
  WIAT-III Essay Composition
  KTEA-II Written Expression
Reading Speed
  WIAT-III Word Reading (Word Reading Speed supplemental score)
  WIAT-III Pseudoword Decoding (Pseudoword Decoding Speed supplemental score)
  WIAT-III Oral Reading Fluency
  KTEA-II Word Recognition Fluency
  KTEA-II Decoding Fluency

THE WIAT-III AND KTEA-II DATA MANAGEMENT AND INTERPRETIVE ASSISTANT

To facilitate the process of interpreting the WISC-IV with the WIAT-III and the KABC-II with the KTEA-II from a CHC perspective, an automated program has been created for this book. This program, the WIAT-III and KTEA-II Data Management and Interpretive Assistant (DMIA), is found on the CD-ROM that accompanies this book. The guiding principles of the WIAT-III and KTEA-II DMIA are those of Cross-Battery Assessment. As mentioned earlier in this chapter, a thorough explanation of the Cross-Battery Assessment approach to test interpretation can be found in the second edition of *Essentials of Cross-Battery Assessment* (Flanagan, Ortiz, & Alfonso, 2007). Readers who are unfamiliar with the interpretive guidelines and underlying principles of this approach are strongly urged to familiarize themselves with these topics prior to using the WIAT-III and KTEA-II DMIA to facilitate interpretation.

What to Expect When Running WIAT-III and KTEA-II DMIA

When the program is opened on your computer, you will see an Introduction ("Intro") screen. This Intro tab includes general information about how to use the program and provides a place for entering the examinee's name, date of birth, and date of evaluation. The program automatically calculates the examinee's chronological age. A tab labeled "Notes" provides information that clarifies how

DON'T FORGET

....

User Qualifications for CHC Tab

- Proper use of the CHC tab requires users to have a complete understanding of the principles and rational underlying Cross-Battery Assessment.
- Detailed information on the Cross-Battery approach is found in *Essentials of Cross-Battery Assessment* (2nd Ed.)(Flanagan, Ortiz, & Alfonso, 2007). This book and its accompanying Cross-Battery Assessment Data Management and Interpretive Assistant (XBA DMIA) program provided the foundation for the CHC tab of the WIAT-III and KTEA-II DMIA.
- If unfamiliar with the Cross-Battery approach, users should consult Flanagan and colleagues (2007) prior to using our CHC tab.

to navigate through the program. Standard score data from the WISC-IV, WIAT-III, KTEA-II, and KABC-II can be entered on separate tabs and will be automatically graphed by the program. In addition, WIAT-III and KTEA-II data can be organized and graphed together, under the IDEA 2004 categories.

The CHC Tab in the WIAT-III and KTEA-II DMIA

A separate tab labeled "CHC" is included to help organize the WISC-IV, WIAT-III, KTEA-II, and KABC-II data into 10 CHC Broad Abilities/processes: *Gc, Gf, Gsm, Gs, Gq, Glr, Gv,* Ga, *Grw-W,* and *Grw-R.* For each Broad Ability, users may enter three standard scores from three subtests (out of any of the four test batteries). The standard scores are converted to a metric with a mean of 100 and a SD of 15. The subtest names are entered by choosing the selected test name via a drop down menu. This CHC tab of the WIAT-III and KTEA-II DMIA can be utilized even if only select subtests from each of the test batteries are administered. That is, complete batteries do not have to be administered in order to calculate CHC Broad and Narrow Ability clusters. However, at least two subtests that comprise a cluster must be administered, as Flanagan, Ortiz, and Alfonso (2007) note: "Because clusters are typically more reliable than scores from single subtests, interpretation of performance on the basis of single subtests is typically not done under the [Cross-Battery approach]" (p. 94). Thus, the interpretive approach that is presented in the WIAT-III and KTEA-II DMIA, which follows cross-battery principles, derives CHC Broad and Narrow Ability cluster scores from two or three subtests.

Calculation of CHC Scores with the WIAT-III and KTEA-II DMIA

The WIAT-III and KTEA-II DMIA allows up to three scores to be entered for each Broad Ability/process listed on the CHC tab. When just two scores are

CAUTION

Prior to using the CHC tab, users should be familiar with the Cross-Battery approach (see Flanagan, Ortiz, & Alfonso, 2007). For example, users of the CHC tab need to bear in mind:

- Cross-Battery Assessment is used when the variation in scores that comprise a cluster is statistically significant and the lower score in the cluster suggests a weakness or deficit.
- When selecting subtests to conduct meaningful Cross-Battery Assessments, practitioners must be familiar with CHC classifications, particularly at the Narrow Ability level.
- The CHC tab of the DMIA is used only when actual norms are not available.

entered, the program will report a cluster when it is unitary and thus interpretable, but will not report a cluster if it is nonunitary and thus not interpretable. After the scores are entered, the program converts all scores to a metric with a mean of 100 and a SD of 15. Then the program determines whether the arithmetic average of the scores is appropriate. The program will report one of three possible outcomes, when two subtest scores are entered into a Broad Ability/processing domain. These three outcomes are the same as those that are produced by the Cross-Battery Assessment (XBA) DMIA (Flanagan, Ortiz, & Alfonso, 2007, p. 95):

1. The program will calculate an average of two standard scores when the difference between them is less than 15 points. These clusters are considered unitary, and therefore interpretable.
2. The program will calculate an average of two standard scores when the difference between them is ≤ 15 points and both scores are within the same normative range (i.e., both scores are either < 85 or ≥ 85 and ≤ 115 or > 115). Although these clusters are nonunitary from a statistical significance standpoint, they are nonetheless interpretable from a clinical standpoint.
3. It will not calculate an average of two standard scores when the difference between them is ≥ 15 and the scores are within different normative ranges (e.g., one score is < 85 and one is ≥ 85). These clusters are both nonunitary and noninterpretable.

When three scores are entered under a Broad Ability on the CHC tab of the WIAT-III and KTEA-II DMIA, the program will report a cluster when it is unitary and thus interpretable, but will not report a cluster if it is nonunitary and thus not interpretable. However, with three scores it is also possible that two of the scores may form a unitary cluster, while the third score is an outlier. This additional outcome is also accounted for by the WIAT-III and KTEA-II DMIA. Specifically, with three subtests entered under a Broad Ability on the CHC tab, there are three instances in which a cluster will be calculated:[3]

1. If all three scores fall within the same normative range (i.e., all three scores are either < 85 or ≥85 and ≤115 or >115), then an average of the three scores is calculated.
2. If the magnitude of the difference between any score with any other scores is < 15, then an average of the three scores is calculated.
3. If one of the following three conditions is true, then the program will calculate a cluster based on the average of two scores, and will report the third score as an outlier. The following explanation from Flanagan, Ortiz, and Alfonso (2007, p. 98) explains these three conditions:
   a. The difference between standard scores for two tests is < 15 and the difference between the third score and both of these scores is ≥15.
   b. Two scores fall within the same normative range (< 85 or ≥85 and ≤115 or >115), and the third score differs from both of those scores by ≥15.
   c. The difference between Standard Score A (SSA) and Standard Score B (SSB) is < 15 and the difference between Standard Score C (SSC) and SSB is < 15 and the difference between SSA and SSC is ≥15, then SSB is averaged with either SSA or SSC, depending on the normative range in which the scores fall. For example, if SSA and SSB were within normal limits but SSC was Above Average, then SSA and SSB would be averaged and SSC would be reported as an outlier.

CLINICAL ANALYSIS OF THE INTEGRATION OF ACHIEVEMENT AND COGNITIVE TESTS

CHC theory and quantitative analyses (which can be conducted by using the WIAT-III and KTEA-II DMIA) provide valuable ways of integrating the WISC-IV with the WIAT-III and the KABC-II with the KTEA-II, but it is important to remember that (a) the KABC-II is built on and can be interpreted from a dual theoretical foundation (Luria's neuropsychological approach as well as CHC psychometric theory), (b) the WISC-IV can be interpreted from multiple theoretical perspectives (Flanagan & Kaufman, 2009), and (c) the

---

3. This procedure is the same as that which is conducted by the XBA DMIA (see Flanagan, Ortiz, and Alfonso, 2007, pp. 97–98).

WISC-IV, WIAT-III, KABC-II, and KTEA-II are individually administered, clinical instruments that afford examiners rich opportunities for qualitative observations. We cannot envision the examiner obtaining the full benefit of an analysis of the WISC-IV, WIAT-III, KABC-II, and KTEA-II without including the important *process and qualitative* information. This information comes from observing a child in a standardized setting that minimizes unnecessary interactions (e.g., wording in instructions) *and* maximizes opportunities to actively engage learning processes (e.g., dynamic subtests like Atlantis and Rebus) with the child.

This section on clinical analysis fully takes into account the neuropsychological processing model developed by Luria and addresses brain functions/processes involved in cognitive *and* achievement tests. For example, the Phonological Awareness test on the KTEA-II is a subtest that requires the child to remember and manipulate sounds and words. Similarly, on WIAT-III Early Reading Skills, the general content domains of Naming Letters, Letter-Sound Correspondence, Phonological Awareness, and Word Reading Comprehension are assessed. These two subtests are wonderful measures of auditory skills (*Ga*). However, the KTEA-II Phonological Processing subtest also taps working memory and cognitive sequencing. These latter skills are specifically measured by the KABC-II Sequential/*Gsm* scale and the WISC-IV WMI, indicating that a complete understanding of the young child's performance on KTEA-II Phonological Awareness or WIAT-III Early Reading Skills requires examiners to compare that performance to the child's success (or lack of it) on KABC-II Sequential/*Gsm* or WISC-IV WMI subtests.

It is not a coincidence that these kinds of tasks reflect years of research based on auditory/sequential skills and the phonemic awareness skills needed for reading (e.g., Hooper & Hynd, 1982; Kamphaus & Reynolds, 1987; Lichtenberger, Broadbooks, & Kaufman, 2000; Lichtenberger, 2001) and associated with left-hemispheric processing (James & Selz, 1997; Lyon, Fletcher, & Barnes, 2003; Reynolds, Kamphaus, Rosenthal, & Hiemenz, 1997).

For each section that follows, discussion emphasizes functional processing abilities that will hopefully help examiners with construct and skill analyses. Both the CHC and Luria theoretical approaches reflect an aspect of comprehensive assessment that needs to be buttressed by qualitative/process information. Furthermore, all cognitive and achievement test data must be interpreted in the context of other important information such as history, medical status, medications, family involvement, quality of teaching, developmental stage, social and emotional functioning, visual-motor functioning, and responses to prior interventions.

Sequential Processing, Short-Term Memory, Phonological Awareness, and Listening Comprehension

As indicated in Rapid Reference 4.12, we believe that WIAT-III Early Reading Skills and Listening Comprehension, and KTEA-II Phonological Awareness and Listening Comprehension are each dependent, to some extent, on the CHC *Gsm* Broad Ability. The process rationale for each subtest follows.

Process Rationale for WIAT-III Early Reading Skills and KTEA-III Phonological Awareness

It is important to understand both the Lurian and CHC ways of interpreting the Sequential/*Gsm* scale because there is a great deal of research literature that combines sequential processing and auditory short-term memory with the type of phonological processing skills that are measured by the KTEA-II Phonological Awareness subtest and the WIAT-III Early Reading Skills subtest (Siegal, 1997; Teeter, 1997). The combination of these phonological awareness tasks and the KABC-II Sequential/*Gsm* subtests or the WISC-IV WMI subtests provides a large window of opportunity for evaluating reading problems and the more phonologically based subtypes of learning disabilities (see the section of this chapter on "Specific Learning Disabilities").

As a primary measure of auditory short-term memory, the KABC-II Sequential/*Gsm* Core subtests and WISC-IV WMI core subtests help the examiner evaluate the critical listening skills that children need in the classroom. The phonological awareness tasks on the achievement tests measure sound-symbol connections, but because of the way they are designed, they also measure auditory short-term memory and sequencing skills. These are interactive tasks where the child has to listen very closely to the examiner and then reproduce sounds, and manipulate word syllables and sounds.

A skilled examiner can retrieve a lot of information by assessing behavioral clues about how well the child can remember sounds and use working memory. Does the child attempt to reproduce the sound? Does the child miss the examiner's cues and ask for repetitions? Is the child shy and too embarrassed to verbalize? Does the child get the sounds right but in the wrong order? When you move to a part of the phonological awareness tasks that needs working memory does the child's behavior shift dramatically? Does the child pay attention or do you have to cue each item?

The reading research literature indicates that many early reading problems stem from a learning disability subtype called "auditory-linguistic or phonological form of dyslexia" (Spreen, 2001; Teeter, 1997). This is not to say that visual and other processing deficits are not important subtypes of reading problems, but for the moment, let us explore the relationship between the processing and production of phonology in young readers.

Phonological processing is basically the ability to understand and use the sound components of language. The KTEA-II Phonological Awareness subtest and the WIAT-III Early Reading Skills subtest include five different activities that correspond to Adams' (1990) five levels of phonemic awareness tasks in ascending order of difficulty: rhyming, sound matching, blending, segmenting, and manipulating phonemes.

Phonological processing is closely related to problems in speech perception, naming and vocabulary ability, and auditory short-term memory with sounds. When phonological awareness deficits are present, reading comprehension suffers because the cognitive processes that are required for comprehension are tied up in decoding and word recognition (Stanovich, 1992). This leaves the child with a myopic focus on the elements of the text and little resources for fluid reading and comprehension.

Young children who have reading problems can be helped by evaluating their ability to understand the phonetic/linguistic parts of reading. If we know which parts are problematic, then we will be able to better describe interventions that are targeted to the child's specific deficit. There is evidence to support interventions in phonemic awareness with young elementary-aged children not only from an academic outcome perspective, but also from neuropsychological growth perspective in that neural networks that support reading can be enhanced with the appropriate instruction (Lyon, Fletcher, & Barnes, 2003).

As indicated, the WISC-IV and KABC-II scales that have an important part in the assessment of phonological awareness skills, especially in younger readers, are the WMI and Sequential/*Gsm* scales, respectively. The primary task of the WMI and Sequential/*Gsm* scales is to measure how the child processes information in a linear, step-by-step fashion. How a child performs on the WMI or Sequential/ *Gsm* scale can illuminate whether the child has the prerequisite auditory sequencing and short-term memory skills to be able to put sounds together with symbols while he or she is decoding a word (Das, Naglieri, & Kirby, 1994; Kirby & Williams, 1991; Naglieri, 2001).

Process Rationale for Listening Comprehension

The KTEA-II Listening Comprehension subtest and the Oral Discourse Comprehension portion of the WIAT-III Listening Comprehension subtest also support the WMI and Sequential/*Gsm* scales because they straddle auditory short-term memory, auditory working memory, and auditory long-term encoding. The tasks are presented in a pure auditory form and therefore should be compared with Phonological Awareness and the WMI and Sequential/*Gsm* Core subtests. Does the child remember well on Phonological Awareness with small, short-term auditory segments and then do very poorly on Listening Comprehension that requires a much higher auditory memory load? Or, the opposite, where the child does not do well with small, pure auditory segments but when the task is put in story form on Listening Comprehension the child performs quite well? Answers to these types of processing questions will help with differential diagnosis later on.

THE WISC-IV PRI AND PSI, KABC-II SIMULTANEOUS/*GV* SCALE AND WRITTEN EXPRESSION

You may wish to compare performance on the WISC-IV PRI and PSI scales and the KABC-II Simultaneous/*Gv* scale with achievement tasks that involve visual-motor ability. For example, examine the visual-motor aspects of KTEA-II Written Expression, WIAT-III Sentence Composition, WIAT-III Alphabet Writing Fluency, and WIAT-III Essay Composition and how they relate to some of the visual-motor activities on the WISC-IV subtests like Block Design, Symbol Search, and Coding or KABC-II subtests like Rover or Triangles. These comparisons may help you figure out why a child has poor handwriting or poor visual organization on writing tasks. Remember back to when you were administering the achievement tests that involved writing. Did you observe the child having trouble holding the pencil? Did the child lose his or her place a lot? Did the child write a lot of words or letters in a reversed way? Were there multiple erasures? Did the child have trouble figuring out where he or she should write the responses even though you were pointing to the correct starting point?

If you do suspect that achievement in writing is partly due to visual-motor issues then it would be appropriate to pursue this hypothesis further by administering tests designed specifically for assessing visual-motor problems. We believe that the WIAT-III subtests, Alphabet Writing Fluency, Sentence Composition, and Essay Composition, and the KTEA-II Written Expression are dependent, to some extent, on the CHC *Gv* Broad Ability (see Rapid Reference 4.13).

Planning, Reasoning, and Executive Functions

Rapid Reference 4.13 indicates that the *Gf* Narrow Abilities of Induction and General Sequential Reasoning (deduction) are measured by WISC-IV's Matrix Reasoning and the *Gf* Narrow Ability of General Sequential Reasoning (deduction) is measured by KABC-II's Rover. Other subtests (three WIAT-III subtests, KABC-II Rebus, four KTEA-II subtests) are mentioned in the "Note" to that Rapid Reference as being dependent, to some extent, on the *Gf* Broad Ability. The process rationale for each of these subtests follows.

Process Rationale for Matrix Reasoning

Matrix Reasoning requires the child to reason with nonverbal visual stimuli. The child must complete the missing portion of a 2 × 2 or 3 × 3 visual matrix by selecting one of five response choices. This subtest also requires secondary cognitive abilities, such as visual acuity, visual discrimination, visualization and working memory, and so on. It is important to first evaluate the role of secondary cognitive capacities to determine whether poor performance on Matrix Reasoning is the result of a weakness in (nonverbal) fluid reasoning.

When you are evaluating the Planning/*Gf* scale, consider the child's performance on Matrix Reasoning. Did the child talk through the Matrix Reasoning items, relying to some extent on verbal reasoning skills? Observe the child's eye movements when solving the problems: Does the child's approach appear systematic or random? Did the child carefully evaluate each problem before answering, or did the child appear to respond impulsively? How easily frustrated is the child? Is the child quick to give a "Don't Know" response? If you note executive function-type weaknesses during Matrix Reasoning, see if these weaknesses were evident on Picture Concepts as well. Make qualitative observations of the child's strategy use and approach to reasoning tasks and then administer other tests of executive functions to support or refute your hypotheses.

Process Rationale for Rover

Rover was designed to explore the child's ability to create numerous ways to solve a problem and then choose the best plan. Like the game of chess, however, Rover also has a visual-spatial component that is just as essential as planning ability to efficiently navigate the game board. When Rover was initially developed, it was intended as a measure of Planning/*Gf*. However, confirmatory factor analyses of National Tryout clearly pinpointed Rover as a measure of simultaneous and visual processing. Because the child has to look for different ways a dog can get to a bone on a map-like game board containing rocks, weeds, and grass, it is ultimately the child's visual mapping ability that plays the most important part in solving the problems.

Nonetheless, Rover was included in the KABC-II because regardless of its scale membership, the task presented an interesting challenge to children and adolescents, measures *both* *Gf* and *Gv* Narrow Abilities, and demands intact executive functions for success. If a child has poor planning or executive functions, performance on this subtest is severely impacted. Even though the child's visual-spatial mapping abilities lead the way, the child still has to figure out several plans, hold them in working memory, and then determine the value of the best plan. The latter is, most definitely, an executive functioning task.

Indeed, in a KABC-II study of 56 children with Attention Deficit/Hyperactivity Disorder (ADHD), a group that is notorious for having deficits in executive functions (Barkley, 2003), the ADHD children had significantly lower scores ($p < .001$) on Rover than their nonclinical peers (Kaufman & Kaufman, 2004a). They also had significantly lower scores on more pure measures of executive functions such as the Planning/*Gf* Pattern Reasoning and Story Completion subtests ($p < .01$).

When you are evaluating the Planning/*Gf* scale, therefore, consider the child's performance on Rover. Was the child organized? Did he/she take the time to look for all of the possible ways, or did he/she just blurt out the first answer? Also look at the style of processing. Did the child take time and think about the routes and then count out the final plan (reflective style), or did the child charge right in and then have to self-correct (impulsive style)? Rover can supplement the Planning/*Gf* scale by helping you look at the differences in subtest scores and including the processing and qualitative aspects of how the child obtained the scores. If you note executive function-type deficits during Rover, also see if these deficits were evident on Pattern Reasoning and Story Completion. Also, examine your qualitative observations of the child's strategy generation and then administer other tests of executive functions to test your hypotheses.

Process Rationale for Rebus

The CHC model places Rebus in the Narrow Ability category of Associative Memory (MA) because the examinee is required to learn the word associated with a particular rebus drawing and then read phrases and sentences composed of these drawings. Although Rebus primarily measures a *Glr* Narrow Ability it still requires a great deal of organization, not just retrieval.

Rebus also measures the process of how a child responds to the teaching/learning situation. Unlike with other subtests (except Atlantis), the child has to learn more and more information and then apply the information. It is similar to a classroom situation only it is strictly controlled and measurable because the examiner gives standardized teaching prompts. This is a subtest where the examiner feeds information and rehearsal to the child step-by-step. The examiner is constrained by only being able to teach in a standardized fashion; however, this constraint also frees the examiner to look at how the child responds to teaching.

This is a dynamic and controlled process and provides key qualitative data to the KABC-II examiner.

The reason why Rebus is considered to depend on *Gf* to some extent is because during administration the test demands executive functions to be at maximum alert. Many researchers (e.g., Goldberg & Bougakov, 2000) liken the executive functions to an orchestra conductor. The first and second functional areas of the brain, if you will, are the actual musicians in the orchestra all designed to play certain instruments at certain times. The orchestra conductor is the third functional area of the brain (frontal lobe area) that has to direct complex cognitive functions that require input, processing, prioritizing, organizing, planning, and output.

Rebus taxes the orchestra conductor because there are many first and second functional unit tasks like paying attention to each tiny word/picture, processing the visual information, processing the auditory information, melding the symbol and sound, only learning exactly what the examiner is teaching at paced intervals, organizing the reading of symbols and their sounds into coherent and meaningful sentences and checking for mistakes and comprehension. It takes quite a conductor to direct the Rebus symphony!

There are many qualitative or behavioral indicators during Rebus that can give the examiner clues as to problems with attention or executive functions. Many young children on Rebus will try very hard to learn the words and their matching symbols and then be completely oblivious to the fact that they are reading meaningful sentences. Therefore if they make a mistake on a word and the meaning of the sentence disappears they do not mentally register the lack of meaning, they simply just continue to read isolated symbols. On the other hand, children who do have developing executive or metacognitive functions will notice the break in comprehension and skip back to where they think they went wrong and try to figure out the mistaken symbol. This behavior is indicative of the orchestra conductor checking where lower functions went wrong, and it also makes for a difference in scores because the child self-corrects.

An alert examiner will know by the presence or absence of self-corrective behaviors if the child has problems with organization. A low score on Rebus could mean that there is a problem with transferring information from short/recent memory to long-term memory (as the *Glr* classification implies), but a low score could also mean that there is trouble with planning/executive functions. Hence, a comparison with the strong planning subtests like Pattern Reasoning and Story Completion is appropriate. Therefore, while Rebus factorially belongs on the *Glr*/Learning Scale of the KABC-II, it can also assist in the exploration of the child's fluid reasoning ability measured on the Planning/*Gf* scale.

Process Rationale for KTEA-II and WIAT-III subtests

There are three subtests on the WIAT-III and four subtests on the KTEA-II that require not only academic knowledge, but organizational, deductive, inductive, and planning skills: WIAT-III Listening Comprehension (Oral Discourse Comprehension component), Reading Comprehension, and Essay Composition, and KTEA-II Written Expression, Reading Comprehension, Oral Expression, and Listening Comprehension. These subtests all require "higher levels of cognition" (Sattler, 2001), "cognitive load" (Raney, 1993), or "higher-complex abilities" (Mather, Wendling, & Woodcock, 2001). Sattler and Mather et al. describe primary academic tasks in a hierarchy ranging from ones requiring low levels of cognition, such as letter identification, to those that require higher levels, such as reading comprehension and the construction of written text. Figure 4.3 illustrates the hierarchical relationship among achievement areas and subtests on the WIAT-III and KTEA-II Comprehensive Form with respect to their level of cognitive processing.

Informally interpreting these subtest scores alongside the subtests that truly measure *Gf* Narrow Abilities acknowledges that the more sophisticated skills needed for these upper-level academic tasks should be assessed in a cognitive processing way. Again, the skilled and observant examiner watches how the child takes these achievement tests and looks for behavioral clues to see if the child has the organization and planning skills to do a good job.

For example, during the WIAT-III or KTEA-II Reading Comprehension subtest, the child has to pick the best of several responses to answer the question about comprehension correctly. Watch for processing style here. Does the child read the passage quickly and impulsively pick an answer (impulsive, inattentive style), or does the child read the passage and then spend quite a bit of time

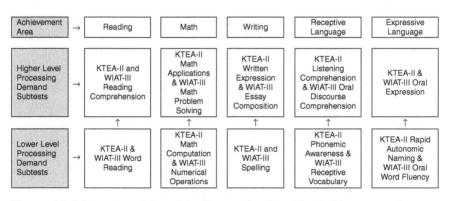

Achievement Area →	Reading	Math	Writing	Receptive Language	Expressive Language
Higher Level Processing Demand Subtests →	KTEA-II and WIAT-III Reading Comprehension	KTEA-II Math Applications & WIAT-III Math Problem Solving	KTEA-II Written Expression & WIAT-III Essay Composition	KTEA-II Listening Comprehension & WIAT-III Oral Discourse Comprehension	KTEA-II & WIAT-III Oral Expression
	↑	↑	↑	↑	↑
Lower Level Processing Demand Subtests →	KTEA-II & WIAT-III Word Reading	KTEA-II Math Computation & WIAT-III Numerical Operations	KTEA-II and WIAT-III Spelling	KTEA-II Phonemic Awareness & WIAT-III Receptive Vocabulary	KTEA-II Rapid Autonomic Naming & WIAT-III Oral Word Fluency

Figure 4.3 Hierarchy of Cognitive Processing Load by Achievement Area.

reading the possible answers and deliberating on the correctness of a response (reflective style)? Does the child have so many problems decoding the reading passage that they miss the overall story? Observe the child's eye movements. Does the child read from left to right with occasional loops back to check for comprehension (fluid movements), or do the child's eyes flicker back and forth, lose place, skip lines, or other nonfluid movements (poor eye tracking/nonfluid movements)? These types of observations can give valuable clues as to what factors bring about a low score on reading comprehension.

Comparing these kinds of observations with other subtests that require organization, executive functions, and fluid reasoning may give the examiner some keys as to why reading comprehension performance is problematic for a child. Perhaps the problem is not that the child does not know math facts, perhaps it is because he or she cannot *organize* the math facts to be able to apply them to a problem. If the child does have problems with organization and other *Gf* subtests, then the remediation plan calls for including prescriptions about organization (not necessarily drilling of math facts).

Similar observations need to be made by the examiner about WIAT-III Listening Comprehension (Oral Discourse Comprehension component) and Essay Composition and KTEA-II Written Expression, Oral Expression, and Listening Comprehension because all of these subtests require the child to have good *Gf* skills. The beauty of comparing these scores with subtests on the Planning/*Gf* scale is that the process of how a child utilizes upper-level cognitive skills to perform academic tasks is being compared, not just the concrete details that the teacher probably already knows about (e.g., reading and math levels).

There is also a quantitative method for examining the child's reasoning ability on the WIAT-III and KTEA-II via its Skills Analysis or Error Analysis procedures, respectively. WIAT-III Reading Comprehension and KTEA-II Reading Comprehension and Listening Comprehension deliberately include items that measure inferential thinking (*Gf*) as well as literal recall of facts. The items on each WIAT-III and KTEA-II subtest have been pre-classified as either "Literal" or "Inferential." The KTEA-II Error Analysis determines whether the child performed at a "Strong," "Average," or "Weak" level on each type of item (Kaufman & Kaufman, 2004b). Hence, if the child's category on the Inferential items of Reading Comprehension and/or Listening Comprehension is classified as "Weak" or "Strong," that classification can be used to corroborate other quantitative and qualitative data about the child's reasoning ability.

From a process point of view, information and data gleaned from the WIAT-III and KTEA-II "high-level" subtests can help the examiner look at how well the "orchestra conductor" organizes complex tasks and large bodies of information.

If you do suspect that the child might have executive function deficits, then it is appropriate to test further with tests that are specifically designed to measure this area. If you do not feel comfortable incorporating measures of executive functions into the Comprehensive Assessment, then a referral to a colleague who is familiar with these measures is an appropriate course of action.

Auditory Processing (Ga) and Several Auditory Tasks on the WISC-IV, KABC-II, WIAT-III, and KTEA-II

The Listening Comprehension subtest on both the WIAT-III and KTEA-II, the WIAT-III Sentence Repetition Portion of Oral Expression, two WISC-IV subtests (Digit Span, Letter-Number Sequencing), and three KABC-II subtests (Riddles, Number Recall, Word Order) are dependent, to some extent, on the CHC *Ga* Broad Ability (see Rapid Reference 4.17). The process rationale for these subtests follows.

Process Rationale for WIAT-III and KTEA-II Listening Comprehension, WIAT-III Sentence Repetition, WISC-IV Digit Span, WISC-IV Letter-Number Sequencing, KABC-II Riddles, KABC-II Number Recall, and KABC-II Word Order

These subtests do not measure the CHC defined auditory processing/*Ga* because they are more to do with auditory memory and the keeping of auditory input long enough to come up with an answer. The primary subtests that measure *Ga*—like KTEA-II Phonological Awareness and WIAT-III Early Reading Skills—are more concerned with the discrimination of sounds and with phonemic analysis and synthesis. Nonetheless, Listening Comprehension, WIAT-III Sentence Repetition, WISC-IV Digit Span, WISC-IV Letter-Number Sequencing, KABC-II Riddles, KABC-II Number Recall, and KABC-II Word Order still all use auditory input as the main processing vehicle and that, by nature, is serial and sequential. Because, most of these auditory processes take place in similar places in the brain, and have resultant brain-behavior similarities (e.g., language problems, reading problems) the examiner should make an effort to distinguish auditory memory from auditory discrimination. Both processes require different intervention strategies and have different influences on academic performance.

Listening Comprehension on both the WIAT-III and KTEA-II, in particular, is a supportive subtest for *Ga* because it measures the kind of listening comprehension that students must do in school—that is, comprehension of relatively formal speech, rather than casual or naturalistic speech. This would serve the purpose of enhancing the relevance of the test score to a school-based evaluation. The Listening Comprehension measures on the WIAT-III and KTEA-II also have a second, important design objective: To parallel the passage items of the respective Reading Comprehension subtests. The primary difference between the listening and reading comprehension subtests from each test is that the listening comprehension measure requires the student to listen to the passages on a CD and then answer questions spoken by the examiner. Because students perform similar tasks in Listening Comprehension and Reading Comprehension, a significantly lower score on the latter subtest may suggest the presence of a reading problem rather than a more general deficit in language development (Stanovich, 1992).

INTEGRATING COGNITIVE AND ACHIEVEMENT TESTS— QUALITATIVE/BEHAVIORAL ANALYSES

By comparing behavioral observations during both cognitive and achievement testing, you can see how a child behaviorally responds to different types of tests. (Qualitative Indicators [QIs] on the KTEA-II and the KABC-II are described in detail in the KABC-II and the KTEA-II manuals.) Examine the following scenarios to determine if there are any differences on performance for each battery.

Look for Differences with Affect and Motivation

Does the child enjoy the novel game-like activities on the WISC-IV or KABC-II but then become quiet, sullen, or bored on the WIAT-III or KTEA-II? Or vice versa? Does he act nervous and unsure on the WISC-IV or KABC-II but cheers up with familiar tasks on the WIAT-III or KTEA-II? Look for changes in behavior going from novel process tasks to familiar academic tasks.

Look for Differences with Self-Confidence

Does the child try hard on the WISC-IV or KABC-II subtests and knows when she performed well? Does she verbalize self-confidence with statements like "I'm good at this!" "This is easy!" Do these self-confident statements reach over into the WIAT-III or KTEA-II test performance? Or does she falter, say self-deprecating statements, or act unsure? Look for changes in behavior (verbalization about the self) when tasks change from process oriented to academic.

Look for Differences Between Modalities

Some children have specific and preferred processing styles. Many times their behavior will reflect these visual, auditory, haptic, and verbal strengths and weaknesses. Look for changes in behavior when the modality of the task changes. Does he pay attention better when he has tasks that are visual and gets fidgety when the tasks are auditory with no visual stimulus? Does he chatter on verbal subtests and act unsure on visual-spatial tasks?

Look for Differences in Behavior with Cognitive Load

Both the WISC-IV and the KABC-II change cognitive load from subtest to subtest and especially from basal to ceiling items on each subtest. The WIAT-III and KTEA-II each have four or five specific subtests that have a higher cognitive load because they require complex skills (see Figure 4.3). Look for changes in behavior when the load level changes or items go from easy to difficult. Does she do well on simple tasks and then get confused on ones where she has to organize? What strategies does she employ on both batteries when she starts to approach ceiling items? Gives up? Gets impulsive? Acts like it is an enjoyable challenge? Gets frustrated, angry, or oppositional?

Look for How the Child Responds When You Teach on the Learning Scale of the KABC-II and Interactive Subtests on the KTEA-II and WIAT-III

Note any changes in behavior when you administer the Atlantis and Rebus subtests on the KABC-II. These subtests are different from the other subtests because they are interactive and the examiner basically teaches the child each item and then requests retrieval of the information. It is important to note how a child responds to the interactive and regimented pace. Atlantis and Rebus are dynamic subtests where there is a more intense social dependency between the examiner and the examinee and the behaviors and social strategies that the child uses in this type of teaching/learning arrangement are valuable information.

You may also want to compare the behavioral observations from tasks that involve actively engaging with the examiner such as on Reading Comprehension, Sentence Composition, Early Reading Skills, Listening Comprehension, and Oral Expression from the WIAT-III, and Written Expression, Phonological Awareness, Listening Comprehension, and Oral Expression subtests from the KTEA-II. They also are interactive subtests where the examiner engages the child throughout the test. Does the child enjoy engaging with you? Is the child nervous about being so interactive with you? Does the child act dependent and need you to lead them? Or is the child defiant, impatient, or oppositional? It would be interesting to mention these types of behaviors to the child's teacher and see if the child's responses are similar in the classroom.

Qualitative observations need to be supported by other data. If you observe behaviors that you believe are disruptive and that hurt the child's performance on the WISC-IV, KABC-II, WIAT-III, or the KTEA-II, check your observations out with staff and teachers to see if these types of behaviors are present in other settings and not just the testing situation. Also, look at the scores for these subtests. If you believe that the behaviors lowered the child's scores, then interventions for those behaviors may help the child perform better in the classroom. Remember, qualitative observations are not just about negative behaviors. Qualitative observations can provide us with valuable information about how a child gets around a disability or weakness. Watching how a child naturally compensates for learning or behavioral deficits is very valuable information, and it should be included in any prescriptive recommendations.

INTEGRATING COGNITIVE AND ACHIEVEMENT TESTS— PROCEDURAL OPTIONS

There are many ways to integrate the results of the WISC-IV with the WIAT-III and the KABC-II with the KTEA-II. At this point in time, there is no definitive method of integrating the results of the two batteries because it may take years of research to define the "best" approach. Even then, no single approach will match the needs of all examiners. Each examiner brings a wealth of experience, internal norms, and beliefs to the use of these tests. Additionally, every examiner has areas of diagnostic specialties and special populations with whom he or she works, and different needs and wants.

The quantitative and qualitative approaches described for integrating the results of cognitive and achievement tests in this chapter have been varied in theoretical foundations, procedural complexity, and utility. It is a good idea for you to look over the different methods that have been offered and decide which work best for you. It is important, and best practice, to incorporate different interpretative systems for different circumstances.

SPECIFIC LEARNING DISABILITIES

To introduce this section on specific learning disabilities (SLD), we give a brief summary of the controversy that has surrounded the use of achievement-ability discrepancies in the diagnosis of learning disabilities, and discuss how that controversy led to legislation that changed the requirements for diagnosis (i.e., PL 108-446). This section also reviews the available research on the WIAT-II and KTEA-II in samples of children with SLD. We specifically examine three types of disability: Reading, Math, and Written Expression.

Controversy Surrounding Cognitive-Achievement Differences in the Diagnosis of Specific Learning Disabilities

The WIAT-III and KTEA-II are frequently used in the process of diagnosing learning disabilities to examine individual achievement and to compare achievement with cognitive ability. The requirements for diagnosing specific learning disabilities (SLD) have been hotly debated in recent years (Kaufman & Kaufman, 2001). Many researchers and clinicians have put forth strong arguments against the use of achievement-ability discrepancies as criteria for determining SLD (Beninger, Dunn, & Alper, 2005; Flanagan et al., 2002; Siegel, 1999; Stanovich, 1999; Vellutino et al., 2000). Now, as has been mentioned throughout this book, 2004 changes to the Individuals with Disabilities Education Act (e.g., PL 108-446) formerly eliminated an achievement-ability discrepancy as a necessary part of determining SLD (Rapid Reference 4.19 lists where more information can be found on PL 108-446). Thus,

---

≡ Rapid Reference 4.19

Resources for the Individuals with Disabilities Education Improvement Act of 2004 (PL 108-446)

National Association of School Psychologists
http://www.nasponline.org/advocacy/IDEAinformation.html

National Center for Learning Disabilities
http://www.ld.org/advocacy/IDEAwatch.cfm

Council for Exceptional Children (CEC): Public Policy and Legislative Information
http://www.cec.sped.org/pp/

Learning Disabilities Association of America
http://www.ldanatl.org/

Council for Exceptional Children (CEC): Summary of Significant Issues in the New IDEA
http://www.cec.sped.org/pp/IDEA_120204.pdf

National Association of State Directors of Special Education (NASDSE) IDEA Side-by-Side: A Comparison of Current Law to the Individuals with Disabilities Education Improvement Act of 2004
http://www.nasdse.org/

Wrights Law: IDEA 2004 Changes in Key Statutes
http://www.wrightslaw.com/law/idea/index.htm

Read the Final IDEA Bill Posted on the Web Site of the Committee for Education and the Workforce
http://edworkforce.house.gov/issues/108th/education/idea/conferencereport/confrept.htm

assessment professionals (depending on how state and local educational authorities decide to implement PL 108-446) no longer need to utilize a rigid discrepancy formula including scores from tests such as the WIAT-III and KTEA-II in conjunction with IQ scores. Rather, WIAT-III and KTEA-II scores may be used as mechanism to determine interindividual academic abilities, and to evaluate how academic deficits are related to or caused by deficits in basic cognitive processes. Procedures for diagnosing SLD without using an achievement-ability discrepancy have been articulated by Berninger and colleagues (Berninger, Dunn, & Alper, 2005; Berninger & O'Donnell, 2005) and Flanagan and colleagues (Flanagan, Ortiz, Alfonso, & Mascolo, 2002; Flanagan, Ortiz, & Alfonso, 2007).

In the following sections, we describe research on specific learning disabilities in the areas of reading, mathematics, and written expression that utilizes the WIAT-III (or WIAT) and the KTEA-II and their conormed tests. For the KTEA-II and KABC-II studies described next, the subjects were diagnosed with learning disabilities based upon a severe discrepancy between performance on an achievement measure and a measure of intellectual ability (the most prevalent definition of a learning disability at the time that the research took place). For the WIAT-III studies described, the students were previously classified as having a specific learning disability, and the classification was verified by evaluating recent test scores. Students were classified based upon meeting either traditional ability-achievement discrepancy criteria and/or inter-achievement discrepancy criteria.

Reading Disability

KTEA-II Study

A sample of 134 students ages 6 to 18 with learning disabilities in reading were administered the KTEA-II Comprehensive Form (mean age 13:1) (Kaufman & Kaufman, 2004a). The scores of these students were compared to those of a nonclinical reference group that was matched on gender, ethnicity, and parent education. Compared to the nonclinical reference group, scores on all KTEA-II subtests and composites were significantly lower ($p < .001$) for the sample with Reading Disabilities. The KTEA-II domain composite scores ranged from highs of 87.1 and 85.0 on the Oral Fluency Composite and Oral Language Composite, respectively, to lows of 76.7 and 76.9 on the Decoding Composite and the Reading Composite, respectively. The mean scores for Written Language, Sound-Symbol, and Reading Fluency Composite were at a level comparable (i.e., about one point different) to the low scores on the Reading Composite and Decoding Composite. Thus, predictably, scores directly measuring reading skill and those related to the fluency of reading as well as phonological awareness (e.g., Sound-Symbol) show the most impairment in the Reading Disability sample. In contrast, scores in the Average range of academic ability on the Oral Language and Oral Fluency Composite (albeit in the lower end of Average) indicate that oral language skills were an area of relative integrity for the Reading Disability sample. Rapid Reference 4.20 shows the scores for this sample on all KTEA-II subtests and composites (as well as other SLD samples).

KABC-II Study

How does the pattern of scores on the KTEA-II compare with those from the conormed KABC-II for children with Reading Disabilities? A sample of 141 students ages 6–18 (M = 13:2 years) with documented Reading Disabilities were administered the KABC-II, and the data were compared to a matched, non-clinical reference group (Kaufman & Kaufman, 2004b). Similar to the results on the KTEA-II, scores on all KABC-II subtests and composites were significantly lower for children with Reading Disabilities than for the nonclinical reference group (all differences were $p < .001$). The Reading Disability sample's mean scores on the Sequential/*Gsm*, Learning/*Glr*, and Knowledge/*Gc* scales bordered between the Below Average and Average classifications (see Rapid Reference 4.21). The largest difference between the nonclinical group and the reading disability group was found on the Learning/*Glr* scale (with a 1 SD difference between the mean scores). Kaufman, Lichtenberger, Fletcher-Janzen, and Kaufman (2005) provide an explanation for this low score in SLD samples:

> The Learning/*Glr* scale is a demanding scale because it requires that all of the cognitive processes work together. Children must use sequential abilities to listen and organize information in a serial manner and learn in a step-by-step fashion; they must use simultaneous processing to look, organize, and remember visual information; and they must use planning abilities to prioritize information processing. The whole process utilized for the Learning/*Glr* scale is very much like a functional symphony where the first and second functional units of the brain (measured by the Sequential/*Gsm* and Simultaneous/*Gv* scales) must interact and take direction and sustain interest from the third functional unit (measured by the Planning/*Gf* scale). A disability in any of these areas can affect scores on the respective scales, but may also affect the performance on the Learning/*Glr* scale where it all has to come together. (pp. 213–214)

WIAT-III Study

A sample of 108 individuals in grades 2–12, aged 7–19 (*M* = 12:1 years), diagnosed with learning disability in reading (LD-R) were administered the WIAT-III (*WIAT-III Technical Manual*, 2009). Their performance was compared to a non-LD control group matched based on sex, age and grade/semester, ethnicity/race, parent education level, and geographic region. Rapid Reference 4.22 reports the mean performance of the

≡ Rapid Reference 4.20

....

KTEA-II Scores for Students with Specific Learning Disabilities

KTEA-II Subtest or Composite	Reading Disability Mean (N = 134)	Math Disability Mean (N = 93)	Writing Disability Mean (N = 119)
Letter & Word Recognition	76.8	76.8	77.2
Reading Comprehension	80.4	79.7	80.8
Reading Composite	**76.9**	**76.8**	**77.4**
Math Concepts & Applications	82.3	78.1	82.5
Math Computation	82.9	79.1	82.3
Mathematics Composite	**81.2**	**77.2**	**81.1**
Written Expression	80.2	78.8	80.0
Spelling	76.9	77.4	76.9
Written Language Composite	**77.5**	**77.2**	**77.5**
Listening Comprehension	89.1	86.4	88.7
Oral Expression	85.2	83.5	85.0
Oral Language Composite	**85.0**	**82.6**	**84.7**
Phonological Awareness	82.8	81.7	82.4
Nonsense Word Decoding	78.9	78.8	79.3
Sound-Symbol Composite	**77.9**	**77.9**	**78.5**
Word Recognition Fluency	77.1	77.1	77.2
Decoding Fluency	78.0	78.5	78.1
Reading Fluency Composite	**77.4**	**77.7**	**77.5**
Decoding Composite	**76.7**	**76.8**	**77.3**
Associational Fluency	90.3	88.0	91.0
Naming Facility (RAN)	88.3	87.8	89.4
Oral Fluency Composite	**87.1**	**85.7**	**88.2**
Comprehensive Achievement	**78.4**	**76.1**	**78.3**

Note: All KTEA-II data on Specific Learning Disabilities (SLD) are from the *KTEA-II Comprehensive Form Manual* (Kaufman & Kaufman, 2004a); Reading Disability data are from Table 7.29, Math Disability data are from Table 7.30, and Writing Disability data are from Table 7.31. All scores from the groups with SLD are significantly lower ($p < 0.001$) than those of the nonclinical reference comparison groups.

≡ Rapid Reference 4.21

Mean KABC-II Index Scores for Children with Reading Disabilities

KABC-II Scale	Reading Disability Mean (N = 141)
Sequential/Gsm	85.4
Simultaneous/Gv	88.1
Learning/Glr	84.3
Planning/Gf	86.8
Knowledge/Gc	84.8
MPI	82.6
FCI	82.2

Source: Adapted from Kaufman and Kaufman (2004a, Table 8.31).

≡ Rapid Reference 4.22

WIAT-III Mean Scores for Students in Grades 2–12 with Specific Learning Disabilities

WIAT-III Subtest or Composite	Reading Disability Mean (N = 108)	Math Disability Mean (N = 90)	Writing Disability Mean (N = 86)
Subtests			
Listening Comprehension	89.1	91.0	93.9
Early Reading Skills	81.6	93.8*	89.2*
Reading Comprehension	83.7	92.5	86.0
Math Problem Solving	86.6	80.5	88.9
Alphabet Writing Fluency	92.6*	85.9	92.6*
Sentence Composition	85.6	87.8	84.2
Word Reading	75.7	87.8	77.3
Essay Composition	92.5	92.2	88.9

(continued)

WIAT-III Subtest or Composite	Reading Disability Mean (N = 108)	Math Disability Mean (N = 90)	Writing Disability Mean (N = 86)
Essay Composition: Grammar and Mechanics[a]	87.2	89.5	82.3
Pseudoword Decoding	78.1	89.0	80.2
Numerical Operations	89.7	82.4	88.9
Oral Expression	88.0	90.5*	89.5
Oral Reading Fluency	77.5	93.0*	80.2
Oral Reading Accuracy[a]	76.8	91.6*	79.0
Oral Reading Rate[a]	77.4	93.7	80.4
Spelling	80.3	85.9	78.3
Math Fluency—Addition	87.4	84.1	87.9
Math Fluency—Subtraction	87.5	81.6	87.3
Math Fluency—Multiplication	87.8	85.0	85.9
Composites			
Oral Language	86.9	89.6	90.4
Total Reading	76.0	89.2	78.5
Basic Reading	76.7	88.0	78.5
Reading Comprehension and Fluency	77.4	91.3	80.5
Written Expression	83.2	86.2	80.7
Mathematics	87.3	80.6	88.1
Math Fluency	86.4	82.4	86.1
Total Achievement	79.5	85.6	81.5

Note: With the exception of the scores with asterisks (*) beside them, all scores from the groups with SLD are significantly lower ($p < 0.01$) that those of the nonclinical reference comparison groups.

Source: All WIAT-III data are from Tables 3.15–3.17 of the WIAT-III Technical Manual, Wechsler Individual Achievement Test, Third Edition (WIAT-III). Copyright © 2009 by NCS Pearson, Inc. Reproduced with permission. All rights reserved. "Wechsler Individual Achievement Test" and "WIAT" are trademarks, in the United States and/or other countries, of Pearson Education, Inc., or its affiliate(s).
[a] Supplemental scores.

two groups. The LD-R group scored significantly lower than the control group ($p <$ .01) on every subtest and composite with the exception of the Alphabet Writing Fluency subtest. The lowest mean scores for the LD group were on the reading subtests (i.e., $M = 75.7$ on Word Reading; $M = 83.7$ on Reading Comprehension;

$M = 78.1$ on Pseudoword Decoding; and 77.5 on Oral Reading Fluency). The highest scores for the LD-R group were on Alphabet Writing Fluency ($M = 92.6$) and Essay Composition ($M = 92.5$). At the composite level, the low score for the LD-R group was in Total Reading ($M = 76.0$), Basic Reading ($M = 76.7$), and Reading Comprehension and Fluency ($M = 77.4$) compared to the non-LD sample ($M = 98.8$, 99.2, 98.9, respectively). The next lowest composite score for the LD-R group was Written Expression ($M = 83.2$) in comparison to the control sample ($M = 100.4$). This is not surprising given that approximately 10 percent of the LD-R students had a co-morbid diagnosis of Disorder of Written Expression. Individuals with reading disorders presented a distinct pattern of scores and overall performance on WIAT-III.

WISC-IV Study

The WISC-IV was administered to 56 children aged 7–13 years who were identified as LD-R according to *DSM-IV-TR* criteria. Rapid Reference 4.23 (from Table 5.25 of the *WISC-IV Integrated Technical and Interpretive Manual* [2004]) reports the means, standard deviations of the WISC-IV subtest, process, and composite scores for the LD-R and a matched control group. When compared to the control group, children with LD-R obtained significantly lower mean scores for all composites, with large effect sizes for the VCI, WMI, and FSIQ. The largest effect size was for WMI. This finding is consistent with research that indicates a relationship between reading achievement and working memory (Swanson & Howell, 2001).

In the WISC-IV LD-R studies, students identified with learning disabilities in reading showed a pattern of lower Working Memory Index and Full Scale IQ scores on the cognitive measure, and a lower Word Reading, Pseudoword Decoding, and Reading Comprehension scores on the WIAT-II when compared to their matching control groups. Further, the WISC-IV study reports significantly lower scores (with large effect sizes) on the Vocabulary, Information, Arithmetic, and Letter-Number Sequencing subtests for the LD-R sample. The lower scores on Vocabulary and Information may reflect, in part, a deficiency in the general fund of information that is usually acquired through reading. The lower scores on Arithmetic and Letter-Number Sequencing suggest the role working memory may play in reading disorders.

The WISC-IV Integrated and the WIAT-II were administered to 102 children aged 7–13 years who were diagnosed with Reading Disorder according to *DSM-IV-TR* criteria. Students with concurrent diagnosis of other learning disorders (i. e., Math LD or Writing LD) were not excluded from the study. Mean scores on the WISC-IV for students with Reading Disorder ranged from 94.7 on the Perceptual Reasoning Index to 88.1 on the Working Memory Index. This Reading Disorder sample's pattern of WIAT-II scores was similar to that

≡ Rapid Reference 4.23

Mean WISC-IV Performance of Reading Disorder and Matched Control Groups

Subtest/ Process Score/ Composite	Reading Disorder		Matched Control Group			Group Mean Comparison			Standard Difference[a]
	Mean	SD	Mean	SD	N	Difference	t value	p value	
BD	9.0	2.4	9.6	2.2	56	.54	1.32	.19	.24
SI	8.8	2.4	10.1	2.4	56	1.34	3.03	<.01	.57
DS	8.0	2.6	9.8	2.5	55	1.80	3.64	<.01	.70
PCn	9.3	2.8	10.1	2.2	56	.73	1.63	.10	.29
CD	8.2	2.5	9.4	2.5	56	1.23	2.47	.02	.49
VC	8.2	2.0	10.4	2.1	56	2.21	6.18	<.01	1.08
LN	7.7	3.3	10.4	2.4	55	2.67	4.64	<.01	.93
MR	8.9	2.2	10.0	2.1	56	1.16	2.71	.01	.54
CO	8.9	2.0	10.2	2.5	55	1.36	3.09	<.01	.61
SS	9.2	2.6	10.1	2.2	56	.91	2.01	.05	.38

PCm	8.9	2.7	10.4	2.5	56	1.52	3.41	<.01	.59
CA	10.1	3.3	9.7	2.8	56	-.43	-.78	.44	-.14
IN	8.2	2.2	10.5	2.2	56	2.25	5.32	<.01	1.01
AR	7.7	1.9	9.9	2.9	35	2.26	4.10	<.01	.92
WR	8.9	2.1	10.1	2.7	56	1.25	2.75	.01	.52
BDN	9.1	2.6	9.6	2.4	56	.50	1.08	.29	.20
DSF	8.4	2.9	9.8	2.7	55	1.40	2.67	.01	.51
DSB	8.5	2.6	9.8	2.5	56	1.38	2.84	.01	.54
CAR	10.3	3.0	9.7	2.7	56	-.68	-1.26	.21	-.24
CAS	9.6	3.3	9.5	2.8	56	-.14	-.29	.77	-.05
VCI	91.9	9.7	100.9	10.6	55	9.00	4.84	<.01	.89
PRI	94.4	11.2	99.3	9.2	56	4.91	2.96	<.01	.48
WMI	87.0	12.9	99.8	10.3	54	12.81	5.62	<.01	1.10
PSI	92.5	11.7	98.6	11.7	56	6.16	2.69	.01	.53
FSIQ	89.1	10.3	99.9	9.7	53	10.79	6.01	<.01	1.08

[a]The Standard Difference is the difference of the two test means divided by the square root of the pooled variance, computed using Cohen's (1996) Formula 10.4.

≡ Rapid Reference 4.24

Correlations between WIAT-II and WISC-IV Integrated Composite Scores for a Reading Disorder Group

WISC-IV Composite	WIAT-II Composite				
	Reading	Mathematics	Written Language	Oral Language	Total Achievement
VCI	.47	.51	.37	.44	.51
PRI	.29	.40	.27	.26	.38
WMI	.30	.35	.15	.23	.31
PSI	.22	.35	.16	.24	.29
FSIQ	.48	.61	.37	.41	.56

Note: Adapted from Table G.1 of the WISC-IV Integrated Technical and Interpretive Manual (Wechsler et al., 2004). VCI = Verbal Comprehension Index; PRI = Perceptual Reasoning Index; WMI = Working Memory Index; FSIQ = Full Scale IQ; N = 102.

reported in the *WIAT-II Manual* (discussed previously). The four lowest mean scores for the WIAT-II were Word Reading (79.5), Spelling (81.7), Pseudoword Decoding (82.8), and Reading Comprehension (83.4). The highest subtest score was a 95.2 on Listening Comprehension. Rapid Reference 4.24 and 4.25 highlight important correlation coefficients for this study. Relative to other index scores, the VCI showed higher correlations with the WIAT-II reading scores (Reading Comprehension .43; Word Reading .41; and Pseudoword Decoding .34). The WMI correlated at the same magnitude as VCI with Reading Comprehension (.43), while there was minimal correlation between WMI and Word Reading (.16) and WMI and Pseudoword Decoding (.13). The PSI showed almost no correlation with WIAT-II reading subtests. One factor that should be considered in light of the low correlation between PSI and the reading subtests is that reading speed and automaticity are not reflected in the subtest scores of the WIAT-II. Instead they are reported in the qualitative observations that should be referenced when a low PSI score is reported. Correlations between the scaled process scores and the WIAT-II composites are higher in the Verbal domain than in the Perceptual and Processing Speed domains. Several of the scaled process scores in the Working Memory domain correlated with Reading Comprehension, including Digit Span Backward, Spatial Span Backward, and the process scores for the arithmetic subtests. These results are consistent with research that suggests

≡ *Rapid Reference 4.25*

Correlations between WIAT-III Subtests and WISC-IV Integrated Composite Score Composites for a Reading Disorder Group

WIAT-II Subtest	VCI	PRI	WMI	PSI	FSIQ
	|___ WISC-IV Integrated Composite ___|				
Word Reading	.41	.16	.16	.12	.34
Reading Comprehension	.43	.32	.43	.25	.51
Pseudoword Decoding	.34	.22	.13	.14	.33
Math Reasoning	.57	.40	.36	.28	.62
Numerical Operations	.38	.34	.29	.38	.52
Spelling	.26	.17	.06	.08	.25
Written Expression	.39	.28	.21	.21	.40
Listening Comprehension	.49	.42	.19	.23	.48
Oral Expression	.27	.08	.20	.19	.26

Note: Adapted from Table G.1 of the *WISC-IV Integrated Technical and Interpretive Manual* (Wechsler, 2004). VCI = Verbal Comprehension Index; PRI = Perceptual Reasoning Index; WMI = Working Memory Index; FSIQ = Full Scale IQ; N = 102, except Written Expression, where N = 96.

children with Reading Disorder have difficulty on verbally mediated tasks and measures of working memory (Stanovich & Siegel, 1994; Wolf & Bowers, 1999).

Math Disability

KTEA-II Study
A sample of 93 students ages 6 to 18 years with learning disabilities in reading were administered the KTEA-II Comprehensive Form (mean age 13:6) (Kaufman & Kaufman, 2004a). Similar to the KTEA-II studies on other SLD, the scores of these students were compared to those of a nonclinical reference group that was controlled for gender, ethnicity, and parent education. Compared to the nonclinical reference group, scores on all KTEA-II subtests and composites were significantly lower ($p < .001$) for the sample with Math Disabilities. An important characteristic to note about this Math Disability sample was that 81 percent had comorbid Reading Disabilities, which contributed to deficits in achievement domains such as reading and writing. Thus, the overall pattern of KTEA-II scores for the Math

Disability sample was similar to that of the Reading Disability Sample, with a notably lower score on the Mathematics Composite for the Math Disability sample (see Rapid Reference 4.20). The lowest average KTEA-II domain composite scores for the Math Disability sample were on the Decoding and Reading Composites (both 76.8) and the Mathematics and Written Language Composites (both 77.2). These low scores were closely followed by standard scores for the Reading Fluency (77.7) and Sound-Symbol (77.9) composites. In the Average range of academic ability was the Oral Fluency Composite (85.7). Rapid Reference 4.20 lists the Math Disability sample's average KTEA-II scores.

KABC-II Study

How do scores on the KTEA-II of children with mathematics disabilities compare with conormed measures of cognitive ability? A sample of 96 students ages 6 to 18 ($M = 13:7$ years) with learning disabilities in mathematics were administered the KABC-II. Like in the Reading Disability sample, all scales were significantly lower for the group with mathematics disabilities than in the matched control group. The nonclinical reference group's average standard score for all scales was about 1 SD higher than that of the Mathematics Disability group. The greatest standard score difference between the mathematics disability group and the clinical reference group (about 16 points) was on the Planning/*Gf* scale (see Rapid Reference 4.26).

≡ Rapid Reference 4.26

Mean KABC-II Index Scores for children with Mathematics Disorders

KABC-II Scale	Math Disability Mean (N = 96)
Sequential/Gsm	83.7
Simultaneous/Gv	84.6
Learning/Glr	83.7
Planning/Gf	82.7
Knowledge/Gc	82.0
MPI	79.8
FCI	79.3

Note: Adapted from Kaufman and Kaufman (2004a, Table 8.32).

Other studies have found that children with mathematics disabilities can be helped by implementing remediation strategies related to planning and fluid reasoning. Examples of such interventions include using meta cognitive approaches, teaching problem-solving rules, and planning solutions to mathematical problems with step-by-step problem solving (Rourke, 1989; Teeter & Semrud-Clikeman, 1998).

WIAT-III Study

WIAT-III was administered to a sample of 90 students in grades 2–12, aged 7–19 ($M = 12{:}8$ years), diagnosed with a learning disability in mathematics. Approximately 9 percent of these students had a comorbid diagnosis of reading disability, which contributed to significant weaknesses in reading and writing subtests as well. Performance was compared to a matched control group (based on sex, age and grade/semester, ethnicity/race, parent education level, and geographic region). The lowest mean scores for the LD group were on the mathematics subtests: $M = 80.5$ on Math Problem Solving; $M = 82.4$ on Numerical Operations; $M = 84.1$ on Math Fluency—Addition; $M = 81.6$ on Math Fluency—Subtraction; and $M = 85.0$ on Math Fluency—Multiplication. At the composite level, the lowest scores for the LD group were Mathematics ($M = 80.6$) and Math Fluency ($M = 82.4$) compared to the non-LD sample ($M = 99.5$ and 100.1, respectively). These results suggest that the WIAT-III may be useful in identifying achievement weaknesses among individuals with learning disabilities in the area of mathematics. Rapid Reference 4.22 lists the Math Disability sample's average WIAT-III scores.

WISC-IV Study

WISC-IV Integrated and WIAT-II were administered to 28 children aged 8–13 years, who were diagnosed with Mathematics Disorder according to *DSM-IV-TR* criteria. Means, standard deviations, and correlation coefficients are reported in Table G.2 of the *WISC-IV Integrated Technical and Interpretive Manual* (Wechsler et al., 2004). Among the WISC-IV Integrated index scores, the VCI and PSI exhibited the highest correlations with the WIAT-II Mathematics Composite (.50 and .56, respectively) as expected. A number of moderate to high correlations are found between WIAT-II math subtest scores and the Arithmetic process scores of the WISC-IV Integrated. The highest correlations are reported between Written Arithmetic and Numerical Operations (.60) and between Written Arithmetic and Mathematics Composite (.60). Given the small sample size of this study, additional research with children diagnosed with learning disability in math is warranted.

Writing Disability

KTEA-II Study

A sample of 119 students ages 6–18 (mean age 13:3 years) with Written Expression Disabilities were administered the KTEA-II along with a matched-sample of students with no noted disability. All KTEA-II scores for the sample with Written Expression Disabilities were significantly lower ($p < .001$) than the nonclinical reference group. Most scores were in the Below Average range, with the lowest scores for the Written Expression Disability sample on the Written Language, Decoding, Reading, Reading Fluency, and Sound-Symbol Composites (all standard scores between 77–78). Though slightly higher, the Mathematics Composite was also in the Below Average range (81.1). Similar to the Reading Disability and Math Disability samples, the oral language skills of this sample with Written Expression Disabilities appeared to be the least affected of all the domains, with average standard scores ranging from 84.7 on the Oral Language Composite to 88.2 on the Oral Fluency Composite.

KABC-II Study

How do scores on the KTEA-II of children with writing disabilities compare with conormed measures of cognitive ability? A sample of 122 students ages 6 to 18 ($M = 13:3$ years) with disorders in the area of written expression were administered the KABC-II. The results of this study were very similar to the results of the sample with reading disabilities, which is not surprising given that about one third of the students with written expression disabilities also had reading disabilities. On all KABC-II scales, the group with writing disabilities scored significantly worse than the nonclinical reference group (which was a sample matched on gender, race, and parent education). The range of mean scores across the KABC-II scales was small (only about 4 points). The lowest index for the writing disability sample was on the Learning/*Glr* scale (see Rapid Reference 4.27). Kaufman, Lichtenberger, Fletcher-Janzen, and Kaufman (2005) provide some insight on why this score may be depressed in children with writing disabilities:

> Written expression does place a large [cognitive] demand on examinees, not only in terms of integrating all levels of information, but also in terms of rapidly changing thoughts and ideas as the material develops. This type of activity stretches every cognitive functional system, and perhaps the Learning/*Glr* scale suffers the most when a child has problems with overall sequential, simultaneous, and planning activities. Indeed, it follows that the evidence-based intervention techniques that work best for children

≣ Rapid Reference 4.27

Mean KABC-II Index Scores for Children with Writing Disabilities

KABC-II Scale	Writing Disability Mean (N = 122)
Sequential/Gsm	84.6
Simultaneous/Gv	87.7
Learning/Glr	83.9
Planning/Gf	86.8
Knowledge/Gc	85.2
MPI	82.1
FCI	82.0

Note: Adapted from Kaufman and Kaufman (2004a, Table 8.33).

with written expression deficits are those that are based on cognitive and metacognitive strategies. (p. 219)

WIAT-III Study

A sample of 86 students in grades 2–12, ages 7–19 ($M = 12:2$ years), diagnosed with a learning disability in the area of written expression were administered the WIAT-III. Performance was compared to a matched control group (based on sex, age and grade/semester, ethnicity/race, parent education level, and geographic region). Approximately 18 percent of the LD students were also identified with a comorbid diagnosis of Reading Disorder, contributing to weaknesses on reading-related subtests. Performance of the LD group was significantly different ($< .01$) from the matched control group on the Sentence Composition, Essay Composition, and Spelling subtests as well as on the Written Expression composite. Specifically, the mean scores of the LD group on Sentence Composition, Essay Composition, and Spelling were 84.2, 88.9, and 78.3, respectively, compared to a mean of 98.7, 98.4, and 99.6, respectively, in the control group. The Written Expression Composite score for the LD group ($M = 80.7$) was significantly lower than for the non-LD group ($M = 98.5$). Rapid Reference 4.21 lists the Writing Disability sample's average WIAT-III scores.

Conclusions from WIAT-III and KTEA-II SLD Studies

The profiles of WIAT-III and KTEA-II scores for the three types of learning disabilities reviewed here are similar to what would be expected based upon the skill deficits commonly present in students with LD. In all of these LD samples, relative weaknesses were seen across the board in specific areas of reading and written expression. In contrast, oral language was an area of relative integrity for all samples with LD. There were no discrete patterns of performance on the WIAT-III or KTEA-II that appeared to distinguish the groups of Reading, Mathematics, and Writing Disorders from one another. However, readers must be cautious in generalizing from the data that we have summarized from the test manuals for several reasons. Most of these LD samples were not homogenous groups; they included students that had disabilities in more than one area (e.g., the WIAT-III and KTEA-II samples with Mathematics Disabilities also had many students with comorbid Reading Disorders). The students were not randomly selected for the studies, and for the KTEA-II and KABC-II studies, independent clinicians were typically responsible for determining whether students fit LD criteria. Finally, these are group data that may not be representative of all individuals in a diagnostic class. Therefore, these data summarized from the manuals of the tests should be considered a preliminary estimate of how LD samples perform on the measures. More research would be a welcome edition to the literature on the new editions of these achievement instruments, using well-defined samples of LD who are assessed using multiple measures.

Models for the Identification of a Specific Learning Disability

Either the KTEA-II and KABC-II or the WISC-IV and WIAT-III may be used as part of a comprehensive evaluation for the identification of specific learning disabilities, either within the context of the traditional ability-achievement discrepancy (AAD) model or within the context of several alternative models for identifying specific learning disabilities. One such alternative is the Modern Operational Definition of SLD developed by Flanagan and colleagues (Flanagan, Ortiz, Alfonso, & Mascolo, 2006; Flanagan, Ortiz, & Alfonso, 2007). Another alternative is the Concordance-Discordance model of SLD identification developed by Hale and Fiorello (2004), which is described in the WIAT-III Technical Manual as the pattern of strengths and weaknesses (PSW) discrepancy model. Each of these models may be used within established cognitive and neuropsychological approaches to assessment (e.g., cognitive hypothesis-testing model, the Cross-Battery assessment approach, Cattell-Horn-Carroll theory, Lurian model).

Modern Operational Definition of SLD

As shown in Figure 4.4, the Modern Operational Definition of SLD specifies several essential elements for identifying a specific learning disability that are organized into three levels: Level I involves specific academic skills measurement and evaluation of exclusionary factors; Level II involves measurement of broad abilities, processes, and learning aptitudes; and Level III involves evaluation of underachievement. Meeting each of these levels of criteria is necessary before a diagnosis of SLD is recommended. The details of levels of this definition of SLD are summarized below.

Level I: Specific Academic Skills Measurement and Evaluation of Exclusionary Factors

For children identified as at-risk by RTI Tier 1 universal screening, learning dysfunction or the presence of academic deficits that fall below normal limits on norm-referenced tests (e.g., standard scores < 85) must be documented at Level I. During this first level, practitioners must also determine whether the academic skill deficits are primarily the result of factors other than cognitive deficit (e.g., cultural or language differences, insufficient instruction, poor motivation, performance anxiety, psychiatric disorders, sensory impairments, medical conditions).

Level II: Measurement of Broad Abilities, Processes, and Learning Aptitudes

The focus of a comprehensive assessment at Level II is on measurement of cognitive abilities, processes, and learning aptitudes. A comprehensive assessment should determine whether an examinee's cognitive abilities or process measures are below normal limits relative to the general population. If these deficits in cognitive abilities or processes exist, then the practitioner should determine whether they are related to the academic skill deficit. (For example, determine whether CHC specific or Narrow Abilities and processes have established relations to academic outcomes). A fundamental part of SLD identification is identifying related cognitive and academic deficits, or *below-average aptitude-achievement consistency*. At Level II, practitioners also must examine comorbid conditions and rule out exclusionary factors as the primary cause for cognitive deficits not evaluated at Level I (e.g., mental retardation).

Level III: Evaluation of Underachievement

When moving to Level III, four necessary conditions for SLD determination should be documented: (a) academic deficit(s), (b) cognitive deficit(s), (c)

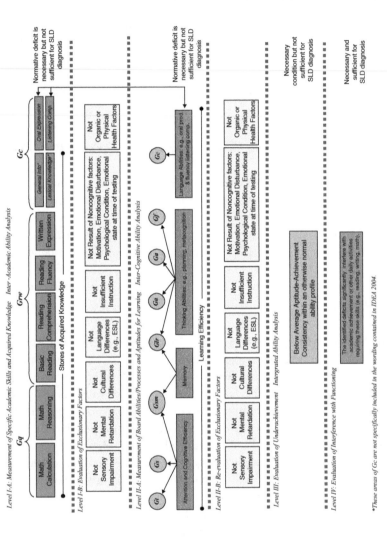

Figure 4.4 Modern Operational Definition of SLD.

Source: Flanagan, Ortiz, and Alfonso (2007).

*These areas of Gc are not specifically included in the wording contained in IDEA 2004.

cognitive and academic deficits are related, and (d) consideration of exclusionary factors. At the third level, all data must be evaluated to determine if the below-average aptitude-achievement consistency exists within an otherwise normal ability profile. That is, in addition to areas of deficit, there must be spared cognitive abilities. The presence of spared cognitive abilities helps distinguish children with SLD from those who have more pervasive cognitive and academic deficits (e.g., slow learners or low achievers).

Pattern of Strengths and Weaknesses (PSW) Discrepancy Model

The PSW model is included in the scoring software capability of the WIAT-III. This model is an alternative research-based procedure to the AAD and response to intervention (RTI) approaches for identifying a specific learning disability as specified by IDEA 2004. The results of the AAD or PSW analysis should be used to generate, support, or disconfirm hypotheses regarding a specific referral question and should be supported by other relevant sources of information before making educational decisions or diagnoses. The PSW analysis requires the identification of a processing weakness, which differentiates a student with a specific learning disability from a student who is underachieving for other reasons, and is a fundamental component of the federal definition of a specific learning disability.

When conducting a PSW analysis, first select a KTEA-II or WIAT-III subtest or composite as the achievement weakness. Selecting a subtest or composite that measures one of the eight areas of achievement specified by IDEA 2004 may be preferable in many settings. If the composite score of interest contains significant discrepancies between subtest-level scores, it may be preferable to use one of the subtest scores that comprise that composite. Next, select two ability index scores, one for the processing strength and one for the processing weakness, from the KABC-II or the WISC-IV. The processing strength should not be empirically related to the achievement weakness, but the processing weakness should be related to the achievement weakness. Measures of processing speed, working memory, short-term memory, or long-term storage and retrieval are not empirically recommended as processing strengths within this model because these scores have lower psychometric g loadings (Prifitera, Saklofske, & Weiss, 2005) and are thought to be less representative of the true nature of SLD. For this reason, the Processing Speed and Working Memory Indexes from the WISC-IV and the Sequential and

Learning Indexes from the KABC-II are not typically recommended cognitive strengths within the PSW model.

As shown in Figure 4.5, in order to meet the criteria of the PSW model for a specific learning disability, two score comparisons must be significantly different (discrepant): the processing strength versus the achievement weakness, and the processing strength versus the processing weakness. If one or both score comparisons are not statistically different, the results do not support the identification of a specific learning disability. If the student is underachieving in more than one area, you may calculate the model more than once. Clinical judgment may be needed for cases that approach significance because some of these students may have a specific learning disability, but the results were not significant due to the student's use of compensatory strategies or due to other psychological processes lowering the cognitive strength. Remember that some differences are clinically significant even if not statistically significant.

As recommended by Hale and Fiorello (2004), the standard error of the difference (SED) is used to evaluate the statistical significance of each score comparison in the PSW model. A standard formula is used to calculate SED, which is available through published references (e.g., Hale & Fiorello, 2004; Rust & Golombok, 1999). SED is preferred over the standard error of the residual (regression method) for comparing a processing strength and weakness because there is no implicit causal relationship between these scores (as in the AAD model). For this reason, and for consistency and simplicity, SED is used to calculate both score comparisons in the PSW model.

A third score comparison requiring consistency between the achievement weakness and the processing weakness is not a statistical requirement of the PSW

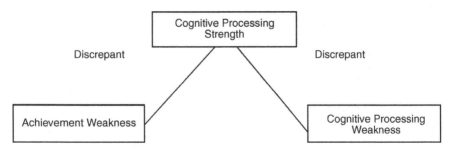

Figure 4.5 Criteria of the PSW Model.

model, but it is important to consider. The cognitive processing weakness should be theoretically related to the achievement weakness to provide an explanation for the learning disability (Hale, Fiorello, et al., 2008). To select a processing weakness that is theoretically related to the achievement weakness, consult relevant research (e.g., Hale, Fiorello, Kavanagh, Hoeppner, & Gaither, 2001; Hale, Fiorello, Bertin, & Sherman, 2003; Fiorello, Hale, & Snyder, 2006) for information regarding theoretical relationships between cognitive processes and achievement domains. A case example that utilizes the PSW model for identifying SLD is provided in Chapter 6.

Achievement Testing in Children with Attention-Deficit Hyperactivity Disorder

Children with Attention-Deficit/Hyperactivity Disorder (ADHD) have tremendous difficulty in their academic performance and achievement. These difficulties include both their work productivity in the classroom and the level of difficulty children have in mastering the expected academic material (Barkley, 1998). Given these difficulties, it is not surprising that ADHD is one of the most common referrals to school psychologists and mental health providers (Demaray, Schaefer, & Delong, 2003). Typically, children who are referred to a clinic for ADHD are doing poorly at school and are underperforming relative to their known levels of ability as determined by intelligence and academic tests. Their poor performance is likely related to their inattentive, impulsive, and restless behavior in the classroom. On standardized tests of academic achievement, children with ADHD typically score 10–30 standard score points lower than their peers in reading, spelling, math, and reading comprehension (Barkley, Dupaul, & McMurray, 1990; Brock & Knapp, 1996; Casey, Rourke, & Del Dotto, 1996). "Consequently, it is not surprising to find that as many as 56% of ADHD children may require academic tutoring, approximately 30% may repeat a grade in school, and 30–40% may be placed in one or more special education programs . . . [and] 10–35% may drop out [of school] entirely" (Barkley, 1998, p. 99).

Specific learning disabilities are often comorbid with ADHD. Estimates of the rates of learning disabilities coexisting with ADHD reveal that 8 to 39 percent of children with ADHD have a reading disability, 12 to 30 percent have a math disability, and 12 to 27 percent have a spelling disorder (Frick et al., 1991; Faraone et al., 1993; Barkley, 1990). Standardized achievement tests administered along with a comprehensive battery (including tests of cognitive ability, behavioral and emotional functioning) can help differentially diagnose ADHD from other learning and psychiatric disorders, and help determine the existence of comorbid disorders.

While achievement tests such as the WIAT-III and KTEA-II and intelligence tests such as the WISC-IV and KABC-II do not, and never were intended to, diagnose ADHD, they are of significant importance in the assessment of children with ADHD. Having knowledge of the specific areas of academic skill deficits coupled with awareness of the cognitive processing abilities of a child with ADHD is a great benefit in planning behavioral and educational programming.

WIAT-III

Given what previous research on children with ADHD has shown, we would predict that children with ADHD tested on the WIAT-III would have significant areas of academic deficit compared to those without ADHD. A study of the performance of students with ADHD on the WIAT-III was not included in the test manual; however, previous studies using the WIAT-II are relevant to testing the assumption that students with ADHD would also demonstrate significant weaknesses on the WIAT-III because of the similarities between the two measures.

The WIAT-II was administered to a group of 178 individuals, ages 5–18 ($M = 13$ years), diagnosed with ADHD, as defined in the *DSM-IV*, and a control group matched on age and grade, gender, ethnicity/race, and parent education level. The lowest scores for the ADHD group were on the Written Expression (92.1) and Spelling (94.0) subtests and the Written Language (92.1) composite. The highest scores for this group were on the Listening Comprehension (100.1) and Oral Expression (98.2) subtests and the Oral Language composite (98.4). Significant differences ($p < .01$) occurred between the two groups across all subtests and composites except the Oral Expression subtest, with actual differences in mean scores ranging from 2.05 (Oral Expression) to 8.17 (Numerical Operations).

In a second study that included 51 children, aged 7–18 ($M = 12$ years), diagnosed with both ADHD and learning disabilities, a very different profile emerged. The differences between mean scores for the ADHD-LD and the control groups are significantly large (ranging from 8.78 for Oral Expression to 25.67 on Spelling). The lowest mean composite score for the ADHD-LD group was on Written Language (80.7), where sustained attention and effort, planning, organizing, and self-monitoring are required. The highest scores for this group were on Listening Comprehension (96.2) and Oral Expression (91.9).

A subsequent study conducted by McConaughy, Ivanova, Antshel, and Eiraldi (2009) investigated test session behavior and performance on the WIAT-II and other measures among 177 children, ranging in age from 6 to 11 years, who were classified as either ADHD–Combined type (ADHD-C), ADHD–Inattentive type (ADHD-I), nonreferred controls, or non-ADHD referred controls (students who were clinically referred for other diagnoses; NON-ADHD-Ref). This study found that, compared to the nonreferred control group, children with ADHD-C and ADHD-I scored significantly ($p < .05$) lower on all three WIAT-II composites that were evaluated: Reading ($M = 96.3$ and 97.9 for each subtype, respectively), Mathematics ($M = 97.4$ and 95.5 for each subtype, respectively), and Written Language ($M = 98.5$ and 97.6 for each subtype, respectively). In addition, there was no significant difference between the ADHD-C and ADHD-I groups in their performance on the WIAT-II composites. These researchers conclude that the WIAT-II was effective in differentiating the performance of children with ADHD and the control group; however, the WIAT-II scores did not differentiate subtypes of ADHD. Only test session observations differentiated ADHD subtypes.

Based upon the WIAT-II research results described here, it is reasonable to expect that students with ADHD are likely to demonstrate significantly lower performance on the WIAT-III reading, written expression, and mathematics subtests and composites; however, research with the newest edition of the WIAT is needed to confirm this finding.

KTEA-II Study

A sample of 51 students, ages 5–18 (mean age 12:11), with ADHD were administered the KTEA-II along with a matched sample of students with no noted disability. All KTEA-II Composite scores for the ADHD sample were significantly lower at the $p < .001$-level than the nonclinical reference group, except for the Oral Fluency Composite ($p < .05$). Unlike the SLD samples whose composite scores were frequently more than 1 SD below the normative mean, the ADHD sample's KTEA-II Composite scores ranged from 3–12 points below the normative mean of 100. The mean Composite scores for Reading (89.5), Mathematics (88.1), and Written Language (87.7) were not highly variable as they differed only by about 2 points. The mean Oral Language Composite was higher at 94.5, and is clearly an area of integrity within the academic profile. The strongest performance for the ADHD group was on the Oral Fluency Composite (97.0), lending further support to the strength of this sample's oral communication skills. Thus, the overall findings from the ADHD sample tested on the KTEA-II do support previous research that found depressed academic functioning for such children. However, this sample was not as impaired as samples of children with SLD, with most of the ADHD sample's mean scores were classified within the average range of ability. Future research administering the KTEA-II together with the KABC-II (and the WIAT-II together with the WISC-IV) to samples of children with ADHD and samples of children with comorbid ADHD and SLD will provide useful information to clinicians who work with such children.

⚔ TEST YOURSELF ⚔

1. **More accurate comparisons can be made between achievement and ability when utilizing conormed tests such as the KABC-II and KTEA-II or correlated tests such as the WIAT-II and WISC-IV.**
   True or False?

2. **Both the Modern Operational Definition of Specific Learning Disabilities and the Pattern of Strengths and Weaknesses Model that were described in this chapter can be used with the WIAT-III and KTEA-II.**
   True or False?

3. **In the WIAT-III Reading-LD and the WISC-IV Reading-LD studies discussed in this chapter, students identified with learning disabilities in reading showed which pattern of scores?**
   (a) VCI was the lowest index scores on the WISC-IV, and Reading Comprehension was the lowest subtest score on the WIAT-II.
   (b) WMI and PSI were the highest index scores on the WISC-IV, and Word Reading, Pseudoword Decoding, and Oral Reading Fluency were the lowest subtest scores on the WIAT-II.
   (c) WMI was the lowest index score on the WISC-IV, and Word Reading, Pseudoword Decoding, Oral Reading Fluency, and Reading Comprehension were the lowest subtest scores on the WIAT-III.
   (d) The lowest WISC-IV index score was PRI, and Word Reading and Pseudoword Decoding were the lowest WIAT-II subtest scores.

4. **Why might a student with a learning disability in reading have a lower score on the Arithmetic subtest of the WISC-IV?**

5. **For students ages 7–18, the KTEA-II Comprehensive Achievement Composite correlated most strongly with the Knowledge/Gc Index, which is not surprising given this index's link to vocabulary and acquisition of facts. Contrary to this finding for 7- to 18-year-olds, which two of the KABC-II scales were among the best correlates of achievement for ages 4 ½ to 6 years?**
   (a) Sequential/Gsm
   (b) Simultaneous/Gv

(c) Learning/*Glr*

(d) a & b

(e) a & c

6. **Administration of which of the following process subtests from the WISC-IV Integrated can be especially important when evaluating a student with a possible language-based learning disorder?**

   (a) Written Arithmetic, Vocabulary, Visual Digit Span

   (b) Block Design No Time Bonus, Digit Span Forward, Digit Span Backward

   (c) Longest Digit Span Forward, Longest Digit Span Backward, Cancellation

   (d) Vocabulary Multiple Choice, Similarities Multiple Choice, and Comprehension Multiple Choice

7. **In addition to five CHC Broad Abilities measured by the KABC-II, the KTEA-II Comprehensive Form measures which three additional Broad Abilities:**

   (a) Auditory Processing (*Ga*)

   (b) Processing Speed (*Gs*)

   (c) Reading and Writing (*Grw*)

   (d) Quantitative Knowledge (*Gq*)

   (e) Speed/Reaction Time (*Gt*)

8. **Which CHC Broad Ability is measured by the WISC-IV and WIAT-III, but *not* by the KABC-II and KTEA-II?**

   (a) Auditory Processing (*Ga*)

   (b) Processing Speed (*Gs*)

   (c) Reading and Writing (*Grw*)

   (d) Quantitative Knowledge (*Gq*)

   (e) Speed/Reaction Time (*Gt*)

9. **The 2004 changes to the Individuals with Disabilities Education Act (e.g., PL 108-446) have formerly eliminated an achievement-ability discrepancy as a necessary part of determining SLD. However, examining WIAT-III and KTEA-II scores alongside their conormed/ correlated tests of cognitive ability may help to determine interindividual academic abilities, and help to evaluate how academic deficits are related to or caused by deficits in basic cognitive processes.**
   True or False?

10. **Although the samples of students with Reading, Mathematics, and Writing disabilities reported in this chapter were not homogeneous groups, the results from the WIAT-III and KTEA-II studies showed that very distinct patterns of academic achievement clearly distinguish the SLD samples from one another.**
    True or False?

(*continued*)

11. **Children with ADHD tend to score highest in which area of achievement measured by the WIAT-III and KTEA-II?**

    (a) Oral Language

    (b) Reading

    (c) Writing

    (d) Mathematics

    Answers: 1. True; 2. True; 3. c; 4. The Arithmetic subtest is a measure of working memory and research demonstrates that there is a close relationship between working memory and the acquisition of reading skills; 5. d; 6. d; 7. a, c, & d; 8. b; 9. True; 10. False; 11. a.

Five

STRENGTHS AND WEAKNESSES OF THE WIAT-III AND KTEA-II

Ron Dumont and John O. Willis

The authors of this chapter judge both the WIAT-III and KTEA-II to be very good instruments. Both of us have had extensive experience with many achievement assessment instruments, and it is with that background that we evaluated the WIAT-III and KTEA-II for this chapter. For both tests, we separate strengths and weaknesses into the following areas: test development, administration and scoring, reliability and validity, standardization, and interpretation. The assets and limitations of each instrument are also summarized in Rapid References 5.1 and 5.2.

STRENGTHS AND WEAKNESSES OF THE WIAT-III

(Cautionary statement: The comments that follow regarding the WIAT-III's strengths and weaknesses are based upon the prepublication standardization version of the test supplied to us before formal publication of the test. Any discrepancies between our comments and the final published version of the test should be considered our mistakes.)

The authors of this chapter believe that, all in all, the WIAT-III is a very good instrument. Both of us have had extensive experience with many other achievement assessment instruments, including the WIAT, WIAT-II, and WIAT-II Update, long before the WIAT-III was published. Because the test has only recently been released, there is no published information regarding how the new test has been accepted by practitioners. Although we find the test to be overall a vast improvement over the prior edition and have welcomed many of the changes in the new edition, we still find several aspects of the test annoying or problematic. Admittedly, we are easily annoyed.

The WIAT-III provides an efficient, thorough, reasonable, and statistically reliable and valid assessment of academic abilities. It is designed with features that enhance useful interpretation.

Rapid Reference 5.1 provides a summary of the WIAT-III strengths and weaknesses. Because of limitations to the length of this chapter, several, but not all, points will be elaborated on below.

≡ Rapid Reference 5.1

Strengths and Weaknesses of the WIAT-III

Test Development

Strengths	Weaknesses
• Improved the floor and ceiling of several subtests.	• Limited ceiling for some subtests for the oldest students in the above average range. Although most subtests have a ceiling that is at least 2 SD above the mean, the ceilings for Sentence Building, Word Reading, Expressive Vocabulary, Oral Reading Accuracy, and Math Fluency (Addition, Subtraction, Multiplication) range from 117–128. At the highest age range, 15 of the 26 possible subtests have ceilings ≤144.
• Expanded the number and type of subtests to measure all eight areas of achievement specified by IDEA 2004 legislation.	
• New or newly separate subtests include Early Reading Skills, Alphabet Writing Fluency, Sentence Composition, Essay Composition, Oral Reading Fluency, and three Math Fluency subtests.	
• The Spelling subtest no longer includes an excessive number of potential homonym confusions.	
• Oral Discourse Comprehension is presented from a CD recording rather than being read aloud by the examiner.	• Limited floor for some subtests for the youngest students with the lowest ability levels. For students age 6, raw scores of zero correspond to standard scores in the "average range" (i.e., SS > 85) for Sentence Combining, Sentence Building, and Math Fluency (subtraction).
• Extensive tryout data using samples with approximately proportional representation by sex and ethnicity.	
• Easel format for presenting many subtest items.	
• Error analysis procedures were expanded.	
• Established links with the most recent Wechsler scales (i.e., WPPSI-III, WISC-IV, WAIS-IV, WNV) and the	

DAS-II to enable clinicians to compare ability and achievement scores.

Standardization

Strengths	Weaknesses
• The standardization sample is well stratified to match the U.S. population. • Data were obtained from a stratified sample of 2,775 students in grades Pre-K–12 (1,375 in the spring of 2008 and 1,400 students in the fall of 2008). From the overall grade sample, an overlapping stratified sample of 1,826 students ranging in age from 4 through 19 was also obtained. • The standardization sample included students receiving special education services. • Very detailed information on standardization procedures and sample are included in the manual. • Extensive (over 500 pages) technical manual is provided as a "green" PDF file rather than a printed manual.	• We hope that examiners will take the time to read, study, and annotate their PDF copies of the technical manual. • There are no college-age norms provided. The *WIAT-II Scoring and Normative Supplement for College Students and Adults* (The Psychological Corporation, 2002) offered very useful two- and/or four-year college norms for grades 13, 14, 15, and 16.

Reliability and Validity

Strengths	Weaknesses
• The average reliability coefficients for the WIAT-III composite scores are all excellent (0.91–0.98). • Average subtest reliability coefficients range from good (0.83–0.89) to excellent (0.90–0.97), with the exception of Alphabet Writing Fluency, which has an average reliability of 0.69. • Correlations between the WIAT-III Total Achievement score and overall cognitive ability scores range from	• No alternative forms are available. • Standard Errors of Measurement (SEM) are high for the Alphabet Writing Fluency (8.35 for fall, spring, and age samples). • The only academic achievement comparison in our prepublication copy was to the WIAT-II.

(continued)

Reliability and Validity

Strengths	Weaknesses
0.60 to 0.82 and are consistent with research-based expectations regarding typical correlations between ability and achievement measures. Such correlations provide evidence of divergent validity, suggesting that different constructs are being measured by the WIAT-III from those measured by each ability test. • Strong face validity based on item content and skill development in reading, writing, and mathematics. • Construct validity indicated by increasing scores across grades and ages.	

Administration and Scoring

Strengths	Weaknesses
• Easel format with tabbed separators simplifies administration. • Starting points and discontinue rules are clearly labeled on the record form for all subtests. • Many test items are scored in a dichotomous manner. • A separate 118-page scoring workbook provides a large number of scoring examples for the subtests that comprise the Written Expression Composite. • Both age and grade norms are provided. • In an effort to improve ease of administration and to shorten administration times, the same reverse rule and discontinue rule is used across all applicable WIAT-III subtests, and the discontinue rule	• The test record form's layout is very busy and crowded in places—particularly on the first two Score Summary pages. • The record form itself is 50 pages long. For those using the WIAT-III with younger children (Pre-K and K), much of the record form is wasted. • When hand scoring and filling in the summary pages, great care must be taken to avoid error. Normative tables are provided as a PDF file, which makes looking up score conversions awkward and at times difficult to read, especially on a small laptop screen. (Some tables are printed in landscape mode, not portrait layout.) • Not all correct or acceptable answers are provided on the record form. Examiners must be diligent to

has been shortened to four consecutive scores of zero.

- New descriptive categories reflect a simpler system of categorizing achievement level based on the test's SD of 15.

- Scoring rules were improved in response to scoring studies, theoretical reviews by expert researchers, and usability reviews by teachers and clinicians.

- There are sufficient scoring examples and a supplemental scoring workbook to assist examiners in learning and using the scoring rules.

- The scoring assistant computer program is a valuable tool for score calculation, graphs, and subtest comparisons, saving time and eliminating possible human-made clerical errors.

- Error analysis for the subtests that have large numbers of skill categories is provided, both in the computer scoring assistant CD and as reproducible worksheets in the examiner's manual.

check the examiner's manual (Appendix B) and the scoring workbook for guidance.

- Several questions appear to have more correct answers than are listed in the record form.

- The new descriptive categories are different than those from the earlier versions of the WIAT as well as many other achievement and ability measures, which may be confusing to those familiar with the old categories. The undifferentiated "average" range, extending from 85 to 115, may make sense statistically and psychologically, but we find it much too broad (more than $2/3$ of the population) for interpreting educational performance.

Interpretation

Strengths	Weaknesses
• Composites and most subtests can be interpreted due to high reliability data.	• Caution needs to be taken when interpreting the scores with a nonoptimal ceiling or floor.
• Error analysis procedures pinpoint specific skill deficits.	• Subtest Score Summary column labeled "Standard Score" contains not only standard scores but weighted raw scores and sum of standard score, leading to possible misinterpretation of the actual numbers.
• The composites and error analysis yield much diagnostic information directly relevant to instructional remediation.	
• Pairs of WIAT-III subtests (i.e., Reading Comprehension and Listening Comprehension, Written Expression and Oral Expression) were developed to have more	• Little information is provided in the WIAT-II technical manual on how to utilize the promised growth scale value (GSV) curves.

(continued)

Interpretation	
Strengths	**Weaknesses**
similar formats than on the WIAT-II, which permits useful comparisons that can help the examiner distinguish specific problems in reading or writing from more general language problems. • The four-point Oral Reading Fluency Prosody Scale is a useful observation. • The WIAT-III Scoring Assistant (beginning in 2010) will allow growth scale values (GSV) from two or more testing sessions to be plotted by grade or age against a curve representing mean growth.	

ASSETS OF THE WIAT-III

Test Development

The revisions made from the WIAT-II to the WIAT-III are, in general, excellent. The graphics and the content of the items appear to be much improved. The three new fluency measures in math, the separate Oral Reading Fluency subtest, the broader coverage of academic achievement areas, vastly improved (or restored) Listening Comprehension subtest, improved scoring rules, a scoring workbook providing real-life examples, and the inclusion of the Scoring Assistant CD all add to the increased utility and user-friendliness of the WIAT-III.

The availability of the computer scoring program packaged with the test serves to alleviate numerical errors often associated with complex tests. The scoring program also offers several extremely useful features, including an enhanced skill analysis for core subtests as well as Intervention goal statements to assist with IEP development. Unique to the scoring program is the research-supported "pattern of strengths and weaknesses discrepancy analysis."

Normative Sample

Normative samples are important for tests, just as for opinion polls. If the normative sample does not resemble the population to whom examinees will be compared, scores will be misleading. The normative sample of the WIAT-III is described in Chapter 2 of the *WIAT-III Technical Manual* (Wechsler, 2009) and we consider it to meet or exceed good current practice and to provide a trustworthy basis for an individual's scores.

Examinee candidates for the normative sample were extensively screened for potentially confounding issues that presumably might impair the validity of test performance. A complete list of the exclusionary criteria for the normative sample is presented in Table 2.1 (p. 15) of the *Technical Manual* (Wechsler, 2009). A representative proportion of students from various special clinical groups was also included in the normative samples to accurately represent the student population as a whole.

Reliability and Validity

The WIAT-III Composite, Indexes, and subtests generally have strong reliability. This topic is discussed at length in Chapter 3 of the *Technical Manual* (Wechsler, 2009). Test scores cannot be trusted unless the tests are internally consistent and likely to yield very similar scores for the same person under similar circumstances, so reliability is an essential foundation for any responsible use of test scores. It is a necessary, but not sufficient, basis for application of test scores. A test can be reliable, but still not valid, for a particular purpose, but without reliability, it cannot be valid for any purpose.

The average reliability coefficients for the WIAT–III composite scores are all excellent (.91 to .98). Short-term (2 to 32 days) stability coefficients for the WIAT–III subtest and composite scores at all grades (Wechsler, 2009, pp. 37 to 38) ranged from .73 (adequate) to .97 (reliable).

Validity data for the WIAT-III are discussed in Chapter 2 of this book and in the WIAT-III *Technical Manual* (Wechsler, 2009, pp. 39 to 59). The subtest intercorrelations confirm expected relations between the subtests within composites and provide evidence of discriminant validity.

Validity evidence from comparisons with tests of academic achievement and cognitive abilities supports the use of the WIAT-III for cognitive assessment and prediction of achievement. The relationships between the WIAT-III and the following cognitive measures were examined: WPPSI-III, WISC-IV, WAIS-IV, WNV, and DAS-II. Unfortunately, the only academic achievement comparison was to the WIAT-II.

Administration and Scoring

The administration of the WIAT-III seems to flow a bit more efficiently, and one reason for this may be the revised discontinue rules (for most subtests there is a consistent discontinuation rule of four consecutive failures), which have for the most part been shortened. Entry points and other essential information have generally been made clear and user-friendly on the record form. Scoring for many tests is made easier because it is dichotomous (0 or 1 point).

The tabbed, two-sided stimulus book contains five subtests and has an easel back that allows it to stand freely on the examination table. Most materials needed to properly administer the WIAT-III are provided and are generally light and do not appear at all cumbersome. It is certainly not unreasonable that the examiner must provide several other materials (e.g., blank paper, CD or MP3 player, stopwatch). One recommendation made in the examiner's manual that we wholeheartedly endorse is to add to the materials for administration a tape recorder to record the person's verbatim responses. Although certainly not needed for the entire test, the proper scoring of four subtests (Word Reading, Pseudoword Decoding, Oral Expression, and Oral Reading Fluency) can be greatly aided by the tape recording.

The inclusion of a CD containing the Oral Discourse Comprehension subtest is a welcome addition. There has always been the problem of different examiners reading a comprehension passage differently from each other or even differently for different examinees. The inclusion of the oral discourse passages on the CD makes the administration of this subtest much more universally standardized so all examinees get the same pronunciation and word emphasis in the recitation of the stories. Many may remember the CHEWIES story on the original WIAT. (That story, as are several other original WIAT stories, is once again used for the Oral Discourse Comprehension passages.) Although the story passage that was to be read aloud to the examinee was printed clearly on the easel, there was no instruction as to whether or not an examiner was to read the passage with a normal tone and without any special emphasis on any passage part or word (despite the fact that the word CHEWIES was always bolded in the story). This problem has been successfully eliminated on the WIAT-III by the use of the CD.

Interpretation

Historically, one wonderful aspect of the original WIAT was the lovely contrast between Reading Comprehension and Listening Comprehension. You had two tests, normed on the same sample, that were (except for the memory demand of Listening Comprehension) nearly identical in format, with one requiring reading and the other only listening. This contrasting pair was tremendously helpful in distinguishing reading comprehension problems from more pervasive language comprehension problems and in documenting the severity of a reading problem compared to an expectation based on oral comprehension. That contrast was lost in the WIAT-II, where the *Listening Comprehension* test was primarily two very brief vocabulary subtests (Receptive Vocabulary and Expressive Vocabulary) with an extremely brief sentence comprehension test thrown in. The WIAT-III now has a much better Listening Comprehension measure made up of the Oral Discourse Comprehension and Receptive Vocabulary subtests. It may still be a bit difficult to interpretively contrast examinee's performance on the Reading Comprehension test to that of the Oral Discourse Comprehension subtest because the tables in the *Technical Manual* (Pearson, 2009c) that provide the relevant critical values and base rate necessary for pairwise comparisons do so only for the Listening Comprehension versus Reading Comprehension measures, but not for the Oral Discourse Comprehension versus Reading Comprehension.

LIMITATIONS OF THE WIAT-III

Poor Instructions for Scoring Certain Tasks

Although the instructions provided in the *Examiner's Manual* (Pearson, 2009b) are typically clear and unambiguous, there remain, in our opinion, several aspects of administration and scoring that need clarification.

Instructions

Some specific instructions may be confusing to examiners. Two examples are for the "Reverse Rules" and for the "Discontinuation Rules."

Four subtests (Oral Discourse Comprehension, Math Problem Solving, Numerical Operations, and Spelling) utilize the reverse rule. This rule states that, if a student scores 0 points on any of the first three items given, administer the items in reverse order from the start point until three consecutive items are passed or item 1 is reached. At that point the examiner should "proceed forward" until the discontinuation rule has been reached. For the Oral Discourse Comprehension subtest, if a student starts at item 6, and passes 6 and 7 but fails 8, the reverse rule should be employed and the examiner must administer items in reverse order, starting with item 5, and continue until three consecutive items are passed. However, because items 8 and 9 are for the same passage, is the examiner really supposed to employ the reverse rule after item 8? If so, do you replay the story again (the record form says "Do not repeat CD tracks"), ask the question associated with item 9 without the child hearing the story again, or administer item 9 even if item 8 is scored as a 0? If the latter is the answer, this may in fact cause more confusion with scoring. What if item 9 is passed, but during the reverse rule administration the child receives four consecutive scores of 0 below item 9? Would the score on item 9 count or not count?

For eight subtests, the discontinuation rule on the record form notes that the examiner is to "Discontinue after 4 consecutive scores of 0." Although technically correct, this applies only to discontinuing when the examiner is moving forward toward establishing a ceiling. However, if an examiner has had to employ the Reverse Rule and administer items in reverse order to establish a basal, it is quite possible that an examinee could have four consecutive failures while being administered the items in reverse order. In such a case, the examiner *should not discontinue* after four consecutive errors since these errors occurred while moving in a reverse order in an attempt to establish a basal.

Item Scoring

Several subtest items appear to have more correct answers than are listed in the record form or *Examiner's Manual*. Clarification of certain responses from the test authors will be helpful.

Reading Comprehension
The *Reading Comprehension* scoring rules should, we think, provide more guidance on querying. Acceptable answers still, as on the WIAT-II, place a premium on the examinee guessing what the question is really asking or what the passage is meant to imply, so there are many possible answers that suggest good understanding but receive no credit and apparently warrant no query. Several questions appear to have more correct answers than are listed in the record form. Examples are listed below:

Item 38 asks that the examinee give the word that "best describes Gobbledeeglue." Several 2-point responses are allowed (no 1-point responses are provided) and answers such as "homemade" or "rolled" are not scored or queried.

Item 54 requires the examinee to give three dangers encountered by the family on their journey. Unfortunately, "getting lost" is not listed as an acceptable answer despite the fact that the story features an Indian guide who helps them survive and guides them to the destination. Also, "Chilkoot Pass" is listed as one of the acceptable dangers that may be encountered—but Chilkoot Pass is merely a location the people in the story must pass through; it is actually the harsh wilderness of Chilkoot Pass that is the danger.

Item 73 requires the examinee to explain what caused whales to begin to make a recovery, and two specific answers are necessary to obtain maximum points. Listed as a possible 1-point response is "Placed on endangered species list." This specific response requires a query by the examiner of "Tell me more." There doesn't appear to be any clear reason why this acceptable 1-point response, followed by either one of the two other acceptable 1-point responses, would not cumulatively be scored as 2 points, but apparently only two of the three 1-point responses is acceptable in the 2-point scoring.

Item 76 requires the examinee to tell "three things that might happen if the zoo prices **are not** raised." The record form provides four possible correct responses. However, the list of correct answers does not include at least three other things that "might happen" according to the story. In the story, Tanisha describes three things that an increase in revenue would support: employees will get a raise; facilities will be kept up; and new animals will be acquired. Notice that each of these three events is a thing that might happen if zoo prices **are** raised. When answering the question about what might happen if the prices are not raised, one need only apply a negative to these three examples and they would be correct answers to the questions (e.g., if prices at the zoo **are not** raised, employees **might not** get a raise).

Math Problem Solving

On item 13 (chip counting), what if the child counts incorrectly but gives the correct total? Could two wrongs may make a right? The child might point wrong (missing a chip) and count wrong (skipping a number) and come up with the right answer.

For Items 24, 26, and 27, the wording for the question ("If you are counting in order, which of these numbers would you say first?") appears to be potentially confusing to the examinee. The problem arises from confusion about just what the intention of the question is and what is meant by "counting in order." Does it mean counting in numerical order (lowest number to highest) or does it mean to count in the order that the numbers themselves have been presented—from left to right? For example, imagine that, instead of numbers, the item was a string of letters (e.g., C B A) and the instructions asked "If you are reading in order, which of these letters would you say first?" If I understood the directions to mean reading in alphabetical order, then I would certainly have to say that "A" would be said first, but, if I take the directions to mean reading in the order that the letters have been presented, then "C" would be the correct answer. Had the item question simply said, "If you are counting in numerical order, which of these numbers would you say first?" there would be little if any confusion.[1]

---

1. Kristina Breaux, WIAT-III Research Director, provides the following response to this criticism: "This item is for grades 1 through 3; thus, the suggested use of this language would not be appropriate. Although reading proceeds from left to right, counting rarely does. This 'confusion about counting in order' was not an issue in the test's tryout or standardization."

Two items (47 and 54) seem to be attempting to measure how well a student knows 90 and 180 degrees respectively, but it also takes a good amount of visualization skills (*Gv*) to do the problem successfully. Reminding the examinee that he or she can use the paper and pencil provided may help alleviate the problem, but there do not appear to be any such cues. Before you start the subtest, you do include the instruction, "You may use this paper and pencil at any time to help work a problem," but there is no indication that this reminder can be given to a student who might be struggling with the problems.

Psuedoword Decoding
One word, *Diminecial*, has two correct pronunciations listed on the record form. Is there actually a third: die-min-e-shel?

Numerical Operations
There appears to be a potential scoring problem with item 2: Item 1 asks the child to count a number of balls and then tell how many there are. Item 2 asks the child to "write the number of the balls you counted" into a box on the record form. How does one score it if the child miscounts the number of balls (e.g., says 4 instead of 5), thus getting item 1 wrong, but then, for item 2, correctly writes in the box "4"? Although the child has done exactly what the directions ask—"write the number of the balls you counted"—the answer key gives 5 as the only correct answer.

Oral Reading Fluency
Although the directions for timing the reading passages are clear in the box at the top of the record form (". . . start timing when the student reads the first word of the passage . . ."), the instructions simply say, "'Start here. Begin.' Start timing." Shouldn't they say "Start timing when the student reads the first word"?

One story, "Amelia the pigeon," seems awfully implausible. A WW1 "tiny camera" being sent to a great-granddaughter is supposed to still work AND have film available to use!

The passage "The Moon" asks, "What does the author like to do by moonlight?" The very first sentence says "I like to watch the moon as it shines at night." Although the Comprehension questions are not scored quantitatively in this subtest, we still wonder is "watch the moon" an acceptable answer?

Tape Recorder
A tape recorder is specified for recording the student's oral responses to several subtests (Word Reading, Pseudoword Decoding, Oral Expression, and Oral Reading Fluency). Will examiners actually do this, since it is a recommendation rather than a requirement? The need to tape record an examinee's responses

increases the amount of equipment needed to correctly administer the test. Given that the Oral Discourse Comprehension subtest requires the use of a separate CD player, examiners are now required to transport to testing sessions both a CD player and a tape recorder or a machine with both functions. We consider this effort to be reasonable, but some examiners may not.

Final Comment on the WIAT-III

Although we have identified some concerns with the new WIAT-III, we definitely consider it a significant improvement over the WIAT-II and, on balance, find it to be a valuable instrument with significant strengths.

STRENGTHS AND WEAKNESSES OF THE KTEA-II

The authors of this chapter consider the KTEA-II to be a very good instrument. Both of us have had extensive experience with the KTEA-II, the WIAT-II, and other achievement assessment instruments, both using them in our own evaluations and teaching them in graduate classes and workshops. One of us (JW) consulted from time to time with the publisher during the development of the KTEA-II and currently uses the KTEA-II more often than other achievement tests, but often supplements and occasionally replaces it with other achievement tests. However, we do, of course, have some complaints and quibbles.

We find the KTEA-II offers an efficient, thorough, practical, and statistically reliable and valid assessment of academic abilities. It is designed with features that enhance useful interpretation. The strengths and weaknesses we perceive in the KTEA-II are listed in Rapid Reference 5.2, which has been slightly updated from Rapid Reference 3.17 in Lichtenberger & Smith (2005).

≡ *Rapid Reference 5.2*

Strengths and Weaknesses of the KTEA-II

Test Development	
Strengths	**Weaknesses**
• Item selection using curriculum consultants and content of widely used textbooks.	• Limited ceiling for some subtests for the oldest students in the above average range. See Table 5.1 for specific data on highest possible

(continued)

Test Development

Strengths	Weaknesses
• Almost all Reading Comprehension questions are appropriately passage dependent (Keenan & Betjemann, 2006).	subtest and composite scores for ages 21–25 and grade 12. Although most subtests have a ceiling that is at least 2 SD above the mean, the ceilings for Spelling, Associational Fluency, and Naming Facility range from 122 to 129. At the highest age range, 12 of the 14 subtests have ceilings ≤ 144.
• Subtests in all eight specific learning disability areas identified in the Individuals with Disabilities Education Improvement Act (IDEA, 2004).	
• Extensive tryout data using samples with approximate proportional representation by gender and ethnicity.	• Limited floor for some subtests for the youngest students with the lowest ability levels. For students younger than age 6, raw scores of zero correspond to standard scores ranging from 82 to 67 for Letter & Word Recognition, from 72 to 81 for Math Computation, from 67 to 77 for Listening Comprehension, from 69 to 77 for Phonological Awareness, from 64 to 72 for Associational Fluency, and from 71 to 83 for Naming Facility. See Table 5.2 for specific data.
• Easel format for presenting subtest items.	
• Reading-Related subtests yielding four Reading-Related Composites.	
• Innovative item types, especially in Reading Comprehension, Written Expression, and Phonological Awareness.	
• Use of extensive item analysis procedures to eliminate biased items (gender or race) and items with poor psychometric properties.	• Error analysis procedures may be difficult for examiners lacking any background in curriculum. In rare instances, examiner knowledge and judgment are required to override potentially misleading error-analysis scores.
• Expanded error analysis procedures with item-level analyses for Reading Comprehension, Listening Comprehension, Written Expression, Oral Expression, Phonological Awareness, Math Concepts and Applications, and Math Computation and within-item analyses for Math Computation (again), Letter & Word Recognition, Nonsense Word Decoding, and Spelling.	
• Conormed with the KABC-II to allow investigation of the student's academic strengths and weaknesses within the context of the student's cognitive abilities.	
• Novel and stimulating artwork is used throughout the test.	

Standardization

Strengths	Weaknesses
• The standardization sample is well stratified to match the U.S. population and included 40 states and the District of Columbia.	• The age-norm sample has smaller adult norm samples than for the younger age samples. For ages 5–14, the samples range in size from 200 to 225; for ages 15–17, the samples are 140 to 145. The age 18 sample is $N = 100$, and the age 19 sample is $N = 80$. $N = 125$ for the sample for ages 20–22, and $N = 125$ for the sample for ages 23–25.
• Stratification included two-way comparisons (e.g., ethnicity and mother's education level).	
• Two separate representative nationwide standardizations were conducted, one in the fall and one in the spring, yielding a large normative group ($N = 3,000$ for the age-norm sample and $N = 2,400$ for the grade-norm sample) for the Comprehensive Form.	
• The standardization sample included students receiving special education services.	• There are no separate norms for post-secondary students. Percentages of those aged 18, 19, 20–22, and 23–25 years in high school or dropped out, graduated from high school with no further education, began two-year post-secondary program, and began four-year post-secondary program roughly approximated U.S. Census data in most cases, but the examiner still lacks norms specifically for students enrolled in post-secondary programs.
• Very detailed information on standardization procedures and sample are included in the Comprehensive Form manual.	
• Expanded age range down to $4\frac{1}{2}$ years for both the Comprehensive and Brief Forms and up to 25 years for the Comprehensive Form and up to 90 years for the Brief Form.	

Reliability and Validity

Strengths	Weaknesses
• High mean split-half reliabilities of subtests and composites. (CAC = 0.97, and other composites range from 0.93 to 0.97, with the exception of Oral Language and Oral Fluency, which range from 0.85 to 0.87.)	• The Oral Language Composite has variable correlations with similar measures on the other achievement instruments. However, this may be due to the very different approaches taken by different test batteries in measuring and defining Oral Expression and Listening Comprehension.
• Two alternate forms are available for the KTEA-II Comprehensive, resulting in reduced practice effects for children who are assessed more than once.	• Standard errors of measurement (SEM) are high for the age-norm

(continued)

Reliability and Validity	
Strengths	**Weaknesses**
• Alternate-form reliability coefficients (adjusted for the variability of the norm group) are very strong, ranging from 0.92 to 0.95 for the CAC. Most composites' alternate-form reliability coefficients range from 0.85 to 0.94. Oral Fluency and Oral Language are the weakest, ranging from 0.59 to 0.81. • The KTEA-II Comprehensive Form manual offers correlational data with four other tests of academic achievement and the original K-TEA. • Moderate to strong correlations between KTEA-II and other measures of achievement for concurrent validity (0.86–0.90). • The KTEA-II CAC correlates approximately 0.80 with the global scores of cognitive ability batteries (e.g., KABC-II and WISC-III). • Strong face validity based on use of textbook content and skill development in reading and mathematics. • Construct validity indicated by increasing scores across grades and ages.	sample for Oral Language (ranging from 4.45–6.96) and Oral Fluency (ranging from 4.25–10.28).

Administration and Scoring	
Strengths	**Weaknesses**
• The test protocol has a user friendly layout. • Easel format simplifies administration. • Starting points and discontinue rules are clearly labeled on the record form and easels for all subtests. • Children find Pepper the puppet very engaging in Phonological Awareness.	• The manual and easel inadvertently fail to note that Pepper, the usually engaging puppet, is recommended but optional, particularly with older students. • Need to write responses phonetically to use error analysis for Letter & Word Recognition and Nonsense Word Decoding, which can be especially challenging when

- Students find the storybook format of Written Expression much less tedious than a more traditionally formatted test of written expression.
- Most test items are scored in a dichotomous manner.
- A large number of Written Expression scoring examples are provided in the manual.
- A large number of Oral Expression scoring examples are provided in the manual.
- A glossary and guide to language rules (examiner's manual, Appendix D) is provided.
- Both age and grade norms are available.
- New descriptive categories reflect a simpler system of categorizing ability level based on the test's SD of 15.
- A separate error analysis booklet is provided for the subtests that have large numbers of skill categories, thereby making the main record form less cumbersome.
- The record form for Letter & Word Recognition and Nonsense Word Decoding includes phonetic pronunciation keys, and, when needed, indicates correct stress of syllables. There is ample space to record the examinee's pronunciations.
- The CD provides correct pronunciations for the examiner.

- testing students who respond very quickly.
- Specific error analysis norms tables are difficult to locate quickly in the manual. Some examiners are tempted to interpret raw error-category scores instead of using norms, which can yield misleading results.
- Need to remember to use conversion table to convert points earned in a set to the raw score for Reading Comprehension, Written Expression, Listening Comprehension, and Oral Expression. Some conversion tables are on the record form, but others are in the test manual.
- Although scoring of most of the Oral Expression and Written Expression items seems clear to us (especially with the aid of the explanations, examples, and glossary), questions from graduate students, colleagues, and workshop attendees suggest that the scoring can be confusing for some examiners.
- When Associational Fluency and Naming Facility are administered, they must be given out of easel order, which is easy to forget for some examiners.
- The new descriptive categories are different than those from the original K-TEA as well as many other achievement and ability measures, which may be confusing to those familiar with the old categories. The undifferentiated "average" range, extending from 85 to 115, may make sense statistically and psychologically, but we find it much too broad (more than $2/3$ of the population) for interpreting educational performance.

(continued)

Administration and Scoring

Strengths	Weaknesses
	• Separate norms for semantic and phonological Associational Fluency and for Naming Facility with colors and objects versus Naming Facility with letters would be helpful, although there is a work-around described next.
	• Even though they would lack sufficient top, norms for Phonological Awareness above age 12 and grade 6 would be helpful with weak readers.
	• It is easy to write the wrong confidence intervals for the Reading-Related Composites.

Interpretation

Strengths	Weaknesses
• Both composites and subtests can be interpreted due to high reliability coefficients.	• Caution needs to be taken when interpreting the scores with a nonoptimal ceiling for ages 21–25 (see Table 5.1) or a nonoptimal floor for children under age 6 (see Table 5.2).
• Error analysis procedures pinpoint specific skill deficits.	
• The composites and error analysis yield much diagnostic information directly relevant to instructional remediation.	• If all of the CAC subtests are not administered, then the Composite Analysis and Subtest Analysis cannot be completed, because the CAC is used in all of these comparisons. However, pairwise composite comparisons or pairwise subtest comparisons are still possible.
• Subtest and battery composite intercorrelations are presented by age and grade in the *KTEA-II Comprehensive Form Manual*.	
• Interpretive procedures were simplified by comparing Composites and subtests to CAC rather than to the mean of all Composites.	• Many evaluators want to know if the component subtests in each Composite are significantly and uncommonly different from each other, which should require cautious interpretation of the Composite score. This information is available in Appendix I of the manual but is buried among all the other subtest comparisons.
• Integrated normative and ipsative comparisons are included in the interpretive process.	
• Pairs of KTEA-II Comprehensive subtests (i.e., Reading Comprehension and Listening Comprehension, Written	

Expression and Oral Expression) were developed to have similar formats to enable useful comparisons that can help the examiner distinguish specific problems in reading or writing from more general language problems.

- Significance and base-rate levels are provided for those and other comparisons.

- Growth scale values (GSV) are provided to provide a mechanism by which a student's absolute (rather than relative) level of performance can be measured.

- The manual encourages examiners to verify hypotheses with other data.

- The KTEA-II record form provides a place to record the basic analysis of the scale composites, including strengths and weaknesses, composite comparisons, subtest comparisons, and ability-achievement discrepancies, as well as behavioral observations. These charts are helpfully labeled with the identifying numbers of the relevant tables in the manual.

- Because it is conormed with the KABC-II, the KTEA-II is easily interpreted within the CHC theoretical framework.

- The comparison between Reading Comprehension and Listening Comprehension is very useful because of the almost identical formats of the two subtests. Differences between the formats of Written Expression and Oral Expression make that comparison less persuasive.

- Little information is provided in the KTEA-II Comprehensive Form manual on how to utilize the growth scale values (GSV).

- Confidence bands can be calculated for age- or grade-equivalent scores (if those scores must be used at all), but this procedure is laborious and is not suggested in the manual.

- According to our calculations, some of the stanine equivalents for standard scores in Table N.8 of the norms book are incorrect: 126 should be stanine 8, 118 should be stanine 7, 111 should be stanine 6, 96 should be stanine 4, 81 should be stanine 2, and 73 should be stanine 1.

ASSETS OF THE KTEA-II

Test Development

Although, as with any test, there are a few weak or debatable items, the publisher's extensive efforts to enlist guidance from curriculum experts, to base items on popular textbooks, and to complete a very thorough tryout produced an instrument with very useful, relevant content for educational assessment in all eight achievement areas specified by IDEA 2004 regulations for assessment of specific learning disabilities. Reading-Related skills are covered extensively, including Reading Fluency, Phonetic Decoding, Phonological Awareness, and Rapid Naming. Reading Comprehension questions are read by the examinee and themselves pose appropriate reading challenges. Unlike some other tests (e.g.,

Keenan & Betjemann, 2006), very few Reading Comprehension questions could be answered correctly on the basis of prior knowledge and deduction without reading the passage. Reading Comprehension also includes some direction-following items, similar to "Turn around in your chair and then stand up."

The Written Expression subtest format of having the examinee fill in missing letters, words, punctuation, and sentences in a storybook as the examiner tells the story and gives instructions, and then write a summary of the entire story, is engaging, and it produces useful data, including the error analysis. There are four different Written Expression levels, three of which require separate storybooks. The need to keep three different storybooks in stock is a mild but worthwhile inconvenience. The artwork in the test easels and the storybook is attractive and appears to appeal to the students whom we have tested.

The extensive error-analysis procedures do require some time and attention if done by hand, but they provide genuinely useful information if the norms are used. The error categories are detailed and educationally meaningful.

The KTEA-II Comprehensive Form is conormed with the KABC-II (Kaufman & Kaufman, 2004b) and the Brief Form with the KBIT-2 (Kaufman & Kaufman, 2004c). Predicted achievement, significant differences, and base-rate data are provided in easily used tables.

Standardization

Please see Chapter 3 for detailed information on the standardization of the KTEA-II, which is also described at length in Chapter 6 of the manual. The large, national sample, with students tested in the fall and in the spring, was stratified to match then-current U.S. Census data, including interactions of variables, such as ethnicity *and* mother's education level. Special efforts were made to ensure randomization within the variables. Students receiving special education and gifted/talented services were included in population-appropriate percentages.

Reliability and Validity

The reliability and validity of the KTEA-II are discussed in detail in Chapter 3. Except for Oral Language and Oral Fluency, the mean split-half and alternate-form are strong. Correlations with four other achievement tests are moderate to strong, showing good concurrent validity. Correlations with global scores on cognitive ability tests are lower, around .80, which indicates divergent validity: An achievement test should correlate reasonably highly with cognitive ability tests, but it should not be 1.

The KTEA-II subtests appear to be legitimate and reasonable measures of the intended constructions (face validity), which is reassuring to examiners, parents, and teachers, and helpful in maintaining the examinee's motivation and cooperation.

Administration and Scoring

The easels, separate stimulus sheets, and record forms are easy to use (with one exception noted below). For the most part, scoring (usually dichotomous) is straightforward with clear explanations and many scoring examples as well as a glossary and Guide to Language Rules (manual Appendix D). The age-based and grade-based norms are readily available and clearly labeled in the *Norms Book*, facilitating scoring and reducing the likelihood of errors. The record form encourages and simplifies the use of confidence bands, which happily do not extend lower than 85 percent confidence.

The KTEA-II uses a simple scheme of only five descriptive categories that (unlike many tests) can easily be found in the table of contents of the manual. As noted below, this simplified system is a mixed blessing.

Error analysis worksheets are included in the record form for subtests with few error categories. A separate error analysis booklet is provided for the subtests that have multiple error categories. Examiners can use the analyses when necessary and omit them when there are no unanswered questions about remediation, as in the case of a high score or when an examinee's weakness in a domain is obvious, extreme, and pervasive. Unlike error analyses on many tests, the KTEA-II weakness-average-strength categories are based on the test norms.

Interpretation

Interpretation of the KTEA-II is enhanced by having subtests and/or composites that measure all eight areas of achievement specified by IDEA legislation as important for identifying and classifying learning disabilities: (a) oral expression (one subtest), (b) listening comprehension (one subtest), (c) written expression (composite based on two subtests), (d) basic reading skill (composite based on two subtests), (e) reading fluency skills (composite based on two subtests), (f) reading comprehension (one subtest), (g) mathematics calculation (one subtest), and (h) mathematics problem solving (one subtest). The KTEA-II also includes subtests of Rapid Automatized Naming (RAN) and Phonological Awareness—two skills considered by many experts to be essential foundations for reading skills (e.g., Wolf & Bowers, 1999), and a subtest measuring Associational Fluency.

The generally high reliabilities of the composites and subtests (please see Chapter 3) permit separate interpretation, and the manual provides the necessary data on significant differences and base rates (as well as intercorrelations).

We find that the subtests, Composites, and error analyses are practical and that the information they provide is educationally meaningful, leading to useful recommendations. The 16-page chapter on interpretation in the manual provides the necessary information in a clear, concise format, and encourages the use of additional data to verify hypotheses.

The Comprehensive Achievement Composite (CAC) excludes (appropriately, in our judgment) Spelling and Oral Expression. If the examiner administers at least the other eight CAC subtests, then each subtest and Composite score can be statistically compared to the CAC in a quick and simple procedure yielding both significant differences and base rates.

Composite and subtest scores can also be compared to each other with readily available data for significant differences and base rates. The contrast between Reading Comprehension and Listening Comprehension is extremely valuable, as the two subtests have essentially identical formats with the only difference being who does the reading. The comparison between Written Expression and Oral Expression is less exact, as the formats differ, but it is still useful.

Growth Scale Values (GSVs) are provided as an Item-Response-Theory-based statistic that would be much better for assessing growth than would be raw scores or grade-equivalent scores.

The record form makes it easy to record both normative strengths and weaknesses and personal (ipsative) ones. There is a simple chart for recording behavioral observations with a very helpful discussion in the manual (pp. 33 to 36) by Elaine Fletcher-Janzen. There is also a table for recording ability–achievement discrepancies. Tables I.9 and I.10 permit comparison of KTEA-II scores with those of the KABC-II as well as other ability measures, which makes it easy to interpret the KTEA-II results within the Cattell-Horn-Carroll framework (e.g., each chart on the record form helpfully lists the identifying number of the table in the manual that is to be used for the scores or comparisons in that chart).

LIMITATIONS OF THE KTEA-II

Although we find the KTEA-II to be a valuable and generally sound test, no test is without limitations.

Test Development

Table 5.1 provides data on the highest possible subtest and composite scores for the oldest examinees and for examinees in grade 12. In most cases, the highest possible score is at least two standard deviations above the mean (standard score ≥ 130; Spelling, Associational Fluency, and Naming Facility reach no higher than 122 to 129 for the highest age and grade groups). At the highest age range, only 2 of the 14 subtests allow scores above 144.

Similarly, there is no sufficient floor on some subtests for students younger than age 6, for whom, as shown in Table 5.2, raw scores of 0 yield standard scores of 67 to 82 for Letter and Word Recognition, 72 to 81 for Math Computation, 67 to 77 for Listening Comprehension, 69 to 77 for Phonological Awareness, 64 to 72 for Associational Fluency, and 71 to 83 for Naming Facility. Before selecting any achievement test for a student, the examiner should always see what scores would be earned by a recently assessed child of the same age as the examinee. (Dumont & Willis, 2009; Goldman, 1989).

Although we find them very useful, and better than those on most other tests, the KTEA-II error analysis procedures may be challenging for examiners who do not have any background in curriculum and instruction. There are occasional instances in which a student may miss an item for the wrong reason (for example, an addition error in the subproducts of an otherwise flawless long multiplication example), which requires the examiner to override the official categorization of the item.

Standardization

The normative samples of adults are smaller than those for the younger students. The number of examinees per year of age prorates to 250 for age 4 (125 for ages 4:6 to 4:11) and is 220 at age 5, 200 for each year from 6 through 14, 145 for age 15, 140 for age 16 and for age 17, 100 for age 18, 80 for age 19, and an average of about 42 for each year from 20 through 25 (250 total for the six years of age).

Had the sample of older students been larger, it would have been helpful to have separate norms for postsecondary students in 2- and 4-year programs. The age-based norms for older students were based on the roughly same proportions as the U.S. Census of high-school students and drop-outs, students who had graduated from high school and not continued their educations, students who had begun 2-year programs, and students who had begun 4-year programs.

Reliability and Validity

As noted under Interpretation, assessment of oral language, especially on achievement tests, is problematical. Consequently, it is not surprising that the Oral Language Composite has variable correlations with the various oral language measures on other achievement tests. Interpretation of oral language achievement measures on tests of academic achievement should always be undertaken carefully and thoughtfully.

Similarly, the reliabilities are low and the Standard Errors of Measurement high for the age-norm sample for Oral Language (SEM 4.45 to 6.96) and Oral Fluency (SEM 4.25 to 10.28). Therefore, differences needed for statistical significance between these tests and between these and other tests are large.

Administration and Scoring

Error analysis for Letter and Word Recognition and Nonsense Word Decoding requires phonetic transcription of the examinee's pronunciations. Unless the examinee reads very rapidly, this is not difficult for examiners with some background in reading instruction or speech pathology, but it might be challenging for those lacking this background.

The norms tables for the error analyses are clear and helpful but not easy to locate quickly in the manual. Examiners will want to make index tabs to help themselves find the tables more easily. It is essential to use the norms for the error analyses. Raw scores in categories can be very misleading.

Raw scores for Reading Comprehension, Written Expression, Listening Comprehension, and Oral Expression are taken from conversion tables based on the item set(s) administered and the number of items passed within the set(s). The tables for Reading Comprehension and Listening Comprehension are in the record form. The tables for Written and Oral Expression are in the manual. The examiner must remember to use the tables.

We do not find significant difficulties with scoring most of the Written Expression and Oral Expression items, but some of our graduate students, workshop attendees, and colleagues report uncertainty in scoring some items, even with the examples, explanations, and glossary.

The three parts of Naming Facility and four parts of Associational Fluency must be administered between pairs of other subtests to allow breaks between parts of the same subtest. This is a good procedure, but it is easy to forget to give one or more parts.

Although the descriptive categories, with "Average" ranging from 85 to 115, are fewer and simpler than the ones found on many other tests, those differences can be confusing when comparing the KTEA-II with other tests that use different classification schemes. For instructional purposes, an undifferentiated "Average" covering more than two-thirds of the population (percentile ranks 16 through 84) seems unhelpfully broad. There is a notable difference between a student functioning in the lowest 16 percent and one functioning in the highest 17 percent on a particular skill.

The instructions for the third and fourth parts of the Associational Fluency subtest tell the examiner to ask the student what sound a certain word starts with and then ask the student to name another word beginning with the same sound. Then the examiner says to name as many words as possible beginning with the same sound as quickly as possible. The manual and easel note that the examiner's example is not given credit if the examinee uses it. They do not make it clear that the examinee is to be given credit if he or she repeats within the time limit the word the examinee offered during the instructions. The publisher confirmed that credit should be given for that word if the examinee uses it during the time limit of the actual test (personal communication, Verena Getahun, April 26, 2006).

The Associational Fluency subtest has two semantic parts (naming words in categories, such as vegetables) and two phonological parts (naming words beginning with a specified sound). Children in or below kindergarten are supposed to take only the two semantic parts. Children in higher grades also take the two phonological parts. For the older children, it would be helpful to be able to compare performances on the two different skills. The norms tables do give scores for the semantic parts alone for all ages, so examiners can compare a score for semantic alone to a score for semantic plus phonological, but it would be even better to be able to compare semantic and phonological fluency directly.

Similarly, the Naming Facility subtest has three parts: naming colors and naming objects for kindergarten and preschool and additionally naming letters for students in or above first grade. Again, the norms allow at any age comparison of total Naming Facility with just colors and objects, but a direct comparison of letters to colors and objects would be helpful.

Norms for Phonological Awareness extend only through age 12 and spring of grade 6. Even though there would be a limited top for scores for older students, norms for Phonological Awareness would be very useful for poor readers at all ages and grades.

On the back of the record form, the **Sound-Symbol Oral Fluency** computation of Reading-Related Composites **Decoding** and **Reading Fluency** is arranged as shown to the right. In Tables N.6 and N.7 of the *Norms Book*, the bands of error (confidence intervals) are listed vertically in the sequence: Sound-Symbol, Reading Fluency, Decoding, Oral Fluency. The potential for writing the wrong confidence interval for a composite is high.

Interpretation

As noted above, under Test Development and in Tables 5.1 and 5.2, examiners must be very cautious when interpreting scores on subtests that limit possible high scores for older examinees and possible low scores for younger ones. Near-perfect raw scores producing only modestly high standard scores and near-zero raw scores with moderately high standard scores must be interpreted with extreme care and may require assessment with another instrument.

If the eight Comprehensive Achievement Composite (CAC) subtests for older students or the four for children in or below kindergarten are not administered, then subtests and other composites cannot be compared to the CAC. However, subtests and composites can still be statistically compared to each other.

Appendix I in the manual lists differences needed for statistical significance and lists base rates for differences among composites and subtests, which is very useful. However, it would have been helpful to highlight the two subtests that make up each composite. Most examiners want to know whether the components of a total score are sufficiently consistent with one another to permit confident interpretation of that total score.

As noted above, the comparison between the Reading Comprehension and Listening Comprehension subtests is extremely valuable diagnostically because the formats of the two subtests are so similar and the correlation between them is fairly high (.63 in grade 5). The comparison between Written Expression and Oral Expression is somewhat less helpful because of substantial differences in test format and a lower correlation (.43 in grade 5) between the subtests.

The Growth Scale Values (GSVs) seem to be potential very useful, but the manual does not explain how they are to be used. The two-paragraph comment in the manual (pp. 32 to 33), although technically accurate, would just confuse or annoy some examiners.

If, for some reason, an examiner wished to report grade-equivalent or age-equivalent scores, it would be helpful to report them as confidence bands rather than as single points. To do this, the examiner must translate the standard scores at the end points of the standard-score confidence bands back to raw scores and then convert those raw scores to age- or grade-equivalent scores—a laborious process often requiring interpolation.

According to our calculations, some of the stanine equivalents for standard scores in Table N.8 of the *Norms Book* are incorrect: 126 should be stanine 8, 118 should be stanine 7, 111 should be stanine 6, 96 should be stanine 4, 81 should be stanine 2, and 73 should be stanine 1. These errors are annoying because the broad "Average" range of standard scores 85 to 115 may induce more examiners to use stanines for classifying KTEA-II scores.

Assessment of oral language is always a vexatious issue. Oral language is tested, of course, in oral language tests, such as the Clinical Evaluation of Language Fundamentals (CELF-4; Wiig, Semel, & Secord, 2003) or *Comprehensive Assessment of Spoken Language* (CASL; Carrow-Woolfolk, 1999), where it is treated as a separate domain. Oral language is also assessed by most cognitive ability measures, such as the *Differential Ability Scales* (DAS-II; Elliott, 2007) or *Wechsler Intelligence Scale for Children* (WISC-IV; Wechsler, 2003), where it is treated as one broad ability within overall cognitive functioning. Oral language is also included in tests of academic achievement, such as the WIAT-III and KTEA-II, where it is a domain of school achievement, comparable to reading or math. This situation is, at best, confusing to evaluators when they attempt to decide whether oral expression or listening comprehension on an achievement test is weaker than would be expected from the student's scores on cognitive ability tests that require very similar speaking and listening skills.

In our opinion, efforts to create good tests of oral language as aspects of academic achievement, as opposed to tests of oral language as its own domain or oral language as part of cognitive abilities, have met with only limited success. The KTEA-II oral language and oral fluency subtests strike us as being as good as any currently available oral language *academic achievement* tests and better than most, but the reliability and validity coefficients are much weaker than those for most other KTEA-II subtests (please see Chapter 3 and Rapid Reference 5.2 in this chapter).

Final Comment on the KTEA-II

Although we have identified some concerns with the KTEA-II, we consider it to be one of the best currently available comprehensive achievement batteries.

Table 5.1 Ceiling for Students Age 21:0–25:11 and Grade 12: Highest Possible Subtest and Composite Scores

KTEA-II Subtest or Composite	Ages 21:0–25:11		Grade 12[a]	
	Form A	Form B	Form A	Form B
Letter & Word Recognition	139	136	140	135
Reading Comprehension	135	131	144	139
Reading Composite	160	160	160	160
Math Concepts & Applications	138	138	160	160
Math Computation	136	136	148	148
Mathematics Composite	153	153	147	147
Written Expression	160	160	160	160
Spelling	129	122	143	133
Written Language Composite	160	160	160	160
Listening Comprehension	134	134	131	131
Oral Expression	140	131	136	130
Oral Language Composite	160	160	160	160
Phonological Awareness	—	—	—	—
Nonsense Word Decoding	134	134	136	136
Sound-Symbol Composite	—	—	—	—
Word Recognition Fluency	144	144	160	160
Decoding Fluency	137	137	140	140
Reading Fluency	160	160	160	160
Decoding Composite	160	160	160	160
Associational Fluency	123	123	135	135

Naming Facility (RAN)	122	122	127	127
Oral Fluency Composite	160	160	160	160
Comprehensive Achievement	160	160	160	160

Note: From Tables N.2, N.3, N.4, and N.5 of the *KTEA-II Comprehensive Form Norms Book* (Kaufman & Kaufman, 2004b). The maximum standard score on all subtests is 160. Scores ≥ 130 (+2 SD) are in the Upper Extreme and scores ranging from 116 to 130 (+1 to +2 SD) are in the Above Average range.

[a] Spring grade norms are reported here. The values for the Fall grade norms (available in Table N.1 of the *KTEA-II Comprehensive Form Norms Book*) for 12th-grade students are very similar to those reported here.

Table 5.2 Floor for Students Age 4:6–4:8 and Grade K: Lowest Possible Subtest and Composite Scores

KTEA-II Subtest or Composite	Age						Grade[a]	
	4:6– 4:8	4:9– 4:11	5:0– 5:2	5:3– 5:5	5:6– 5:8	5:9– 5:11	K	1
Letter & Word Recognition	82	79	76	73	70	67	59	44
Reading Comprehension	—	—	—	—	—	—	—	63
Reading Composite	—	—	—	—	—	—	—	44
Math Concepts & Applications	60	59	58	57	54	50	50	43
Math Computation	—	—	81	78	75	72	66	52
Mathematics Composite	—	—	42	42	42	42	46	46
Written Expression	48	40	40	40	40	40	40	40
Spelling	—	—	—	—	—	—	—	62
Written Language Composite	—	—	—	—	—	—	—	46
Listening Comprehension	77	74	71	69	68	67	67	61

(continued)

Table 5.2 (Continued)

KTEA-II Subtest or Composite	Age						Grade[a]	
	4:6–4:8	4:9–4:11	5:0–5:2	5:3–5:5	5:6–5:8	5:9–5:11	K	1
Oral Expression	68	65	63	63	62	61	55	50
Oral Language Composite	42	42	42	42	42	42	46	46
Phonological Awareness	—	—	77	73	69	67	63	53
Nonsense Word Decoding	—	—	—	—	—	—	—	76
Sound-Symbol Composite	—	—	—	—	—	—	—	40
Word Recognition Fluency	—	—	—	—	—	—	—	—
Decoding Fluency	—	—	—	—	—	—	—	—
Decoding Composite	—	—	—	—	—	—	—	40
Associational Fluency	72	70	69	67	65	64	53	46
Naming Facility (RAN)	83	81	79	76	73	71	68	45
Oral Fluency Composite	40	40	40	40	40	40	40	40
Comprehensive Achievement	40	40	40	40	40	40	40	43

Note: From Tables N.2, N.3, N.4, and N.5 of the *KTEA-II Comprehensive Form Norms Book* (Kaufman & Kaufman, 2004b). The minimum standard score on all subtests is 40. Scores ≤ 69 (–2 SD) are in the Lower Extreme and scores ranging from 70 to 84 (–1 to –2 SD) are in the Below Average range. Data are reported for Form A only. However, in most cases the data for Form B are equivalent to Form A or only 1 to 2 points different. Values shown here are standard scores corresponding to raw scores of zero.

[a]Spring grade norms are reported here. The values for the Fall grade norms (available in Table N.1 of the *KTEA-II Comprehensive Form Norms Book*) for kindergarten and first grade students are very similar to those reported here.

🪶 TEST YOURSELF 🪶

....

1. **The revised discontinue rules for the WIAT-III provide a consistent discontinuation rule of four consecutive failures for most subtests.**

   True or False?

2. **The WIAT-III scoring program offers which of the following among its useful features**

   a) an enhanced skill analysis for core subtests

   b) intervention goal statements to assist with IEP development

   c) a research-supported pattern of strengths and weaknesses discrepancy analysis

   d) all of the above

3. **A tape recorder is specified for recording the student's oral responses to several WIAT-III subtests including**

   a) Math Problem Solving

   b) Word Reading

   c) Pseudoword Decoding

   d) Reading Comprehension

   e) Oral Expression

   f) Oral Reading Fluency

   g) Oral Discourse Comprehension

4. **Unlike error analyses on many tests, the KTEA-II categories of weakness-average-strength are based on the test norms.**

   True or False?

5. **Both the KTEA-II and the WIAT-III have having subtests and/or composites that measure all eight areas of achievement specified by IDEA legislation as important for identifying and classifying learning disabilities.**

   True or False?

Answers: 1. True; 2. d; 3. b, c, e, f; 4. True; 5. True

Six

ILLUSTRATIVE CASE REPORTS

T his chapter presents case studies of three children who were referred for psychoeducational evaluation or who participated in WIAT-III standard-ization. The first child, Luke, age 8, was referred for an evaluation due to concerns about his ability to follow oral directions and his difficulties with reading comprehension and written expression. He was administered the WISC-IV and WIAT-III. The second child, Ryan, age 12, was administered the KTEA-II and KABC-II, as well as measures of his neuropsychological and behavioral functioning, to evaluate concerns regarding his attentional difficulties, along with his receptive and expressive language problems. The third child, Anika, age 10, demonstrated difficulties in the areas of basic reading, reading fluency, and written expression. She was administered the WIAT-III, KABC-II, and KTEA-II.

The goals of this chapter are to bring all other facets of this book together to demonstrate how the WIAT-III and KTEA-II may be used as part of a comprehensive battery, and to demonstrate the cross-validation of hypotheses with behavioral observations, background information, and supplemental test scores. The basic outline for each report includes the following: reason for referral, background information, appearance of client and behavioral observa-tions, tests administered, test results and interpretation, summary diagnostic impression, and recommendations. All of the test data are presented in a psychometric summary at the end of each report.

As in all illustrative cases presented throughout this book, the identifying data of the clients have been changed to protect their confidentiality.

CASE REPORT 1: LUKE, AGE AT EVALUATION: 8 YEARS, 0 MONTHS, GRADE: 2, NORMS USED: AGE BASED

Purpose of the Evaluation

Luke's parents sought this evaluation to determine whether processing weaknesses may be interfering with his achievement and performance in certain areas. He has been struggling with following oral directions, reading comprehension, and letter reversals. This evaluation assessed his mental ability, thinking skills, oral language, early reading, writing, and mathematics skills, and some nonverbal processes.

History and Background

Luke's mother and father provided information regarding his educational and developmental history. Luke is an only child who lives with both parents. His parents reported that he met developmental milestones at age-appropriate times, and his mother described him as an easy baby. His medical history is unremarkable. According to a central auditory evaluation and a visual processing evaluation completed last year, Luke's hearing is within normal limits and his vision is 20/20 in each eye.

Luke's parents reported that he began struggling with reading comprehension this year and he does not enjoy reading at home. In addition, he reverses many of his letters during writing tasks. His parents indicated that when they ask him to follow a sequence of directions, he will follow the directions incorrectly or do some, but not all, of the behaviors requested. Luke's teacher reported that Luke is a well-behaved, cooperative student with strong social skills. His teacher also reported that he needs reminders to stay on task, particularly during reading activities.

Behavioral Observations

Luke was polite, attentive, and cooperative throughout testing. Rapport was easily established, and overall, Luke was able to communicate effectively and establish a positive, friendly relationship with the examiner. Luke maintained good eye contact during conversation and responded appropriately during social interactions. He did not use a great deal of gesture when communicating, but his style did not detract from his ability to communicate well.

Upon entering the testing environment, his intellectual curiosity was immediately apparent as he inquired about several objects in the room. He was attentive to details in his surroundings. Luke smiled frequently and displayed a delightful sense of humor. Praise and periodic breaks were offered to Luke, but, in general, he did not seem dependent upon them to sustain motivation. Only on tasks that were especially difficult for him did he display some avoidance behaviors (e.g., asking for frequent breaks, getting out of his seat). Luke appeared to take pride in his work and seemed confident in his responses.

Luke was systematic and persistent in his approach to tasks. In general, he did not become easily frustrated or distractible on difficult items; periodically, he would simply say he did not know the answer. Luke was meticulous and deliberate, particularly on performance tasks involving a visual-motor component, and proceeded at a steady pace. He was generally thoughtful and not overly impulsive in his responses. However, on some occasions, he attempted to begin tasks without waiting for the instructions to be read. Despite his eagerness to begin, Luke demonstrated adequate comprehension of all administered tasks.

Luke was able to follow directions and understand tasks without significant problems, he exhibited no visual or auditory problems that negatively affected his performance, and he appeared to put forth his best effort on the administered tasks. Thus, the results of this evaluation are believed to accurately reflect Luke's current ability and achievement level.

TESTS ADMINISTERED

Wechsler Intelligence Scale for Children–Fourth Edition (WISC-IV)
Wechsler Individual Achievement Test–Third Edition (WIAT-III)

Test Results

Cognitive Ability

Luke was administered the Wechsler Intelligence Scale for Children–Fourth Edition (WISC-IV) to assess his overall cognitive ability and processing strengths and weaknesses. Ten WISC-IV subtest scores were grouped into four global areas, or index scores, that reflect various processing skills. The four indexes include: Verbal Comprehension, which measures the depth of knowledge acquired from one's culture; Perceptual Reasoning, which involves solving problems nonverbally by perceiving, storing, and manipulating visual patterns; Short Term Memory, which involves taking in and holding information to use within seconds; and Processing Speed, which measures cognitive processing efficiency. Significant scatter was exhibited between Luke's index scores, with his abilities varying between Average range and Below Average range. Thus, his

WISC-IV Full Scale IQ score of 94 (34th percentile; Average range of function-ing) does not provide a good estimate of his overall cognitive ability because it represents a combination of very diverse abilities. A better understanding of his cognitive skills can be gleaned by interpreting his individual index scores.

Luke's ability to demonstrate knowledge that he has acquired from his culture and reason with acquired information was overall in the Below Average range, as evident from his Verbal Comprehension Index (VCI) standard score of 83 (13th percentile). However, his abilities within this domain were variable, indicating that his abilities were not equally well developed. He showed Average perform-ance in his ability to understand and explain societal norms (Comprehension = 25th percentile) and identify similarities between verbal concepts (Similarities = 37th percentile), but his ability to define vocabulary words was in the Below Average range (Vocabulary = 2nd percentile) compared to his peers. Due to the significant variability in his performance on the Verbal Comprehension tasks, his VCI represents the midpoint of a diverse set of verbal abilities.

In contrast to his variable skills evident on the Verbal Comprehension Index, Luke demonstrated consistently well-developed skills on the Perceptual Reason-ing Index (PRI). His abilities to solve problems nonverbally by perceiving, storing, and manipulating visual patterns were in the Average range, and were evident from his PRI standard score of 108 (70th percentile). Luke's nonverbal problem-solving skills were assessed with three tasks: arranging blocks to match a model (Block Design = 63rd percentile), matching pictures that belong together based on common characteristics (Picture Concepts = 50th percentile), and completing patterns within a matrix of nonverbal stimuli (Matrix Reasoning = 84th percentile). His Average range performance on these tasks that tapped nonverbal skills was consistent with Luke's parents' report that he has no repor-ted difficulties with nonverbal skills, such as left-right or spatial orientation, time orientation, or social perception. No problems were detected with perceptual-motor skills or gross-motor skills during the evaluation.

Similar to his nonverbal reasoning skills, Luke's ability to perform simple, clerical-type tasks quickly was in the Average range. This ability was evident from his Processing Speed Index (PSI) of 103 (58th percentile). His abilities in this domain were assessed by two tasks: coding symbols according to a key (Coding = 37th percentile), and determining whether one of two symbols was present in a row of different symbols under timed conditions range (Symbol Search = 75th percentile).

Luke also demonstrated Average range ability to take in and hold information to use within seconds. His short-term memory skill was apparent from his performance on the Working Memory Index (WMI) (standard score = 91; 27th percentile). When Luke was required to recall an orally presented string of random digits, he performed within the Average range (Digit Span = 50th percentile). He also performed in the Average range when required to recall and sequence an orally presented string of letters and digits, first saying the digits in increasing order, then saying the letters in alphabetical order (Letter-Number Sequencing = 16th percentile).

A significant and rare discrepancy of 25 points was identified between the VCI and the PRI scores, occurring in approximately 3.7 percent of the population. A significant and uncommon discrepancy was also identified between the VCI and the PSI, occurring in 11.6 percent of the population. In addition, a significant and uncommon discrepancy was identified between the PRI and the WMI, occurring in 13.6 percent of the population. Overall, these scores indicate significant variability among Luke's processing abilities, which range from Below Average to Average, with a significant relative weakness in the area of verbal comprehension.

Academic Achievement

Similar to the variability noted within his cognitive abilities, Luke demonstrated variability in his performance on tests of academic achievement. He was administered the Wechsler Individual Achievement Test—Third Edition to gather information about his academic skills across several domains, which are described below.

Oral Language

Luke's receptive (listening) and expressive (speaking) language skills were evaluated at the level of vocabulary, sentence, and discourse using a variety of tasks. This is an area of mixed achievement.

Auditory Receptive Language

To assess his comprehension of single words, Luke was administered the Receptive Vocabulary component of the WIAT-III Listening Comprehension subtest. He was asked to point to the picture that corresponded to each administered word. His score was within the Average range (standard score = 94).

To assess receptive language skills at the sentence and discourse levels, Luke was administered the Oral Discourse Comprehension component of the WIAT-III Listening Comprehension subtest. He was asked to listen to one or more sentences from an audio CD and then answer open-ended comprehension questions. Luke did not appear to be listening carefully during this task. His responses to the comprehension questions were often not based on the information presented. Inferential questions were particularly difficult for him. His performance was in the Below Average range (standard score = 80).

Overall, Luke displayed variability in his receptive language skills. His understanding of single words was in the Average range. At the sentence and discourse level, his comprehension of oral discourse was Below Average.

Auditory Expressive Language

Throughout our evaluation, Luke tended to respond to questions with complete, well-formulated sentences and mature vocabulary. For example, his response to one question was, "I'm not quite sure about that." After using coins to figure out a math problem, he commented, "That was useful."

The Expressive Vocabulary component of the WIAT-III Oral Expression subtest assessed Luke's expressive vocabulary by requiring him to look at pictures, listen to an oral definition, and then name each concept presented. His performance was at the high end of the Average range (standard score = 112). The Oral Word Fluency component of the same subtest was administered to assess Luke's word retrieval skills and flexibility of thought processes. He was asked to name things belonging to a given category (e.g., animals) within a time limit. His performance was within the Average range (standard score = 105).

To assess expressive syntax and memory for sentences, Luke was administered the Sentence Repetition component of the WIAT-III Oral Expression subtest. He was asked to listen to sentences of increasing length and repeat them back. He scored at the high end of the Average range (standard score = 115).

Overall, Luke's expressive language skills are within the Average range, commensurate with his mental ability.

Reading

Luke's achievement in the area of reading was assessed both silently and orally and with single words and words in context. Assessment also included measures of phonological processing skills, which have been shown to be important for reading achievement.

When administered a test that required him to read single words aloud (WIAT-III Word Reading subtest), his reading indicated that he knows some sight words; however, when decoding unfamiliar words, he does not usually attempt to construct a meaningful word. His reading of multisyllabic words was somewhat dysfluent, and he needed to be reminded to blend the sounds together. Overall, Luke scored within the Average range (standard score = 90). Luke was also administered a Pseudoword Decoding subtest (WIAT-III) that required him to decode single non-words. His performance was within the High Average range (standard score = 113). His speed of word reading and pseudoword decoding was slower than approximately 95 percent and 90 percent, respectively, of his same-age peers.

Luke's oral reading in context was measured by the Oral Reading Fluency subtest of the WIAT-III, which required him to read passages aloud under timed conditions. His fluency score was in the Below Average range (standard score = 83). His errors suggest that he was reading for meaning as he often inserted words that were semantically acceptable and made several repetitions to establish fluency and cohesion. He also made several errors that were graphically similar (e.g., rest instead of nest), but often self-corrected when his errors changed the meaning of the sentence. The rate and accuracy with which he read the passages were both in the Below Average range (standard scores = 83, 82, respectively).

To assess his silent reading in context, he was administered the Reading Comprehension subtest (WIAT-III), which required him to read grade-appropriate narrative and expository passages and answer open-ended comprehension questions by providing an oral response. His performance was in the Below Average range (standard score = 83). Inferential comprehension questions were particularly difficult for him.

Luke was administered the Early Reading Skills subtest of the WIAT-III to assess his proficiency in many of the subskills that may contribute to reading achievement. He performed well on rhyming tasks, but had some difficulty on items requiring him to recognize ending sounds of words and items requiring him to blend sounds together to make a whole word. He scored within the Average range (standard score = 100).

Overall, Luke's performance in the area of reading and reading-related skills ranges from Below Average to Above Average. His word attack skills are a relative strength, but he struggled with reading comprehension and oral reading fluency. Luke demonstrated phonological processing skills in the Average range.

Writing

At the outset of his evaluation, Luke indicated that writing is his favorite subject. He seemed to enjoy all the writing tasks he was administered and commented periodically on his ability to write stories and reports well. Throughout this evaluation, Luke wrote using his left hand and an adaptive, tripod grip. He preferred to write in cursive on all tasks except those that were timed. Luke appeared to take pride in his manuscript, using slow, deliberate strokes. His manuscript was meticulous and legible, but his print was often difficult to read. His letter and number formations were well planned, but Luke sometimes reversed letters when writing in print (e.g., b instead of d, q instead of p). No reversals were made in Luke's cursive writing.

Luke was administered a test of Alphabet Writing Fluency (WIAT-III), which required him to write as many letters of the alphabet as possible within 30 seconds. He printed nine letters using a combination of upper and lower case; he only received credit for six letters because three letters were reversed (b, d, f). His performance was in the Below Average range.

On a test of written spelling (WIAT-III Spelling subtest), Luke scored well within the Average range (standard score = 110). His performance suggests that he has acquired strong orthographic awareness and usually represents all the sounds within words.

To assess Luke's written language at the sentence level, he was administered the Sentence Composition subtest (WIAT-III) that required him to combine sentences into one sentence that means the same thing (Sentence Combining component) and to write sentences using a target word (Sentence Building component). His performance was within the average range (SS = 108), but he performed much better on Sentence Combining (SS = 113) than Sentence Building (SS = 89). On Sentence Building, he seemed to have some difficulty thinking of sentences to write and did not always use the target word with appropriate context. His performance reflected strong spelling skills and consistent use of capitalization and ending punctuation; however, he alternated between writing in manuscript and in print, and he was penalized for letter reversals when printing.

In summary, Luke's overall performance in the area of writing ranges from Below Average to Average. His manuscript is adequate, but legibility and letter reversals were problematic when Luke wrote in print. His performance was strong on tests of spelling and sentence combining. However, he struggled with alphabet writing fluency and sentence building.

Mathematics

Luke's teachers report that math is an area of relative strength; however, during the evaluation, Luke indicated that math was his least favorite subject. Despite his feelings about math, he was thoughtful and worked diligently on every problem. His performance in this area was consistent and his scores ranged from Average to Above Average.

On a written test of math calculation (WIAT-III Numerical Operations subtest), Luke was able to correctly add single- and double-digit numbers, carrying numbers when needed, and subtract single numbers. He was only able to subtract double-digit numbers that did not require borrowing. When borrowing was necessary, he simply subtracted the smaller number on the top from the larger number below. He was able to work problems presented both horizontally and vertically. Luke's performance on this test was within the Average range (standard score = 99).

To assess mathematics reasoning and computation, Luke was administered the Math Problem Solving subtest (WIAT-III) that required him to view pictures and word problems and listen as each problem was read aloud to him. He was provided with a pencil and piece of paper, which he chose to use on a few occasions. Even though the text was printed in front of him, at one point he asked for a word problem to be repeated. As problems were read aloud to him, Luke preferred to listen without following along. He often used his fingers for counting and on one occasion, used coins from his pocket to solve a problem. Luke's performance on this test was within the Above Average range (standard score = 118).

To assess Luke's math fluency, he was administered the Math Fluency—Addition and Subtraction subtests from the WIAT-III. He tested within the Average range on both subtests.

Overall, Luke's performance in the area of mathematics ranges from Average to Above Average. These scores are consistent with his High Average performance on the arithmetic subtest of the WISC-IV. Despite his strong mathematical skills, Luke's weaknesses in reading comprehension and avoidance of reading tasks are likely to interfere with his performance on word problems when working independently.

Summary

Luke is an 8-year-old second grader who was referred for an evaluation by his parents to determine whether processing weaknesses may be interfering with his achievement and performance in certain areas (i.e., following oral directions, reading comprehension, and letter reversals.) The results of the evaluation indicate that Luke's cognitive abilities are significantly variable, ranging from Average level skill in solving nonverbal problems, short-term memory, and cognitive processing efficiency, to Below Average level skill in his ability to acquire and reason with information from his culture. Considerable variability was also found within and across many areas of achievement, ranging from Below Average to Above Average. Luke demonstrated academic abilities in the Average range consistently across tasks of mathematics and mathematics fluency, as well as basic reading skills. However, his skills in the academic domains of Oral Language, Written Expression, and Reading Comprehension and Fluency were more variable with some areas of weakness noted. Specifically, consistent weaknesses were demonstrated in the areas of reading comprehension and reading fluency (both Below Average). Written expression is an area of mixed achievement for Luke. He demonstrated strong performance in spelling and sentence combining and weak performance in the areas of alphabet writing fluency and sentence building. In the domain of Oral Language, he demonstrated Average range oral expression abilities, but had Below Average performance on Oral Discourse Comprehension. To evaluate whether Luke's pattern of strengths and weaknesses across his ability and achievement profile are consistent with a specific learning disability, a pattern of strengths and weaknesses (PSW) discrepancy analysis was conducted in the achievement areas of reading comprehension and fluency (see Tables 6.1–6.5).

Analysis for the Identification of a Specific Learning Disability

Children with specific learning disabilities typically show a cognitive processing weakness that is contributing to their academic achievement weakness. In Luke's case, he has an academic weakness in the area of reading comprehension, which was evident in his Reading Comprehension and Fluency composite standard score of 79. In contrast, Luke showed evidence of a cognitive processing strength in his WISC–IV PRI standard score of 108. Theory and research have not established a strong relationship between perceptual reasoning and reading comprehension and fluency; thus, it would be expected that a child with a specific learning disability would have significantly different scores when comparing this cognitive processing strength to the achievement weakness. In Luke's case, a significant difference ($p = .01$) was indeed found between the processing strength (PRI) and the achievement weakness (Reading Comprehension and Fluency).

In addition to the significant difference between cognitive processing strengths and achievement weaknesses, children with specific learning disabilities typically show a pattern of significant difference between their cognitive processing strengths and their cognitive processing weaknesses. Luke's WISC-IV VCI standard score of 83 represented his processing weakness, as it is in the Below Average range and is relatively low compared to most of his other cognitive abilities (all in the Average range). Verbal comprehension is theoretically and empirically related to reading comprehension and fluency performance so it would be expected to be consistent with his achievement deficit, while also being significantly different from his cognitive processing strength. In Luke's case, a significant difference ($p = .05$) was found between the processing strength (PRI) and the processing weakness (VCI). Overall, the results from the analysis of Luke's pattern of strengths and weaknesses support the identification of a specific learning disability in the areas of reading comprehension and reading fluency.

Recommendations

Oral Language

1. Listening comprehension and inferential skills might be strengthened by asking Luke to answer factual and inferential questions about stories and paragraphs that have been read to him.
2. Luke's grammatical understanding and speaking skills may be improved by focusing on his comprehension and use of morphology and irregular past tense verbs. Reading and writing can be used to support instruction in this area.
3. Luke's ability to discriminate between the sounds within words and correctly perceive spoken words is facilitated by his effective use of context. Instruction in the area of oral language should be provided in the context of longer units of meaningful discourse (e.g., phrases, sentences).

Reading

1. Reading instruction should emphasize meaningful units of discourse and context. Luke's reading fluency may be improved by increasing his sight vocabulary of familiar words and phrases and combining them to form sentences. He should be encouraged to continue reading for meaning and making predictions.
2. Reading comprehension might be strengthened by increasing Luke's attention span through the use of stimulating material that he enjoys. Taking turns reading paragraphs aloud with Luke and each person asking comprehension questions about each paragraph (i.e., reciprocal reading) may be useful for sustaining his attention and increasing his awareness of important content.
3. Luke's silent reading comprehension and inferential skills can be monitored and strengthened by asking him questions after he reads. Questions should emphasize prediction, cause and effect, main ideas, and supporting details.
4. Luke's comprehension of mathematics word problems should be carefully monitored. It is recommended that word problems be used to encourage reading for meaning, ensuring that he understands the correct meaning of mathematics terminology.

Writing

1. Writing activities that are meaningful and functional will continue to foster Luke's love of writing. Writing productivity may be increased by allowing him to type some longer units of discourse on a computer.
2. It is recommended that Luke receive help and practice using specific words to construct sentences. These activities can incorporate work on grammar and morphology.
3. Luke's use of print may be improved with instruction focusing on legibility and correcting letter reversals.

PSYCHOMETRIC SUMMARY FOR LUKE

Table 6.1 Wechsler Intelligence Scale for Children–Fourth Edition (WISC–IV) Scores

Index/IQ Subtest	Score	95% Conf. Interval	Percentile Rank	Descriptive Category
Verbal Comprehension	83	77–91	13	Below Average/ Normative Weakness
Similarities	9		37	
Vocabulary	4		2	
Comprehension	8		25	
Perceptual Reasoning	108	100–115	70	Average Range/ Within Normal Limits
Block Design	11		63	
Picture Concepts	10		50	
Matrix Reasoning	13		84	
Working Memory	91	84–99	27	Average Range/ Within Normal Limits
Digit Span	10		50	
Letter-Number Sequencing	7		16	

(continued)

Table 6.1 (Continued)

Index/IQ Subtest	Score	95% Conf. Interval	Percentile Rank	Descriptive Category
Processing Speed	103	94–112	58	Average Range/ Within Normal Limits
Coding	9		37	
Symbol Search	12		75	
Full Scale IQ	94	89–99	34	Average Range/ Within Normal Limits

Note: WISC-IV Indexes have a mean of 100 and a standard deviation of 15. WISC-IV subtests have a mean of 10 and a standard deviation of 3.

Table 6.2 WISC-IV Index Level Discrepancy Comparisons

Index Comparisons	Scaled Score 1	Scaled Score 2	Diff.	Critical Value	Sig. Diff. Y/N	Base Rate
VCI–PRI	83	108	−25	10.6	Y	3.7%
VCI–WMI	83	91	−8	11.38	N	
VCI–PSI	83	103	−20	12.11	Y	11.6%
PRI–WMI	108	91	17	11.76	Y	13.6%
PRI–PSI	108	103	5	12.47	N	
WMI–PSI	91	103	−12	13.14	N	

Note: Base rate by overall sample; statistical significance (critical values) at the 0.05 level.

Table 6.3 Wechsler Individual Achievment Test–Third Edition (WIAT-III) Scores

Composite/ Subtest/ Subtest Component	Standard Score	95% Confidence Interval	Percentile Rank	Qualitative Description
Oral Language	95	86–104	37	Average
Listening Comprehension	83	71–95	13	Below Average
Receptive Vocabulary	92	—	30	Average
Oral Discourse Comprehension	80	—	9	Below Average

Composite/ Subtest/ Subtest Component	Standard Score	95% Confidence Interval	Percentile Rank	Qualitative Description
Oral Expression	110	99–121	75	Average
Expressive Vocabulary	107	—	68	Average
Oral Word Fluency	105	—	63	Average
Sentence Repetition	112	—	79	Average
Total Reading	89	85–93	23	Average
Reading Comprehension	83	73–93	13	Below Average
Word Reading	90	86–94	25	Average
Pseudoword Decoding	113	108–118	81	Average
Oral Reading Fluency	83	75–91	13	Below Average
Basic Reading	100	97–103	50	Average
Word Reading	90	86–94	25	Average
Pseudoword Decoding	113	108–118	81	Average
Reading Comprehension and Fluency	79	72–86	8	Below Average
Reading Comprehension	83	73–93	13	Below Average
Oral Reading Fluency	83	75–91	13	Below Average
Written Expression	95	86–104	37	Average
Alphabet Writing Fluency	80	64–96	9	Below Average
Sentence Composition	101	92–110	53	Average
Sentence Building	89	—	23	Average
Sentence Combining	113	—	81	Average
Spelling	111	104–118	77	Average
Mathematics	110	102–118	75	Average
Math Problem Solving	118	108–128	88	Above Average
Numerical Operations	100	90–110	50	Average
Math Fluency	97	90–104	42	Average
Math Fluency—Addition	98	87–109	45	Average

(continued)

Table 6.3 (Continued)

Composite/ Subtest/ Subtest Component	Standard Score	95% Confidence Interval	Percentile Rank	Qualitative Description
Math Fluency— Subtraction	94	85–103	34	Average
Total Achievement	96	92–100	39	Average
Early Reading Skills	92	80–104	30	Average

Table 6.4 WIAT-III Cumulative Percentages

Supplemental Score	Cumulative Percentage
Word Reading Speed	5%
Pseudoword Decoding Speed	10%

Table 6.5 WIAT-III Supplemental Subtest Score Summary

Score Name	Standard Score	95% Confidence Interval	Percentile Rank	Qualitative Description
Oral Reading Accuracy	83	71–95	13	Below Average
Oral Reading Rate	82	74–90	12	Below Average

CASE REPORT 2: RYAN P., AGE: 12 YEARS, 2 MONTHS, EDUCATION: 6TH GRADE

Reason for Evaluation

Ryan P. is a 12-year-old boy who attends the sixth grade at Hillside Elementary School. Ryan lives at home with his parents, his 10-year-old brother, and his 8-year-old sister. This evaluation was initiated at his parents' request due to their concerns regarding Ryan's attentional difficulties, along with some receptive and expressive language problems identified on speech and language testing. Ryan has had some partial assessments done in the past; however, he has never had a full, comprehensive neuropsychological evaluation. He has been diagnosed with a mood disorder, and he is currently on Trileptal and Seroquel. His parents are eager for information regarding any specific neurocognitive deficit that Ryan may be displaying, and what can be done to help him in this regard. This assessment will evaluate Ryan's cognitive status as well as assess any specific academic and emotional difficulties.

Background Information

Developmental History and Health

According to Mr. and Ms. P., Ryan is the product of a normal, full-term pregnancy, and a normal labor and delivery. He weighed 8 lbs. 11 oz. at birth. Ryan was described as a very fussy, colicky baby who did not eat or sleep well and suffered from "stomach problems." His mother indicated that he was nursed for 6 months. Ryan suffered from frequent ear infections until age two. No other health problems or behavior difficulties were noted as an infant. According to Ryan's parents, he reached all his developmental milestones on time. No significant deficits in self-help skills or adaptive behavior were reported.

As noted above, Ryan is currently on Trileptal and Seroquel, which were prescribed for his mood disorder. He has had no head injuries or concussions. Ryan complains of frequent stomach aches, nausea, and frequent bowel movements. His parents indicated that these complaints are related to anxiety. Ryan's parents indicated that he displays irregular sleeping patterns, and he has asked his mother for Benadryl to help him fall asleep at night. Although he has difficulty falling asleep at night, once he is asleep, he sleeps deeply. However, he has trouble staying awake in the classroom, and constantly falls asleep during class. His parents voiced concerns about Ryan's difficulty following auditory instruction, although they do not suspect a hearing loss, and his hearing was recently checked at school. Ryan displays a moderate impairment in articulation.

Ryan's parents described him a talented athlete with good gross and fine coordination skills. He participates in several sports, including soccer, football, and skating, and he excels in these areas. Ryan demonstrates some significant sensory sensitivities. He cannot tolerate tags in his clothes, and he insists of wearing a specific type of sock. He also displays some motor tics, including switching his shoulder and eye blinking.

Ryan's family history has notable instances of psychological problems. His mother reported that she is currently medicated for depression, as well as possible ADHD. She also indicated that Ryan's maternal grandmother has a history of depression and suicide attempts. Ryan's father reported symptoms of high anxiety, some inattention, as well as processing problems. He noted that Ryan's paternal grandfather suffered from mood swings and anger control difficulties.

Academic History

Ryan began preschool at age 3 ½ and kindergarten at age 5. He reportedly had some mild difficulty learning his letters and numbers, but his teachers reported that he was functioning at appropriate levels for his age. Ryan began attending

Hillside Elementary School at first grade. His parents noted that no behavior difficulties were reported, aside from some overactivity in the lunch line and the tendency to blurt out answers in class. Through second grade, he reportedly did well academically, and his grades were consistently As and Bs.

However, in third grade, Ryan's parents noted the demands of his very performance-oriented school increased, and they indicated that Ryan demonstrated some academic difficulty and organizational problems at this school. He forgot his assignments, he did not complete homework, and he appeared to cover up his embarrassment about not understanding the work by hiding assignments in his desk. Ryan expressed significant anxiety to his parents in relation to the statewide group standardized tests, although his overall results were average for his age. His fourth grade teacher told Mr. and Ms. P. that movement and sounds in the classroom easily distracted Ryan and that "even things on the wall distract him." As a result, Ryan was tested through the school district at the beginning of fifth grade. These results indicated that Ryan's intellectual functioning was in the Low Average range (Full Scale IQ = 83), and receptive language difficulties and articulation problems were reported. As a result of this testing, Ryan received speech pathology services at school until the end of the school year.

Ryan apparently has done better academically during his sixth grade year. However, his parents reported that he continues to struggle to complete his homework assignments and that he is extremely disorganized. He typically does his homework at the kitchen table, where there are numerous distractions from his younger sister. His father noted that there are many unnecessary materials on the table at this time, and that it is an extremely disorganized environment. Ms. P. voiced her concern about both Ryan and her own organizational difficulties, and she expressed eagerness for any assistance in this regard. In an interview with Ryan's sixth grade teacher, she noted that her greatest concerns about Ryan were his inability to focus, his poor study and organizational skills, and his sleepiness. She noted that he is unable to stay awake between 9 am to 10:30 am when the class is working on reading, and that she finds it is very unusual for a student to be sleepy at this time. She indicated that Ryan "is wired" after lunch and is fidgety and more distractible. She reported that Ryan is strong in math and spelling skills, but that he is "overwhelmed" by writing tasks and is unable to complete these tasks in the classroom. She described Ryan as having a pleasant and sweet personality, a good sense of humor, and a willingness to participate in new things, and she noted that he is very popular among his peers. According to his teacher, Ryan is never uncooperative or defiant in class, and aside from some aggressive behavior on the playground, she has not noted any inappropriate conduct from him.

In an interview with Ryan, he expressed an acute awareness about his difficulty remaining awake at school. He noted: "If I read, I won't fall asleep, but if they read I get tired." When asked if he can anticipate himself falling asleep, he indicated that "I kind of know . . . I stay up and listen to it . . . my eyes are closed, I am half asleep, I can hear what is going on, I usually know what is going on." He also indicated that in the past he had experienced significant memory problems, but that "it is better now for a few weeks or months." He was unable to express what had changed to improve his memory abilities.

Currently, his parents described Ryan as extremely distractible and displaying poor sustained attention. However, his attention span is better if he is interested in the subject matter. His father indicated that, when Ryan focuses, "he completes his work and tasks amazingly," but that he is rarely focused. His processing speed is reported to be inconsistent. His parents indicated that he has adequate problem-solving skills and intact visual-spatial ability. His expressive language is reported to be variable and deficits in his receptive language have been noted. His parents are unsure whether this reflects inattention, auditory processing difficulties, or an undetected hearing deficit. According to Mr. and Ms. P., Ryan demonstrates very concrete thought processes, he does not display the capacity for abstract reasoning, and he is very literal in his interpretation of events and expressions.

Emotional and Social Development

Mr. and Ms. P. reported that Ryan has always been a very irritable child who would lose control over small details, such as his trousers being too pressed, or the sun being in his eyes. In third grade, Ryan apparently began displaying more intense temper outbursts, mood instability, and volatility. He also began having extreme difficulty with transitions. His parents indicated that at this time the family was experiencing a high level of stress due to moving home, building and selling another home, and living with Ryan's grandparents. Ryan was apparently displaying significant anger problems that were "creating rifts in the family." He was also extremely anxious, and he had significant difficulty getting organized in the morning.

Ryan began psychiatric treatment at this time. His psychiatrist recommended that a course of Tripleptal and Seroquel be prescribed as his medication regime. The medication appeared to have a positive effect.

From a social point of view, Ryan is reported to be very popular and has several good friends. His mother described him as having a "very loving heart," and she reported that he likes to take care of the elderly, as well as a Down's syndrome child at his school. His father noted that he is "very considerate, willing to please, quick witted, and funny." Ryan apparently gets along well with his brother, although there is reported to be some competition and friction between them at times. His parents noted that he used to "adore" his sister and was very responsible with her. However, he now tends to antagonize his sister, as well as the family dog, and that he can be very aggressive in this regard. His parents wondered whether this could be a means for Ryan to release his frustration after a day at school.

Behavioral Observations

Ryan presented himself as a cute and friendly 12-year-old boy. Rapport was easily established, and Ryan cooperated and worked diligently. He made no complaints about the length of testing, and he did not request additional breaks beyond those suggested by the examiner. However, on the first day of testing, Ryan reported being very tired when he arrived, which he attributed to having had a late night the evening before. On this day, he was noted to be fairly fidgety, and he frequently played with his watch, which he reported was new and needed to be reset. However, these behaviors were not evident during the second testing session. In general, Ryan's performances were extremely slow. He did not appear to rush through any task or to feel pressured on timed tests.

During the first day of testing, although Ryan gave the appearance of being attentive on many tasks, he demonstrated some significant difficulty remaining alert. On several occasions, he would become completely unresponsive while completing a task, and he would sit staring ahead and blinking repetitively. On one occasion, Ryan appeared to fall asleep right after this episode. He was unable to explain what he had been experiencing, merely stating that he was unable to think of any further responses to the task at hand. He did not appear to be confused, and he was alert immediately after the episode. Although he was unable to complete the task he had been working on, he was able to respond to a new task. This was most noticeable on language-based tasks, and on tasks that did not require him to make extensive verbal or motor responses, but rather to focus on verbal information presented by the examiner. These episodes lasted a few seconds to a minute. With the exception of these incidents, Ryan did appear to be attentive and focused during the testing. In contrast, Ryan appeared to be completely alert during the second day of testing, and none of the episodes described above were observed. It should be noted that Ryan did not take his dose of Trileptal on the second day, and his dose of Seroquel had been increased at that time. In addition, he reported going to sleep earlier the night before, and he certainly appeared more vigilant and attentive. In addition, Ryan chewed gum during his second day of testing, and he reported that this helped him remain alert.

Ryan appeared to put forward his best effort at all times. On the basis of these behavior observations, this assessment appears to be a valid measure of Ryan's neuropsychological functioning at this time.

ASSESSMENT PROCEDURES & TESTS ADMINISTERED

- Clinical interview with Mr. and Ms. P.
- Clinical interview with Ryan
- Kaufman Assessment Battery for Children–Second Edition (KABC-II)
- A Developmental Neuropsychological Assessment (NEPSY): Selected Subtests
- Kaufman Test of Educational Achievement–Second Edition (KTEA-II)
- IVA Continuous Performance Test (IVA)
- Children's Depression Inventory (CDI)
- Piers-Harris Children's Self-Concept Scale 2 (PHSCS2)
- Revised Children's Manifest Anxiety Scale (RCMAS)
- Rorschach
- Sensory Profile
- Achenbach Child Behavior Checklist/6–18 (CBCL)
- Achenbach Teacher's Report Form/6–18 (TRF)
- Conners' Parent Rating Scale–Revised: Long Version
- Conners' Teacher Rating Scale–Revised: Long Version

Test Results

Intellectual Abilities

To assess Ryan's intellectual ability, he was administered the Kaufman Assessment Battery for Children–Second Edition (KABC-II), which is an individually administered test of a child's intellectual ability and cognitive strengths and weaknesses. One of the objectives of this test is to provide a more fair assessment of the processing abilities of children with receptive language disorders. There are four scales that are administered to such children: Sequential/Short-term Memory (*Gsm*), Simultaneous/Visual Processing (*Gv*), Learning/Long-term Retrieval (*Glr*), and Planning/Fluid Reasoning (*Gf*). The Mental Processing Index (MPI) is the global scale that is considered the most representative estimate of global intellectual functioning when administered to children with language processing problems. Ryan's general cognitive ability is within the Average range of intellectual functioning, as measured by the MPI of 89 (90 percent confidence interval = 84–94). His overall thinking and reasoning abilities exceed those of approximately 23 percent of children his age. This score is consistent with the results of the assessment conducted two years ago, which yielded a WISC-IV Full Scale IQ of 83 (90 percent confidence interval = 79–88). In addition, additional subtests of the KABC-II were administered to calculate a Nonverbal Index (NVI). He scored a global IQ score of 80 on this scale (9th percentile), which is in the Low Average range. Therefore, even with the minimization of language factors on the KABC-II, Ryan's intellectual functioning is consistently in the Low Average to Average range.

Ryan's sequential processing abilities, as measured by the Sequential/*Gsm* scale, are in the Average range, at the 50th percentile (Standard Score = 100). This scale is designed to measure the ability to process information in a serial or temporal order, and to hold information in immediate awareness and then use that information before it is forgotten. Ryan's scores on the subtests contributing to the Sequential/*Gsm* scale are extremely variable. His performance was intact when required to repeat a series of numbers in the same sequence as the examiner said them (63rd percentile), as well as on a subtest assessing his ability to touch a series of silhouettes in the same order as the examiner said their names (37th percentile). He had significantly more difficulty on a task requiring him to copy a sequence of hand movements made by the examiner (5th percentile). Although no overt signs of inattention were evident on this subtest, Ryan had great difficulty remembering the examiner's hand movements, and he was only able to complete some very basic items on this subtest. This reflects notable problems with sequential processing and short-term memory in the visual-motor channel.

Ryan's simultaneous processing abilities as measured by the Simultaneous/*Gv* Scale are in the Average range, at the 16th percentile (Standard Score = 85). This scale is designed to measure the visual processing of information, spatial manipulation of visual stimuli, and nonverbal reasoning. Ryan had no difficulty on a task of spatial scanning assessing his ability to plan the quickest route for a dog to take to get to a bone (50th percentile). However, he struggled on a measure of spatial visualization in which he was required to assemble several triangles together to match a picture of an abstract design (5th percentile). His responses on this task appeared to be somewhat random, and he displayed considerable difficulty manipulating the triangles and matching the colors on the triangles with the target design. He had further difficulty on another subtest of visual orientation with regards to spatial relationships in which he was required to count the number of blocks in a stack in which some blocks were hidden from view (5th percentile). This reflects problems with the spatial management of visual stimuli, difficulties mentally organizing visual information presented spatially, and difficulties analyzing part-whole relationships among spatial information.

Ryan demonstrated a significant weakness on the Learning/*Glr* Scale (Standard Score = 84, 14th percentile). He struggled on a task measuring his ability to learn nonsense names for pictures of fish, plants, and shells (16th percentile). He had similar difficulty on a task assessing his ability to learn words associated with particular drawings, and to "read" aloud sentences composed of these drawings (16th percentile). His recall of these names and words after a delay was also impaired (16th and 5th percentiles). This is indicative of considerable problems storing information in long-term memory and retrieving this information in an efficient manner, both after an initial presentation of the information, as well as after a delay.

On the Planning/*Gf* scale, Ryan demonstrated an intact ability to solve novel problems with flexibility, to draw inferences and understand implications, to apply inductive or deductive reasoning, and to plan his course of action (Standard Score = 99, 47th percentile). He displayed Average ability on a subset requiring him select from a set of pictures, those that are needed to complete a story, and to place the missing pictures in their correct locations (37th percentile). His performance was also intact on a subtest of abstract categorical reasoning ability requiring him to complete a pattern by selecting the correct stimulus from an array (63rd percentile). He worked slowly on these tasks, he did not display any impulsivity, and he appeared to plan his responses carefully.

Attention and Executive Functions

In order to assess his attention, Ryan was administered selected subtests from the NEPSY and the D-KEFS. Ryan demonstrated variable performances on these subtests of attention and executive functioning. His performance was Average (50th percentile) on a subtest assessing his nonverbal planning and problem-solving abilities. On this task, Ryan was required to move three colored balls to target positions on three pegs in a prescribed number of moves. He was able to complete some very difficult problems on this subtest, yet he struggled on some easier ones.

On a NEPSY subtest of selective auditory attention, Ryan's performance was also in the Average range (63rd percentile). This task required Ryan to maintain selective auditory attention and to regulate his responses to conflicting stimuli. The first phase of this task required him to maintain auditory vigilance to words presented on a tape and then place the target object in a box when its name was called out. On the next phase, he had to do the same, but with three target objects. In addition, on two of the three objects, Ryan was required to do the opposite of what he was told (e.g., put the red chip in the box to the command "yellow"). Ryan demonstrated a very strong performance on the initial phase of this task, and he was attentive and focused throughout this phase. He had slightly more difficulty on the second phase of this task, although his performance was still within the Average range. His performance on this subtest reflected no problems with inattention or impulsivity, as evident by his very low number of omission and commission errors.

In contrast to these strong performances, Ryan demonstrated great difficulty on a test of selective visual attention assessing his ability to attend to a visual stimulus and locate target pictures quickly in an array (9th percentile). Although Ryan worked accurately both when required to detect one target stimulus and when searching for two target stimuli, his speed was much slower than expected. Ryan's slow processing speed was noted consistently throughout the testing.

Ryan's motor inhibition was Average as evident by his performance on a subtest assessing self-regulation and inhibition (26–75th percentile). His impulse control and inhibition were Low Average (11–25th percentile) on a subtest assessing his ability to sustain a position over a 75-second interval. Ryan displayed some difficulty inhibiting the impulse to respond to auditory distraction on this task.

On the D-KEFS, Ryan demonstrated some significant problems with cognitive flexibility. This is indicative of some rigid and concrete thinking, and was identified by Mrs. P. when she noted that Ryan tends to be very literal and to lack the capacity for abstract thinking. This was noted particularly on sequencing trail-making tasks, but was also evident on an executive functions test of verbal interference assessing inhibition of verbal response and cognitive flexibility. Despite his difficulties, Ryan demonstrated the ability to monitor and modify his behaviors in order to produce correct responses. He did not demonstrate an impulsive response style or any visual scanning difficulties, and there were no problems noted in maintaining cognitive set.

Ryan's performance was extremely impaired on the IVA Continuous Performance Test (IVA). This task is intended to be mildly boring and demanding of sustained attention over a 13-minute period of time. On this task Ryan was required to respond to target stimuli (the number "1" presented either auditorily or visually on the computer) and refrain from responding to non-target stimuli (the number "2" presented in the same formats). During the administration of this test, Ryan's back was to the examiner, and she was therefore unable to determine his level of alertness throughout the task. A diagnosis of Attention-Deficit/Hyperactivity Disorder, Combined Type was indicated by his performance on the IVA. Ryan was unable to validly respond to visual stimuli, and therefore his response pattern to visual stimuli could not be analyzed or interpreted. This reflects significant problems with Ryan's visual attention span. Ryan also displayed problems with his general auditory attentional functioning, and he demonstrated an impaired ability to accurately and quickly respond in a reliable manner to auditory stimuli. He had significant difficulty remaining vigilant to auditory stimuli, and he also demonstrated problems with impulse control in response to auditory stimuli. This indicates that Ryan most likely is overreactive to and distracted by auditory stimuli in his environment. His pattern of responding indicated that Ryan experiences periods of random, idiopathic, impulsive responses to non-target auditory stimuli. The impact of this deficit is likely to be significant, manifesting as impulsive responses to auditory stimuli in his home and school environments. He also demonstrated poor Fine Motor Regulation, indicating problems with self-control. Ryan demonstrated some lapses in his auditory attention, along with very poor auditory processing speed. His performance on this task indicates a tendency to make unusual, careless errors, problems remembering rules, and a likelihood that he engages in behaviors that are distracting and annoying to others.

Further measures of Ryan's attentional functioning were obtained by the Conners' Parent Rating Scale–Revised, the Conners' Teacher Rating Scale–Revised, the Achenbach Child Behavior Checklist/6–18 (CBCL), and the Achenbach Teacher's Report Form/6–18 (TRF). On the Conners' Parent Rating Scale–Revised, the profiles generated by Mr. and Ms. P.'s reports were almost identical, reflecting a high level of consistency in the way in which they view Ryan. Both parents expressed concerns regarding Ryan's level of inattention, organizational problems, and difficulty completing tasks. They also reported a significant level of hyperactivity, restlessness, and impulsiveness, and they identified Ryan as meeting the diagnostic criteria for ADHD, Combined Type. These concerns were also noted on the CBCL. Ryan's teacher was asked to complete the Conners' Teacher Rating Scale–Revised and the TRF. The profile generated by his teacher on the Conners' was indicative of some inattention and a significant level of restlessness and impulsiveness. She identified Ryan as being "at risk" for ADHD, Combined Type. These Conners' profiles were compared to the Conners' profiles generated by Ryan's mother and his third-grade teacher from a previous assessment. The profiles were extremely consistent, although it appears that Ms. P. is currently noting more significant problems with hyperactivity than she did a year ago.

Overall, Ryan's attention span on structured neuropsychological tests is extremely variable. Although his behaviors were not indicative of a high level of inattention or impulsivity, he clearly demonstrated variable ability to stay on task due to significant problems remaining alert. It is very likely that his level of alertness impacts his performances and confounds the diagnosis of attention difficulties. It is essential to determine whether any neurological or medical factors are responsible for the level of inattention noted by Ryan's parents, as well as the variability in his test results.

Language

Ryan's language skills have been previously identified as an area of weakness. On the NEPSY, he had some significant difficulties in these areas. His comprehension of verbal instructions was significantly impaired on a subtest assessing his ability to process and respond quickly to verbal instructions of increasing complexity (2nd percentile). Ryan was only able to complete some very basic items on this subtest. On multi-step instructions, Ryan was able to follow the first part of the instruction, but he was unable to complete the entire sequence of instructions. As the instructions became more complex, Ryan failed to make any response at all. He had somewhat less difficulty, performing in the Low Average range, on a subtest of phonological processing (25th percentile), as well as on a subtest assessing his ability to access and produce familiar words in alternative patterns rapidly (16th percentile). Although he was able to name the words accurately with little difficulty, his performance was fairly slow, which is indicative of his slow processing speed.

Sensorimotor

Ryan's performances were Low Average to Average on most subtests of sensorimotor functioning. He demonstrated some problems on measures of finger dexterity and on measures requiring Ryan to imitate hand and finger positions (25th percentile on both). He had even greater difficulty on a subtest assessing his ability to imitate a series of rhythmic movement sequences using one or both hands (3–10th percentile). In contrast, his performance was Average on a task requiring Ryan to remain inside a curved track while drawing a line between these tracks (50th percentile). His speed was surprisingly fast on this subtest, although he had some difficulty remaining inside the lines as the track became more narrow. Overall, these results are consistent with his Low Average to Average cognitive abilities are do not appear to reflect significant problems with fine-motor coordination or difficulty monitoring motor output.

In order to further examine Ryan's sensory processing abilities, his mother was asked to complete the Short Sensory Profile. Results indicated that Ryan demonstrates a high number of sensation-seeking behaviors. He frequently seeks to add sensory input in his daily experiences, which may reflect an over-reactive neural system that may make Ryan aware of every stimulus that is available, along with an inability to habituate to these stimuli. Results further indicated some inconsistencies in Ryan's ability to screen out sounds in daily life. While his mother indicated a high sensitivity to sounds, she also noted some hyporesponsiveness to sounds, reflecting a difficulty in paying attention to relevant auditory input.

Visuospatial

Ryan consistently demonstrated relative difficulties on measures of his visuospatial functions. He scored at the 9th percentile on a task requiring him to copy two-dimensional geometric figures of increasing complexity, and at the 25th percentile on a task assessing his ability to judge line orientation. His difficulties in these areas were further noted earlier on the KABC-II on which he had great difficulty mentally organizing visual information presented spatially. It should be noted, that the KABC-II subtests were presented on the first testing session, during which Ryan had great difficulty remaining alert. However, even during the second day of testing, Ryan consistently struggled on tests of visuospatial skills, reflecting some relative difficulties in these areas.

Memory

Ryan demonstrated impaired memory functions in all areas with the exception of recognition memory. While he excelled on a task assessing his memory for faces (75th percentile), he had significant difficulties on subtests measuring his memory for names (16th percentile), narrative memory (5th percentile), and verbal memory span (16th and 5th percentiles). His performances indicate a poor recall of verbal labels, difficulties in his ability to organize and retrieve details from prose, impaired auditory short-term memory for language, and an impaired ability to learn over a series of trials. However, Ryan consistently demonstrated a significantly stronger performance on delayed memory than initial memory. This was noted on both tasks of recognition memory and verbal recall and is a very unusual memory pattern. This appears to indicate that Ryan has some significant difficulties encoding new information.

Assessment of Academic Abilities

Ryan was administered the Kaufman Test of Academic Achievement–Second Edition (KTEA-II) to assess his academic skills. He demonstrated a significant variability across his skills in the different academic domains. Although Ryan's abilities in some areas such as math and reading were Average levels, other abilities such as his oral language skills and written expression were below expected levels. His specific academic abilities are described in the following sections.

Reading

Ryan's performances on all subtests of reading were consistent with his cognitive ability. He performed comparably on tasks that required him to correctly read a series of printed words (47th percentile), read sentences and paragraphs and answer questions about what was read (39th percentile), and correctly apply phonetic decoding rules when reading a series of nonsense words (47th percentile). However, he demonstrated the need for frequent repetition of questions on the reading comprehension task, and he had great difficulty remaining alert during this subtest. His passage reading speed was significantly below expected levels.

Mathematics

Ryan's skills in mathematics are diverse and may not be adequately summarized by a single number. He performed much better on tasks that evaluated his ability to add and subtract one- to three-digit numbers and multiply and divide two-digit numbers (86th percentile) than on tasks that required him to understand number concepts, consumer math concepts, geometric measurement, basic graphs, and solve one-step word problems (34th percentile). His skills in the area of mathematical calculations are a personal strength for him, and a normative strength compared to other children his age. However, it is clear that Ryan resists performing calculations with a paper and pencil, and he prefers to do mental math. As a result, he is not always accurate and makes careless errors. Ryan's lower score on the Math Concepts and Applications subtest resulted from his difficulty comprehending auditorily presented word problems, and he requested frequent repetition of these items. This is consistent with his problems with receptive language processing.

Oral Language

Ryan performed in the Below Average to Lower Extreme range in overall language skills, and his skills in this area exceed those of only 2 percent of students his age. He struggled on tasks assessing his expressive and receptive vocabulary, and he had great difficulty on a subtest of sentence comprehension requiring him to identify the picture that best represents an orally presented descriptor. His overall performance on these tests of Listening Comprehension was in the Low Average range (10th percentile). In addition, his performance was significantly impaired on expressive language tasks requiring him to generate words within a category, describe scenes, and give directions, and he was unable to complete several of these tasks (1st percentile). In addition, Ryan was observed to display problems remaining alert on these tasks, and his behavior was extremely concerning.

Ryan's performance on the Oral Expression subtest was a normative weakness and a personal weakness when compared to his average level of academic ability. Typically children with learning disabilities show patterns of relative weaknesses in some domains paired with "normal" functioning in other academic domains. Also indicative of a learning disability is the presence of a cognitive processing deficit among otherwise normal areas of cognitive functioning. Ryan's KABC-II Learning/*Glr* score of 84 (a normative weakness) is evidence of a processing deficit, while many of his other cognitive abilities are intact. Thus, his personal and normative weaknesses in both Listening Comprehension and Oral Expression, when coupled with his cognitive processing deficit in Learning/*Glr*, is indicative of a learning disability in the areas of Oral Expression and Listening Comprehension.

Written Language

Ryan's performances on tasks of Written Expression that required him to generate words within a category, generate sentences to describe visual cues, combine sentences, and compose an organized paragraph were in the Below Average range (12th percentile). His sentences and paragraph were not well written, several punctuation errors were noted, he omitted some essential information in his writing, and he frequently changed the meaning of the sentences when combining them to create a new sentence. His writing was poorly organized, and his use of vocabulary words was extremely elementary. Ryan was noted to having difficulty remaining alert on this subtest, particularly on a test of written word fluency. In comparison, he was alert and attentive of the Spelling subtest and he scored within the Average range (34th percentile). Ryan's abilities in the area of Written Expression are considered Below Average range, and when coupled with his cognitive processing deficits in the visual-spatial domain, provides evidence of a learning disability in the area of written expression.

Emotional Functioning

Ryan completed the Rorschach, the Piers-Harris Children's Self-concept Scale 2, the Revised Children's Manifest Anxiety Scale, and the Children's Depression Inventory. His parents each completed the Conners' and the Achenbach Child Behavior Checklist. Ryan's teacher completed the Conners' and the Achenbach Teacher Report Form.

As noted earlier, on the CBCL and the Conners' Ryan was rated by his parents as displaying a significant level of inattention and hyperactivity, and as meeting the diagnostic criteria for ADHD, Combined Type. His parents also reported some significant concerns about Ryan's high level of rule-breaking behaviors and aggression at home. They further noted that Ryan displays a high level of anxiety, frequent somatic complaints, and some social problems. In contrast, his teacher did not report noting significant oppositional behaviors, and she also did not report social concerns or anxiety to be relevant issues on the TRF. However, on the Conners' she did rate Ryan as displaying a moderate level of anxiety characterized by a sensitivity to criticism and a high level of emotionality.

On measures of emotional functioning, Ryan demonstrated a moderate level of situational guardedness and a reluctance to be forthcoming. He appears to be purposefully avoiding self-focusing, and he is fairly unwilling to process emotional stimulation or to become engaged in affectively charged situations. He also displays some evidence of oppositional tendencies that are likely to be associated with transient irritation and situational reactions to his responsibilities and obligations.

Although Ryan certainly does not avoid interpersonal relationships, his relationships with others tend to be distant and detached rather than close and intimate. He may avoid more involved relationships out of concern that they will make more demands on him than he can handle. Testing was also indicative of some impairment in his reality testing capacity, whereby Ryan tends to misperceive events and to form mistaken impressions of people and the significance of their actions. This adaptive liability may result in poor judgment in which Ryan fails to anticipate the consequences of his actions and misconstrues what constitutes appropriate behavior. He demonstrates some confusion in separating reality from fantasy. This results in some inappropriate behaviors, which may lead to chronic and pervasive adjustment difficulties in life. In addition, it is evident that many of his breakdowns in reality testing are prompted by feelings of anger or resentment. Therefore, it is likely that when anger clouds his judgment, Ryan may demonstrate some confusion in separating reality from fantasy.

On personality testing, Ryan tended to respond in a socially desirable direction. His responses are indicative of a lack of realistic self-appraisal and a strong need to be viewed by others in a positive manner. He denied any problematic behaviors, he expressed confidence in his intellectual and academic abilities, he expressed a high level of satisfaction with his physical appearance, and he indicated a high level of perceived popularity. He also denied experiencing any anxiety or depression. However, as indicated above, his self-reports reflected a defensive denial of behavior problems in order to mask real difficulties and a high need for social acceptance.

Summary and Recommendations

Ryan is a 12-year-old boy who was referred for an evaluation of his neuro-psychological and emotional status. A primary aim of this evaluation was to determine if his Low Average intellectual ability, as determined by a pervious assessment, is an accurate assessment of his cognitive functioning, or if receptive and expressive language difficulties impacted his performance on earlier testing. Ryan is being treated by a pediatric psychiatrist for a mood disorder. He is currently on Seroquel and Trileptal. During the first day of the evaluation, Ryan demonstrated significant difficulty remaining alert and oriented to the testing. On numerous occasions, he sat blinking, staring straight ahead blankly, and was unresponsive to questions. After a few seconds, he was able to resume testing. On one occasion Ryan appeared to fall asleep right after this episode. However, these behaviors were not noticeable during the second testing session during which Ryan was attentive and alert. There had been a change to his medication regime before this second testing session, and Ryan also indicated that he had had more sleep the night before. He also chewed gum during this session, which he indicated increased his alertness.

The results of this assessment indicate that Ryan's intellectual ability is consistently in the Low Average to Average range, even when tested with instruments designed to minimize the impact of language abilities (see Tables 6.6–6.9). His KABC-II MPI of 89 does not differ significantly from his previously measured WISC-III FSIQ of 83, indicating other factors, aside from language, impact his performance on cognitive testing. Ryan demonstrated significant difficulty organizing visual information presented spatially. He also had struggled on measures of learning ability and memory. In fact, Ryan's short-term memory in the visual-motor and verbal channels was consistently impaired. However, his recognition memory was intact, and his delayed memory was an area of relative strength. Ryan displayed intact planning ability, although some deficits were noted in his cognitive flexibility. He demonstrated variability on measures of attention, which appeared to be highly dependent on his level of alertness at the time of testing, rather than on an inconsistent attention span. Further difficulties were noted on measures of receptive and expressive language ability, and Ryan meets the criteria for specific learning disabilities in the areas of oral expressions, listening comprehension, and written expression.

On personality testing, Ryan tended to display a high level of situational guardedness and to deny any problematic behaviors. He demonstrated a reluctance to process emotional content, and he also displayed evidence of some situational-based oppositional tendencies. Testing also indicated some reality testing difficulties whereby Ryan forms mistaken impressions of others. This is more apparent in situations that trigger Ryan's anger or oppositionality, and it appears to significantly impact his coping skills.

Recommendations

On the basis of these findings, the following recommendations are made:

Neurological and Medical Evaluation

It is imperative that Ryan's neurological status be thoroughly evaluated to determine whether his current functioning is being impacted by any undetected neurological factors. His difficulties remaining alert are extremely unusual and are concerning to his parents, teacher, and to the examiner. It is recommended that Mr. and Ms. P. contact a neurologist who would be able to rule out any contributing neurological condition. In addition, it is essential that his parents ensure that the vision and hearing assessments conducted through his school adequately assess any difficulties in this regard. A thorough medical evaluation is strongly recommended to rule out any possibilities of sleep apnea.

Ongoing Psychotherapy

Ongoing psychotherapy sessions are strongly recommended. Intervention focused on anger resolution may play an important role in improving his reality testing. In addition, the development of coping skills and stress management may be extremely beneficial.

Ongoing Pharmacological Intervention

Ryan appears to be benefiting from his current medication regime. However, it is essential to determine whether these medications could be impacting his level of alertness, and creating further difficulties for him in the classroom. It is strongly recommended that his psychiatrist be informed about the results of any neurological evaluation and that she continue to modify and monitor Ryan's medications as needed.

Biofeedback

Biofeedback training may be useful for Ryan in teaching him effective ways to control his difficulties remaining alert and attentive. EEG biofeedback is a way to train those areas of the brain involved in arousal and focus. In EEG biofeedback training, Ryan will develop an understanding about the connection between what is happening in his cortex and what is recorded on the EEG. He will then learn how to gain control over his brain waves and therefore to regulate his behavior. A psychologist specializing in biofeedback will be able to further assist Ryan in this regard should it be determined that this intervention is appropriate after assessing his neurological status.

Educational Therapy

Ryan would benefit from ongoing assistance with his organizational and study skills. He needs help to meaningfully organize his study time, study materials, and the information that is to be learned. An educational therapist would be useful in helping Ryan learn to maintain his planner to keep track of his assignments and to schedule daily study periods. Assistance with memory strategies would also be extremely beneficial. His teacher has indicated that there is an educational therapist at Ryan's school whose services are available for an additional charge. Alternatively, there are a number of educational therapists who would be appropriate to work with Ryan in this regard, several of whom can meet with Ryan at his home or school. I would be happy to make this referral at the request of Mr. and Ms. P.

Speech Pathology Services

It is recommended that Mr. and Ms. P. consult with Ryan's speech pathologist, to determine recommendations on oral language development and effective teaching approaches for Ryan. Based upon these test results, it appears that he would benefit from ongoing language therapy, and the speech pathologist may be able to offer further advice to his teacher regarding classroom modifications for language disabled students.

Classroom Recommendations

Ryan's Expressive Language Disability qualifies him for special educational services. In addition, his significant difficulties remaining alert, his inconsistent attentional abilities, his impaired short-term memory, and his extremely slow processing speed will make it particularly difficult for him to keep up with the pace of information being presented in a normal classroom setting. Children with Ryan's learning difficulties usually benefit from a learning environment that is carefully planned and consistently implemented in terms of the physical arrangement, schedule of activities, and expected behaviors. Consequently, it is recommended that Ryan receive classroom accommodations that include the following:

- Placement in a small classroom setting where he can receive more immediate and individual attention and consistent monitoring of his behavior is strongly recommended.
- He will learn much more effectively in a slower-paced classroom that will allow him to acquire knowledge in a much more repetitive and less pressured environment.

- Ryan will benefit from preferential seating in the front of the classroom where his teacher can monitor him.

- Whenever possible, minimize distractions in Ryan's study area. For example, place Ryan's desk near the teacher, facing a wall, or in an area with minimal classroom traffic.

- His teacher should be informed about the nature of Ryan's language difficulties and how it affects his academic functioning. She should be encouraged to provide Ryan with both written and oral instruction whenever possible. He may often need to have instructions repeated. Thus, encourage Ryan to ask for such repetition if he initially has difficulty understanding. In instances of more elaborate instruction, allow Ryan to tape record the information to permit relistening at a later stage. Nonverbal input and visual reinforcement such as gestures, drawings, and modeling is essential. When giving directions, make frequent eye contact and stop at various points to ensure that Ryan understands. It would be useful to discuss task requirements with Ryan to ensure that he has an accurate interpretation of what is expected of him. Make sure that Ryan feels comfortable to ask for clarification and repetition of instructions. Provide him with visual guide-lines such as checklists to help him understand the specific steps he must take to complete assignments and other classroom tasks. Ryan will benefit from having most books on tape as well as recordings from more lecture-oriented courses. Ryan could also be provided with a copy of the notes of a student who is a good note taker to supplement his own notes.

- Due to Ryan's slow processing speed, he certainly would benefit from untimed or extended time on tests. He would also benefit from having his assignments reduced in length so that he can complete his work in class rather than taking assignments home.

- Ryan would benefit from being taught strategies to improve his memory functioning. Discuss with him what strategies he uses to recall information and help him identify and learn other strategies to enhance recall. Teach him a strategy for active listening by having him learn to attend to keywords that signal that important information is about to be administered, such as "first," "most important," or "in summary." When Ryan is learning infor-mation for a test, direct his attention to the information to be remembered and indicate the importance of this information. Discuss with him ways in which he would be most likely to learn and remember this information. Do not require a rapid recall of facts until Ryan understand and is able to demonstrate the underlying concepts. Before teaching new information, review previous information from the last lesson and check for mastery.

When teaching Ryan factual information, provide as much review and repetition as possible, and provide frequent opportunities for practice.
- Continue consistent contact between teachers and parents via a homebook. Encourage Ryan to highlight important material (e.g., key words, instructions, main ideas) in texts or handouts. Help Ryan establish a regular time for him to do homework. During this time, family members should be available to provide assistance, while limiting distracting behaviors.
- Ryan's impaired visuospatial abilities will interfere with his ability to learn more complex nonverbal ideas, such as geometry. Also, he may have difficulty reading nonverbal communication cues, such as body language and vocal intonation, resulting in his failing to respond to salient social cues in his environment. He may therefore require additional assistance in this regard.

Michelle Lurie, Psy.D.
Clinical Psychologist

PSYCHOMETRIC SUMMARY FOR RYAN P.

Table 6.6 Kaufman Assessment Battery for Children–Second Edition (KABC-II)

Scale or Subtest	Standard Score	90% Confid. Interval	Percentile Rank	Descriptive Category
Sequential/Gsm	100	92–108	50	Average
Number Recall	11		63	
Word Order	9		37	
Hand Movements	5		5	
Simultaneous/Gv	85	78–94	16	Average
Rover	10		50	
Triangles	5		5	
Block Counting	5		5	
Learning/Glr	84	78–92	14	Below Average
Atlantis	7		16	
Rebus	7		16	
Atlantis Delayed	7		16	
Rebus Delayed	5		5	

Table 6.6 (Continued)

Scale or Subtest	Standard Score	90% Confid. Interval	Percentile Rank	Descriptive Category
Planning/Gf	99	90–108	47	Average
Story Completion	9		37	
Pattern Reasoning	11		63	
Mental Processing Index	89	84–94	23	Average

Note: KABC-II Scales have a mean of 100 and a standard deviation of 15. KABC-II subtests have a mean of 10 and a standard deviation of 3.

Table 6.7 Kaufman Test of Educational Achievement–Second Edition (KTEA-II) Comprehensive Form A

Composites & Subtests	Standard Score (Age-Based)	90% Confidence Interval	Percentile Rank
Reading	96	91–101	39
Letter & Word Recognition	99	93–105	47
Reading Comprehension	96	89–103	39
Decoding[a]	99	95–103	47
Nonsense Word Decoding	99	94–104	47
Math	104	99–109	61
Math Computation	116	110–122	86
Math Concepts & Applications	94	87–101	34
Written Language	87	81–93	19
Spelling	94	87–101	34
Written Expression	82	74–90	12
Oral Language	70	60–80	2
Listening Comprehension	81	70–92	10
Oral Expression	67	55–79	1
Comprehensive Achievement Composite	92	88–96	30

[a] The Decoding composite includes Nonsense Word Decoding and Letter and Word Recognition

Table 6.8 A Developmental Neuropsychological Assessment (NEPSY)

Subtest	Standard Score	Percentile Rank
Attention/Executive		
Tower	10	50
Auditory Attn. and Resp. Set	11	63
Visual Attention	6	9
Statue	—	11–25
Knock and Tap	—	26–75
Language		
Phonological Processing	8	25
Speeded Naming	7	16
Comprehension of Inst.	4	2
Sensorimotor		
Fingertip Tapping	8	25
Imitating Hand Positions	8	25
Visuomotor Precision	10	50
Manual Motor Sequences	—	3–10
Visuospatial		
Design Copying	6	9
Arrows	8	25
Memory		
Memory for Faces	12	75
Memory for Names	7	16
Narrative Memory	5	5
Sentence Repetition	7	16
List Learning	5	5

Table 6.9 Delis-Kaplan Executive Function System (D-KEFS)

Trail Making Test: Primary Measure	Scaled Score
Condition 1: Visual Scanning	10
Condition 2: Number Sequencing	11
Condition 3: Letter Sequencing	8
Condition 4: Number-Letter Switching	1
Condition 5: Motor Speed	6

Color-Word Interference Test: Primary Measures	Scaled Score
Condition 1: Color Naming	7
Condition 2: Word Reading	8
Condition 3: Inhibition	6
Condition 4: Inhibition/Switching	7

CASE REPORT 3: ANIKA, AGE AT EVALUATION: 10 YEARS, 3 MONTHS, GRADE: 4, NORMS USED: AGE BASED

Purpose of the Evaluation

Anika's language arts teacher referred her for an evaluation to determine whether processing weaknesses may be interfering with her achievement and performance in the areas of basic reading, reading fluency, and written expression. The results of the evaluation will be used to develop a targeted plan for intervention based upon her individual processing strengths and weaknesses. The evaluation included an assessment of mental ability, listening comprehension, oral expression, basic reading, reading comprehension, and written expression. Mathematics was not assessed because Anika has demonstrated Average to Above Average achievement in this area.

History and Background

Anika is an African-American student who comes from a multiracial family. Her expressive language does not incorporate features of African-American English dialect. Anika's parents are divorced, and she lives with her mother, two younger brothers, and grandparents. Her mother works as a nurse and her father is a self-employed electrician. Her father performs well in his current job, but reported having difficulty learning to read and write as a child. He stated that he "did not enjoy school and struggled to complete high school," but he has never received a formal evaluation for a learning disability. Anika's mother reported doing very well throughout her schooling, and also said that Anika's brothers are performing well in school. Anika was described by her mother as a quiet child who was slow to begin talking. She began crawling and walking "sooner than most children her age," and has well-developed gross motor skills. Anika began playing sports at a young age, and currently plays basketball and soccer.

Anika's medical history has been unremarkable. She has experienced no major illnesss or injuries, and is described by her parents as being generally "healthy." Anika has received regular hearing and vision tests since first grade, and all test results have indicated that Anika's hearing and vision is within normal limits.

Anika's parents reported that her teachers first expressed concern about her reading performance last year, and she started having difficulty with writing this year. She does not enjoy reading for pleasure and avoids writing activities. Last year she began receiving small-group reading instruction in a resource room setting for 30 minutes, three times per week. She has also been attending after-school tutoring twice a week to help her keep up with her homework demands. This year, she has been receiving intensive instruction with a reading coach for 40 minutes, four times per week, focusing on decoding and fluency. Anika's language arts teacher describes her as friendly and mild-mannered. Her teacher reported that Anika follows directions and completes assignments, but she reads slowly and has difficulty answering reading comprehension questions. In addition, her handwriting is neat and easy to read, but her written work is typically very brief with many spelling errors. Anika loves math and has always excelled in this academic area. Her math teacher reports that she is performing very well in the classroom.

Behavioral Observations

Anika was cooperative throughout testing and seemed to try her best. Anika was friendly and good humored throughout most of the testing session, which made rapport easy to establish. She did not initiate conversation very often, but she maintained good eye contact and responded appropriately during social interactions.

She said that math is her favorite subject because she's "good at it," but she doesn't enjoy her other classes. During two of the reading tasks, she asked how much more she would have to read. Anika took several short breaks, particularly in between reading and writing tasks.

Anika was consistent in her approach to tasks. She tended to work at a relatively slow and steady pace. She would typically try to solve every problem, even when she admitted not knowing how. Her approach to tasks and her persistence in working through problems was similar to her approach to school work.

Anika asked for directions to be clarified on a few occasions. However, hearing and vision problems did not seem to interfere with her performance during testing at any time. When asking for directions to be clarified, she did not seem to have trouble hearing the directions; rather, she wanted the directions reworded to ensure that she understood them. She demonstrated adequate comprehension of all administered tasks. The results of this evaluation are believed to accurately reflect Anika's current ability and achievement level.

TESTS ADMINISTERED

Kaufman Assessment Battery for Children–Second Edition (KABC-II)
Kaufman Test of Educational Achievement–Second Edition (KTEA-II) Comprehensive Form, Form A
Wechsler Individual Achievement Test–Third Edition (WIAT-III)

Results

Cognitive Abilities

Anika was administered the KABC-II to assess her overall cognitive ability. In Anika's case, the KABC-II yielded scores for five separate scales, and one score that represented her global level of cognitive functioning. However, Anika's cognitive abilities were quite variable, ranging from the Below Average range (9th percentile) on a scale measuring short-term memory to the Average range (77th percentile) on a scale measuring planning and reasoning. Due to this variability across cognitive domains, the KABC-II's measure of her overall cognitive ability (her Fluid-Crystallized Index standard score of 87), represents nothing more than the midpoint of her diverse skills. Thus, more valuable information about her cognitive strengths and weaknesses is available by examining the separate scales that comprise the KABC-II.

Anika demonstrated Below Average abilities in two cognitive domains: (a) sequential processing and short-term memory, and (b) long-term storage and retrieval of newly learned or previously learned information. Her first Below Average ability was evident from her standard score of 80 (9th percentile) on the

Sequential/*Gsm* Index, which represents a relative processing weakness that is not infrequent in the normative sample. Her second Below Average ability was evident from her standard score of 81 (10th percentile) on the Learning/*Glr* Index, which represents a relative processing weakness that is not infrequent in the normative sample. Taken together, these results indicate that Anika has a disorder in the basic psychological processes of short-term memory, as well as long-term storage and retrieval. These processes are strongly related to performance in reading, writing, and the retention of oral directions.

In contrast to her Below Average short-term memory and long-term storage and retrieval abilities, Anika demonstrated consistently Average level functioning in her abilities to (a) process information visually, (b) solve novel problems, and (c) demonstrate the breadth and depth of her knowledge. Specifically, her performance on the Simultaneous/*Gv* Index (standard score = 94; 34th percentile) was evidence of her Average level ability to complete tasks involving visual processing (perceiving, storing, manipulating, and thinking with visual patterns). Her performance on the Planning/*Gf* Index, a measure of fluid reasoning ability when solving novel problems, was also within the Average range (standard score = 111); this score represents a relative processing strength that was demonstrated in less than 5 percent of the normative sample. Finally, her performance on the Crystallized Ability/*Gc* Index, a measure of the breadth and depth of knowledge acquired, was within the Average range (standard score = 90). Overall, Anika's performance on the KABC-II suggests processing weaknesses in the areas of short-term memory and long-term storage and retrieval with a processing strength in the area of fluid reasoning.

Academic Achievement

Similar to the variability noted within her cognitive abilities, Anika demonstrated variability in her performance on tests of academic achievement. She was administered select portions of two achievement test batteries to gather information about her academic skills across several domains. The results from both the Kaufman Test of Educational Achievement–Second Edition (KTEA-II) and the Wechsler Individual Achievement Test–Third Edition (WIATI-III) are described in the sections that follow.

Oral Language

Anika's receptive (listening) and expressive (speaking) language skills were evaluated at the level of vocabulary, sentence, and discourse. Her overall oral language composite score on the WIAT-III was within the Average range (standard score = 92); however, this is an area of mixed achievement.

Auditory Receptive Language

To assess her comprehension of single words, Anika was administered the Receptive Vocabulary component of the WIAT-III Listening Comprehension subtest. She was asked to point to the picture that corresponded to each administered word. Her score was within the Average range (standard score = 110). To assess receptive language skills at the sentence and discourse levels, Anika was administered the Oral Discourse Comprehension component of the WIAT-III Listening Comprehension subtest. She was asked to listen to one or more sentences from an audio CD and then answer open-ended comprehension questions. Anika said she was getting tired of listening during this task. Her responses to the comprehension questions were sometimes based upon prior knowledge, rather than the information presented. She performed similarly on both literal and inferential questions. Her performance was in the Average range (standard score = 86). Overall, Anika's Listening Comprehension subtest performance was within the Average range (standard score = 98).

Auditory Expressive Language

To assess Anika's expressive language at the level of the word and sentence, the WIAT-III Oral Expression subtest was administered. The Expressive Vocabulary component required her to look at pictures, listen to an oral definition, and then name each concept presented. On several items, she guessed incorrectly, providing tangentially related words. Her performance was within the Average range (standard score = 87). The Oral Word Fluency component provided a measure of Anika's word-retrieval skills and flexibility of thought processes. She was asked to name things belonging to a given category (e.g., animals) within a time limit. Her performance was within the Average range (standard score = 108). To assess expressive syntax and memory for sentences, Anika was administered the Sentence Repetition component of the WIAT-III Oral Expression subtest. She was asked to listen to sentences of increasing length and repeat them back. As the sentence length increased, she had difficulty remembering the sentence. She often gave the gist of the sentence, but could not remember the exact words used. She scored in the Below Average range (standard score = 75). Her overall subtest performance was within the Average range (standard score = 87).

To assess Anika's expressive language at the sentence and discourse level, the KTEA-II Oral Expression subtest was administered. This subtest measures oral expressive pragmatics, semantics, syntax, and grammar in the context of various real-life scenarios. Anika struggled with the sentence formulation tasks, frequently asking for the instructions to be repeated. Her responses often omitted important information. Anika scored in the Below Average range (standard score = 75).

Anika's listening skills are in the Average range; however, she demonstrated a relative weakness in expressive language when the tasks required auditory short-term memory, particularly when the information required verbatim memory. This finding is consistent with the relative processing weakness in the area of short-term memory identified by the KABC-II.

Reading

Anika's achievement in the area of reading was assessed both silently and orally and with single words and words in context.

When administered a test that required her to read single words aloud (KTEA-II Letter and Word Recognition subtest), her reading indicated that she knows some sight words. When decoding unfamiliar words, she would attempt to sound out the words and take a guess; however, her responses were not typically real words. Her performance was in the Below Average range (standard score = 78). Anika was also administered a Nonsense Word Decoding subtest (KTEA-II) that required her to decode single non-words. Her perform-ance was within the Below Average range (standard score = 83). Skills analysis results from both subtests revealed that Anika tends to insert and/or omit sounds, and has difficulty sequencing the sounds within words and reading words with diphthongs and consonant blends. She did well reading consonant digraphs.

Anika's oral reading in context was measured by the Oral Reading Fluency subtest of the WIAT-III, which required her to read passages aloud under timed conditions. Her fluency, accuracy, and rate scores were within the below average range (standard score = 76, 77, and 78, respectively). Her reading errors suggest that she tries to read for meaning, attempting to self-correct sentences that don't make sense. The majority of her errors were graphically similar substitution errors (e.g., leg for length). Generally, Anika read the passages with appropriate prosody, but her word identification difficulties sometimes interfered with her ability to read with appropriate phrase boundaries.

Anika's silent reading comprehension skills were assessed with two measures. The KTEA-II Reading Comprehension subtest required her to read the passages and the questions and respond with open-ended and multiple-choice answers. The WIAT-III Reading Comprehension subtest required her to read the passages and give open-ended responses, but the questions were read to her by the examiner. On the WIAT-III subtest, Anika was administered the third-grade item set because the grade-appropriate item set was too difficult for her and she did not answer any items correctly on the first passage. Reversing to a lower item set allowed her to demonstrate her reading comprehension skills with passages at a lower reading level. Her performance on the KTEA-II subtest was at the lower end of the Average range (standard score = 85), and her performance on the WIAT-III subtest was in the Average range (standard score = 100). Skill analysis results from both subtests indicated similar performance on both literal and inferential questions.

Overall, Anika's performance in the area of reading ranges from Below Average to Average. Her reading comprehension skills are in the Average range; however, weaknesses in word recognition and decoding skills interfere with her performance on reading comprehension and reading fluency tasks.

Writing

Anika used a right-handed, adaptive, tripod grip. She preferred writing in print, rather than cursive. Her handwriting was legible, but she wrote slowly and with effort. After writing more than a few sentences, she often became tired and shook her hand.

On a test of written spelling (KTEA-II Spelling subtest), Anika scored in the Below Average range (standard score = 80). She spells with good phonetic representation of all sounds within words, but a skills analysis results revealed that she tended to misspell diphthongs, unpredictable patterns, and silent letters.

To assess her writing of sentences and discourse, Anika was administered the Written Expression subtest (KTEA-II) and the Essay Composition subtest (WIAT-III). The KTEA-II Written Expression subtest required her to write words to complete sentences, write sentences that use or omit target words, and write an essay that retells a story that was presented. In particular, she demonstrated weaknesses in punctuation, word form (grammar), and sentence structure (syntax). Her essay contained faulty sentence structure. In addition, her essay did not follow a logical flow and was not organized in correct sequence. She scored within the Below Average range (standard score = 71). The WIAT-III Essay Composition subtest measured spontaneous writing skills by requiring her to write an essay about her favorite game within a 10-minute time limit. Her overall performance was within the Below Average range (standard score = 83). She wrote a short, one-paragraph, 32-word essay about the game of soccer; her productivity was at the lower end of the Average range relative to her same-age peers. The content of her essay was scored for theme development and text organization. She provided a basic introduction to the essay, but she did not write a conclusion. In addition, she did not use transitions to connect sentences nor did she elaborate on her reasons. Her score was Below Average. Her essay was also scored for grammar and mechanics. Misspelled words, omitted commas, fragments, and run-on sentences contributed to her Below Average score (standard score = 80).

In summary, Anika's overall performance in the area of writing is consistently Below Average. She demonstrated weaknesses in spelling, sentence writing, and essay writing. Specifically, Anika needs further instruction in spelling, punctuation, grammar and syntax, and essay writing skills, including use of transitions, theme development, and text organization.

Summary and Data Integration

Anika is a 10-year-old fourth grader referred for an evaluation to determine whether processing weaknesses may be interfering with her achievement and performance in the areas of basic reading, reading fluency, and written expression. The results of the evaluation indicate that Anika's cognitive abilities are variable, which was evident from her scores on the KABC-II that ranged from the Below Average range (9th percentile) on a scale measuring short-term memory to the Average range (77th percentile) on a scale measuring planning and reasoning (see Tables 6.10–6.13). Within her set of cognitive skills, a relative processing strength was identified in the area of fluid reasoning (Planning/Gf). In contrast, relative processing weaknesses were identified in the areas of short-term memory (Gsm) and long-term storage and retrieval (Glr). These two relative weaknesses are indicative of disorders in the basic psychological processes of short-term memory and long-term storage and retrieval. Anika's performance on the achievement tests administered revealed normative weaknesses in the areas of basic reading, contextual oral reading fluency, and written expression. Oral expression is an area of mixed achievement for Anika; she demonstrated weaknesses on tasks that placed demands on auditory short-term memory, which is consistent with the processing weaknesses identified. Anika's academic history and the results of this evaluation reveal that she has Average (to Above Average) abilities in mathematics and Oral Language.

Anika has been receiving reading intervention at school for one year (i.e., small-group reading instruction for 30 minutes, three days a week), as well as private after-school tutoring twice a week to help with homework. Despite these interventions, Anika continues to demonstrate Below Average achievement in basic reading, reading fluency, and written expression. The results of this comprehensive assessment indicate that Anika's Below Average academic skill deficits are consistent with a constellation of her cognitive processing deficits (short-term memory and long-term storage and retrieval). Overall, her specific pattern of strengths and weaknesses (both academic and cognitive) are consistent with the criteria for a Specific Learning Disability. Based on the findings of this evaluation, it seems clear that the interventions implemented by Anika's school thus far are insufficient to adequately address her Specific Learning Disability. A review of these data coupled with her academic history suggests the need for remediation, interventions, and accommodations that are more intensive and frequent than currently being provided.

Recommendations

Basic Reading
Anika would likely benefit from instruction that builds upon her sight word vocabulary and utilizes her relatively strong vocabulary skills. She also needs to acquire strategies for segmenting and sequencing the sounds within words and identifying orthographic features within words (e.g., onset, rime, prefix, suffix). Tasks that require careful inspection of visually similar words may be helpful (e.g., visual matching of words with similar-looking foils). Instruction should also focus on reading words that contain diphthongs and consonant blends. When reading single words or words in context, instruction should emphasize reading for meaning and attending to the meaning of words to build upon Anika's reading comprehension skills.

Reading Fluency
Anika demonstrated weaknesses in oral, contextual reading fluency, accuracy, and rate. She tends to make graphically similar substitution errors and usually attempts to self-correct sentences that don't make sense. Instruction should encourage her to continue reading for meaning and reading with appropriate prosody. Instruction should integrate single-word reading and reading in context at the level of the phrase, sentence, and paragraph. Instruction goals should include improving both speed and accuracy.

Written Expression
Anika is relying heavily upon a phonological strategy for spelling, but needs instruction that emphasizes orthography and the relationships between phonology and orthography. Contextual writing instruction should emphasize punctuation, grammar and syntax, theme development, and text organization. Specifically, she needs work on writing complete sentences and combining sentences to form paragraphs. At the paragraph and essay level, she needs instruction on writing an introduction and conclusion, and a cohesive body paragraph, clearly stating reasons using transition words, and elaborating upon the main points of her essay. Increasing her written productivity should also be an instructional objective.

PSYCHOMETRIC SUMMARY FOR ANIKA

Table 6.10 Kaufman Assessment Battery for Children–Second Edition (KABC-II) Scores

Scale Subtest	Standard Score	95% Confidence Interval	Percentile Rank	Descriptive Category
Sequential/Gsm	80	71–91	9	Below Average
Number Recall	4		2	
Word Order	3		1	
Hand Movements	6		9	
Simultaneous/Gv	94	84–104	34	Average
Rover	5		5	
Triangles	7		16	
Block Counting	6		9	
Learning/Glr	81	74–90	10	Below Average
Atlantis	5		5	
Rebus	2		0.5	
Atlantis Delayed	4		2	
Rebus Delayed	2		0.5	
Planning/Gf	111	99–121	77	Average
Story Completion	13		84	
Pattern Reasoning	11		63	
Crystallized Ability/Gc	90	82–98	25	Average
Riddles	6		9	
Verbal Knowledge	10		50	
Fluid Crystallized Index (FCI)	87	81–93	19	Average

Note: KABC-II Scales have a mean of 100 and a standard deviation of 15. KABC-II subtests have a mean of 10 and a standard deviation of 3.

Table 6.11 Kaufman Test of Educational Achievement–Second Edition (KTEA-II) Scores

Composite Subtest	Standard Score	95% Confidence Interval	Percentile Rank	Qualitative Description
Reading	83	77–89	13	Below Average
Letter and Word Recognition	78	72–84	7	Below Average
Reading Comprehension	85	80–90	16	Average
Decoding*	84	79–89	14	Below Average
Nonsense Word Decoding	83	76–90	13	Below Average
Letter and Word Recognition	78	72–84	7	Below Average
Written Language	74	66–82	4	Below Average
Spelling	80	72–88	9	Below Average
Written Expression	71	59–83	3	Below Average
Oral Langauge	—	—	—	—
Oral Expression	75	64–86	5	Below Average

*The Decoding composite includes Nonsense Word Decoding and Letter and Word Recognition.

Table 6.12 Wechsler Individual Achievement Test–Third Edition (WIAT–III) Scores

WIAT-III Composite	Standard Score	95% Confidence Interval	Percentile Rank	Qualitative Description
Oral Language	92	84–100	30	Average
Total Reading	83	79–87	13	Below Average
Basic Reading	84	80–88	14	Below Average
Reading Comprehension and Fluency	84	77–91	14	Below Average

WIAT-III Subtest Subtest Component	Standard Score	95% Confidence Interval	Percentile Rank	Qualitative Description
Listening Comprehension	98	87–109	45	Average
Receptive Vocabulary	110	—	75	Average

Oral Discourse Comprehension	86	—	18	Average
Reading Comprehension*	99	89–109	47	Average
Essay Composition	83	73–93	13	Below Average
Word Count	86	—	18	Average
Theme Development and Text Organization	82	—	12	Below Average
Oral Expression	87	76–98	19	Average
Expressive Vocabulary	87	—	19	Below Average
Oral Word Fluency	108	—	70	Average
Sentence Repetition	75	—	5	Below Average
Oral Reading Fluency	76	68–84	5	Below Average

*Based on below-grade level (3rd grade) reading passages

Table 6.13 Supplemental Subtest Score Summary

Score Name	Standard Score	95% Confidence Interval	Percentile Rank	Qualitative Description
Essay Composition: Grammar and Mechanics	80	67–93	9	Below Average
Oral Reading Accuracy	77	65–89	6	Below Average
Oral Reading Rate	78	68–88	7	Below Average

References

Adams, M. (1990). *Beginning to read: Thinking and learning about print.* Cambridge, MA: The MIT Press.

Alexander, A., Andersen, H., Heilman, K., Voeller, K., & Torgesen, J. (1991). Phonological awareness training and remediation of analytic decoding deficits in a group of severe dyslexics. *Annals of the Orton Society, 41,* 193–206.

Altemeier, L., Jones, J., Abbot, R., & Berninger, V. (in press). Executive functions in becoming writing-readers and reading-writers: Note-taking and report writing in third and fifth graders. *Special Issue of Developmental Neuropsychology.*

Archer, R. P., Maruish, M., Imhof, E. A., & Piotrowski, C. (1991). Psychological test usage with adolescent clients: 1990 findings. *Professional Psychology: Research & Practice, 22,* 247–252.

Barkley, R. A. (1990). *Attention-deficit hyperactivity disorder: A handbook for diagnosis and treatment.* New York: Guilford Press.

Barkley, R. A. (1998). *Attention-deficit hyperactivity disorder: A handbook for diagnosis and treatment* (2nd ed.). New York: Guilford Press.

Barkley, R. A. (2003). Attention-Deficit/Hyperactivity Disorder. In E.J. Mash & R.A. Barkley (Eds.), *Child Psychopathology* (2nd ed., pp. 75–143). New York: Guilford Press.

Barkley, R. A., DuPaul, G. J., & McMurray, M. B. (1990). A comprehensive evaluation of attention deficit disorder with and without hyperactivity. *Journal of Consulting and Clinical Psychology, 58,* 775–789.

Berninger, V. (1999). Coordinating transcriptions and text generation in working memory during composing: Automatized and constructive processes. *Learning Disability Quarterly, 22,* 99–112.

Berninger, V. (1998). *Process Assessment of the Learner (PAL): Guides for intervention in reading and writing.* San Antonio: The Psychological Corporation.

Berninger, V. (2007). *Process Assessment of the Learner Diagnostic (PAL II).* San Antonio, TX: The Psychological Corporation.

Berninger, V. (2001). *Process Assessment of the Learner (PAL) Test Battery for Reading and Writing.* The Psychological Corporation, San Antonio, TX.

Berninger, V. (2000). *Process Assessment of the Learner: Test for Reading and Writing manual.* San Antonio: The Psychological Corporation.

Berninger, V. (2005). Research-supported differential diagnosis of specific learning disabilities. In A. Prifitera, D. Saklofske, L. Weiss & E. Rolfhus (Eds), *WISC–IV clinical use and interpretation.* New York: Academic Press.

Berninger, V., & Abbott, S. (2003). *PAL research-based reading and writing lessons.* San Antonio: The Psychological Corporation.

Berninger, V., & Amtmann, D. (2003). Preventing written expression disabilities through early and continuing assessment and intervention for handwriting and/or spelling problems: Research into practice. In H. L. Swanson, K. Harris, and S. Graham (Eds.), *Handbook of research on learning disabilities* (pp. 345–363). New York: Guilford Press.

Berninger, V., Dunn, A., & Alper, T. (2005). Integrated multilevel model of branching assessment, instructional assessment, and profile assessment. In A. Prifitera, D. Saklofske, L. Weiss, & E. Rolfhus (Eds.), *WISC–IV Clinical use and interpretation* (pp. 151–185). San Diego: Academic Press.

Berninger, V., Nagy, W., Carlisle, J., Thomson, J., Hoffer, D., Abbot, S., Abbott, R., Richards, T., & Aylward, E. (2003). Effective treatment for dyslexics in grades 4 to 6. In B. Foorman (Ed.), *Preventing and remediating reading difficulties: Bringing science to scale* (pp. 381–417). Baltimore: York Press.

Berninger, V., & O'Donnell, L. (2005). Research-supported differential diagnosis of specific learning disabilities. In A. Prifitera, D. Saklofske, L. Weiss, & E. Rolfhus (Eds.), *WISC–IV Clinical use and interpretation* (pp. 189–233). San Diego: Academic Press.

Berninger, V., Stage, S., Smith, D., & Hildebrand, D. (2001). Assessment for reading and writing intervention: A three-tier model for prevention and remediation. In J. Andrews, D. Saklofske, & H. Janzen (Eds.), *Handbook of psychoeducational assessment. Ability, achievement, and behavior in children.* (pp. 195–223). New York: Academic Press.

Berninger, V., Vaughn, K., Abbott, R., Brooks, A., Abbott, S., Reed, E., Rogan, L., & Graham, S. (1998). Early intervention for spelling problems: Teaching spelling units of varying size within a multiple connections framework. *Journal of Educational Psychology, 90*, 587–605.

Berninger, V., Whitaker, D., Feng, Y., Swanson, H. L., & Abbott, R.D. (1996). Assessment of Planning, Translating, and Revising in Junior High Writers. *Journal of School Psychology, 34*(1), 23–52.

Bley, N. & Thornton, C. (1989). *Teaching mathematics to the learned disabled.* Austin, TX: Pro-Ed.

Braden, J.P., & Weiss, L. (1988). Effects of simple difference versus regression discrepancy methods: An empirical study. *Journal of School Psychology, 26*, 133–142.

Brock, S. W., & Knapp, P. K. (1996). Reading comprehension abilities of children with attention-deficit/hyperactivity disorder. *Journal of Attention Disorders, 1*, 173–186.

Bryant, D., Ugel, N., Thompson, S., & Hamff, A. (1999). Instructional strategies for content-area reading instruction. *Intervention in School and Clinic, 34*, 293–302.

Carroll, J. B. (1993). *Human cognitive abilities: A survey of factor-analytic studies.* Cambridge, UK: Cambridge University Press.

Carroll, J. B. (1997). The three-stratum theory of cognitive abilities. In D. P. Flanagan, J. L. Genshaft, & P. L. Harrison (Eds.), *Contemporary intellectual assessment: Theories, tests, and issues* (pp. 122–130). New York: Guilford Press.

Carrow-Woolfolk, E. (1996). *Oral and Written Language Scales.* Circle Pines, MN: AGS Publishing.

Carrow-Woolfolk, E. (1999). *Comprehensive Assessment of Spoken Language.* Circle Pines, MN: American Guidance Service.

Casey, J. E., Rourke, B. P., & Del Dotto, J. E. (1996). Learning disabilities in children with attention deficit disorder with and without hyperactivity. *Child Neuropsychology, 2*, 83–98.

Cattell, R. (1943). The measurement of adult intelligence. *Psychological Bulletin, 40*, 153–193.

Cattell, R. (1963). Theory of fluid and crystallized intelligence: A critical experiment. *Journal of Educational Psychology, 54*, 1–22.

Cattell, R., & Horn, J. (1978). A check on the theory of fluid and crystallized intelligence with description of new subtest designs. *Journal of Educational Measurement, 15*, 139–164.

Clay, M. (1972). *The early detection of reading difficulties.* Auckland, NZ: Heinemann.

Cohen, B. H. (1996). *Explaining psychological statistics.* Pacific Grove, CA: Brooks/Cole.

Cohen, J., Cohen, P., West, S. G., & Aiken, L. S. (2003). *Applied multiple regression/correlation analysis for the behavioral sciences.* Mahwah, NJ: Erlbaum.

Das, J. P., Naglieri, J. A., & Kirby, J. R. (1994). *Assessment of cognitive processes.* Needham Heights, MA: Allyn & Bacon.

Demaray, M. K., Schaefer, K., & Delong, K. (2003). Attention-deficit/hyperactivity disorder (ADHD): A national survey of training and current assessment practices in the schools. *Psychology in the Schools, 40*(6), 583–597.

DiPerna, J., & Elliott, S. (2000). *Academic Competence Evaluation Scales*. San Antonio, TX: The Psychological Corporation.

Donders, J. (1997). Sensitivity of the WISC-III to injury severity in children with traumatic head injury. *Assessment, 4*, 107–109.

Dumont, R., & Willis, J. O. (2009). *The evaluation of Sam McGee*. Retrieved July 13, 2009, from http://alpha.fdu.edu/~dumont/psychology/McGee.htm.

Dunn, A. (2002, Fall). Partnership and problem solving to promote early intervention in literacy: Using the PAL. *CASP Today, 51*(1).

Dunn, A. (in press). Los Angeles Unified School District (LAUSD) school psychology project bridging special and general education. *CASP Today, 53*.

Dunn, L. & Dunn, L. (1997). *Peabody Picture Vocabulary Test* (3rd ed.) Circle Pines, MN: American Guidance Service.

Ehri, L. C., Nunes, S. R., Stahl, S. A., & Willows, D. M. (2001). Systematic phonics instruction helps students learn to read: Evidence from the national Reading Panel's meta-analysis. *Review of Educational Research, 71*, 393–447.

Elliott, C. (1990). *Differential Ability Scales*. San Antonio, TX: The Psychological Corporation.

Elliott, C. D. (2007). *Differential Ability Scales* (2nd ed.). San Antonio: The Psychological Corporation.

Elliott, S., DiPerna, J., & Shapiro, E. (2001). *Academic Intervention Monitoring System*. San Antonio, TX: The Psychological Corporation.

Faraone, S. V., Biederman, J., Lehman, B. K., & Spencer, T. (1993). Intellectual performance and school failure in children with attention deficit hyperactivity disorder and in their siblings. *Journal of Abnormal Psychology, 102*(4), 616–623.

Fiorello, C. A., Hale, J. B., & Snyder, L. E. (2006). Cognitive hypothesis testing and response to intervention for children with reading problems. *Psychology in the Schools, 43*(8), 835–853.

Flanagan, D. P., & Kaufman, A. S. (2004). *Essentials of WISC-IV assessment*. New York: Wiley.

Flanagan, D. P., & Kaufman, A. S. (2009). *Essentials of WISC-IV assessment* (2nd ed.). Hoboken, NJ: John Wiley & Sons.

Flanagan, D. P., McGrew, K. S., & Ortiz, S. O. (2000). *The Wechsler intelligence scales and Gf-Gc theory*. Boston: Allyn & Bacon.

Flanagan, D. P., & Ortiz, S. O. (2001). *Essentials of cross-battery assessment*. New York: Wiley.

Flanagan, D. P., Ortiz, S. O., & Alfonso, V. C. (2007). *Essentials of cross-battery assessment* (2nd ed.). Hoboken, NJ: John Wiley & Sons. See also the official site of the CHC Cross-Battery Approach by Dawn P. Flanagan and Samuel O. Ortiz at http://facpub.stjohns.edu/~ortizs/cross-battery, retrieved February 29, 2008.

Flanagan, D. P., Ortiz, S. O., Alfonso, V. C., & Mascolo, J. T. (2002). *The achievement test desk reference (ATDR): Comprehensive assessment and learning disabilities*. Boston: Allyn & Bacon.

Flanagan, D. P., Ortiz, S. O., Alfonso, V. C. & Mascolo, J. T. (2006). *Achievement test desk reference (ATDR-II): A guide to learning disability identification* (2nd ed.). Hoboken, NJ: Wiley.

Frick, P. J., Kamphaus, R. W., Lahey, B. B., Loeber, R., Christ, M. A. G., Hart, E. L., & Tannenbaum, L. E. (1991). Academic underachievement and the disruptive behavior disorders. *Journal of Consulting and Clinical Psychology, 59*, 289–294.

Frith, U. (1980). Unexpected spelling problems. In U. Frith (Ed.), *Cognitive processes in spelling*. London: Academic Press.

Fry, A., & Hale, S. (1996). Processing speed, working memory, and fluid intelligence: Evidence for a developmental cascade. *Psychological Science, 7*, 237–241.

Gathercole, S., Pickering, S., Ambridge, B., & Wearing, H. (2004). The structure of working memory from 4 to 15 years of age. *Developmental Psychology, 40*, 177–190.

Glutting, J., Oakland, T., & Konold, T. (1994). Critetion-related bias with the guide to the assessment of test-session behavior for the WISC–III and WIAT: Possible race/ethnicity, gender, and SES effects. *Journal of School Psychology, 32*(4), 355–369.

Goldberg, E., & Bougakov, D. (2000). Novel approaches to the diagnosis and treatment of frontal lobe dysfunction. In A. Christensen & B. P. Uzell (Eds.), *International handbook of neuropsychological rehabilitation* (pp. 93–112). New York: Kluwer/Plenum.

Goldman, J. J. (1989). On the robustness of psychological test instrumentation: Psychological evaluation of the dead. In G. G. Ellenbogen (Ed.), *The primal whimper: More readings from the Journal of Polymorphous Perversity*. New York: Ballantine, Stonesong Press.

Goodman, Y. & Burke, C. (1972). *Reading miscue inventory: Procedure for diagnosis and correction*. New York: Macmillan.

Gottfredson, L. (1998). *The general intelligence factor. Scientific American*, November, 1–10. Retrieved February 5, 2002, from www.scientificamerican.com/specialissues/1198intelligence/1198gottfred.html.

Gough, P.B., & Tunmer, W. E. (1986). Decoding, reading, and reading disability. *Remedial and Special Education, 7*(1), 6–10.

Hale, J. B., & Fiorello, C. A. (2004). *School neuropsychology: A practitioner's handbook*. New York: Guilford Press.

Hale, J. B., Fiorello, C. A., Bertin, M., & Sherman, R. (2003). Predicting math achievement through neuropsychological interpretation of WISCIII variance components. *Journal of Psychoeducational Assessment, 21*, 358–380.

Hale, J. B., Fiorello, C. A., Miller, J. A., Wenrich, K., Teodori, A., & Henzel, J. N. (2008). WISCIV interpretation for specific learning disabilities identification and intervention: A cognitive hypothesis testing approach. In A. Prifitera, D. H. Saklofske, & L. G. Weiss (Eds.), *WISC–IV clinical assessment and intervention* (2nd ed., pp. 109–171). San Diego, CA: Academic Press.

Hammill, D. D., Fowler, L., Bryant, B., & Dunn, C. (1992). *A survey of test usage among speech/language pathologists*. Unpublished manuscript.

Hasbrouck, J. & Tindal, G. (1992). Curriculum based oral reading fluency norms for students in grades 2 through 5. *Teaching Exceptional Children, 24*(3), 41–44.

Henry, M. (2003). *Unlocking literacy. Effective decoding and spelling instruction*. Baltimore: Paul H. Brookes Publishing.

Hooper, S. R., & Hynd, G. W. (1982, October). *The differential diagnosis of developmental dyslexia with the Kaufman Assessment Battery for children*. Paper presented at the meeting of the National Academy of Neuropsychologists, Atlanta, GA.

Horn, J. (1991). Human cognitive capabilities: Gf-Gc theory. In D. Flanagan, J. Genshaft, & P. Harrison (Eds.), *Contemporary intellectual assessment: Theories, tests, and issues* (pp. 53–91). New York: Guilford Press.

Hutton, J. B., Dubes, R., & Muir, S. (1992). Assessment practices of school psychologists: Ten years later. *School Psychologist Review, 21*, 271–284.

Individuals with Disabilities Education Act Amendments of 1997, 20 U.S.C. 1400 et seq. (Fed. Reg. 64, 1999).

Individuals with Disabilities Education Act-section 602 (15) (1991). *Compilation of Federal Education Laws Vol. V*. U.S. Government Printing Office, Washington, D.C.

Individuals with Disabilities Education Improvement Act (IDEA) of 2004, Pubic Law No. 108–446.

James, E. M., & Selz, M. (1997). Neuropsychological bases of common learning and behavior problems in children. In C. R. Reynolds and E. Fletcher-Janzen (Eds.), *The handbook of clinical child neuropsychology* (2nd ed., pp. 157–203). New York: Kluwer-Plenum.

Johnson, D. (1982). Programming for dyslexia: The need for interaction analyses. *Annals of Dyslexia 32, 61–70*. Baltimore, MD: The Orton Dyslexia Society.

Johnson, D. J. & Myklebust, H. R. (1967). *Learning disabilities: Educational principles and practices.* New York: Grune & Stratton.

Johnson, M., Kress, R. & Pikulski, J. (1987). *Informal reading inventories* (2nd ed.). Newark, IL: International Reading Association.

Joint Committee on Testing Practices (2004). *Code of Fair Testing Practices in Education.* Washington, DC: American Psychological Association.

Kail, R., & Salthouse, T. (1994). Processing speed as a mental capacity. *Acta Psychologica, 86,* 199–225.

Kamphaus, R. W., & Reynolds, C. R. (1987). *Clinical and research applications of the K-ABC.* Circle Pines, MN: AGS.

Kaufman, A. S., & Kaufman, N. L. (1985, 1997). *Kaufman Test of Educational Achievement.* Circle Pines, MN: AGS.

Kaufman, A. S., & Kaufman, N. L. (2001). *Specific learning disabilities and difficulties in children and adolescents.* New York: Cambridge University Press.

Kaufman, A. S., & Kaufman, N. L. (2004a). *Kaufman Test of Educational Achievement, Second Edition Comprehensive Form Manual.* Circle Pines, MN: AGS.

Kaufman, A. S., & Kaufman, N. L. (2004b). *Kaufman Assessment Battery for Children, Second Edition Manual.* Circle Pines, MN: AGS.

Kaufman, A. S., & Kaufman, N. L. (2004c). *Kaufman Brief Intelligence Test, Second Edition Manual.* Circle Pines, MN: AGS.

Kaufman, A. S., & Kaufman, N. L. (2005a). *Kaufman Test of Educational Achievement, Second Edition Brief Form Manual.* Circle Pines, MN: AGS.

Kaufman, A. S., Lichtenberger, E. O., Fletcher-Janzen, E., & Kaufman, N. L. (2005). *Essentials of KABC-II assessment.* New York: Wiley.

Kavale, K. A., & Forness, S. R. (1995). *The nature of learning disabilities: Critical elements of diagnosis and classification.* Mahwah, NJ: Erlbaum.

Kavale, K., Holdnack, J., & Mostert, M. (2005). Responsiveness to intervention and the identification of specific learning disability: A critique and alternative proposal. *Learning Disability Quarterly, 28*(4), 2–16.

Keenan, J. M. & Betjemann, R. S. (2006). Comprehending the Gray Oral Reading Test without reading it: Why comprehension tests should not include passage-independent items. *Scientific Studies of Reading, 10*(4), 363–380.

Kirby, J. R., & Williams, N. H. (1991). *Learning problems: A cognitive approach.* Toronto: Kagan and Woo.

Kuhn, M. & Stahl, S., (2000). *Fluency. A review of developmental and remedial practices (CIERA Report #2-0008).* Ann Arbor: University of Michigan, Center for Improvement of Early Reading Achievement.

Laurent, J., & Swerdlik, M. (1992). *Psychological test usage: A survey of internship supervisors.* Paper presented at the annual meeting of the national Association of School Psychologists, Nashville, TN.

Lennon, J. & Slesinski, C. (1999). Early intervention in reading; Results of a screening and intervention program for kindergarten students. *School Psychology Review, 28*(3), 353–364.

Lichtenberger, E. O. (2001). The Kaufman tests- K-ABC and KAIT. In A. S. Kaufman & N. L. Kaufman (Eds.), *Specific learning disabilities and difficulties in children and adolescents* (pp. 283–306). New York: Cambridge University Press.

Lichtenberger, E. O., Broadbooks, D. Y., & Kaufman, A. S. (2000). *Essentials of cognitive assessment with KAIT and other Kaufman measures.* New York: Wiley.

Lichtenberger, E. O., & Smith, D. R. (2005). *Essentials of WIAT-II and KTEA-II assessment.* Hoboken, NJ: Wiley.

Lovett, M. (1987). A developmental approach to reading disability: Accuracy and speed criteria of normal and deficient reading skill. *Child Development, 58,* 234–260.

Luria, A. R. (1966). *Human brain: An introduction to neuropsychology.* New York: Basic Books.

Luria, A. R. (1970). The functional organization of the brain. *Scientific American, 222,* 66–78.

Luria, A. R. (1973). *The working brain: An introduction to neuro-psychology.* London: Penguin Books.

Lyon, G., Fletcher, J. & Barnes, T. (2003). Learning Disabilities. In E. J. Mash & R. A. Barkley (Eds.), *Child Psychopathology* (pp. 390–345). New York: Guilford Press.

Lyon, G. R., Shaywitz, S. E., Shaywitz, B. A. (2003). Defining dyslexia, comorbidity, teachers' knowledge of language and reading: A definition of dyslexia. *Annals of Dyslexia, 53,* 1–14.

Markwardt, F. C., Jr. (1989, 1998). *Peabody Individual Achievement Test, Revised.* Circle Pines, MN: AGS Publishing.

Masterson, J., Apel, K., & Wasowicz, J. (2002). *SPELL: Spelling Performance Evaluation for Language & Literacy: A prescriptive assessment of spelling on CD-ROM.* Evanston, IL: Learning by Design.

Mather, N., Wendling, B. J., & Woodcock, R. W. (2001). *Essentials of WJ III Tests of Achievement Assessment.* New York: Wiley.

Mather, N., & Woodcock, R. W. (2001). *Woodcock-Johnson III Tests of Achievement Examiner's Manual.* Itasca, IL: Riverside.

McConaughy, S. H., Ivanova, M. Y., Antshel, K., & Eiraldi, R. B. (2009). Standardized observational assessment of attention deficit hyperactivity disorder combined and predominantly inattentive subtypes. I. Test session observations. *School Psychology Review, 38*(1), 45–66.

McGrew, K. S., & Flanagan, D. P. (1998). *The intelligence test desk reference (ITDR): Gf-Gc cross-battery assessment.* Boston: Allyn & Bacon.

Moats, L. C. (1995). *Spelling: Development, disabilities, and instruction.* Baltimore, MD: York Press, Inc.

Moats, L. C. (2001). Spelling disability in adolescents and adults. In A. Bain, L. Bailet, and L. Moats (Eds.), *Written language disorders: Theory into practice* (2nd ed., pp. 43–75). Austin, TX: Pro-Ed.

Mylkebust, H. (1960). *Psychology of Deafness.* New York: Grune & Stratton.

Naglieri, J. A. (2001). Using the Cognitive Assessment System (CAS) with learning disabled children. In A. S. Kaufman & N. L. Kaufman (Eds.), *Specific learning disabilities and difficulties in children and adolescents* (pp. 141–177). New York: Cambridge University Press.

National Council of Teachers of Mathematics (2000). *Principles and Standards for School Mathematics.* Reston, VA: Author.

National Institute of Child Health and Human Development (NICHHD, 2000). *Report of the National Reading Panel. Teaching children to read: An evidence-based assessment of the scientific research literature on reading and its implications for reading instruction (NIH Publication No. 00-4769).* Washington, DC: U.S. Government Printing Office.

National Reading Panel. (2000). *Teaching children to read: An evidence-based assessment of the scientific research literature on reading and its implications for reading instruction* (NIH Publication No. 000-4754). Washington, DC: National Institute of Child Health and Human Development.

Nunnally, J. C. (1978). *Psychometric theory* (2nd ed.). New York: McGraw-Hill.

Pearson. (2009a). *The Wechsler Individual Achievement Test* (3rd ed.) San Antonio, TX: Pearson.

Pearson. (2009b). *Wechsler Individual Achievement Test–Third Edition Examiner's Manual.* San Antonio, TX: Author.

Pearson. (2009c). *Wechsler Individual Achievement Test–Third Edition Technical Manual.* San Antonio, TX: Author.

Perlow, R., Jattuso, M., & Moore, D. (1997). Role of verbal working memory in complex skill acquisition. *Human Performance, 10*, 283–302.

Prifitera, A., Saklofske, D. H., & Weiss, L. G. (2005). *WISC-IV clinical use and interpretation.* San Diego: Elsevier Academic Press.

Psychological Corporation (2007). *Process Assessment of the Learner, Diagnostic for Reading and Writing* (PAL-II RW) (2nd ed.). San Antonio, TX: The Psychological Corporation.

Psychological Corporation, The. (1992). *Wechsler Individual Achievement Test.* San Antonio, TX: Author.

Psychological Corporation, The. (1999). *Wechsler Abbreviated Test of Intelligence.* San Antonio, TX: Author.

Psychological Corporation, The. (2001). *Wechsler Individual Achievement Test-Second Edition–Abbreviated* (WIAT-II—A). San Antonio, TX: Author.

Psychological Corporation, The. (2002). *Wechsler Individual Achievement Test-Second Edition.* San Antonio, TX: Author.

Psychological Corporation, The. (2002). *WIAT-II Scoring and Normative Supplement for College Students and Adults.* San Antonio, TX: Author.

Rack, J., Snowling, M., & Olson, R. (1992). The nonword reading deficit in developmental dyslexia: A review. *Reading Research Quarterly, 27*(1), 28–53.

Raiford, S., Weiss, L., Rolfhus, E., & Coalson, D., (2005). *WISC–IV technical report #4: General abilities index.* San Antonio, TX: The Psychological Corporation.

Raney, G. E. (1993). Monitoring changes in cognitive load during reading: An event-related brain potential and reaction time analysis. *Journal of Experimental Psychology: Learning, Memory & Cognition, 19*, 51–69.

Rayner, K., Foorman, B. R., Perfetti, C. A., Pesetsky, D., & Seidenberg, M. S. (2001). How psychological science informs the teaching of reading. *Psychological Science in the Public Interest, 2*(2), 31–74.

Reitan, R. M. (1988). Integration of neuropsychological theory, assessment, and application. *The Clinical Neuropsychologist, 2*, 331–349.

Reynolds, C. R., Kamphaus, R. W., Rosenthal, B. L., & Hiemenz, J. R. (1997). Applications of the Kaufman Assessment Battery for Children (K-ABC) in neuropsychological assessment. In C. R. Reynolds & E. Fletcher-Janzen (Eds.), *The handbook of clinical child neuropsychology* (2nd ed., pp. 253–269). New York: Kluwer-Plenum.

Roberts, M., Turco, T., & Shapiro, E. (1991). Differential effects of fixed instructional ratios on student's progress in reading. *Journal of Psychoeducational Assessment, 9*, 308–318.

Rourke, B. (1989). Significance of Verbal-Performance discrepancies for subtypes of children with learning disabilities: Opportunities for the WISC-II. In A. Prifitera & D. Saklofske (Eds.), *WISC-II clinical use and interpretation* (pp. 139–156). San Diego, CA: Academic Press.

Rust, J., & Golombok, S. (1999) *Modern psychometrics: The science of psychological assessment* (2nd ed.). New York: Routledge.

Samuels, S. (1988). Decoding and automaticity: Helping poor readers become automatic at word recognition. *The Reading Teacher, 48*(8), 756–760.

Sattler, J. (2001). *Assessment of children: Cognitive applications* (4th ed). San Diego, CA: Author.

Scruggs, T. E., & Mastropieri, M. A. (2002). On babies and bathwater: Addressing the problems of identification of learning disabilities. *Learning Disability Quarterly, 25*, 55–168.

Semel, E., Wiig, E. H., & Secord, W. A. (2003). *Clinical Evaluation of Language Fundamentals* (4th ed.). San Antonio, TX: The Psychological Corporation.

Shinn, M. R. (2007). Identifying students at risk, monitoring performance, and determining eligibility within response to intervention: Research on educational need and benefit from academic intervention. *School Psychology Review, 36*(4), 601–617.

Siegal, M. (1997). *Knowing children: Experiments in conversation and cognition* (2nd ed.). Hove, England: Psychology Press.

Siegel, L. S. (1989). IQ is irrelevant to the definition of learning disabilities. *Journal of Learning Disabilities, 22,* 469–478.

Siegel, L. S. (1999). Issues in the definition and diagnosis of learning disabilities: a perspective on Guckenberger v. Boston University. *Journal of Learning Disabilities, 32,* 304–319.

Siegel, L. S. (2003). IQ-discrepancy definitions and the diagnosis of LD: Introduction to the special issue. *Journal of Learning Disabilities, 36,* 2–3.

Smith, D. K. (2001). *Essentials of individual achievement assessment.* New York: Wiley.

Spreen, O. (2001). Learning disabilities and their neurological foundations, theories, and subtypes. In A. S. Kaufman & N. L. Kaufman (Eds.), *Specific learning disabilities and difficulties in children and adolescents* (pp. 283–306). New York: Cambridge University Press.

Standards for educational and psychological testing. (1999). Washington, DC: American Psychological Association.

Stanovich, K. (1985). Explaining the variance in reading ability in terms of psychological processes: What have we learned? *Annals of Dyslexia, 35,* 67–96.

Stanovich, K. E. (1992). Developmental reading disorder. In. S. R. Hooper, G. W. Hynd, & R. E. Mattison (Eds.), *Developmental disorders: Diagnostic criteria and clinical assessment* (pp. 173–208). Mahwah, NJ: Erlbaum.

Stanovich, K. E. (1999). The sociopsychometrics of learning disabilities. *Journal of Learning Disabilities, 32,* 350–361.

Stanovich, K., E. & Siegel, L. (1994). Phenotypic performance profile of children with reading disabilities: A regression-based test of the phonological-core variable-difference model. *Journal of Educational Psychology, 86,* 24–53.

Sternberg, R. (1995). *In search of the human mind.* Fort Worth, TX: Harcourt Brace College Publishers.

Stinnett, T. A., Havey, J. M., & Oehler-Stinnett, J. (1994). Current test usage by practicing school psychologists: A national survey. *Journal of Psychoeducational Assessment, 12,* 331–350.

Swanson, H. (1996). Individual and age-related differences in children's working memory. *Memory & Cognition, 24,* 70–82.

Swanson, H., & Howell, M. (2001). Working memory, short-term memory, and speech rate as predictors of children's reading performance at different ages. *Journal of Educational Psychology, 9,* 720–734.

Teeter, P. A. (1997). Neurocognitive interventions for childhood and adolescent disorders: A transactional model. In C. R. Reynolds and E. Fletcher-Janzen (Eds.), *The handbook of clinical child neuropsychology* (2nd ed., pp. 387–417). New York: Kluwer-Plenum.

Teeter, P. A., & Semrud-Clikeman, M. (1998). *Child clinical neuropsychology: Assessment and interventions for neuropsychiatric and neurodevelopmental disorders of childhood.* Boston: Allyn & Bacon.

Torgesen, J., Wagner, R., & Rashotte, C. (1994). Longitudinal studies of phonological processing and reading. *Journal of Learning Disabilities, 27*(5), 276–286.

Van Leerdam, M., Bosman, A., & van Orden, G. (1998). The ecology of spelling instruction: Effective training in first grade. In P. Reitsma, & L. Verhoeven (Eds.), *Problems and Interventions in Literacy Development* (pp. 307–320). Dordrecht: Kluwer Academic Publishers.

Vellutino, F. R., Scanlon, D. M., & Lyon, G. R. (2000). Differentiating between difficult-to-remediate and readily remediated poor readers: more evidence against the IQ-achievement discrepancy definition of reading disability. *Journal of Learning Disabilities, 33,* 223–238.

Wechsler, D. (1975). Intelligence defined and undefined: A relativistic appraisal. *American Psychologist, 30,* 135–139.

Wechsler, D. (1981). *Wechsler Adult Intelligence Scale–Revised.* San Antonio, TX: The Psychological Corporation.

Wechsler, D. (1989). *Wechsler Preschool and Primary Scale of Intelligence–Revised.* San Antonio, TX: The Psychological Corporation.

Wechsler, D. (1991). *Wechsler Intelligence Scale for Children* (3rd ed.) San Antonio, TX: The Psychological Corporation.

Wechsler, D. (1997). *Wechsler Adult Intelligence Scale* (3rd ed.) San Antonio, TX: The Psychological Corporation.

Wechsler, D. (2001). *Wechsler Individual Achievement Test* (2nd ed.). San Antonio, TX: The Psychological Corporation.

Wechsler, D. (2002). *Wechsler Individual Achievement Test–Second Edition Supplement for Adults and College Students.* San Antonio, TX: The Psychological Corporation.

Wechsler, D. (2002). *Wechsler Preschool and Primary Scale of Intelligence* (3rd ed.) San Antonio, TX: The Psychological Corporation.

Wechsler, D. (2003). *Wechsler Intelligence Scale for Children* (4th ed.). San Antonio, TX: The Psychological Corporation.

Wechsler, D. (2008). *Wechsler Adult Intelligence Scale* (4th ed.). San Antonio, TX: The Psychological Corporation.

Wechsler, D., Kaplan, E., Fein, D., Kramer, J., Morris, R., Delis, D., & Maerlender, A. (2004). *WISC-IV Integrated technical and interpretive manual.* San Antonio, TX: Harcourt Assessment, Inc.

Wechsler, D., & Naglieri, J. A. (2006). *Wechsler Nonverbal Scale of Ability.* San Antonio, TX: The Psychological Corporation.

Wilkinson, G. S. (1993). *Wide Range Achievement Test–Third Edition administration manual.* Wilmington, DE: Wide Range, Inc.

Wilson, M. S. & Reschley, D. J. (1996). Assessment in school psychology training and practice. *School Psychology Review, 21,* 9–23.

Wolf, M., & Bowers, P. (1999). The double-deficit hypothesis for the developmental dyslexias. *Journal of Educational Psychology, 91,* 415–438.

Woodcock, R. & Johnson, B. (1990). *Woodcock-Johnson Psycho-Educational Battery–Revised, Tests of Achievement.* Chicago, IL: Riverside Publishing.

Woodcock, R. W., McGrew, K. S., & Mather, N. (2001). *Woodcock-Johnson III.* Itasca, IL: Riverside Publishing.

Zachary, R. (1990). Wechsler's intelligence scales: Theoretical and practical considerations. *Journal of Psychoeducational Assessment, 8,* 276–289.

Annotated Bibliography

Berninger, V., Dunn, A., & Alper, T. (2005). Integrated multilevel model of branching assessment, instructional assessment, and profile assessment. In A. Prifitera, D. Saklofske, & L. Weiss (Eds). *WISC–IV Clinical use and interpretation* (pp. 151–185). San Diego: Academic Press.

This chapter presents a multilevel approach to integrated assessment. It discusses methods for integrating results from achievement and cognitive measures with students' response to intervention. The final goal of the assessment approach is to provide the most useful information that is relevant to instructional planning.

Flanagan, D. P., & Kaufman, A. S. (2009). *Essentials of WISC-IV assessment* (2nd ed.). New York: Wiley.

This book details administration, scoring, and interpretation of the WISC-IV. It provides a theory-driven approach to integrating the WIAT-II and WISC-IV in the assessment of learning disabilities. Case reports are presented that exemplify how to integrate the WIAT-II with the WISC-IV, and a CD-ROM is provided to automate the book's interpretive method.

Flanagan, D. P., Ortiz, S. O., & Alfonso, V. C. (2007). *Essentials of cross-battery assessment* (2nd ed.). New York: Wiley.

This second edition provides a comprehensive set of guidelines and procedures for organizing assessments based on contemporary CHC theory and research, integrating test results from different batteries in a psychometrically defensible way, and interpreting test results within the context of research on the relations between cognitive and academic abilities and processes. Also includes guidelines for assessing culturally and linguistically diverse populations and individuals suspected of having a specific learning disability. This book includes a CD-ROM containing three software programs for assisting in data management and interpretation, making decisions regarding specific learning disability, and discerning difference from disability in individuals whose cultural and linguistic backgrounds differ from the mainstream.

Flanagan, D. P., Ortiz, S. O., Alfonso, V. C., & Mascolo, J. (2006). *The achievement test desk reference (ATDR): A guide to learning disability identification.* Boston: Allyn & Bacon.

This book provides comprehensive information about the most important psychometric, theoretical, and qualitative characteristics of the major achievement batteries, including the WIAT-II, KTEA-II, and WJ III. In addition, test characteristics are summarized for brief/screening measures as well as special-purpose batteries that are used to assess specific academic skill areas such as reading, math, writing, oral language, and phonological processing. In addition, this book offers a comprehensive framework for LD determination and provides practitioners with a step-by-step decision-making process in responding to learning-related referrals.

Hale, J. B. & Fiorello, C. A. (2004). *School neuropsychology: A practitioner's handbook.* New York: Guilford Press.

This book is a user-friendly guide for understanding the practical role of neuropsychology in the schools with a focus on interpreting assessment results and linking assessment to intervention within the framework of a cognitive hypothesis-testing model. Special emphasis is given to the assessment and treatment of disorders in the areas of reading, mathematics, and written language. It introduces the rationale behind the author's concordance-discordance model of learning disability determination and explains how to conduct the analysis using a case example.

Kaufman, A. S., & Kaufman, N. L. (2001). *Specific learning disabilities and difficulties in children and adolescents.* New York: Cambridge University Press.

This book contains 13 chapters written by experts in the field of learning disabilities. History and traditions are examined along with alternative cognitive approaches to learning disabilities assessment and remediation. In addition, several chapters focus on neuropsychological assessment and remediation and the assessment of memory. A summary chapter reviews current controversies and future issues.

Kaufman, A. S., & Kaufman, N. L. (2004a). *Kaufman Test of Educational Achievement– Second Edition (KTEA–II): Comprehensive Form.* Circle Pines, MN: American Guidance Service.

The manual of this test (included in the test kit) gives detailed information about KTEA-II test development, standardization, and the test's psychometric properties. It describes all of the subtests and scales, and instructs examiners on how to score and analyze the KTEA-II data. Because the KTEA-II was conormed with the KABC-II, this manual provides a wealth of correlational data and information about how the tests are related.

Kaufman, A. S., Lichtenberger, E. O., Fletcher-Janzen, E., & Kaufman, N. L. (2005). *Essentials of KABC-II assessment.* New York: Wiley.

Covers thoroughly the administration, scoring, and interpretation of the KABC-II, including treatment of how it can be integrated with the KTEA-II. It includes sample case reports exemplifying use of the KTEA-II with the KABC-II.

Lichtenberger, E. O., Mather, N., Kaufman, N. L., & Kaufman, A. S. (2004). *Essentials of assessment report writing.* New York: Wiley.

This book reviews the essential elements and structure of well-written psychological and psychoeducational reports. It covers all aspects of preparing a written report and provides numerous illustrative examples of clear, informative reports. It includes the case reports of Xander, a 5-year-old who was administered the WPPSI-III and the WIAT-II, and of Brianna, an 18-year-old diagnosed with ADHD, who was assessed with the KABC-II and KTEA-II.

Pearson (2009). *Wechsler Individual Achievement Test–Third Edition.* San Antonio, TX: Author.

The Examiner's Manual of this test (included in the test kit) gives detailed information about WIAT-III test development, standardization, and the test's psychometric properties. It describes all of the subtests and scales, and instructs examiners on how to score and analyze the WIAT-III data. The Technical Manual CD (included in the test kit) provides a wealth of correlational data and information about how the WIAT-III is related to other tests.

Swanson, H. L., Harris, K., & Graham, S. (Eds.) (2003). *Handbook of research on learning disabilities.* New York: Guilford.

This handbook reviews the major theoretical, methodological, and instructional advances that have occurred in the field of learning disabilities over the last 20 years. With contributions from leading researchers, the volume synthesizes a vast body of knowledge on the nature of learning disabilities, their relationship to basic psychological and brain processes, and how students with these difficulties can best be identified and treated. Findings are reviewed on ways to support student performance in specific skill areas—including language arts, math, science, and social studies—as well as general principles of effective instruction that cut across academic domains.

INDEX

About the Authors

Elizabeth O. Lichtenberger, PhD, has worked as an Adjunct Faculty member at Alliant International University in San Diego and a researcher at the Laboratory for Cognitive Neuroscience at The Salk Institute for Biological Studies in La Jolla, CA. Her work at The Salk Institute focused on the cognitive and neuropsychological patterns in children with genetic developmental disorders. Because of her expertise in psychological, psychoeducational, and neuropsychological assessment, Liz also serves as a psychoeducational test/measurement consultant and trainer for organizations and provides consultation to individual psychologists.

Liz is a published author of numerous books, book chapters, and articles on assessment and assessment instruments, including many books in the *Essentials* series, as well as *Assessing Adolescent and Adult Intelligence (3rd Ed)*. In addition, Liz served as a consulting editor of the second edition of the *Encyclopedia of Special Education: A Reference for the Education of the Handicapped and Other Exceptional Children and Adults* and is currently on the editorial board of the journal *Psychology in the Schools*.

Kristina C. Breaux, PhD, led the research and development of the WIAT®-III. She is a licensed special educator and learning disabilities specialist. Kristina has worked as a special education teacher, diagnostician, and remediation clinician. She is currently a research director with Pearson.

About the CD-ROM

This appendix provides you with information on the contents of the CD that accompanies this book. For the latest information, please refer to the ReadMe file located at the root of the CD.

System Requirements

A computer with a processor running at 120 Mhz or faster

- At least 32 MB of total RAM installed on your computer. For best performance, we recommend at least 64 MB
- A CD-ROM drive

NOTE: Many popular spreadsheet word processing programs are capable of reading Microsoft Excel files. However, users should be aware that a slight amount of formatting might be lost when using a program other than Microsoft Excel.

Using the CD with Windows

To install the items from the CD to your hard drive, follow these steps:

1. Insert the CD into your computer's CD-ROM drive.
2. The CD-ROM interface will appear. The interface provides a simple point-and-click way to explore the contents of the CD.

If the opening screen of the CD-ROM does not appear automatically, follow these steps to access the CD:

1. Click the Start button on the left end of the taskbar and then choose Run from the menu that pops up.
2. In the dialog box that appears, type *d:***start.exe**. (If your CD-ROM drive is not drive d, fill in the appropriate letter in place of *d*.) This brings up the CD Interface described in the preceding set of steps.

Using the CD with Macintosh

To install the items from the CD to your hard drive, follow these steps:

1. Insert the CD into your computer's CD-ROM drive.
2. The CD icon will appear on your desktop; double-click to open.
3. Double-click the Start button.
4. Read the license agreement and click the Accept button to use the CD.
5. The CD interface will appear. Here you can install the programs and run the demos.

What's on the CD

The following sections provide a summary of the software and other materials you'll find on the CD.

Content

This book's accompanying CD-ROM consists of worksheet files written and programmed in Microsoft Excel that allow readers to enter WIAT-III and KTEA-II data along with other specific test data and have it analyzed following the steps outlined in Chapter 4 of this book. Programmed by Elizabeth O. Lichtenberger, the first Excel program is the **WIAT-III and KTEA-II Data Management and Interpretive Assistant** (WIAT-III and KTEA-II DMIA.) Users of the WIAT-III and KTEA-II DMIA are strongly cautioned not to use the CHC tab until they have obtained a solid understanding of Cross-Battery Assessment principles and rationale (e.g., found in Flanagan, Ortiz, & Alfonso, 2007).

It is important to note that the WIAT-III and KTEA-II DMIA does not convert tests' *raw scores* to any metric. Users of this program are responsible for following the test publisher's administration and scoring guidelines. All test scores entered into this program must be derived from the norms and procedures provided by the test publisher.

Also included on the CD-ROM is the **KTEA-II GSV Score Analysis Program**. This Microsoft Excel worksheet allows users to record GSV scores over multiple administrations of the KTEA-II. This data can then be used to help determine whether an individual is showing academic growth over time on certain KTEA-II subtests.

In addition, the CD-ROM includes the **WIAT-III Scoring Tutorial,** a PowerPoint slide presentation that helps examiners learn to score the Theme Development and Text Organization for the WIAT-III Essay Composition subtest.

Note for Starting the Excel Programs:

If you receive a "Security Warning" about macros when opening either Excel program, you must click on the "Enable Macros" option. If you do not select this option, you will lose some functionality and the program will not operate correctly.

Applications

The following applications are on the CD:

Adobe Reader
Adobe Reader is a freeware application for viewing files in the Adobe Portable Document format.

OpenOffice.org
OpenOffice.org is a free multi-platform office productivity suite. It is similar to Microsoft Office or Lotus SmartSuite, but OpenOffice.org is absolutely free. It includes word processing, spreadsheet, presentation, and drawing applications that enable you to create professional documents, newsletters, reports, and presentations. It supports most file formats of other office software. You should be able to edit and view any files created with other office solutions.

Note: OpenOffice.org requires at least 256 MB of total RAM installed on your computer. For best performance, we recommend at least 512 MB.

Shareware programs are fully functional, trial versions of copyrighted programs. If you like particular programs, register with their authors for a nominal fee and receive licenses, enhanced versions, and technical support.

Freeware programs are copyrighted games, applications, and utilities that are free for personal use. Unlike shareware, these programs do not require a fee or provide technical support.

GNU software is governed by its own license, which is included inside the folder of the GNU product. See the GNU license for more details.

Trial, demo, or evaluation versions are usually limited either by time or functionality (such as being unable to save projects). Some trial versions are very sensitive to system date changes. If you alter your computer's date, the programs will "time out" and no longer be functional.

CUSTOMER CARE

If you have trouble with the CD-ROM, please call the Wiley Product Technical Support phone number at (800) 762-2974. Outside the United States, call

1(317) 572-3994. You can also contact Wiley Product Technical Support at **http://support.wiley.com**. John Wiley & Sons will provide technical support only for installation and other general quality control items. For technical support on the applications themselves, consult the program's vendor or author.

To place additional orders or to request information about other Wiley products, please call (877) 762-2974.